Remaking Asia

The Pantheon Asia Library
New Approaches to the New Asia

No part of the world has changed so much in recent years as Asia, or awakened such intense American interest. But much of our scholarship, like much of our public understanding, is based on a previous era. The Asia Library has been launched to provide the needed information on the new Asia, and in so doing to develop both the new methods and the new sympathies needed to understand it. Our purpose is not only to publish new work but to experiment with a wide variety of approaches which will reflect these new realities and their perception by those in Asia and the West.

Our books aim at different levels and audiences, from the popular to the more scholarly, from high schools to the universities, from pictorial to documentary presentations. All books will be available in paperback.

Suggestions for additions to the Asia Library are welcome.

REMAKING ASIA

Essays on the American Uses of Power

EDITED BY

MARK SELDEN

PANTHEON BOOKS
A Division of Random House
NEW YORK

"Japan: The Roots of Militarism," by Herbert P. Bix, was originally published in the *Bulletin of Concerned Asian Scholars.* "Dependence and Imperialism in India," by Thomas E. Weisskopf, was originally published in the *Review of Radical Political Economics.*

Grateful acknowledgment is made to the following for permission to reprint previously published material:

Pacific Basin Reports: for an excerpt from pages 83–85 of *Pacific Basin Reports,* April 1, 1971.

Aoki Shoten: for the chart on page 306 of Moriya Fumio, *Sengo Nihon shihonshugi—sono bunseki to hihan.*

Library of Congress Cataloging in Publication Data
Selden, Mark.
    Remaking Asia: Essays on the American Uses of Power.

    (The Pantheon Asia Library)
    Includes bibliographical references.
    1. Asia—Foreign relations—United States.
    2. United States—Foreign relations—Asia.
    3. Asia—Foreign economic relations—United States.
    4. United States—Foreign economic relations—Asia.
    I. Title.
DS33.4.U6S44   327.73′05   73–7011
ISBN 0–394–48186–0
ISBN 0–394–70670–6 (pbk.)

First Edition

*To the people of Indochina and
to men and women everywhere who
have linked arms in their struggle.*

Contents

Preface ix

Introduction by Harry Magdoff 3

PART I

OIL IMPERIALISM IN SOUTHEAST ASIA 21
by *Malcolm Caldwell*

THE INTERNATIONAL MONETARY FUND
AND INDONESIAN DEBT SLAVERY by *Cheryl Payer* 50

THE ASIAN DEVELOPMENT BANK: An Imperial Thrust
into the Pacific by *Richard de Camp* 71

THE VIETNAM WAR AND THE CIA-
FINANCIAL ESTABLISHMENT by *Peter Dale Scott* 91

PART II

THE PHILIPPINES: A Case History of Neocolonialism
by *William J. Pomeroy* 157

DEPENDENCE AND IMPERIALISM IN INDIA
by *Thomas E. Weisskopf* 200

MODERNIZATION AND PEASANT RESISTANCE
IN THAILAND by *Ralph Thaxton* 247

OKINAWA AND AMERICAN SECURITY IMPERIALISM
by *Mark Selden* 279

PART III

JAPAN: The Roots of Militarism *by Herbert P. Bix*   305

NOTES ON THE CONTRIBUTORS   363

INDEX   367

Preface

Asia and the United States stand at the brink of a new era defined by the relative decline of American power and the emergence of powerful competitors:

- The United States' defeat by popular forces in Indochina has forced large-scale *military* withdrawal from much of the area and an overall cutback of its armed forces based in Asia.
- President Nixon's normalization of relations with the People's Republic of China marks the final collapse of the *political* cornerstone of two decades of Asian policy predicated on the encirclement of China.
- In the *economic* sphere, the twenty-seven-year reign of the dollar as an international currency collapsed on August 15, 1971, as the United States abandoned gold convertibility of the dollar. Subsequent abortive efforts to halt the decline have further exposed the dollar's weakness, and successive protectionist trade moves reflect an overall erosion of American economic supremacy.
- On the *ideological* level the banner of freedom and democracy has been unobtrusively furled (consonant with increasing U.S. support for military dictatorships), and even

ix

the rhetoric of militant anti-Communism has yielded to vague sentiments of peace (consonant with U.S. efforts to neutralize the Soviet Union and China by means of the carrot as well as the stick) .

Nevertheless, it is only on the basis of analysis of the patterns of postwar history, shaped in large measure by American power, that we can grasp the significance of the era that is presently unfolding.

In the aftermath of World War II the United States replaced the entire gamut of colonial nations, all of them ravaged by war, to become the supreme power in Asia. This hegemony was destined to be short lived. By the 1960s American supremacy was challenged simultaneously by liberation movements and by the reemergence of Japan, Europe, the Soviet Union, and, most recently, China. No longer can illusions of unilateral American hegemony be sustained save by hard-core ideologues of empire. We are witnessing the passage of the American era in Asia and throughout the world. But what is to replace it?

Studies abound of America's expansion and the foreign policy process which directed it. What is striking—if scarcely surprising—is their ethnocentric quality, their overwhelming preoccupation with the *American* experience. Asia remains but dimly perceived, a blur hovering on the periphery of American consciousness. If the violence of the Indochina War has aroused the conscience of many Americans, most remain oblivious to the myriad ways in which the United States government, business, and military interests shape the daily lives of people in other lands.

The focus of the present study is the transformation and attempted transformation of Asia wrought by the American economic, military, political, and cultural thrust since World War II. The essays gathered here explore the distinctive contours of the American impact on the national experience of Japan, India, the Philippines, Indochina, Okinawa, Indonesia, and Thailand; they analyze in addition key American-created or -dominated international institutions and forces, including the International Monetary Fund, the Asian Development Bank, and international oil interests. The authors have sought, not a single key which unlocks all doors to the uses of American power in remaking Asia, but an understanding of the interrelationship of (sometimes conflicting) forces and an appreciation of certain unique elements of national experience. The evidence nevertheless discloses the distortion and repression of Asian societies, the systematic thwarting of their prospects for development, and above all the *human* costs imposed by the American presence in its manifold aspects.

Can we identify distinctive features of the American era in postwar Asia? Three elements emerge with particular force. First is the characteristic American opposition to classical colonial patterns of domination. It is not sufficient to talk of informal empire. The United States did not reject colonialism outright— as its long rule in Okinawa and its continued control of Micronesia and (closer to home) Puerto Rico demonstrate. Nor has the United States been alone in its recognition of the necessity to settle for indirect hegemony in the postwar era. The wave of anticolonial struggles which began after World War I reached its global peak in the aftermath of World War II, leading to the dismantling of the great empires. In China, North Korea, and North Vietnam the result was genuine national liberation premised on the elimination of foreign domination. Elsewhere, however, including most of the nations of Asia discussed in the present study, "independence" merely marked a change of masters and of modes of domination. Following World War II the United States confronted two major obstacles to its economic and military hegemony in Asia: wars of national liberation on the one hand, and the reconstitution of classical colonialism on the other. In the name of national independence the United States selectively lent its support to Asian anticolonial movements and then promptly stepped in with armies, bases, and economic aid or investment to establish its own hegemony.

Second, the intricate global system of multilateral institutions initiated by American planners at the end of World War II and developed in subsequent decades provided one of the characteristic features of what we might call the internationalization of American power. I am thinking of a range of institutions including the World Bank, the International Monetary Fund, the Southeast Asian and North Atlantic Treaty Organizations, regional development banks, and even the United Nations, in addition to other trade, industrial, financial, and military organizations operating on a regional and global scale. All of these have in common the fact that they were formed with a high degree of U.S. initiative, dominated (at least in the early postwar decades) by the United States, and served to rationalized the global expansion of U.S. capital and military power. Thus, for a quarter of a century the United States defined, created, and dominated the multilateral institutions which provided the framework for capitalist development and insured the continued dependence of other countries on its power.

Finally, the maturation of the multinational corporation as the characteristic institution of international economic supremacy typifies both the era in general and the mode of American economic penetration in particular. This theme, touched on in a number of essays in this volume, is one which requires extensive further analysis. Here it is sufficient to note that the imperialism of colonies and resource plunder has in part given way to an infinitely more complex global phenomenon. Denied access to major international markets by tariff and other protective barriers, particularly in the advanced capitalist countries of Europe and Canada, U.S. corporations created a network of branch plants throughout the globe. U.S.-based conglomerates now produce sophisticated manufactured goods from electronic components to automobiles in dozens of different countries where cheap labor and tax shields provide attractive lures.

We are witnessing a variant of the classical pattern in which resources from the colonies fuel factories located in the metropolitan countries. The control of strategic resources remains in foreign (since World War II primarily American) hands. And they are being supplied at an accelerated rate to foreign-owned factories, most of which are still located in the industrialized countries. What is new is the proliferation of substantial foreign export industries located throughout the Third World. Such a pattern has already begun to develop in Hong Kong, Singapore, Taiwan, and South Korea. And it will advance much further if the multinational corporations attain their goal: unfettered movement across national boundaries to exploit economic opportunities on a global scale. The consequence of these developments for the poor nations of Asia has been the penetration of powerful foreign corporations into critical sectors of the economy, crushing native industry where it had begun to develop, intensifying the exploitation of natural resources, and reinforcing the dependence of the local economy on international markets.

But that is not the whole story. The global expansion of U.S.-based multinational corporations has increased contradictions between *American* workers and the corporations over the loss of jobs flowing abroad and wage ceilings imposed by the availability of cheap foreign labor. The expansion of multinational corporations has also heightened tensions between government and the corporations over such issues as balance of payments and the stability of the dollar. For example, since 1971, while the government sought to prevent the collapse of the dollar, U.S.-based multinational corporations bought immense quantities of German marks and Japanese yen on international currency markets. The dominant pattern nevertheless remains—and will remain—a hand-in-glove partnership between the U.S. government and the multinational corporations, at the expense simultaneously of Asian and American workers.

The present volume offers new light on U.S. goals and policies in contemporary Asia. But it also explores the crucial (if subordinate) role of Asian elites in facilitating and shaping the American era. Asian business and government elites have shared in the feast prepared by international economic interests even if their share has been limited to little more than some large crumbs. To be sure, a handful of Asian entrepreneurs and politicians with connections to U.S. interests have accumulated vast personal fortunes—dictators Marcos of the Philippines and Thieu of South Vietnam among the most prominent examples. However, nowhere has the American era launched the agrarian nations of Asia on a path of economic development which holds out the hope of breaking patterns of foreign domination or passing on the benefits of industrialization to the poor and disenfranchised. The genius of neocolonialism, the perpetuation of foreign domination in an era of nominal political independence, lies precisely in reducing political liabilities and costs of empire by passing the burdens of administration and pacification to local ruling groups with a stake in preservation of the status quo.

If the saga of neocolonialism in Asia was primarily an American one in the initial postwar decades, by the mid-1960s a powerful new force had entered the scene: Japan, brought to its knees in World War II, reemerged as the dominant Asian *economic* power searching for new trade and investment opportunities in Asia and globally. These essays explore the nature of the emerging U.S.–Japan hegemony since the sixties, and the mounting tensions between the two powers as the basic premise of their relationship—Japanese subordination to U.S. interests—began to disintegrate. The continued Japanese economic and military surge in the seventies, coupled with the waning of absolute American supremacy, emerges as a central feature of great power economic involvement in Asia in the present era. Japan remains, for the time being, dependent on U.S. military power, and, despite efforts at diversification, her economy is firmly tied to the United States. But this situation is changing rapidly, opening new possibilities of an independent and more aggressive Japanese role.

Is the American debacle in Indochina and the reduction of American troops in Asia the cutting edge of a full-scale withdrawal from Asia? The studies in the present volume make abundantly clear that the answer is no. The United States emerges from the Indochina conflict badly scarred and confronting multiple challenges at home and abroad. Yet it remains the single most powerful country in Asia, committed to the same fundamental hegemonic goals. And it is presently rationalizing and streamlining its farflung network of bases and client regimes. While the United States has greatly expanded the military role of Asian mercenaries and pressed for an expanded Japanese (non-nuclear) military role within the framework of American power, the direct American military presence is not about to fade away. In Japan, Okinawa, South Korea, and Taiwan, in Thailand, the Philippines, and Micronesia, and in the oceans and skies, American naval and air power continues to expand, providing some of the sinews for empire in Asia. Moreover, the United States has been able to exploit intense Sino–Soviet antagonisms and divisions among its other major competitors to its own advantage. Nor is its economic stake in the Pacific Basin, since the sixties probably the fastest-growing market region in the world, diminished. Asia is nevertheless entering a new and dynamic stage in which American dreams of hegemony must yield to a reality in which several major powers and blocs vie with the forces of revolution and national liberation to shape the future. If the final outcome of these struggles remains open, this volume should provide new perspectives on the forces and interests which will be decisive.

The present attempt to explore the nature and impact of

American power in Asia extends the analysis initially developed in *America's Asia: Dissenting Essays on Asian-American Relations* (Pantheon and Vintage, 1971). Like *America's Asia,* this volume was jointly conceived by Edward Friedman and myself, and the initial framework elaborated during a summer workshop held in Cambridge in 1971. Although other commitments eventually forced Ed to withdraw as co-editor, the volume reflects many of his insights and is much the richer for his probing criticisms of the essays. I would like to thank all the participants in the Cambridge workshop and colleagues in the Committee of Concerned Asian Scholars and throughout Asia who contributed directly and indirectly to the realization of this project.

Mark Selden
Tokyo

August 1973

Remaking Asia

INTRODUCTION

HARRY MAGDOFF

The explorations of the situation in Asia contributed to this volume are distinguished by their marked departure from traditional academic studies. Their novelty is not due to innovations in technique or because of greater or lesser depth of scholarship. What is new and invigorating here is the use of an alternate frame of reference, and with it a significant broadening of the questions asked as well as an opening up of new areas of investigation. Unshackled from customary inhibitions and such rationalizations of the status quo as are found among even severe critics of foreign policy, the authors represented here are able to look full face at today's imperialism, including the imperialism of their own country. In addition, they can boldly recognize that underlying the myriad of problems contained in the issue of social and economic development in Asia rests the clear, although far from simple, choice by the people between either a socialist or capitalist social system. The purpose of this essay is to suggest an avenue of approach and advance some hypotheses that may help in the search for an historical and theoretical perspective of major themes discussed in subsequent chapters.

Toward the end of the nineteenth century the British Empire was celebrated in a popular history, *The Expansion of England* by J. R. Seeley. While this book is generally ignored by modern

3

scholars, its epigrammatic summation lives on: "We seem, as it were, to have conquered and peopled half the world in a fit of absence of mind."[1] This theme, along with its corollary that the British were reluctant imperialists, has penetrated the literature of empire, providing the kernel of more sophisticated formulations. Not as a witticism but as a summary of sober historical analysis, a modern British specialist puts it this way: "In short, the modern empires lacked rationality and purpose: they were the chance products of complex historical forces operating over several centuries, and more particularly during the period after 1815."[2]

Now that U.S. scholars and publicists are beginning to acknowledge the reality of an American empire, they too seem to find comfort, or significance, in the elements of chance and reluctance that pervade history. Thus two diplomatic correspondents who have recently published a book tracing, quite superficially, the roots of U.S. interest in Asia back to 1784, entitle their opening chapter, with no hint of satire, "The Reluctant Imperialists."[3] In a more scholarly and penetrating study, *Pax Americana,* Ronald Steel recites the extensive U.S. military involvement around the globe and recalls James Reston's words that these are "commitments the like of which no sovereign nation ever took on in the history of the world." But Steel is quick to point out, "These entanglements happened more by accident than by design. . . . We had no intention of virtually annexing Okinawa, of occupying South Korea, of preventing the return of Taiwan to China, of fighting in Indochina, or of remaining in Western Europe. If someone had said in 1947 that twenty years later there would be 225,000 soldiers in Germany, 50,000 in Korea, and a half million Americans fighting in Vietnam, he would have been considered mad."[4]

Both accident and reluctance are of course ever present in empire-building. Hitler, and Kaiser Wilhelm before him, must surely have experienced some reluctance: it would have been safer and more efficient to obtain Germany's long-standing goals of empire without the costs and risks of war. And it is equally probable that the U.S. decision-makers are reluctantly bombing Vietnam: they would most likely prefer to exert their will in Southeast Asia without ruining the people and land of Vietnam and without war-induced domestic social and economic problems. As for the influence of chance, it should be obvious that in the absence of omniscience and omnipotence all of history in one sense consists of a series of accidents. Or as Trotsky, a firm believer in the existence of laws in history, observed, "The entire historical process is a refraction of historical law through the accidental." Faced with the reality of empire-building, as with any other recurring phenomenon in history, the analyst needs to discover, or try to understand, why through the very operations of accident history moves in one direction rather than another. One might even ask why some countries or social organisms are more accident prone than others or why at certain times rather than at other times.

While it should go without saying that, given the shortcomings of astrology and the flaws in crystal balls, no one in 1947 could have foreseen the specific future configuration of U.S. global involvement, it is nevertheless essential to recognize that the policies and pressures that produced the U.S. drive to global hegemony were far from accidental and were in evidence long before 1947. In fact, the mainsprings of U.S. global strategy during the past quarter century had already taken shape well before the Second World War was over.[5] But even more important, the striving for empire stretches back to the earliest days of the Republic, and even into colonial times.

"Man's character is his fate" said Heraclitus, the ancient Greek philosopher. The same may be said of nations. And the key to the character of the U.S. social organism which has determined its destiny—modified and adapted, to be sure, in reaction to chance events and to complex historical forces—has been its persistent urge to expand. Taking the long view, Professor Van Alstyne in *The Rising American Empire* sees this urge as one of "direction and unbroken continuity in the history of the United States":

> The early colonies were no sooner established in the seventeenth century than expansionist impulses began to register in each of them. Imperial patterns took shape, and before the middle of the eighteenth century the concept of an empire that would take in the whole continent was fully formed. A drive south into the Spanish Caribbean was also in progress, with the ultimate goal in view of converting the Caribbean into an American lake. In the Revolution the spirit of conquest was a powerful force, and it took about a century thereafter to satisfy the territorial ambitions of the United States. Except for the

internal dissension which was a constant factor during the first half of the nineteenth century, and which finally exploded into a civil war of vast proportions, it seems probable that these ambitions would have been pursued more persistently and energetically, that indeed they would have been pushed to the limit. But by the time of the Mexican War, the controversy between the North and South developed into an obsession; and further conquests became for the time being impossible. On the North American continent American expansion reached its maximum limits by 1867, the process of advance having been delayed long enough to enable the Canadians to develop the necessary counter-moves. The two related drives, south into the Caribbean and westward to China via Cape Horn, continued to the end of the century, when a burst of energy finished off the process in a war against Spain.[6]

While the focus of attention in U.S. history books is on continental expansion, the conquest of the Indians, and the acquisition of Mexican territory, they often overlook the fact that the so-called frontier was not only on land but on the seas as well, and that the absorption of the Far West was considerably influenced by desire to control the Pacific Ocean and thus to widen trading opportunities in Asia. The early United States was not only an agricultural but also a mercantile and seafaring society. This was especially so of the New England states, where a relative poverty of natural resources meant the lack of suitable agricultural or mineral export products that could be exchanged for European manufactures. The road to prosperity was found in commerce, bringing with it the dominance of a merchant class that spread its interests around the globe: not only in the rum–molasses trade with the West Indies, the marketing of African slaves, and the coastal traffic, but also in whaling, sealing, and trade (including opium) in the Pacific. To facilitate and expand this commerce, U.S. business firms spread to Asia during the earliest days of the Republic: "In the Pacific, Americans established themselves in the Sandwich Islands, 1787, Nootka Sound, 1788, Marquesas, 1791, Fanning, 1797, and Fiji, 1800. American interest in the North Pacific was in whale fisheries, which encouraged the start of an American settlement in Honolulu. The consul to Canton, Major Samuel Shaw, started the firm of Shaw & Randall in that city in 1786, only two years after the Chinese port had been opened to American trade."[7]

These commercial stakes in Asia may seem puny by today's

standards, but not if judged in the perspective of the world economy in the eighteenth and early nineteenth centuries. For this spread into the Pacific, in addition to the Caribbean and the slave trade, spurred the emergence of a competitive merchant marine, a supportive navy, and the sort of trade that brought not only wealth to the merchant classes in North Atlantic ports but also nurtured the roots of eventual economic as well as political independence of the nation as a whole.

At the heart of the current economic underdevelopment of most Asian countries, as well as former colonies and semi-colonies throughout the world, are the enormous economic and social distortions imposed by Western nations: the transfer of the traditional international trade of these countries into European hands and their eventual adaptation to serve as raw materials and food suppliers for the industrializing nations and as markets for their manufactured products. And it is in this respect that the history of the United States differs so strikingly from that of other colonial or excolonial territories. For, instead of becoming a victim of the colonial system, this country emerged at an early stage as an active participant and rival in seeking a share of the profits from the growing world commerce and the forcible opening up of new business opportunities in the non-Western world.

An important ingredient of U.S. ability to compete in the ever-widening sphere of imperialist influence was the attainment, for a variety of reasons, of a high degree of independence as a shipbuilder, trader, and shipper. This was the very opposite of the situation in the colonial areas which at that time, as well as in the future, were transformed into adjuncts of militarily superior powers, an outstanding characteristic of colonial and semi-colonial countries being the concentration of import and export shipping in foreign hands. It is noteworthy that the ability of American merchants and shippers to compete with those of the mother country contributed significantly to the tensions and resulting struggle leading up to the final separation. In 1790, U.S.-owned ships already handled fifty-nine percent of its foreign trade. By 1807 this proportion rose to ninety-two percent. The forward push to economic as well as political independence provided by the American Revolution was strengthened by the opportunities arising from the subsequent wars between European powers. Thus a large part of the shipping business at the end of the eighteenth century fell to U.S. entrepreneurs during the war years: ". . . several new routes, on which the profits were very high, developed during the war years. These were the trade in the Dutch East Indies, which first assumed significant proportions in 1797, and the China trade, frequently in conjunction with the fur trade of the American Northwest. The latter route was initiated in 1784, but expanded in the 1790s, when the United States became the major shipper of tea to Europe during the war."[8]

Trade, fishing, and shipping were only the initial nuclei of expansion. Traders became investors; missionaries discovered untold numbers of pagans; and the U.S. navy found steadily increasing duties as the protector of businessmen and missionaries in foreign lands, as explorer of new trade routes, and as opener of additional doors for commerce. (The U.S. Navy Pacific Squadron was organized in 1821, the East India Squadron in 1835. These were in addition to the Mediterranean, West India, and Brazil, or South Atlantic, Squadrons during the early nineteenth century.)

There were thus two strands of empire-building: a maritime domain in addition to the better-known acquisition of land across the continent. These were often complementary and mutually supporting, rather than conflicting, movements. Such a complementary relationship manifested itself especially in the struggle for control of the Pacific coast. Jefferson and Adams both saw the Pacific Northwest "as the American window on the Pacific, the corridor across the continent which would give the United States the advantage of a direct route to the great trade routes of Asia."[9] As commercial relations with China grew and rivalry with Britain, Russia, and France for control of Pacific ports and trade routes mounted, ownership of the coastal ports (stretching down to San Francisco, Los Angeles, and San Diego) became an ever more urgent consideration in determining the boundaries the United States sought with Mexico and Canada.[10] Annexation of the coastal ports, however, did not mark the end of western expansion. They became, instead, safe harbors for the growing trade on the long and arduous route around Cape Horn to Asia, and home ports for the U.S. navy operating in the Pacific.

The road to empire in Asia was not built in a continuous and methodical fashion. It proceeded in fits and starts, tempered by competing demands on limited resources (e.g., for the Indian,

Mexican, and Civil wars) and by constraints imposed by rival empire-seekers, most especially the British with their dominant navy during the nineteenth century and, beginning at the turn of the twentieth century, the expanding naval power of Japan. Still, the United States didn't miss too many opportunities—for example: taking advantage of Britain's breakthroughs (via the Opium wars) to obtain treaty ports and extraterritorial rights in China; sending Commodore Perry to force open ports in Japan; pushing for special position in Korea; helping to put down the Boxer Rebellion; stretching U.S. frontiers northward to Alaska and the Aleutians, and westward to Hawaii, Midway, Samoa, Wake, Guam, and the Philippines; imposing the Open Door Policy, and continuing to enforce this policy with the use of the U.S. marines and by patrolling nearly 2000 miles of the Yangtse River with gunboats.

Seen in this historical context, U.S. imperialist activities in Asia since the Second World War appear less as the result of a combination of accidents and more as the fruition under favorable circumstances of its long-standing imperial strivings. With Japan, the main Pacific rival, utterly defeated, with Russia, a potential rival, severely weakened, and with Great Britain lacking the resources to create the air force and aircraft carriers needed under modern conditions to dominate the Pacific, it was perfect weather for the United States to spread its sails. Obviously, the contraction of the world imperialist system due to the emergence of socialist societies and the threat of further contraction arising from spreading national liberation movements spurred U.S. interest and active involvement in Asia and other areas of the underdeveloped world. But there is no denying the continuous path of empire-building in Asia and elsewhere throughout U.S. history, independent of the "red menace."

It is important to understand that this expansionism is not the result of some mystical force inherent in the character of the American people. On the contrary, expansion was central to the evolving social system and its remarkable productivity and wealth. Expansion played a major role at each historical stage and helped to mold the resulting economic structure and the cultural environment—both of which reinforced the drive for further expansion. Enterprising capitalists, supported by an energetic state, kept pushing forward in the search for more opportunities for profit; in turn, each new frontier fired the ambition of restless businessmen and spurred the imagination of political leaders dreaming of national wealth and glory.

In interpreting this process of dynamic expansion it is important to recognize that the opportunities for capital formation and accumulation do not make their appearance in the smooth self-generating manner implicitly assumed in the neat mathematical models which economic theorists like to design. While such models may be useful in exploring the mechanisms of coordination which must be present in an anarchic economic system, they overlook certain crucial facts: 1) that such progress as actually does take place is never continuous and orderly, and 2) that unbalanced development is an integral, one might even say necessary, aspect of capitalist growth.

The most obvious feature of this spasmodic development is the alternating cycle of prosperity and depression. But perhaps more important for understanding the process of expansion are the longer waves in which periods of rapid growth are followed by slow and sluggish growth. Based on evidence for the United States since the 1830s, Professor Moses Abramovitz summarizes this phenomenon as follows:

> The economic growth of the United States has taken place in a series of surges during which growth was especially rapid followed by relapses when growth proceeded much more slowly. In periods of rapid growth, output has increased at rates two, and often three, times as fast as in periods of slow growth. . . . The long waves in the rate of growth reflect similar waves in the rate of growth of resources, both labor and capital; in the rates of growth of productivity; and in the intensity with which resources are utilized.[11]

Underlying these phenomena—both the ordinary boom—bust cycle and the longer swings of alternating galloping and crawling growth—are certain essential characteristics of capitalist development: 1) The speed of growth and even the presence or absence of growth depend in the final analysis on the aggregate investment decisions of businessmen; 2) Capitalist enterprise inevitably entails taking risks, even risks that might end in total loss of invested capital. These risks are generally not incurred unless the odds are right, that is, unless the profit prospects are so encouraging that they far outweigh the danger of loss.

It should go without saying that capitalist societies thrive best when stimulated by exceptionally good profit opportunities, and especially so during waves of speculative fervor and "reasonable" inflation. But these favorable circumstances are not always present. They appear in clusters and are due to various causes, as, for example, a major technological innovation, an upsurge in urbanization, sudden access to new domestic and/or foreign markets, an arms buildup, or war and its aftermath. The impact of any one or a combination of these stimulants can propel the economy forward at a feverish pace. But the factors that induce accelerated growth have an inherent tendency to peter out. It is true that new opportunities for capital investment tend to have a cumulative effect, for they spur related lines of business activity and prolong boom times. But these stimulants are self-limiting. The main canals and railroad lines get completed; areas of settlement are occupied; competing nations encroach on new trade routes; the more independent foreign nations erect tariff walls. And running like a red thread through all the ups and downs of capitalist development is the fundamental paradox: the very process of capital accumulation (the primary engine of growth) generates an imbalance between consumer demand and the output resulting from capital investment; if profits are to be high enough to warrant the risks of enterprise, the flow of income to the mass of consumers must be limited.

So far it has been stressed that capitalist development is characterized both by "normal" business cycles and by longer waves of speedup and slowdown in the rate of growth. But these two kinds of fluctuations are not unrelated. During the longer upswings booms are strong and depressions weak, while the reverse is true during the long downswings. The latter are therefore periods of more or less continuous stagnation which threaten not only the economy but the health of the society as a whole. It is hence not surprising that it is precisely in these periods of stagnation (or slow growth) that new stimuli are sought, and that business and political leaders should be especially receptive to whatever opportunities for foreign expansion may present themselves—or may be created by those with the necessary imagination and daring. This is by no means the exclusive component of the expansionary urge. Other pressures keep coming up, ranging over the centuries—from land speculators promoting acquisition and settlement of new territory; to merchants, farmers, and manufacturers seeking new markets; to monopoly firms desiring control over their sources of raw materials and privileged market conditions. The cause is advanced, and sometimes initiated, by daring, far-sighted political and ambitious military chiefs who foster expansion for the sake of their own "personal politics," their notions of patriotism, or their vision of what is needed to increase the power and wealth of their country.

But with all of this, it is still important to recognize that these policies are arrived at in a capitalist environment that time and again is faced with the need for stimulants to rev up the engine. The stimulants pounced upon are not always effective; they frequently fail to produce all the hoped-for results. Moreover, domestic political strife may emerge over the choice of strategy and tactics concerning the mode, pace, and geographic concentration of expansion as well as over the preferred method of exercising influence and control—differences that may reflect variations in judgment and/or interpretation of self-interest. But in light of the limited alternatives available for stimulating growth in a profit-oriented society, and the pressure to cope with competing nations also confined to similar limited alternatives and hence pursuing analogous policies, the road to empire becomes well-trodden.

It is not uncommon for traditional historians and economists to ridicule the notion that the foreign policies of capitalist powers are strongly influenced by stagnation or the threat of stagnation. Thus, in dealing with the burst of U.S. imperialist expansionism at the end of the nineteenth century, they point to the great internal growth of the United States during the twentieth century as proof that there had been plenty of outlets for domestic savings in the last quarter of the nineteenth century. The weakness of this approach is that it interprets history unhistorically. The capitalists and politicians of the 1890s may have dreamed about their country's great and glorious future, but their urgent task was to deal with the present. They may even have made stimulating commencement-day addresses about the country's youth and potential for development, but what faced them the day after commencement was the threat of business failure against the backdrop of repetitive depressions. One of the longest depressions in U.S. business history lasted from October 1873 to March 1879. Indeed, about half the years in the last quarter of the nineteenth century were years of depression.

The point is that theoretical economists and historians do not make decisions about how the nation's savings are to be disposed of. Such decisions are made by practical business people who are very alert to the profit-and-loss potential of opportunities actually available to them. Furthermore, the professorial hindsight that can now identify the enormous investment outlets which materialized in the twentieth century has a way of overlooking the extent to which the Spanish-American War and the subsequent two world wars contributed to the creation of these enlarged domestic investment opportunities.

Just as many economic and other historians are still perplexed by what seems to them the narrow-mindedness and lack of vision of those who masterminded the burst of U.S. imperialist activity in Latin America and Asia at the close of the nineteenth century, there are now many who have little appreciation of the impact of the depression of the 1930s on the decision-makers before, during, and after the Second World War. Once again hindsight calls attention to the very substantial growth of the postwar period and casts doubt on the judgment of those in the thirties and forties who had so little faith. It may therefore be worthwhile to review the dimensions of the dilemma of those years. Just to get a sense of what was at stake, let us look at the fluctuations in the production of steel—an indispensable input for the construction, machinery, autos and other consumer goods, and armaments industries.

STEEL INGOTS AND CASTINGS PRODUCED
(*Millions of Long Tons*)

Year		Year	
1929	56.4	1944	80.0
1932	13.7	1946	59.5
1937	50.7	1948	79.1
1938	28.3	1949	69.6
1939	47.1	1950	86.5
1941	74.0		

(SOURCE: U.S. Bureau of the Census, *Historical Statistics of the United States, Colonial Times to 1957*, Washington, D.C., 1960, p. 416.)

The most striking change, of course, is the drastic drop from 1929 to 1932, with production in 1932 less than one-fourth the previous high. This decline reflects the extent of the crisis in the users of steel. Not all production went down so precipitously, but this kind of contraction was typical of the machinery and construction industries. Thus, residential construction, measured in 1947–1949 prices, slid from $11.6 billion in its peak year of 1926 to $1.7 billion in 1932. Despite the efforts of the New Deal, the recovery reached in 1937 still did not create a demand for steel as high as that of 1929. And this recovery, as can be seen in the figure for 1938, was at best a shaky one. Ten years of depression, during which population and labor productivity kept increasing, left steel production still considerably below 1929. The so-called domestic outlets for savings were surely there, but only on paper. As far as the business community was concerned, there was no point in speculating on the profitability of these theoretical domestic outlets. It was only in 1941 that steel output shot ahead—in response to the war needs of Europe and the heavy armaments program undertaken by the United States in view of the probability that it would soon participate in the Second World War.

There is no intention here to draw the inference that the United States went to war, or encouraged others to go to war, as a crisis-remedy; the issues are much more complex. But what is important and too often neglected is that the depth and persistence of depression, the apparent inability of the system to snap out of its illness either through a so-called normal recovery or acceptable government measures, dominated all policy-making in those years.

Opinions differed strongly on the proper road to eventual full recovery, but the range of policy recommendations was necessarily limited, since the choice had to remain within the conditions imposed by capitalist economics. For example, only when mobilization for war, and more especially the war itself, imposed its priorities on the system did the American people get fed more or less properly and the agricultural surpluses disappear. Surplus food and the potential for producing even more food were both present throughout the depression. But it took the mobilization of twelve million men and women into the armed forces, fed by the government, and full employment of the remaining civilian population, made possible by a war-directed economy, to generate the income flows and effective demand that wiped out plaguing agricultural surpluses. Short of war, the policy alternatives had been limited to methods of re-stimulating market demand. But, since domestic markets proved time and again to be too sluggish either to feed the population or stimulate business enterprise growth, the capture of foreign markets (including the issue of how to handle the closing down of market opportunities by aggressive rival powers) necessarily rose on the list of policy priorities.

Despite the lift to the U.S. economy given by the war, the experience of the depression and fear of recurrence of stagnation weighed heavily on postwar policy-making. It was clear at the end of the war that the economy was ripe for a new and significant upturn. This optimism was, however, moderated by uncertainty over how long the recovery would last, along with grave doubts about the ability of the private economy to generate enough jobs for the vast number of returning servicemen. The way the war had been financed created large reserves of cash throughout the economy; workers, perhaps for the first time in history, had substantial savings accounts, and veterans benefits added additional temporary stimuli. At the same time, the backlog of consumer demand was extraordinary, piled up after a long drought of housing construction and some five years of almost no new civilian passenger car production. Yet, despite the omens of a new wave of prosperity, the economy began to turn down only three years after the war. As can be seen in the above table, steel production in 1949 fell back to below the 1941 prewar high. While the first postwar decline was short lived, and the recovery reinforced on the way up by the Korean War and a new wave of military spending, the experience nevertheless reconfirmed the dangers of stagnation.

It was against the still vivid background of a prolonged depression and an accompanying breakdown of world financial and commercial markets that the United States sought to reconstitute a postwar world order. To reap the potential profits made possible by the war-created deferred demand, industrialists would need to invest vast sums to quickly create new capacity. The temptations (and the competitive pressure) for such expansion was great, but so was the fear, supported by the recollection of the recent 1930s, that the mouth-watering profit prospects might be transformed into devastating losses just as soon as the effects of the proposed demand wore off. Added assurance of long-term growth was needed to justify the risk of spiraling new investment. This was in the cards if the potential foreign markets could also be tapped. But in order to convert the potential into effective and sustained demand it was necessary to restore the health of traditional trading partners, to overcome the limitations imposed by the dollar and gold shortage outside the United States, and to replace the complex national trade, exchange, and investment barriers that had been erected in self-defense during the depression. The methods adopted to solve these problems fitted in admirably with the long-run striving for hegemony in the capitalist world, reaching fruition as the U.S. dollar became the key currency in foreign trade and New York the hub of world banking and the international money market. The components of the new capitalist world order, built on the ruins of war and the disruption of the preceding protracted economic crisis, fell into place like the pieces of a jigsaw puzzle, influenced by the long history of U.S. empire-building, the ever-present threat of stagnation, the U.S. emergence from the war as the unquestioned dominant military and economic power, and the revolutionary upsurge in the colonial world.

The world economic, financial, and political system erected after the Second World War is under special stress these days as the United States, its designer and leader, exposes its feet of clay. The inability to suppress the revolution in South Vietnam, the quaking of the world financial system, originally based on the inviolability of the dollar, and the thrust of rival powers, notably Japan and Germany, to attain more competitive and independent positions vis-à-vis the United States—these are all signs of a transition to a new stage. These changes, however, do not as yet portend an alteration of fundamentals: both the struggle for hegemony in Asia and the basic social problems of the underdeveloped countries are still with us and will continue to be for the visible future.

To understand developments in the American empire and, looming on the horizon, the Japanese empire in Asia, one must comprehend the basic contradictions in the opportunities for development of the subordinate countries, whether or not they formerly had the status of colonies. Neither the transfer of advanced technology nor injections of foreign aid has succeeded in shaking them out of the morass of poverty, persistent mass unemployment, and misery. They are stuck on the capitalist road, but the options that had been available to the successful capitalist countries in past centuries—options which helped pull them out of impending, recurrent periods of stagnation—are out of the question. Conquest of territory, providing new surges of investment, is impossible. Nor is there, as in the past, the opportunity to dispose in new areas of settlement of surplus populations generated by the agricultural and industrial revolutions. At the same time, the economic and financial structure shaped by a long and continuing history of dependence on the more advanced capitalisms, imposes additional limits on the possibility of bootstrap-lifting via the route of profit-seeking capital investment.

It is hard to avoid the conclusion that, more and more, the only real alternative facing these peoples is whether to accept their lot of misery and its accompanying wastage of human lives or to revolutionize their societies so that labor can be fully utilized to begin to meet the real needs of the people.

N O T E S

1. J. R. Seeley, *The Expansion of England.* London: Macmillan, 1883, p. 8.

2. D. K. Fieldhouse, *The Colonial Empires, A Comparative Survey from the Eighteenth Century.* London: Weidenfeld & Nicolson, 1966, p. 239.

3. Marvin Kalb and Elie Abel, *Roots of Involvement: The U.S. in Asia 1784–1971.* New York: W. W. Norton, 1971. The theme of reluctance is one of the most pervasive explanations found in histories of colonialism. A characteristic example, in this case referring to South Africa, is the following: "The border . . . remained too thinly settled to provide real protection; the area instead became an irresistible attraction to Bantu cattle rustlers with grievances against the newcomers. Settlers and tribesmen could not be kept apart; both moved to and fro across the boundary. Governments then tried to enforce security by more advanced lines of demarcation, but each new boundary further compressed the territory of the indigenous tribes and ultimately led to further conflicts, with the result that the imperial power, regardless of its original intentions, reluctantly kept adding to its commitments." (From: L. H. Gann and Peter Duignan, *Burden of Empire, An Appraisal of Western Colonialism in Africa South of the Sahara.* New York: Praeger, 1967, p. 19.)

4. Ronald Steel, *Pax Americana.* New York: Viking Press, 1968, pp. 10–11.

5. This theme is thoroughly explored in two valuable studies: Gabriel Kolko, *The Politics of War: The World and United States Foreign*

Policy, 1943–1945 (New York: Random House, 1969) , and Joyce and Gabriel Kolko, *The Limits of Power, The World and United States Foreign Policy, 1945–1954* (New York: Harper & Row, 1972) .

6. R. W. Van Alstyne, *The Rising American Empire.* Chicago: Quadrangle Paperbacks, 1965, p. v.

7. Mira Wilkins, *The Emergence of Multinational Enterprise: American Business Abroad from the Colonial Era to 1914.* Cambridge, Mass.: Harvard University Press, 1970, p. 7.

8. The quotation as well as the preceding percentages are from: Douglas C. North, *The Economic Growth of the United States 1790–1860.* Englewood Cliffs, New Jersey: Prentice-Hall, 1961, pp. 41–42.

9. Van Alstyne, *op. cit.,* p. 93.

10. Professor Graebner puts the case forcefully: "What [the] traditional approaches overlook is the essential fact that the expansion of the United States was a unified, purposeful, precise movement that was ever limited to specific maritime objectives. It was the Pacific Ocean that determined the territorial goals of all American presidents from John Quincy Adams to Polk. From the beginning, travelers, traders, and officials who concerned themselves with the coastal regions had their eyes trained on ports. The goal of American policy was to control the great harbors of San Francisco, San Diego, and Juan de Fuca Strait. . . . But mercantile interests in the Pacific provided more than a contributing motive to American expansionism. They determined the course of empire. Maritime calculations first defined the objectives of American statesmen on the distant shore. Next, they augmented the strong inclination of British and American officials to seek a peaceful solution of the Oregon controversy. And, finally, they fused Oregon and California into one irreducible issue and created a vision of empire that encompassed both regions. The sea made the settlement of the Oregon question contingent upon the acquisition of California in the fulfillment of the American purpose." (Norman A. Graebner, *Empire on the Pacific, A Study in American Continental Expansion.* New York: Ronald Press, 1955, p. vi.)

11. *Hearings before the Joint Economic Committee, Congress of the United States, Employment, Growth and Price Levels,* Part 2, April 7–10, 1959. Washington, D.C.: Government Printing Office, 1959, p. 412.

PART I

OIL IMPERIALISM IN SOUTHEAST ASIA

MALCOLM CALDWELL

To what extent is there an energy crisis? How significant is Southeast Asia in the global energy equation? These are the questions to which I address myself. Certainty is, of course, out of the question in matters such as projections of future energy needs and the adequacy of reserves to meet them. Assessments vary widely, from the bland reassurances of The Institute of Petroleum (London), to the mathematical jeremiads of *The Limits to Growth*. The first declares that:

> ... far more oil still remains in the earth than has so far been produced and adequate supplies should certainly be available to satisfy foreseeable needs for many decades... Despite the fact that, like all minerals, oil is a wasting asset, proven reserves are now greater than ever before. Tremendous advances have been made in the past in the technique of finding, producing and refining crude oil and the proportion which can be extracted from individual oilfields has been greatly increased. This trend will doubtless continue, making more and more petroleum available. Meanwhile, various alternative raw materials provide further assurance as to future supplies.[1]

On the other hand, the authors of the Club of Rome study estimate that, even allowing for reserves five times those known at present, the exhaustion period with exponential growth of consumption would be no more than fifty years, while applying the same consumption growth rate to known reserves reduces the exhaustion period to twenty years.[2]

Two points should constantly be borne in mind. First, a situation of crisis arises with respect to access to nonrenewable resources long before the point of actual exhaustion. Indeed, we may say that as soon as the end is sighted and this fact is freely bandied about the crisis has begun. Second, it is not global availability that counts, but availability in relation to need, to profits, and to military power—in relation, that is, to the geography of imperialism. This is startlingly true in particular of oil. Over two-thirds of known reserves are situated in Asia (including the "Middle East" or West Asia), while the United States, Western Europe, and Japan together account for over seventy-eight percent of non-Communist consumption.[3] No placatory mystifications ought to be allowed to obscure these striking facts, so pregnant with implications. Those who discount the reality of an energy and resource crisis must explain satisfactorily Japan's lunge into Southeast Asia in the Pacific war, America's ruthless paring away of British power and influence in the Middle East at the war's end,[4] the overthrow of Mossadegh in Iran, the Suez war, and the long, continuing, Southeast Asian war, in other terms, terms equally convincing and persuasive. As the Kolkos have shown in massive detail, anti-Communist rationalizing rhetoric was only called in by the Americans to mask their global economic expansionism in the years following the Second World War *after* the plans had been carefully laid and partially implemented—precisely to ease both domestic and international acceptance of what could not otherwise fail to appear as naked buccaneering imperialism.[5] Of all the raw materials involved, oil was by far the most important in American business and official eyes, and, since the two conceptually distinguishable sectors—industry and government—interlocked functionally in practice (the same person frequently moving from one role to the other, or indeed fulfilling both roles simultaneously), the pursuit of reserves was bound to be a priority objective of postwar U.S. policy. During the war and in the years immediately after, those ultimately responsible for guaranteeing America's raw material inputs—up to and including the President—were involved in conducting numerous inventories of key items: in 1943 Secretary of State Cordell Hull, for instance, appointed a petroleum advisory committee, with major oil company personalities playing a leading role in its deliberations.[6]

It has been urged against the raw material crisis thesis—notably by apologists for U.S. foreign policy but also by others unfamiliar with the facts and bolstered by faith in the power of science to transcend all apparent limitations to global growth (and therefore, of course, to enable interclass and international harmony to be theoretically achievable) —that in each particular case some alternative will emerge in the future as in past instances of threatened real resource scarcity. In the field of inanimate energy, it does appear at first glance as if possible alternatives to the principal fossil fuels (oil, coal, and gas) are numerous and highly promising. I have attempted elsewhere to refute this optimism, which appears to me facile and largely unwarranted.[7] And since per capita consumption of inanimate energy correlates in an almost linear way with per capita GNP (i.e., per capita consumption of the major raw materials), availability of inanimate energy sources defines the contours of future world growth, regardless of the relevance of recycling, substitution, and synthetics to the future availability of other major resource inputs. Oil at this moment in time constitutes the critical core of the problem.

In turning to regional oil problems, I shall start with the major consuming countries. The United States so dominates the international oil scene that one must begin there. America is a major oil-producing country in her own right. As recently as 1950, she produced fifty-two percent of the world total and broadly satisfied her domestic demand; but by 1970 her share of world production had fallen to twenty-one percent and nearly a quarter of domestic needs was being met by imports, mainly from Venezuela and Canada.[8] In the immediate postwar years, America dramatically increased her sphere of oil operations at the expense of the declining European imperialist powers while tying up reserves and prospects for the future. Thus U.S. penetration of the Middle East[9] and establishment of the frontier of her Pacific empire in Korea and Vietnam (and Thailand).[10]

In recent years the dimension of domestic need has encroached more and more urgently upon the attention of Washington. U.S. planners now foresee the prospect of having to import one-third of home needs from the Middle East by 1980.[11] Yet bountiful though the reserves of the Middle East may appear, even they will be strained to accommodate such an additional demand (estimated at 8.5 million b-d[12]) on top of Western Europe's anticipated doubling consumption (from twelve-million b-d now to twenty-six million by the end of the century) and Japan's leap from three million to twelve million b-d over the same period.[13] These facts are well known, and lie behind keen American interest in alternative sources of supply, including Siberia and South and East Asia, the more so as the Alaskan supply may never fulfill expectations, and Canada is now firmly restricting exports of oil and natural gas in her own long-term interests.[14]

Bleak as the American energy future appears, it is comparatively speaking bright when set against the import-dependence and domestic resource-depletion of Western Europe as a unit and of Japan. But this is an unreal formulation. America has to reconcile her own insatiable needs for raw materials with the needs of those other major components of the imperialist sphere, since collapse of economic activity as a result of import difficulties in her rivals (for third markets, investment opportunities, guaranteed access to raw materials) would ultimately redound to her own grave disadvantage. In other words, America's leaders must try to maximize U.S. profit in intrametropolitan trading in raw materials, by control of resources and distribution, while at the same time taking ultimate responsibility for preserving the American empire as widely as possible in geographical terms in order that international capitalism *as such* may continue to function. This requires continued access to and disposal of all the raw material inputs which, like oil, alone make industrial activity possible. The energy crisis is a crisis for imperialism as a system, with the United States (or, more accurately, her top decision-makers) almost alone in possessing the drive to hold together a crumbling "free world" empire (with minor help from client states such as Australia and outright satrapies such as Thailand), and certainly alone in possessing the capacity to execute the necessary measures whatever they might entail.

Western European oil consumption represents about a third of the non-Communist world total; but indigenous production (and potential production) of crude oil was negligible until the North Sea bonanza altered the picture. At the same time, it would require a miracle for the North Sea to yield enough to sustain Western Europe's rapid growth without imports from outside the area. Western European demand, rising at over thirteen percent per annum, is growing at a pace well above the world average. In a recent summing up of prospects for Europe in the light of the North Sea finds, the industrial editor of the *Sunday Times* (London) concluded: "The harsh truth is that the Western world now has no defence against a really effective Arab embargo, and the North Sea does not alter this."[15] So the countries of Western Europe too have much more than a detached interest in the discovery and development of reserves of fossil fuels which will lower dependence upon the Middle East. It has been suggested, for example, that the enlarged Common Market might ultimately have to ship coal from Australia. In the meantime, the EEC countries strive to retain a stake in the Asian energy race. West Germany negotiated oil agreements with Burma in 1970.[16] Total Indonesia, a French company, is engaged in offshore exploration and drilling around Indonesia.[17] Holland and Britain, of course, retain important interests in the region.

Japan, of all the highly industrialized countries, is in the most acute and exposed position, with a disastrous recent experience of oil deprivation still in the forefront of national consciousness. (At the end of the Pacific war the allied blockade paralyzed the economy.) Almost all the country's essential oil is imported from sources not controlled by Japan—ninety percent of it from the Middle East, shuttled to Japanese ports by 280 giant tankers straggling in a 10,000-mile crocodile from the Persian Gulf.[18] In Japan itself, the stock of oil constitutes only forty-five days' supply, so that any cessation for whatever reason—an embargo by the OPEC powers, for instance, or closure of the vital Strait of Malacca—would instantly resurrect the nightmare of economic thrombosis. Still, oil climbs in importance in provision of inanimate energy: as late as 1950 coal still accounted for sixty percent of the total, but by 1970 oil provided seventy percent. Moreover, the Americans forced upon Tokyo oil agreements violating traditional Japanese determination to exclude foreign control over critical sectors of the economy and won for the big U.S. oil companies the permanent right to supply crude. The United States controls nearly two-thirds of Middle East oil, despite strenuous Japanese efforts since 1957—against implacable obstruction on the part of the oligopolies—to obtain a toehold in the region, so vital to her interests.

But Middle East oil is in some ways unsuitable to Japan's needs, as well as being precarious. It has a high sulfur content, and therefore particularly exacerbates Japan's pollution problem, which is the worst in the world. This further steels Japanese determination to search out alternative sources of supply. Indonesian and Siberian oil (in both of which Japan is intensely interested), aside from being more conveniently sited, are of low sulfur content. Japan, in conjunction with South Korea and Taiwan, is also actively exploring prospects in the promising offshore area centering on the Tiao-yu (Senkaku) Islands. China has, however, vigorously protested against any claim made by the Ocean Development Corporation, formed in Tokyo in 1970, to rights in an area held by Peking to belong to the People's Republic.[19] Japan's leaders understand full well that as far as oil control is concerned nothing talks remotely like concentrated economic power backed up by military might. For this reason re-cartelization and re-militarization have been proceeding hectically in Japan in recent years.[20] This process is expected to accelerate and to embrace all the kinds of modern equipment—up to and including nuclear weapons—hitherto eschewed.[21]

Japan's immediate neighbors are understandably restive at the specter of resurgent armed might in their midst. Apprehensions are strengthened by other aspects of the current scene, notably by Japanese economic penetration accompanied by rhetoric uncannily reminiscent of the "Greater East Asia Co-prosperity Sphere"[22] and by Japanese plans to participate in the policing of Taiwan, Korea, and the Strait of Malacca.[23] In all of this, oil plays a preponderant role: "I think the problem of oil is most important, not only to Japan but to the world at large," Taro Yamashita (first president of Japan's Arabian Oil Company) told a Tokyo newspaper in 1958. "Think of the Pacific War. Its cause was the blockade or prevention of movements of only some two million tons of oil. It is oil that dominates the world."[24]

In this context, Siberian oil—and Russo-Japanese cooperation in its development (most probably with United States participation, despite unconvincing disclaimers) —is of some significance. Estimates by Japanese experts suggest that the Tyumen oil field contains proven reserves of at least forty million tons of oil a year for at least twenty years; this would provide eight percent of Japan's estimated annual energy requirements in the 1980s.[25] The extent to which such cooperation, involving Russia, America, and Japan, forms a pattern, or is on a strictly ad hoc basis is still a matter of dispute. My own view, which I have expressed elsewhere, is that the cooperation is systematic enough to warrant use of the term "the new RAJ in Asia" (*R*ussia–*A*merica–*J*apan) .[26] Joint interest in the Siberian oil pipeline is only one aspect of it. Both Washington and Moscow have also supported Japan's aggressive assertion of rights of navigation in the Strait of Malacca over the counterproposals of the geographically responsible powers, Malaysia, Indonesia, and Singapore. More importantly, all three "RAJ" powers support both General Suharto of Indonesia and General Lon Nol of Cambodia against the revolutionary struggles of their respective peoples—which one may interpret as a common interest in "containment of China" or in limiting the spread of peasant revolutionary movements in the area aimed at eliminating "Great Power" influence (or both).[27] The facts are hardly in question; it is in the interpretation to be put upon them that differences arise among commentators.

It may be as well, in passing, to point out that although the Soviet Union is a major oil producer (second only to the United States), harbors vast reserves, and plans to increase her already extensive exports to the rest of the world, her ultimate status in the world's oil markets will depend upon the extent to which she becomes a truly high mass consumption society on the American pattern, particularly in ownership of private automobiles. At the moment, the lag is very great, but the growth pattern of the private automobile suggests the possibility that the Soviet Union may choose to conserve her own reserves or even import oil[28] as the United States is now increasingly obliged to do despite her once seemingly inexhaustible reserves.

Recent reports of vast oil discoveries in China are also of obvious interest to Japan, since domestic Chinese consumption is bound to be low for the foreseeable future—forever, if certain unnecessary petrol-consuming technological gadgets (such as the private motor car) are to be foregone by deliberate choice, as appears to be the case.[29] Already Japan–China barter agreements have involved the exchange of Chinese oil for Japanese machinery.[30] This kind of transaction could develop into something of importance for both parties, but business considerations alone do not define the future of Sino-Japanese relations: we need only recall the clash over Senkaku-centered offshore oil; again, China jumped to the defense of Malaysia and Indonesia— much to their surprise and confusion—in their joint struggle to keep a Japanese military presence out of the Malacca Strait; China has also supported the OPEC powers in their confrontations with the Western powers.

China and the Indian subcontinent afford an interesting and instructive parallel. The story of the Chinese oil industry is well known in outline. Before the revolution, the impression was

fostered that China was poorly endowed with indigenous petroleum reserves. It was part of Western global oil strategy at the
time to keep the Chinese market for oil products attuned to
importing from Western-dominated production facilities in
neighboring and accessible Pacific territories. By this means,
pricing policies optimizing profits could be pursued without
threat of domestic competition. Since the revolution, however,
intense effort devoted to surveying and development has led to a
situation where China is self-sufficient in oil—and even, as we
have seen, in a position to export.[31]

India, Bangla Desh, and Pakistan, in contrast, still find themselves victims of a strategy common to the major oil companies of
consistently extorting prices well above the prevailing world
market rates, playing upon the supposition that the countries of
the subcontinent are deficient in petroleum reserves.[32] For the
future, the portents are mixed. On the one hand, the growing
bargaining strength of the OPEC country elites suggests that they
will progressively wrest price concessions from the oil giants,
thereby even further raising the prices the latter charge to customers such as India.[33] Further, in the absence of revolutionary
social change, the private motor car will no doubt continue as
the regional status symbol—in marked contrast with China—
thus sustaining additional inessential demand and weakening
the subcontinental bargaining position. On the other hand,
India has been, and will doubtless continue, developing contacts
outside the capitalist oligopolies which lend her leaders some
countervailing power: Russia, for instance, has given important
help in locating and exploiting indigenous oil potential. In addition, India has explored the possibility of making direct deals
with major oil producers such as Iraq; the terms of the proposed
agreements would effectively circumvent the obstruction of the
Western concerns.[34] The fact remains, however, that—at least as
far as our present (prerevolutionary) knowledge goes—all three
countries of the subcontinent seem to be relatively poorly endowed with oil, and therefore vulnerable.[35] Only time can tell
whether the current appraisal is culturally bound or not.[36]

We may now turn to the question of the oil resources of Southeast Asia, which have figured so greatly in recent discussion, both
academic and polemical. Below I summarize the readily available
bare statistical facts about Southeast Asian oil (together with
some relevant comparative data from elsewhere in Asia) :

COUNTRY	Est. reserves, thousands of barrels, 1970	% world reserves	Crude prod., thousands of barrels, 1970	% world prod. '70	Reserves- prod. ratio	Demand for refined, thousands of barrels, 1970	Refining cap., thousands of barrels/ day, 1970	% world refining cap.
Brunei-Malaysia	650,000	0.12	54,020	0.33	12.03	(b)	(d)	(d)
Burma	48,000	0.01	6,150	0.04	7.80	n.a.	26.3	0.1
Indonesia	18,000,000	3.37	310,483	1.81	57.97	41,068	251.2	0.5
Philippines	—	—	—	—	—	58,286	205.0	0.3
Singapore-Malaysia	(a)	(a)	(a)	(a)	(a)	97,865	313.5	0.6
South Vietnam	n.a.	n.a.	—	—	—	62,713 (c)	n.a.	n.a.
Thailand	500	0.00	n.a.	n.a.	n.a.	36,923	43.5	0.1
OTHER ASIAN								
Formosa	19,200	0.00	587	0.00	32.71	34,599	118.0	0.2
India	261,191	0.05	49,275	0.29	7.50	124,294	544.4 (e)	1.0 (e)
Japan	26,962	0.01	5,840	0.03	4.62	1,186,173	3,698.8	7.0
Pakistan	34,900	0.01	3,234	0.02	10.79	34,874	(f)	(f)
South Korea	—	—	—	—	—	54,010	250.0	0.5
China	5,669,000	1.06	76,000	0.46	74.59	n.a.	n.a.	n.a.

Notes: a. See above under "Brunei-Malaysia"; Singapore has no known reserves.
   b. See below under "Singapore-Malaysia."
   c. Includes Cambodia.
   d. Included with "Singapore-Malaysia" below.
   e. Includes Pakistan.
   f. See above, included with India.

Notation: Est. = Estimated; prod. = production; '70 = 1970; cap. = capacity; n.a. = not available.

(SOURCE: E. L. DeGolyer and L. W. MacNaughton, *Twentieth Century Petroleum Statistics 1971* (Dallas: DeGolyer and MacNaughton, 1971), pp. 1, 60, 90.)

Scrutiny of the table hardly reveals—at least at first glance and by itself—anything sensational enough to justify the excitement at Asian, and specifically Southeast Asian, oil prospects which swept through the ranks of the industry in the late 1960s and which was subsequently reflected in the press and in left-wing political circles. But it should be added in explanation, first, that if we exclude from the calculations the five special cases (United States, U.S.S.R., Saudi Arabia, Kuwait, and Iran) in the matter of reserves, the Southeast Asian estimate comes to a far from insignificant ten percent of the remainder. Second, there is no doubt that the frantic prospecting and other activities of the oil giants and of adjunct organizations such as CCOP (Committee for Coordination of Joint Prospecting for Mineral Resources in Asian Offshore Areas—an organization of the leading imperialist powers and their neocolonies) in the area reflects a general expectation that, when more is positively and firmly established about the relevant physical properties of the region, its estimated reserves will be progressively reassessed upward. Certainly the evidence is too overwhelming to require elaboration that the Americans are determined to hold at whatever cost the broad frontiers of empire so that such imperialist activities can continue unabated.[37]

Before concentrating on Indonesia, which is the heart of the Southeast Asian matter as far as the Americans are concerned (and has been for the better part of three decades), and which was the objective of the Japanese "Strike South" strategy in the Pacific and again attracts the particular attention of Tokyo, I will discuss briefly some of the issues raised by international competition for oil elsewhere in the region.

Despite the savagery of the assault consequent upon Nixon's decision to escalate in Indochina in the winter–spring of 1971–1972, few can harbor any illusions that oil will ever flow (if indeed there are any reserves of significance there) to the big Western oil giants from concessions offshore from South Vietnam and Cambodia.[38] But this does not mean that everything for which U.S. business and government have fought since the Second World War is being or will be abandoned. Far from it: the very intensity of U.S. aggression in Indochina mirrors determination to wrest something from the wreckage, in order to consolidate in Thailand, Indonesia, and elsewhere. South Vietnamese oil as such is a fantasy that can be relinquished. It is important to understand, however, the role that oil has played in the Indochina war. For instance, one of the first things attended to by the Lon Nol regime immediately after the overthrow of Sihanouk in 1970 was the coordination of conditions for the leasing of Cambodian offshore oil leases with Bangkok and Saigon. Even before the coup, pressure had been exerted upon Cambodia to participate in the work of ECAFE's CCOP. Significantly, since the 1970 coup U.S. petroleum statistics simply include Cambodian estimates with those of South Vietnam (see table above). Further, it was Pertamina, the notorious Indonesian oil enterprise, which paid the expenses of the Djakarta conference of regional neocolonial powers which attempted to "stabilize" post-coup conditions in Cambodia in order to permit the United States to derive some benefit from the long-planned deposition of Sihanouk.[39] The port of Sihanoukville would obviously have been of some interest to oil companies prospecting offshore locally, affording facilities almost halfway between those of Bangkok and Saigon, eight hundred miles apart by sea.

Thailand presents quite a different picture, however. An insurgency that has shown steady progress notwithstanding, the oil-hungry countries, headed by the United States, have pushed ahead in extracting the right to exploit their oil. It was announced in May 1972 that the Thai Petroleum Committee was considering inviting bids from foreign companies for the survey of oil deposits in the deep sea of more than 200 meters on the west coast of Thailand (in the southern narrow neck of the Kra Isthmus).[40] This was in addition to the granting of concessions for the survey of offshore oil deposits in six areas around the Gulf of Siam. Japan, as the biggest single foreign investor in Thailand, is interested and in a position to exert some leverage. Tokyo has a secondary interest: the possibility of constructing a canal or pipeline across the narrowest part of the Kra Isthmus in order to carry Middle Eastern crude by a route circumventing the increasingly hazardous and potentially hostile Strait of Malacca. (The biggest Japanese tankers now navigate the Strait only with difficulty and in favorable circumstances; talks are in progress between Japan, Malaysia, Indonesia, and Singapore about possible measures, such as dredging, designed to increase the safety margin.) But whether it is Kra canal or Kra pipeline that is at the moment being the more seriously considered, it seems unlikely to come to fruition, for the area it would have to traverse is guerrilla country, only partially under Bangkok's control (and slipping further all the time). Moreover, as Thai forces become more deeply enmeshed in the Indochina War— invading Laos and Cambodia on behalf of the United States— long-term prospects must assume a gloomier mien discouraging to investors contemplating expensive projects with a long-term payoff.

In neighboring Burma, there are other complications besides insurgencies. As a result of a peculiarly disastrous colonial experience, Burma since independence has pursued policies designed as far as possible to exclude foreigners (especially Westerners) and to minimize dependence upon other countries (especially the rich Western countries). In the sphere of oil, this has dictated a number of maneuvers. First, the British-owned Burmah Oil was nationalized (though it continued to operate elsewhere in the world), becoming first the People's Oil Company and later Myanma Oil. Acceptable compensation was paid, and it appears the action was—most untypically where oil "seizures" are concerned—absorbed by the international oil giants with a shrug, no doubt with the expectation that such a small rural country would be unable on its own to work its oil, and that therefore one or other of the giants would soon be invited back in. But, second, the Burmese government has played off foreign oil interests quite astutely one against the other in the intervening years, and has as a result retained much of its deeply craved independence.

Specifically, Burma has shunned the biggest oil concerns, and has particularly taken care to shut out American interests. The country's contacts with foreign oil organizations have been restricted to soliciting such financial and technical assistance as has been deemed essential to raising domestic production, which still falls short of domestic requirements. American representatives in Burma, noting these limitations, have advocated "low-profile" local activity, if any is allowed, operating through foreign companies if necessary.[41] In 1970 the West German government signed two aid agreements which help finance the development of existing fields and the opening of new ones, and provide technical assistance in the form of experts and equipment. The Burmese government has also bargained very hard. For this reason the Japanese, although interested, have so far made no progress: the Burmese refused to enter into a percentage-share arrangement with them with respect to offshore oil, offering instead a specified return on any investment undertaken.

Because of this adamantly nationalistic attitude, speculation has long been rife that when former Burmese premier U Nu started an armed struggle against the regime he was financed by American oil interests. His guerrillas were armed and trained by the CIA, but it now appears that the funding came from a non-American oil company operating in Southeast Asia. What the state of the game is at the present moment is hard to gauge; U Nu recently relinquished his titular leadership of the guerrillas; the latter in any case seem to have made negligible progress when compared with the Communist-led guerrillas, who have been in action for over two decades and have made major steps toward coordination with the various minority-group rebellions. Burma's assertion of independence in exploiting her own oil has not been taken lying down by the oil giants, who will undoubtedly go on trying to find ways of penetrating the country and prizing loose its oil, by unseating General Ne Win if necessary.

Malaysia and Brunei constituted, until recently, a fairly secure economic enclave for the British. Brunei, with the largest offshore oil field in Asia (in terms of current production), is still a British dependency, and Shell dominates its economy. The whole is a caricature of neocolonialism. British troops put down a nationalist revolt in 1962–1963. Shell until recently paid one of the lowest prices in the world per barrel for the oil it took out of the country (though recently it has guiltily improved its terms). The government is a feudal relic. The best prospects for change in all respects—independence, economic autonomy, domestic democracy, and socialism—lie with the Communist guerrillas who already control large areas of neighboring Sarawak and incorporate units of the Brunei insurgents put down by the British a decade ago. But for the moment the British and their oil company remain. Britain also retains the major share of Sarawak's economy, and Shell has all the local concessions. Sabah has been prospected by a variety of companies, including Japanese. Japan is interested in this area, which it occupied during the Second World War. Mitsubishi is currently cooperating with Shell in the construction of a natural gas liquefication plant in Brunei.

But if Britain clings to northern Borneo, West Malaysia is in the process of "changing masters";[42] increasingly U.S. interests, cuckoolike, nudge British from the comfortable neocolonial nest. As part of this transformation, there has been an international scramble for offshore oil concessions. But there is some doubt about the potential, and some companies have already pulled out, ostensibly in protest against Malaysia's demand for fifteen percent participation if oil is discovered. Clearly, whatever the truth ultimately revealed by further prospecting, Malaysia for strategic reasons alone must remain an object of profound concern for the oil companies and the governments of countries dependent upon them.

Indochina, Thailand, and Burma are the frontier of Southeast Asia, but Malaysia is a corridor leading to the very heartland, as far as imperialist interests are concerned: Indonesia. The left in Malaya posed a serious military challenge to the British in the years from 1948 to the fifties, and now again a major insurgency is in progress. British Special Forces, Australian, and New Zealand troops posted in the country, and the British-trained and -advised Malaysian armed forces are all engaged.

Although Singapore boasts no oil resources of its own, it is necessary to say something about it since it has emerged as very much the nerve center of oil imperialism in the region. For an oil firm casting about for a suitable local anchorage, Singapore offered from the very beginning of the boom unparalleled facilities. Some of the major advantages of the island may be listed as follows: first, a private enterprise-oriented government securely in power, with control exercised by a single-party legislature, a network of "community" organizations, and a highly efficient secret police (known as the Special Branch);[43] second, labor legislation virtually eliminating industrial action by workers and deliberately pushing down the rate of growth of wages below those of such competitors as Taiwan and South Korea;[44] third, ample capacity of an appropriate kind, in the form of office buildings, docks, marine repair works, and communications facilities; fourth, available lower managerial, clerical, and skilled labor with relevant experience (or adaptability); fifth, excellent accommodations for expatriate Western families in one of the healthiest countries of the world; and, sixth, the incentive of need induced in Singapore's government by British military withdrawal. The conjuncture was irresistible.

Singapore's oil boom was well under way by the start of the

1970s as foreign companies swarmed in to capitalize on these (and other) advantages, and local entrepreneurs frantically diversified to fit in the better with new demands. Existing refining capacity was extended (it had long served the needs of the American military in Indochina and Thailand), and the government itself underwrote provision of manufacturing, constructional, and repair facilities relevant to the servicing of the offshore rigs. Although there have been attempts by some neighboring countries—notably Indonesia—to attract away some of the direct and indirect business generated by the oil bonanza, so far Singapore has preserved its clear lead. As a result of the September 1972 general elections, in which the ruling People's Action Party took almost seventy percent of the vote and all the seats, it seems Singapore will keep its lead. Internal security is notably greater than elsewhere in the region. Moreover, both geography and economic history, which dictated that the island would act as the colonial entrepôt for the whole Southeast Asian area (and even beyond), still exert a determining influence in selection of Singapore as the hub of international neocolonialist (imperialist) activity locally, not least in the complex interchanges necessitated by the oil industry.[45]

The Philippines, as one would expect, is tied up by American oil interests. Geologically, the prospects for finding domestic resources seem good, but up to the present the U.S. companies have preferred to make easy profits on Middle Eastern oil sold at inflated prices in a tax-avoidance haven where the private car is a supreme status symbol. Nationalist sentiment certainly exists against this situation, but much of it boils down to the envy of local interests, covetously eyeing the profits seeping abroad. Others—to the left—see the problem in its true light: how to acquire the capital and expertise to uncover and utilize domestic resources, and at the same time cut away all unnecessary consumption. In the words of a leading Filipino intellectual, Renato Constantino: "We shall realise our folly all the more if we consider certain developments in China. ... China has achieved self-sufficiency in the production of crude oil and will soon join the ranks of oil-exporting nations ... her own requirements are increasing at a very moderate rate. This is due in large part to a well-established socialist policy which correctly places a high priority on the development of a rational public transport system and a very low priority on private car ownership."[46] Revolutionary armed struggle is already well advanced in the Philippines—but tens of thousands of U.S. troops are at hand, and militarily resurgent Japan is also very close. The special economic arrangements with America terminate in 1974 (in theory) ; that the Philippines will be caught up in the resolution of intra-imperial and anti-imperialist contradictions in the area in the near future is therefore certain.

But ultimately it is Indonesia that defines the Southeast Asian situation in this context: Indonesia is the prize for imperialism, and Indonesia provided and provides the pretext for pushing out the regional boundaries of empire to their militarily "logical" limits. The sufferings of Indochina and Indonesia in the postwar period of U.S. economic, political and military hegemony in the region have differed in kind, but in the last analysis stem from the same source—the greedy determination of American imperialism to command the lion's share of world raw materials and to dominate as much of the world as possible for markets, investment opportunities, and optimum juggling of assets generally.

The Indonesian oil industry is of long standing. The nineteenth-century pioneers succeeded not only in establishing a flourishing industry but also in showing that the theoretically favorable terrain could live up to its promise where adequately prospected, worked, and made accessible by provision of the necessary infrastructure. The lesson was not lost on those intent on dominating the world's oil industry. The terrain is not easy to survey and prospect, so that it was not until modern methods became available that satisfactory assessments of Indonesia's potential could be undertaken. Toward the close of the interwar period, interested oil concerns undertook extensive aerial mapping of the inaccessible and largely unexplored tracts of Sumatra, Borneo, and New Guinea—three of the largest islands in the world and among the most impenetrable by reason of swamp, mountain, and jungle. The Netherlands New Guinea Oil Company (NNGPM) survey of what is now West Irian was—at the time it was conducted—". . . probably the most complete one ever made anywhere in the world."[47]

The NNGPM was a joint enterprise, run by and for Royal Dutch Shell, Standard Vacuum (Stanvac), and California Standard and Texas Company (Caltex), the two American components controlling sixty percent. Elsewhere in the archipelago the

American share varied, but the foot was firmly in the door. Just before the Second World War promising finds were made in various parts of Indonesia, suggesting that eventual production might well be far above anything formerly anticipated. It was with this knowledge available to a limited number of oil people, including Americans, that the war interrupted any further work. Indonesian oil, long coveted by the Japanese, now fell into their hands, but insurmountable difficulties—principally logistic but also arising from a shortage of appropriate skilled and experienced oil men—prevented them from making much use of the prize.

The postwar history of Indonesia can be written, too, in terms of a fluctuating international struggle for the archipelago's rich resources. Indonesian oil, tin, rubber, bauxite, and a wide range of other raw materials figure repeatedly in American leaders' wartime and postwar articulations of their economic foreign policy. Constantly, in formulating the domino theory, reference is made to warding "Communism" away from Indonesia, thus justifying the struggle in Vietnam. To preserve Southeast Asia for the "free world" demanded, however, a certain amount of flexibility. If the old colonial power still showed the will and the strength to crush "Communism" (indigenous social revolution, that is), then the United States would not oppose restoration, with—of course—the quid pro quo of enhanced economic opportunities and access for U.S. interests in return for any necessary assistance in the way of arms and aid.

The Dutch were totally dependent upon U.S. aid for their war against the Indonesian people. But it was not the cost that bothered Washington; it was the inability of the Dutch to achieve their ends. Therefore, when the nationalist leadership showed its true colors with the crushing of Tan Malaka (an independent revolutionary with great popular appeal) and subsequently (in 1948, in the so-called Madiun affair) the Communist party of Indonesia (PKI), and confirmed this by displaying a readiness to make humiliating and expensive concessions to the Dutch, U.S. leaders drew the correct conclusions. By threatening to withdraw all aid they forced Holland to concede independence. The new leaders of independent Indonesia could go on making as many fiery "anti-imperialist" speeches as they cared, but the Americans knew that this posed no threat to their economic penetration, made easier by undercutting the Dutch position.

In 1940, Indonesian oil production had totaled 7.9 million metric tons; by 1946 it had fallen to a mere 300,000. Now Stanvac and Caltex poured money into reconstruction and reactivation of the industry. By 1951 prewar production had been surpassed, and by 1957 had been doubled. The American companies' top competitor, Royal Dutch, was knocked out in the latter year, when it was nationalized as part of President Sukarno's campaign to recover West Irian (retained by the Dutch after the rest of Indonesia had been given independence). Sukarno wanted to move forward to further measures of nationalization, but his "radical" rhetoric provoked a conservative rebellion by Western-influenced Indonesian elites. They staged it in Sumatra, where much of the oil was produced. This put the United States in a dilemma. On the one hand, it helped the rebels by supplying arms, planes, and some personnel (such as pilots). The United States also prepared to invade the areas of Sumatra where it held oil rights.[48] But, on the other hand, it could see that the rebellion had no popular backing, and that even the army—as conservative as the bankers and Western-educated economists who led the revolt—held firm to Djakarta and had no difficulty in crushing the revolt. (In doing so Indonesian armed forces succeeded in shooting down an American pilot flying for the rebels—awkward evidence of oil imperialism in practice.) From this point on, the U.S. government changed its strategy from dismembering Indonesia and taking the lucrative and oil-rich parts, to building up influence and support inside the army preparatory to taking maximum advantage of any eventuality favorable to freer and more profitable economic access.

For Sukarno's policies were restrictive. They were intended to divert Indonesian attention from economic chaos and stagnation rather than to implement anything recognizable as socialism. Nevertheless, they did impinge upon the valued freedoms of Western and other capitalist enterprises working in the country: the freedom to repatriate profits; the freedom to use earnings to buy and import whatever was wanted; freedom from nationalization or threat of it; freedom from local competition; and all the other desiderata of companies operating internationally. Nevertheless, it is important to grasp that, even within the framework of Sukarno's "Guided Economy," instituted in 1957, American power could be—and was—used to wrest differential economic advantage for U.S. concerns. Thus, while Royal Dutch Shell withdrew altogether from participation in the Indonesian oil industry as a result of government measures in the years 1958 to 1963, American threats of withdrawing economic aid effectively safeguarded the position of Caltex and Stanvac. As a result of postwar maneuvering, the American oil companies had nudged their rivals completely out.

From September 1963, Caltex and Stanvac had to accept terms which made them contractors for two state-owned concerns—Permina, which supervised all exploration and production, and Pertamina, which undertook distribution. In March 1965, the government progressed further to ". . . supervision of operations of foreign oil companies as a 'new revolutionary measure' imposed on foreign capital and on vital projects. This was followed in July when the Government took over local sales of the foreign oil companies. . . ."[49] Clearly, the writing was on the wall. The United States was prepared to tolerate any quantity of theoretical leftism and radical rhetorical bluster, but when threatened with substantial losses it acted quickly. Sukarno fell from power shortly afterward in circumstances still riddled with question marks.[50] What is certain is that the outcome could not have been better for the oil companies and imperialist interests generally. Step by step the restrictions shackling free operation were removed. American advisers and American-trained Indonesian economists set about recasting the laws relating to foreign investment, repatriation of profits and dividends, and other matters vital to lucrative foreign investment.[51]

The fall of Sukarno could hardly have been more propitiously timed. Indonesia stands on the largest continental shelf in the world. Geologists had long been aware of the oil potential of the world's continental shelves. But until the early part of the 1960s technical difficulties hampered actual exploration and exploitation. These problems were progressively overcome in the 1960s. At a stroke, Indonesia became one of the lushest oil plums in the world. The question then was: Into whose lap would it fall?

The United States, having emerged victorious over the Japanese in the war and usurped the Dutch thereafter, started as the clear favorite. Indeed, as a result of the Suharto coup and the coming to power of the "Berkeley Mafia,"* the U.S. position seemed assured and unassailable. With American agents in power,[52] America dominating the "Inter-Governmental Group on Indonesia,"[53] and American business hogging the major share of post-1967 foreign investment,[54] the United States imperial grip seems impregnable. But we ought to look a little more closely at the position and prospects, in particular at the complex, mutually distrustful—yet mutually dependent—accommodation between U.S. imperialism and Japanese imperialism.

Japan, as we have seen, desperately needs to reduce her present dependence upon U.S.-controlled oil. The government-owned Japan Petroleum Development Corporation provides financial and technical assistance to Japanese companies engaged in a frantic international search for oil. The aim is to have thirty percent "yen oil" by 1985. This would mean uncovering in areas open to them reserves sufficient to produce between three and four million barrels a day—equivalent to total consumption at the present moment. Recent OPEC price rises and oil nationalizations have galvanized the Japanese into sharp awareness of their predicament. In the absence of proved alternative energy sources, dependence on imported crude will continue for the foreseeable future.

With this in mind it is not difficult to appreciate the intense Japanese interest in Indonesian developments. Fifty percent of Indonesia's current crude output—seventy percent of its crude exports—already goes to Japan. Official Indonesian expectations are that 1973 production will be two million barrels per day. Japan is now second only to the United States in granting aid to Indonesia, and accounts for roughly a third of the total. Much of it is directly oil related (such as the loan extended to Pertamina in 1971 by Mitsui and Marubeni-Iida for building oil tankers and pipelines in Western Java), and to be repaid in crude. Also, the Japanese have vigorously pushed their own interests in the carve-up of Indonesian offshore areas among the big foreign oil companies. On- and offshore, Japanese firms now hold something more than 60,000 square miles of Indonesian land and shelf.

---

* "Berkeley Mafia" refers to American and American-trained Indonesian scholars who were involved in preparing for, and subsequently taking advantage of, the Indonesian coup of 1965. The phrase arises from the title of the David Ransom article cited in note 50.

Japanese firms have also been trying to buy into other foreign companies operating around the archipelago, and have succeeded in at least five known cases. Recent economic disputes with the United States have sharply accentuated the precariousness of Japan's position were Washington, for any reason, to threaten a raw materials embargo.

It is in this light that we can assess Japanese prospects in Indonesia. The disadvantages are obvious enough. Memories of the occupation years linger here as well as elsewhere in Southeast Asia, and apprehensions are freely expressed about the resurgence of ominously familiar features: rearmament, economic penetration, and the expression of ambitions uncannily like those of the prewar Greater East Asia Co-prosperity Sphere.[55] But Japan also has advantages. First and foremost is the fact that America's capacity to wage large-scale and protracted counter-revolutionary warfare has been badly damaged by the Indochina War. More and more, Washington will have to rely upon Asianization—getting Asians to undertake necessary ground control—while the United States continues its air war strategy. In this context Japan is by far the most important country in the region, though undoubtedly extension of a Japanese counterinsurgency presence to Southeast Asia would have to develop cautiously and to some extent indirectly at first.

This latent Japanese counterrevolutionary capacity is a powerful bargaining counter for Tokyo—facing a Washington whose capacity is tangibly ebbing, but whose need of empire in the region is as strong as ever. Japanese suspicions have been that U.S.-dominated oil companies have been taking up concessions which they have no serious intention of working simply to prevent their falling to Japanese companies. Up to the present the Japanese-owned concessions in Indonesia have not been markedly fortunate (which explains the eagerness to buy into other companies: the French Total Indonesia, Pertamina, and Japex working in harness in June 1972 struck oil off East Kalimantan). But the U.S. companies may be forced to back down further and allow Japan to cut in more deeply in Indonesian oil, and relinquish some concessions not yet worked. In this kind of process, it would be natural to see Pertamina favoring Japanese aspirations, since between them a deal might emerge eliminating the oil giants and their profits. A further new factor is the willingness of the Japanese government's Export and Import Bank to extend finance to permit Japanese oil companies to buy into the giants (witness the Japex–Union Oil Corporation joint enterprise, also off East Kalimantan). It should be borne in mind that Japan has, since 1968 or so, accumulated a mammoth foreign exchange surplus, now available for investment, as a result of priming a strong trade surplus with the U.S. and Southeast Asia.

Nor should it be forgotten, though the point will not be developed here, that many Indonesian leaders were strongly influenced in their formative years by their Japanese occupiers.[56] Suharto himself, for instance, joined Peta (Pembela Tanah Air—the Fatherland Defense Force) on its formation in 1943. In 1944 he was promoted to Chūdanchō (company commander). A number of Japanese military leaders during the occupation worked hard to make friends among the younger generation of Indonesians, feeling certain that Indonesia would soon win independence, and that in the postindependence period such friendships would be of the utmost value. Rear Admiral Tadashi Maeda in particular cultivated these friendships. After the war he returned to Indonesia, along with some formerly prominent military colleagues, as an oilman[57] and was able at once to pick up the threads, threads stretching by now very widely through the political and administrative structure. It is true that the United States, with the CIA acting as Black Dragon,* has also its equivalent network, but it ought not to be overlooked that, whereas Maeda and his colleagues were from the first preaching anti-imperialist, anti-Western nationalism, congenial to a whole cross-section of Indonesians seized with that emotion in the first place, American influence has worked only with an elite Westernized handful, alienated already by that status from the mass of the people, and has assumed a form readily portrayed as antagonistic to Indonesia's long-run national interests. Furthermore, the American presence, in its various manifestations, is markedly more dissonant, in respect of its compatibility with Indonesian traditions and sensibilities, than a muted Japanese presence. It is notable that U.S. Special Forces stationed in Indonesia have had to be tucked away out of sight as much as possible. But the elaborate facilities that have had to be provided to

---

* Black Dragon was the Japanese secret service/secret society involved in the prewar Japanese penetration of Southeast Asia as a prelude to taking it over.

attract U.S. oilmen and other businessmen away from their bases in Singapore to settle in Indonesia have already violently offended the people and provoked a number of serious clashes by demonstrators with the authorities. It takes no great insight to see this kind of thing escalating and serving to politicize those originally protesting from pure chauvinism or religion-influenced puritanism.

The intra-imperialist struggle over Indonesia has no predetermined outcome. That it will intensify and assume additional forms is self-evident. America's assets, in terms of effective and relevant regional power and influence, are declining, Japan's increasing. But we should also look at a third party to the struggle: the Communist Party of Indonesia (PKI). Decimated and all but annihilated as a consequence of the Suharto coup, the party has now firmly embraced protracted revolutionary armed struggle based on the countryside. There seems little doubt that it is once again gaining ground steadily, with a secure base area in West Kalimantan and guerrilla groups in various islands of the archipelago. The difficulties in its path are very great, but the leadership is taking a realistic and long-term perspective. Developments in the area may rapidly transform prospects—for example, further guerrilla gains in Sarawak, Mindanao (Southern Philippines), and West Malaysia affording enhanced supply, courier, training, and sanctuary facilities. The PKI repeatedly denounces Suharto's auctioning off of Indonesia's natural resources to the giant international companies, and in this it is in chorus with the liberation struggles throughout the area.[58]

This is a factor af major importance in surveying Southeast Asia's prospects. It is not simply a question of Japan and the United States, with their respective clients and bought men, fighting over the real resources of a passive and inert Southeast Asia. Let the academic and journalistic commentators quibble all they like about the comparative economic prospects of Japan and the United States. But we should be clear that the true future of the area and its real resources lies with the armed liberation struggles, representing the patriotic and democratic instincts and aspirations of the entire people.

NOTES

1. Institute of Petroleum Information Service, *Oil—The World's Reserves* (London: Institute of Petroleum, 1967), p. 5.

2. Dennis L. Meadows *et al., The Limits of Growth* (London: Earth Island, 1972), p. 58.

3. E. L. DeGolyer and L. W. MacNaughton, *Twentieth Century Petroleum Statistics 1971* (Dallas: DeGolyer and MacNaughton, 1971), pp. 1, 60.

4. To Washington, Saudi Arabia (with the bulk of the Middle East's oil reserves) was a place "where the oil resources constitute a stupendous source of strategic power, and one of the greatest material prizes in world history." U.S. Department of State, *Foreign Relations of the United States, 1945*, vol. 8, p. 45, cited in Joyce and Gabriel Kolko, *The Limits of Power* (New York: Harper & Row, 1972), p. 71.

5. Joyce and Gabriel Kolko, *Limits of Power, passim,* and, e.g., pp. 65, 69.

6. Gabriel Kolko, *The Politics of War* (London: Weidenfeld & Nicolson, 1969), pp. 296 ff., and, for the importance of oil and other raw materials to American elites in the mid-1940s, *passim*.

7. See Malcolm Caldwell, "The Energy Crisis," in Ken Coates, ed., *Socialism and the Environment* (Nottingham: Russell Press, 1972).

8. DeGolyer and MacNaughton, *Petroleum Statistics*, p. 3.

9. Kolko, *Limits of Power*, pp. 69 ff., 235 ff., 403 ff.

10. Malcolm Caldwell, "Oil and Imperialism in East Asia," *Journal of Contemporary Asia* (London), vol. 1, no. 3, 1971.

11. *Daily Telegraph* (London), February 7, 1972.

12. b-d = barrels per day; 1 barrel = 42 U.S. gallons; 7.33 barrels = 1 metric ton. To convert b-d into tons per year multiply by 49.8; to convert tons per year into b-d multiply by 0.0201. George Lincoln, director of the U.S. Office of Emergency Preparedness, estimated at the 1972 convention of the American National Coal Association that oil and gas imports could cost the United States $27 billion by 1985; the estimate may be on the low side.

13. "As far as future energy needs are concerned, the Energy Council has now revised its forecasts of demand made in 1967 and is looking for a total energy consumption in fiscal year 1975 equivalent to 8.6m. b-d of oil, and 18.3m.–20.1m. b-d in fiscal year 1985. Within this framework, the Council expects oil to provide approximately 68 percent of the total, hydro-electricity 2.5 percent, nuclear energy 9.5, coal 17 and other sources, mainly gas, about 3 percent." *Financial Times* (London), March 7, 1972.

14. *International Herald Tribune,* November 23, 1971.

15. May 14, 1972.

16. *Special Report of the U.S. Embassy* (Rangoon), December 15, 1970, discusses this matter.

17. *Indonesian News* (London), November 5, 1971.

18. Many of the statistics and facts in the section on Japan are drawn from an unpublished manuscript on the oil industry in Asia by Leon Howell, Michael Morrow, and Malcolm Caldwell.

19. "If they (the Senkakus) are parts of the sedimentary basin, they presumably belong to China, which was awarded them after World War II." Robert E. King, of the Woods Hole Oceanographic Institute, in *The Oil and Gas Journal,* April 27, 1970.

20. See Jon Halliday and Gavan McCormack, *Japanese Imperialism Today—"Co-prosperity in Greater East Asia"* (London: Penguin Books, 1973).

21. See *Daily Telegraph,* April 14, 1972.

22. See letter by a number of Filipino academics in *Sunday Times* (Manila), April 18, 1971; also "Greater East Asia Co-prosperity Sphere Once Again," *AMPO* (Tokyo), no. 12, March 1972; *Financial Times,* January 4, 1972. See also two important articles on "Japan's Economic Grip in Asia" by James P. Sterba, *International Herald Tribune,* August 30 and 31, 1972.

23. *Daily Telegraph,* April 4, 1972.

24. Cited in the Howell, Morrow, and Caldwell manuscript, note 18 above.

25. *Daily Telegraph,* September 5, 1972.

26. Malcolm Caldwell, "Russland, Indonesien und das neue Raj in Asien," *Sudostasien Korrespondenz* (Bonn), March 1971.

27. Russian economic and military aid to the reactionary Suharto regime was confirmed during the June 1971 visit to Moscow of Indonesian Foreign Minister Adam Malik; the Djakarta regime in turn supplies aid to the beleaguered Phnom Penh clique and the Soviet Union refuses recognition to Sihanouk's government, maintaining relations with the U.S.-backed Lon Nol—even offering to set up a "legal communist party" for him in Phnom Penh! (see, e.g., *Le Monde Diplomatique,* April 4, 1972).

28. *International Herald Tribune,* December 23, 1970.

29. *International Herald Tribune,* January 17, 1972.

30. See *AMPO,* November 1971.

31. Press reports subsequent to Nixon's attempted imposition of a blockade of North Vietnam in 1971–1972 suggested that stepped-up Chinese overland exports of oil to Vietnam were being replenished by Soviet tanker supplies to Chinese ports; see, e.g., *International Herald Tribune,* September 2–3, 1972.

32. See Biplab Dasgupta, *The Oil Industry in India* (London: Frank Cass & Co., 1971).

33. See *Indian Oil News 1972*, article by P. T. Sethi, India's Minister for Petroleum and Chemicals.

34. See *Financial Times*, January 5, 1972.

35. See Institute of Petroleum Information Service, *Oil—The Far East* (London: Institute of Petroleum, 1967), pp. 4–5.

36. The concept of "cultural appraisal" as regards resources is well known in geography and refers to the relationship between sociopolitical structure and both knowledge of and capacity to utilize resources.

37. The importance of Thailand as a linchpin of U.S. empire in Southeast Asia has recently been discussed in Kolko, *Limits of Power,* pp. 75–76; see also Michael Morrow, "Thailand: Bombers and Bases—America's New Frontier," *Journal of Contemporary Asia,* vol. 2, no. 4, 1972; and Wolfgang Wehner, "Thailand and U.S. Involvement," *Journal of Contemporary Asia,* vol. 3, no. 3, 1973.

38. See "Saigon Calls Off Plan for Coastal Oil Bidding" in *Los Angeles Times,* May 29, 1972; it is true that subsequently bidding for and allocation of leases actually took place in Saigon (see *Daily Telegraph,* July 16, 1972), but it is inconceivable that the successful companies in the bidding will ever bring in oil in profitable quantities in the time available to them before the final total liberation of Indochina.

39. See Malcolm Caldwell and Lek Tan, *Cambodia in the Southeast Asian War* (New York: Monthly Review Press, 1973).

40. *Thai News,* London, May 17, 1972.

41. See Howell, Morrow, and Caldwell manuscript, note 18 above, section on Burma.

42. See Ron Witton, "Malaysia: Changing Masters," *Journal of Contemporary Asia,* vol. 2, no. 2, 1972; Anonymous, "Hunting with Huntingdon," *Dissent* (Melbourne), no. 27, Autumn 1972.

43. See Iain Buchanan, *Singapore in Southeast Asia* (London: G. Bell & Sons, 1972); Anonymous, "The Coming General Election in Singapore—Will It Be the Last One?" *Journal of Contemporary Asia,* vol. 2, no. 3, 1972.

44. See Buchanan, *Singapore,* for an extensive discussion; see also Helen Hughes and You Poh Seng, *Foreign Investment and Industrialisation in Singapore* (Canberra: ANU Press, 1969). The Hughes and You volume gives much data on American, Japanese, and other foreign investment in Singapore.

45. See my "Oil and Imperialism in East Asia," *Journal of Contemporary Asia,* vol. 1, no. 3, 1971.

46. *The Manila Chronicle,* July 1, 1971; for a discussion of the role of oil in the September 1972 coup in the Philippines, see Malcolm

Caldwell, "ASEANisation," in AREAS, *The Philippines—End of an Illusion* (London, 1973).

47. R. W. Van Bemmelen, *The Geology of Indonesia* (The Hague: Government Printing Office, 1949), vol. 2, p. 8.

48. The pretext would have been protection of U.S. citizens, or evacuation of their dependents, or one or another of the now familiar rationalizations for imperialistic aggression. "The Eisenhower-Dulles administration had secretly ordered a troop landing on Indonesian soil. Last May 15 (1965), just after the U.S. intervened in Santo Domingo, the *Indonesian Herald,* semiofficial organ of the Foreign Ministry, reminisced about the near miss in a long article entitled 'Lesson on Pakanbaru and Dominica.' Pakanbaru is a city in Sumatra at the very center of the oil-rich area. The facts of the incident are not in dispute. Oil exports are the country's major source of foreign exchange. These next three paragraphs are a direct quote from the *Indonesian Herald* of May 15, 1965: 'On March 12, 1958, at 7 A.M., the combined forces of the Indonesian Armed Forces landed in Pakanbaru . . . not only to crush foreign-supported rebellion, but also to prevent the imminent intervention by American and possibly British troops. At 9 A.M., the ships from the Seventh Fleet were sighted off the coast. The Commander of the Seventh Fleet flotilla, Rear Admiral Roy Benson, admitted to the press that he had consulted with the British High Commissioner concerning possible joint operations in Indonesia. . . . Direct armed intervention by the Seventh Fleet was, in the case of Pakanbaru, prevented due to the timely intelligence report and quick action of the government in immediately landing her troops there. Otherwise, the Americans might have used the pretext of protecting the lives of several hundred foreign citizens there to land the Marines in Pakanbaru. After having landed, it was not unlikely that, as in the present case in the Dominican Republic, the American forces might stay on long enough, with another pretext of protecting American properties, to tip the war balance on the rebels' side.' " William Worthy in *The Silent Slaughter* (New York: Youth Against War and Fascism, 1966), pp. 17–18.

49. Azhari Zahri, *Indonesia: Public Control and Economic Planning* (Singapore: MPH Publications, 1969), p. 173.

50. Nobody now disputes that the official Indonesian version of Sukarno's downfall is unsatisfactory. However, establishing the truth will take time. Two lines of research, at least, need pursuing: 1), the complicity in the coup of Suharto himself; and 2), the complex direct and indirect links connecting various Indonesian personalities and groups prominent in the coup and the CIA and the United States generally. Suharto served both the Dutch colonialists and the Japanese

invaders, so it comes as no surprise to see him now presiding over the auction of his country to the Americans. His complicity in the coup is discussed in W. F. Wertheim, "Suharto and the Untung Coup—The Missing Link," *Journal of Contemporary Asia,* vol. 1, no. 2, 1971. On the American role in the coup see David Ransom, "The Berkeley Mafia and the Indonesia Massacre," *Ramparts,* October 1970; and Deirdre Griswold, *Indonesia—Second Greatest Crime of the Century* (New York: Youth Against War and Fascism, 1969). Two of the top army men in the coup had been cleared by the CIA and trained in the United States —Colonel Sahirman (Fort Leavenworth) and Brigadier-General Supardjo (Fort Bragg). The alleged agent of the *Biro Chusus* (Special Bureau) of the PKI said to have been detailed to foment the coup, "Sjam" (Kamarusaman bin Ahmed Mubaidah), had in fact been in Suharto's battalion during the Independence struggles, and had later been associated (1951–1955) with the Socialist party (PSI)—a party notoriously saturated with CIA influence. Later still, he was in the army intelligence section, attached to the crack Siliwangi Division until 1960. He evaded arrest for eighteen months after the coup, probably through top army protection. Suharto obviously cannot afford to bring him to trial.

51. For a description of the relevant legislation, frank to the point of cynicism, see Department of Trade, *Indonesia: Investment—Policies, Procedure, Fields of Investment & Progress Report,* 2nd ed. (Djakarta: Japenda Foreign Languages Publishing Institute, 1969). See also Asian Development Bank, *Southeast Asia's Economy in the 1970's* (London: Longmans, Green & Co., 1971), pp. 373–81.

52. See, besides the David Ransom article cited in note 50 above, Hugh Mabbett, "The Return of the Berkeley Mafia?" *Straits Times* (Singapore), November 5, 1971.

53. The "Inter-Governmental Group on Indonesia" consists of the United States, Japan, Australia, Canada, the Netherlands, West Germany, France, Belgium, Italy, and Denmark. It bails out Indonesia in return for economic privileges—a combination of pauperization and rape. It is expected to pay some three-quarters of the costs of the Five-Year Development Plan, a charter, and *carte blanche* for private foreign investment devised by American "economists" (i.e., business consultants) and their Indonesian apprentices. Cf. Cheryl Payer's analysis of IGGI in this volume.

54. Up to the end of 1972, the Indonesian government had approved foreign investments totaling 2.3 billion U.S. dollars, spread over 543 projects; $923 million of this came from the United States and $345 million from Japan. Another $278 million came from the Philippines, a sum which in effect can be added to the American total, a consideration which applies to part of the rest of the investment originating in

U.S.-dominated Asian neocolonies. In addition, in the period 1967–1972, fifty-five foreign firms, nationalized by Sukarno, were restored to their former Western owners. See *Indonesian News,* London, June 5 and July 5, 1973.

55. See "Greater East Asia Co-prosperity Sphere Once Again," *AMPO,* March 1972, no. 12. The *Financial Times* (London) reported on January 4, 1972, that Japan was planning to try to establish a yen settlement union as a step toward developing a yen economic bloc in Southeast Asia. At the moment ninety percent of all Japanese trade is dollar-financed, though Japan is beginning to write in settlement in yen in some export agreements. It is also felt in Japan that the 1971 Group of Ten arrangements foreshadow a future of blocs and that it "should hurry to form its own bloc in South East Asia." See also the important reference cited in note 20 above.

56. Benedict R. O'G. Anderson, *Java in a Time of Revolution* (Ithaca, N.Y.: Cornell University Press, 1972); G. McT. Kahin, *Nationalism and Revolution in Indonesia* (Ithaca, N.Y.: Cornell University Press, 1952); Harry J. Benda, *The Crescent and the Rising Sun —Indonesian Islam* (The Hague: Van Hoeve, 1958).

57. Maeda had been engaged in oil negotiations on behalf of the Japanese government in both Holland and the then Netherlands East Indies even before the outbreak of war; he was also at that time engaged in military spying. See Anderson, *Java,* p. 427.

58. See, for instance, *OISRAA Bulletin,* Peking, vol. 5, no. 3, October 1971 (OISRAA: Indonesian Organization for Afro-Asian Peoples' Solidarity); see also the reference cited in note 10 above. The Provisional Revolutionary Government of South Vietnam has announced that "all natural resources in South Vietnam are sacred and inviolable property of the South Vietnamese people. . . . Any agreements signed between the Saigon puppet administration and whatever country, whatever foreign firm or organization, have no value and are not binding to the South Vietnamese people." Radio Hanoi, commenting on offshore oil leases, has said: "The Vietnamese people will not let the imperialist Americans and any other reactionaries use Thieu-Ky to get Vietnamese national resources" (both cited in the Howell, Morrow, and Caldwell manuscript, note 18 above).

THE INTERNATIONAL MONETARY FUND AND INDONESIAN DEBT SLAVERY

CHERYL PAYER

The International Monetary Fund (IMF) is one of the most powerful supranational organizations in the world today. The resources it controls and its ability to interfere in the internal affairs of member nations gives it real power of which United Nations advocates can only dream. Only the U.S. military establishment with its client armies can rival the IMF as the key institution of imperialism in the world today, and their functions are complementary. The discipline imposed by the IMF has often eliminated the need for direct military intervention in order to preserve a climate friendly toward foreign investment.

The IMF must be seen as the keystone of a total system. Its power is made possible not only by the enormous resources (about $28 billion) which it adminsters directly in short-term lending to cover balance-of-payment fluctuations, but more significantly as a result of its function as an international credit agency. All major sources of credit in the developed capitalist world, whether private capital, bilateral government aid (of which U.S. aid is by far the most important) or other multilateral institutions such as the World Bank and regional development banks, will refuse aid to a country which persists in defying IMF "advice." The real importance of the IMF lies in the authority delegated to it by the governments and capital markets of the entire capitalist world.

The IMF's power over the underdeveloped countries derives from their economic weakness, as reflected in their chronic foreign exchange difficulties. The lack of foreign exchange is the *major external constraint* on the development programs of poor countries[1] and is derived from several factors: declining prices for their raw materials exports; the huge proportion (as much as forty percent for some countries) of export earnings that must go to debt service and to the remittance of profits from private investment, and their critical need for capital goods and raw materials for industry, food for their urban population, and consumer goods which they cannot manufacture themselves.

The IMF and its client institutions have the resources to ease these payment difficulties, but they will grant credit only if the borrowing country institutes a stabilization program to control inflation. Arguing that it is chiefly inflation which is responsible for balance-of-payments difficulties, the IMF enforces a program which invariably contains three main elements:

1) The elimination of as many direct controls on foreign exchange expenditure as possible, which usually necessitates frequent devaluation of the nation's currency relative to the world's major trading currencies.

2) Domestic anti-inflationary policies, including the reduction of government spending and the contraction of bank credit. This necessitates a curtailment of public expenditures for welfare and of government investment in development projects. It inevitably results in economic recession; the failure of many domestic businesses and their forced sale to foreign speculators; and a large unemployment problem resulting from both curtailed government expenditures and business recession.

3) Policies encouraging foreign investment, which range from antistrike legislation (and action) through tax benefits to guarantees on profit remittance.

The IMF claims that the aim of this stabilization package is long-term balance-of-payments stability, but its effect in practice has been reinforcement of the dependence on raw material exports which was the basic cause of instability to begin with. Governments which implement these IMF policies are rewarded, not with aid for developing a healthy and diversified economy, but with temporary relief for immediate exchange difficulties. This relief typically takes the form of new loans to the government, rescheduling of old loans when repayments become burdensome, and credit for the import of consumer goods.

Governments unwilling to take IMF advice face severe sanctions in the form of inability to obtain credit anywhere in the capitalist world. The system can be compared point by point with peonage on an individual scale. In peonage, or debt slavery, the worker is unable to use his nominal freedom to leave the service of his employer, because the latter supplies him with credit (for overpriced goods in the company store) necessary to supplement his meager wages. The aim of the employer–creditor–merchant is neither to collect the debt once and for all, nor to starve the employee to death, but rather to keep the laborer permanently indentured through his debt to the employer. The worker cannot run away, for other employers and the state recognize the legality of his debt; nor has he any hope of earning his freedom with his low wages.

Precisely the same system operates on the international scale. Nominally independent countries find that their debts, and their continuing inability to finance current needs out of export earnings, keep them tightly leashed to their creditors. The IMF orders them, in effect, to continue laboring on the plantation while it refuses to finance their efforts to set up in business for themselves. For these reasons the term "international debt slavery" accurately describes their situation.

The stabilization program imposed by the IMF precludes the adoption of socialist policies, and is hostile even to mild social welfare measures, whether direct subsidies such as government pensions or consumer subsidies such as public utilities operated at a deficit. All such programs are considered distortions of free market forces, and thus undesirable, by IMF advisers, who prescribe instead policies which penalize the average citizen by reducing his income and raising the price of essential goods and services.

Domestically controlled and financed enterprises are particularly hard hit, and often bankrupted, by the measures demanded by the IMF. Tight credit restrictions make domestic financing extremely difficult to obtain; devaluation increases the local cost of both imports and existing loans; and domestic markets are usurped by the unrestricted imports financed by external credit.

These conditions give foreign firms a strong relative advantage. A foreign firm's capital resources are not affected by the local depression; devaluation means its dollars can buy more in local assets; and, if it is chiefly interested in export enterprises rather than consumer goods, its potential markets are not affected by the depression. Because the general level of employment and wages in the host country is depressed, the foreign firm can assure itself of a stable, docile labor force at bargain prices by paying slightly more than the general low level of wages.

Additionally, the IMF requires specific incentives for foreign investment. Underlying all IMF recommendations is its fundamental hostility to any type of development which is not carried out by, through, and for private foreign capital. To this end the policies it enforces systematically veto any possibility of domestically controlled industrial growth, whether under public or private auspices. In addition, the type of speculative foreign investment which is encouraged by the IMF does not represent the transfer of resources from rich countries to poor, but rather the *transfer of resources within the poor countries from domestic to foreign ownership*. And, although foreign investment and foreign aid may provide some temporary relief to the balance of payments, in the long run they add to the burden as profits are remitted to the investing country and loans must be repaid with interest.

One Asian nation now in the throes of an IMF austerity program is the Philippines. The enormous government spending which was used to generate votes for President Ferdinand Marcos' reelection in 1969 helped precipitate a foreign exchange crisis, which Marcos met by capitulating to IMF conditions so he could obtain more aid. The underlying cause of the crisis, however, was the basic weakness and foreign trade dependence of the Philippine economy—conditions which an earlier program, supported by the IMF in 1962, did much to exacerbate.

The 1962 program included such typical IMF staples as the elimination of restrictions on currency convertibility; the end of import and export controls; free exchange rates; fiscal and monetary restraints on the government and domestic private enterprise; and devaluation of the peso. These policies, however, did not achieve their professed goal of balance-of-payments equilibrium. Rather, dismantling controls on foreign exchange allowed the invisible dollar outflow (mostly profit remittances) to rise from $200 million in 1961 to $990 million in 1966. These deficits were eased by American loans; the external government debt rose from $275 million in 1961 to $737 million by 1968.[2] Largely because of the pressures of this crushing debt, the Philippines is now being forced through the same wringer which has proved so destructive to national industry, and so powerless to achieve its professed aims, in the past. The price level, which crawled upward at the modest rate of two percent per annum in the 1950s, had shot up by twenty percent in 1971 after a few doses of IMF-sponsored "stabilization."

This inflation which surges ahead despite supposedly deflationary policies has been termed "deflationary inflation."[3] This paradox can largely be explained by examining the effects of the devaluation which is another component of the "comprehensive stabilization program." In orthodox economic theory, a devaluation is expected to improve the balance of trade by encouraging exports and discouraging imports. For example, the 1971 U.S. devaluation predictably raised the price and thus discouraged the purchase of Toyotas and Japanese stereo components. This theory assumes, however, that the productive capacities of the various nations are basically comparable and consumer tastes nearly identical, so that a decline in imports will benefit domestic producers of similar goods.

Whatever its validity for industrialized nations, in the case of underdeveloped countries dependent on raw materials exports this assumption cannot hold. The poor countries and the rich countries simply do not produce the same type of goods for the world market. Imports of capital goods and manufactures are necessary to the poor country's economy, but not available from domestic sources, while export markets do not expand automatically when prices fall. The effect of devaluation in these countries is thus to worsen the already disadvantageous terms of trade, which forces the country to export more to pay for essential imports, and raises the internal price level because imported goods comprise such a large part of the economy. Devaluation benefits three groups: exporters (typically either local landowning oligarchs or foreign corporations owning mines or plantations) whose earnings are in foreign currency; foreign consumers of these exports who can buy them more cheaply; and foreign companies buying up local businesses hit by the recession. In this way a program ostensibly introduced to check inflation and improve the balance of payments may have just the opposite effect.

It is important to understand that the various elements of the IMF stabilization program are closely related. The IMF charter gives it no power to control the domestic policies of borrowing nations. The power to intervene was arrogated in practice, when Latin American countries began to borrow from the Fund in the early 1950s. It was justified with the argument that balance-of-payments problems could not be controlled in the presence of inflation.

There is in fact another way to control payments deficits, a way which socialist countries have adopted and many bourgeois nationalist governments would prefer if given a choice: this is the use of exchange controls. To be sure, controls administered by a corrupt government become another focus of corruption. Nonetheless, they offer the only way a weak economy can protect itself by setting its own priorities on the use of scarce foreign exchange. However, the IMF charter commits it to promote currency convertibility, the necessary condition of capitalist penetration of other countries via investment and trade. In practice, a weak economy cannot hope to achieve full convertibility. The IMF recognizes this through its category of so-called "Article 14" countries, which are permitted to retain some controls. The IMF nevertheless exercises constant pressure for decontrol and tries to insure that foreign investors and importers of foreign goods get priority treatment in the distribution of exchange permits.

It is the systematic linkage of control of inflation with devaluation and currency convertibility plus incentives for foreign investment which effectively shuts off all alternatives for autonomous national development and therefore precludes economic independence in the long run. If a government is willing to abandon the quest for a fully convertible currency, a whole new range of possibilities appears. With the significant exceptions of currency convertibility and hospitality to foreign investment, China, not a member of the IMF, has developed with conservative financial and anti-inflationary policies but without currency convertibility or direct foreign investment. Japan provides a capitalist example of an economy that has achieved both growth and currency stability while sharply restricting foreign investment. The policies Japan followed to become the second largest capitalist economy would never have been sanctioned by the IMF if it had been permitted to interfere.[4]

The truth is that the IMF plays an intensely political role in its dealings with economically weak countries, not an impartial technical one. This is best illustrated by the role it has played in the subversion of social revolutions which have been attempted in several Third World countries.

In this context it is irrelevant whether a would-be revolutionary government came to power legally or illegally, via elections, military coup, or armed popular revolution. The dilemma that any government will face if it is genuinely nationalist (let alone socialist) is a result of its foreign exchange weakness, the burden of debt inherited from previous governments, and the rising expectations of its supporters. Such a government faces the choice of going through one of two types of economic wringer: either submission to an IMF austerity program; or a choice to go it alone with a self-imposed austerity program conditioned by the lack of foreign exchange for imports. The latter choice will require that the government move rapidly leftward in order to curb upper-class consumption and to mitigate austerity by equalizing the benefits that are available.

The difficulties of this choice must not be underestimated. To give just one example: when large food imports are necessary to feed the urban population, people may go hungry before even the best-intentioned government can expand its nation's agricultural production sufficiently. The penalties, in forced restrictions of imports, of defiance of the IMF are so heavy that many revolutionary governments are forced to change course and bow to the will of international capital. India was forced by a foreign exchange crisis in 1957 to abandon its nationalist and social welfare policies as a condition of foreign exchange relief.[5] The same story has been repeated many times, for the pattern is inexorable: no country with a foreign exchange program can avoid the choice between the two types of austerity program.

The recent history of Indonesia provides a prime example of the intermediary role played by the IMF and of the consequences of the type of development it enforces.

Indonesia, although endowed with enough natural and human resources to make it one of the richest countries on earth, is in fact one of the poorest insofar as the livelihood of its people is concerned. The economic structure imposed by Dutch colonialism and the exploitative nature of international economic relations in the post-colonial era have combined to keep Indonesia one of the least industrialized nations in the world, heavily dependent on a handful of raw material exports for its earnings in the world market.

The failure to develop has been commonly attributed in the Western press to the disastrous economic policies pursued in the Sukarno era of "guided democracy" (1959–1965). There is some truth to this charge, but it must be viewed in perspective. During its first decade of independence, Indonesia labored under the necessity of repaying huge debts to the Netherlands—obligations which it had been forced to accept as the price of independence; and its major businesses (mostly export-oriented) remained under Dutch ownership and thus outside the effective control of the Indonesian government.

The Dutch debts were unilaterally repudiated by Indonesia in 1956 and the Dutch firms nationalized in 1958, but the island nation remained pathetically vulnerable to world economic conditions over which it had no control. The price of natural rubber, Indonesia's major foreign exchange earner, fell drastically from 38.5 cents/lb. in 1960 to only 25.7 cents/lb. in 1965.[6] This drop of thirty-three percent in the price of the commodity which provided sixty percent of Indonesia's total export value contributed to Indonesia's economic crisis as surely as did the government's policies.

It is nevertheless true that Sukarno does deserve criticism for his failure to recognize Indonesia's critical economic situation and to employ his political gifts in finding a permanent way out of the crisis. Rather than make hard political decisions about the distribution of the country's resources, he chose to finesse the problem by allowing unrestrained government spending which caused the severe inflation of the mid-1960s. The so-called "aid" he obtained from both the Communist and the capitalist world continues to haunt his successors in the form of billion-dollar debts.

As Sukarno squandered foreign loans on consumption goods, prestige projects, and armaments, so he wasted the nation's dwindling export earnings of foreign exchange because the government had become dependent on a complicated system of multiple exchange rates for the major part of its revenue. Indonesia had inherited from the Dutch colonial government a system of absolute control of foreign exchange, in which exporters were required to deposit all foreign exchange earnings with the government and receive in return a *rupiah* payment at a rate of exchange determined by the government. The government then sold the exchange in excess of its own needs to importers, at a higher rate of exchange, and kept the difference in *rupiah* proceeds as its own revenue. Over time this system became extremely complex, with rates set at many different levels to encourage selected categories of exports and imports. The effect of this system was to tax exporters for the benefit of both government revenues and those importers privileged enough to obtain the scarce foreign exchange permits.

The problem was that exchange controls became less and less effective as a means of conserving and allocating scarce foreign exchange as the government became more dependent upon them for revenue. In the Sukarno era the government began to sell "free" foreign exchange which could be used for luxury imports (i.e., outside the regular regime of controls which prohibited such imports) to obtain more revenue. Although Sukarno seemed to be moving in the direction of state control of the economy, in this critical sector he countenanced "a denial of economic planning and a return to an intrinsically laissez-faire method of allocating precious foreign exchange."[7]

Sukarno's success in playing off Communist and capitalist aid-givers against each other lasted only a few short years, and by 1963 he found himself pressured by both sides to choose between them. Although his anti-Western statements and threats to nationalize Western-owned oil companies in Indonesia[8] provoked the U.S. Congress into banning economic and military aid to that country, the State Department and the Agency for International Development (AID) remained very interested in using Western aid to steer Indonesia into economic policies favorable to the Western bloc.

In a striking "dress rehearsal" for the events of 1966–1967, the United States used the IMF as an intermediary between itself, the Indonesian government, and a prospective consortium of Western aid donors. An Economic Survey Team from the United States visited Indonesia and issued a report in November 1962, recommending a five-year, $390-million aid program of which the United States would contribute $233 million. These amounts are minuscule compared to the sums Indonesia has obtained in aid each year since 1966, but at the time the promise of long-term aid seemed very attractive. The aid, however, was contingent on Indonesia's cooperation with respect to devaluation of the *rupiah* and budgetary restraint. An IMF mission went to Djakarta to help the Indonesian government devise a stabilization program. In March 1963, the United States offered a ten-year $17-million loan, repayable in dollars, to finance imports needed for the Economic Stabilization Program.[9] In May the Indonesian government announced a series of regulations which amounted to de facto devaluation of the *rupiah* and the elimination of many government price controls and government subsidies. In June a consortium of prospective aid donors met under the auspices of the Development Assistance Council of the Organization for Economic Cooperation and Development, to raise $400 million to help Indonesia cover its balance-of-payments gap.[10] In August 1963, Indonesia entered into a standby arrangement with the IMF which would enable it to draw up to $50 million over the coming year if it continued to follow IMF advice.[11]

In September, however, Sukarno's anger at the proposed federation of Malaysia led him to seize British-owned businesses in Indonesia; whereupon the United States and the IMF announced the cancellation of their recently concluded aid arrangements. At this point Sukarno began to realize the political price he would have to pay for future economic aid. In his National Day address on August 17, 1964, Sukarno expressed admiration for the self-reliant economic policies followed by North Korea, saying that Korea had completely solved her problem of food and clothing "enabling her both politically and culturally not to depend on anybody at all." He added, "Indonesia does not want to stay behind."[12]

The year 1965 was one of mounting hostility to foreign investment, and looming economic disaster due to the lack of foreign exchange for consumption imports, for factory spare parts, and for the payment of foreign debts. In early 1965 most remaining foreign-owned enterprises with the exception of the oil companies, nationalized. On May 27 the law guaranteeing foreign investments was repealed. The trade unions and the Indonesian Communist Party (PKI) pressed the government to take over the oil companies, and the government obliged halfway by placing the companies under government supervision "without prejudice to property rights." The government announced plans to take control of the foreign trade sector.

In his National Day speech on August 18, 1965, Sukarno announced Indonesian withdrawal from the IMF and the World Bank and declared that the coming year would be "A Year of Self-Reliance." According to the speech, this meant a socialist-style austerity program tailored to the necessity of conserving foreign exchange and preserving the nation's political independence, by cutting imports to a minimum, stressing domestic investment and home production of import substitutes, and accepting only those foreign credits which did not prejudice national control of the economy. It meant "the acceptance of hardship as the price of revolutionary achievement."[13]

There is reason to doubt that Sukarno had the determination to carry through such a politically difficult program. The mere threat, however, must have alarmed many vested interests both inside and outside the country. In the event, Sukarno did not hold on to his power throughout the year, so his policy of self-reliance never had a real trial. The events leading to his eclipse —the murder of six army generals, with alleged Communist collusion, on October 1; the subsequent decimation of the PKI and the massacres, under army sponsorship, of hundreds of thousands of Indonesians; the March 11, 1966, order in which Sukarno, under compulsion, transferred extensive powers to General Suharto—all had their logic in the tense internal politics of Indonesia. But they were closely related as well to the foreign exchange crisis and disagreements about its solution.

One month after the March 11 transfer of power to General Suharto, the new Minister of Finance announced the reversal of Sukarno's policy of hostility toward private enterprise and foreign investment. Six days later the United States offered an $8.2 million credit for the purchase of rice, and this gesture was soon followed by offers from the United Kingdom and Japan.

Despite this indication of tentative support, the new Indonesian leaders found that the Americans did not automatically rush to support the anti-Communist regime. Instead, the formula chosen closely resembled that of the abortive 1963 stabilization program. The United States wanted to see evidence of specific new economic policies before pledging support, and backed the IMF (which Suharto's government hastened to rejoin) as the adviser and referee of those new policies. An "initially reluctant

Indonesia" had to be persuaded by "intensive diplomatic activity" to accept a consortium of all the creditor countries as the instrument for negotiation of debt rescheduling, and for badly needed new credits.[14]

In the late summer of 1966 an IMF mission arrived in Indonesia to work out a new stabilization program, and soon the IMF advice became apparent in new government policies. One of the most important of these was the shift of most foreign exchange transactions from control of the Central Bank to the open market on October 3, 1966, the first major step in the decontrol of foreign exchange transactions. The government, rather than setting priorities for the use of scarce foreign exchange (which it admittedly had handled badly in the past), was to abdicate this function to market forces of supply and demand. A weak economy could not afford to take such a step without massive new injections of foreign aid, but these were forthcoming in support of the decontrol measures.

The IMF advisers also worked out a familiar package of anti-inflationary measures as the necessary complement to the decontrol of foreign exchange: a balanced budget, limitation of government expenditures to no more than ten percent of national income, improvement in the tax collection system, a "realistic" exchange rate, the end of subsidies, a review of pricing policies of state enterprises, reductions in the number of government employees, and severe limitations on the creation of bank credit.[15]

The government also hastened to give substance to its promise of a friendlier climate for foreign investment. A new Foreign Investment Bill guaranteed prospective investments against nationalization for a period of twenty years (thirty in the case of agricultural estates), promised reasonable compensation in the case of nationalization after the stated periods, assured freedom to remit profits and to repatriate capital, and provided generous tax concessions. In December, three days before a crucial meeting of Indonesian creditors, the government announced its intention of restoring the foreign-owned companies nationalized since 1963 to their former owners.

The Western nations responded to these proofs of obedience by offering $174 million in ad hoc credits to get Indonesia through its annual crisis for 1966, and by arranging for debt rescheduling. The need for rescheduling was acute because fully $534 million in repayments were falling due or in arrears by 1967, which represented sixty-nine percent of anticipated export earnings for that year. Unless some of the payments were deferred, any new credits extended to Indonesia would simply go down the drain of debt repayment, leaving the new anti-Communist government just as economically vulnerable as was Sukarno's. Therefore, when the Western creditor nations met in Paris in December 1966 they agreed to a moratorium until 1971 on repayments of all principal and interest on long-term debts contracted before June 1966. After 1971, Indonesia was to repay her debts in eight installments: five percent in 1971, ten percent per year in 1972–1974, fifteen percent in 1975–1977, and twenty percent in the last year, 1978. Similar terms had been negotiated separately by the Soviet Union and the other Communist-bloc creditors, who had not been invited to the first capitalist creditors' meeting in September.

Members of the "Paris Club" creditors' consortium were the United States, Britain, Japan, Australia, France, West Germany, Italy, Netherlands, the World Bank, the Organization for Economic Cooperation and Development (OECD), and the International Monetary Fund. The IMF, with U.S. pressure clearly discernible behind its efforts, vigorously supported lenient terms for the debt rescheduling and pressed for the creation of an aid consortium which would mobilize new credits for Indonesia.

The Intergovernmental Group on Indonesia (IGGI) was duly formed in early 1967. Similar consortia or "consultative groups" for major countries have been favored by the United States since the early 1960s as a means for persuading other capitalist nations to assume a share of the aid burden proportionate to the benefits in investment and trade which the latter derive from the Pax Americana. In the case of Indonesia, the target of the U.S. share-the-burden campaign was Japan, whose large and growing economic stake in the rest of Asia still depended on U.S. determination to preserve the security of the area.

The IGGI has regularly met twice a year in the Netherlands—the former colonial power in Indonesia. At the first meeting, late in the calendar year, Indonesia, supported by the IMF, presents the aid donors with its estimates of the aid needed to finance its deficit in the coming fiscal year. At the second meeting, in the following April, after the annual Indonesian budget has been presented and the IMF has renewed its standby arrangement, the consortium members agree among themselves who is to supply the needed credits. In the pattern, which has by now become well established, the United States leads the bidding with an offer of one-third of the needed sum in the expectation that Japan will supply another third and the rest of the consortium will provide the remainder. In 1968 the United States refused to put up its one-third until Japan did the same—which resulted in a six-month delay of aid deliveries and serious difficulties for the Indonesian government.[16]

It is probably significant that the aid pattern matches precisely the proportions of actual and intended foreign investment in Indonesia from 1967 to 1971, with the United States and Japan (if the nominally Philippine investment is attributed to Japan, the real source of capital) both supplying one-third of the investment capital.[17]

The debt rescheduling formula of 1966 had only postponed the problem, and, as 1971 approached, the Paris Club commissioned West German financier Hermann Abs to study the Indonesian debt problem. His recommendation, that the "Sukarno debts" be repaid in thirty installments between 1970 and 1999, was approved by the creditors in April 1970 and lightened the repayment burden for the 1970s significantly. The agreement included a "most favored nation" clause which prevented Indonesia from repaying the Soviet-bloc countries at a faster rate than the Western creditors.

Significantly, this debt deferment closely followed an Indonesian devaluation and exchange reform enthusiastically supported by the IMF, which left Indonesia with one of the "freest" exchange systems in the world. Since April 1970, the unitary exchange rate has meant that imports designated as "essential" no longer enjoy a preferential exchange rate, but must compete in profitability on the open market with all other categories of imports, including luxury goods. Without the record $600 million of new loans agreed to by the IGGI in the same month, Indonesia's balance of payments could not have afforded such a liberalization. It should not have been done at all in terms of development priorities; but that is a problem related to the type of "development" which is sponsored in Indonesia by the IMF and the IGGI.

The Suharto regime and its supporters talk continually of the economic miracle which has brought Indonesia out of the Sukarnoist dark ages, but on closer examination the real miracles appear to be a result of accounting, public relations, and the ever-mounting annual IGGI credits rather than any substantial structural reforms. The main claims to success are based on three achievements: control of inflation, a balanced budget, and the stable external value of the *rupiah*.

These claims have some truth when comparison is made with the Sukarno era, although nonofficial price indices show a current rate of inflation of twelve percent and the *rupiah* was devalued three times in 1970 and 1971 in order to maintain its free convertibility with foreign currencies.

The telling fact, however, is that all three "achievements" have been possible only because the IGGI has so far been willing to provide the enormous loans necessary to support the balance of payments and the budget. It works in this way: The IGGI credits finance hundreds of millions of dollars of imports each year which Indonesia would not be able to pay for with its foreign exchange earnings.* The country's foreign payments are thus "balanced" by foreign loans, and the debts are piling up rapidly. At IMF insistence, the IGGI agreed that their aid credits would be handled in an unprecedented manner: the government *sells* the aid (in the form of import credits) on the free market to importers and uses the sale proceeds as budget revenue. Thus, not only has the government relinquished its right to control its foreign exchange *earnings* (by the decontrol measures of October 1966) but it auctions its government-to-government *aid* for *rupiahs* on the free market as well. Finally, the sale of aid-financed imports controls inflation by absorbing excess currency and diverting it to the use of the government.

Thus annual doses of substantial aid produce three "miracles" simultaneously—miracles which have nothing to do with the real development which would promote the country's economic independence, but on the contrary make Indonesia far *more* dependent on continued injections of aid. In 1967, when IGGI aid totaled only $200 million, this aid financed twenty-eight percent of all imports; and the import credits, sold by the government to private importers, generated more than thirty percent of govern-

---

* In fact, imports and exports of goods have been roughly in balance ever since independence. It would be more accurate to say the aid is financing "invisible" and "unrequited" payments: debt repayment, repatriation of foreign investment profits, etc. See figures for Indonesia in the IMF annual report for 1971, Table 76, pp. 200–201.

ment revenue. By 1970 the annual figure had risen to $600 million, three times the 1967 amount, and the government projected that no less than $910 million would be needed for fiscal year 1973–1974, the last year of the current Five-Year Plan.[18] The government claims that its "regular budget" is now completely financed by its own revenues and that aid revenues all go into the "development budget"; but, even if this is not simply an accounting trick, it is doubtful that the so-called development budget is contributing to Indonesia's potential for financial independence. For example, some of the development expenditures reportedly go into refurbishing of government offices and acquisition of official cars, which is described as "infrastructure development."

The Suharto government points to new foreign investments and a modest growth of exports since 1967 as proof of the efficacy of its economic policies. The major export growth has occurred in the two main commodities—petroleum and timber—which have attracted the lion's share of new foreign investment. In fact, the government's future hopes of foreign exchange earnings, from which the massive old and new debts will eventually have to be repaid, rest squarely on the fate of its extractive and raw materials exports, mainly petroleum. Many economists doubt that prospective earnings will in fact cover the nation's future foreign exchange needs, but, apart from that, the nation's precious natural resources are being dissipated, with massive profits to investors, substantial revenues for the government in power, but little or no investment in a diversified economy for the future.

Timber exports, which amounted to only $10 million in 1966, had expanded to a rate of $160 million a year in the first quarter of 1971. This is cited as proof of the success of the improved returns to exporters under the liberalized foreign exchange system; but it may be questioned, however, whether foreign companies earning forty or fifty percent annual return on their investment need additional incentives.[19] Indonesia's rich timber stands are falling victim to the same wasteful and exploitative cutting which has denuded the Philippine Islands, threatening its water resources and agricultural lands as well as the forests— and at the hands of the same American, Japanese, and Philippine logging companies which have destroyed the ecological balance in the Philippines.

There is no systematic plan for industrial development. Domestic producers suffered bitterly, and predictably, from the effects of the IMF-sponsored stabilization program, particularly contraction of bank credit and competition from the avalanche of aid-financed imports and other goods made available under the liberalized foreign exchange allocation system. One report claimed that 9517 Indonesian firms collapsed between 1964 and 1970.[20] The local textile industry was left "demoralized" by the use of foreign credits to import huge amounts of finished textiles, while Indonesian factories stood idle for lack of working capital.[21] Thus the price of a stable price index and increased government revenue was a drastic slowdown in domestic production.

While domestic entrepreneurs were forced out of business by competition from imports, foreign owners of industrial plants (restored to their owners after the nationalizations of 1963–1965) received special protection from the Indonesian government. When the Goodyear tire factory at Bogor stopped production in September 1968, blaming its problems on excessive tire imports, the government thoughtfully removed tires from the list of imports which could be bought at a favorable exchange rate, reduced the sales tax on home-produced tires, and banned tire imports by government agencies.[22] The automobile assembly industry similarly flourishes under the protection of prohibitive tariffs and taxes on the importation of assembled automobiles, although Indonesia's Minister of Trade has acknowledged that "the foreign exchange required to import components [for assembly plants] will frequently exceed that required to import complete items."[23] In his reasoning, the foreign exchange wastage is justified by the creation of employment opportunities—a strange argument since a few thousand more jobs will scarcely touch Indonesia's enormous unemployment problem. In 1968, the Ministry of Industries closed some manufacturing sectors to new foreign investment, but the effect in several of these sectors was to protect the existing foreign-owned factories. The foreign investor in Indonesia today enjoys more privileges and immunities than his native competitor.

Despite these inducements, there has been almost no new foreign investment in manufacturing industries. The nation's population, although numerically large, is still too poor on the whole to make an attractive market and imported goods preempt the opportunities which exist. Djakarta has been recently blessed with two new soft drink factories; and the Surabaja Investment Information Office reports that potential investors are interested in nightclubs, bars, steam baths, massage parlors, restaurants, and bowling alleys—but not in productive investment.[24]

Indonesia has also put out the welcome mat for foreign banks. Under World Bank sponsorship, new development banking facilities and a private development finance corporation are being set up. This can hardly be called foreign investment, as the intent is to mobilize local (*rupiah*) savings and put them at the disposal of the foreign investors who do not want to bring in more foreign exchange than necessary.[25]

Mass dismissals of employees by the government and by private firms were a logical consequence of the IMF austerity program and have added to an already staggering unemployment problem. The rate of unemployment was estimated at thirteen to fifteen percent in 1967, and no one claims that the situation has improved or that any solution is in sight since the foreign investment projects, existing or contemplated, are not labor intensive and any employment which they provide can be only a drop in the bucket compared to what is needed. Suharto's New Order has continued Sukarno's policy of holding down rice prices through direct controls as well as massive imports, since rice is an important component of the carefully watched cost-of-living index; but the policy has depressed the earnings of the rice-producing rural sector. Other consumer subsidies, however, have been ended—the government-controlled prices of gasoline products, for example, were raised sharply in 1966, 1968, and 1970; and fuel prices are an important component, through transportation and energy costs, of the prices of most basic goods.

Aside from the changes discussed above, the remarkable thing about Suharto's New Order is the number of problems which have remained unsolved, or worsened, since the Sukarno era. Residents of Djakarta aver that corruption and income inequality are markedly more blatant than before, as the generals hobnob with foreign oil magnates. Despite much fanfare about tax reform, there has been no basic restructuring; most of the improvement in government finance can be attributed to expansion of the oil industry, which it is estimated will contribute forty percent of government revenue in 1972, and to taxes on imports and exports, which are politically and technically the easiest to collect.

Indonesia remains one of the least industrialized countries of the world, almost 100 percent dependent on a few raw-material-exports for its international earnings. In 1970 petroleum and rubber accounted for sixty percent of the total exports by value, with lumber, tin, and coffee adding another twenty percent and the remainder contributed by various other raw materials. Despite the extremely low level of wages, none of Indonesia's manufactures shows prospects of being competitive on the world market.

The most significant irony, however, is that the much-maligned "Sukarno debts" are rapidly paling into insignificance relative to the debts that the Suharto government is blithely incurring under IMF sponsorship. Sukarno left a legacy of over $2 billion in debts; but the *new* debts of the Suharto regime, plus projected foreign financing of the remainder of the Five-Year Plan to 1974, add up to *more than $4 billion,* with the annual rate of new credits expanding from $175 million in 1966 to an estimated $910 million in 1973–1974.[26] So far the IGGI has provided all the aid that Indonesia, with IMF backing, has requested; whether its members will continue to do so indefinitely at an ever-expanding rate, even to protect valuable petroleum, timber, tin, copper, and bauxite investments, is an interesting question.

There can be no question, however, that Indonesia stands virtually no chance of climbing out from under her debt burden via any means but repudiation. It may well be rescheduled again and again, at intervals of perhaps a decade, but it will not be paid off at the present rate. Indonesia's vast natural riches are mortgaged for an indefinite future to subsidize an oppressive military dictatorship and to pay for imports which support the lavish life-style of the generals in Djakarta.

This is international debt slavery on a vast scale. Indonesia is considered the greatest "success story" of the IMF, and illustrates the real intentions of that institution and international capitalism toward the development of the Third World. Poor nations today have little or no autonomous control over their own fiscal, financial, and exchange rate policies, and for this reason are likely to become even poorer. The developed capitalist "aid" donors, through the mediation of the IMF, effectively control the most important economic decisions of these only nominally sovereign nations.

NOTES

1. This is a major theme of the Pearson report, *Partners in Development*, report of the Commission on International Development sponsored by the World Bank (New York: Praeger Publishers, 1969).
2. Bruce Nussbaum, "So Little Hope," *Far Eastern Economic Review*, September 19, 1970.
3. Eprime Eshag and Rosemary Thorp, "Economic and Social Consequences of Orthodox Economic Policies in Argentine in the Post-War Years," *Bulletin of the Oxford University Institute of Economics and Statistics*, vol. 27, no. 1, February 1965, pp. 3–44.
4. See "Consider Japan," *The Economist*, September 1, 1962, pp. 787–819, for details of Japan's program for dealing with exchange crises.
5. Michael Kidron, *Foreign Investment in India* (London: Oxford University Press, 1965), pp. 120, 157 and *passim*. For other examples of IMF programs throughout the underdeveloped world see Cheryl Payer, "The Perpetuation of Dependence," *Monthly Review*, September 1971, pp. 37–49.
6. Bank of Indonesia, Report for the Financial Years 1960–1965, p. 93.
7. J. A. C. Mackie, *Problems of the Indonesian Inflation* (Ithaca: Cornell University Modern Indonesia Project, 1967), p. 35.
8. This dispute was settled quickly to the delight of the oil companies, with the assistance of a personal envoy from President Kennedy, in July 1963. See Roger Hilsman, *To Move a Nation* (Garden City: Doubleday, 1967), p. 390.
9. Usha Mahajani, *Soviet and American Aid to Indonesia 1949–68* (Athens, Ohio: Ohio University Center for International Studies, Southeast Asia Program, 1970), p. 22.
10. U.S.A. National Advisory Council on International Monetary and Financial Policies, *Special Report to the President and Congress on The Indonesia Debt Rescheduling*, March 1971, p. 1; and Economist Intelligence Unit, *Threemonthly Economic Report: Indonesia*, no. 46, October 1963.
11. Mahajani, *loc. cit.*
12. Quoted in Guy J. Pauker, "Indonesia in 1964: Towards a 'Peoples' Democracy'?" *Asian Survey*, vol. 5, no. 2, February 1965, p. 95.
13. *Bulletin of Indonesian Economic Studies* (hereinafter cited as *BIES*), [vol. 1], no. 2, September 1965, p. 1.
14. Mahajani, *op cit.*, p. 34; and BIES, [vol. 2], no. 4, June 1966, p. 6.
15. *BIES*, [vol. 3], no. 6, February 1967, p. 11.
16. Robert Shaplen, *Time Out of Hand* (New York: Harper & Row, 1969), p. 167.

17. *BIES*, vol. 8, no. 1, March 1972, p. 6. Japan's reliance on imports from Indonesia has expanded sharply in the 1960s. In the first nine months of 1971 Japanese imports amounted to $611.8 million, compared with only $161.7 million going from Indonesia to the United States. The corresponding export statistics for the same period were $210.2 million for the United States and $305.9 million for Japan. (IMF and World Bank statistics published in *Direction of Trade,* February 1972.)

18. *BIES*, vol. 6, no. 2, July 1970, p. 17.

19. Robert Coats, "Indonesian Timber," *Pacific Research and World Empire Telegram,* vol. 2, no. 4, May–June 1971, p. 10.

20. *BIES*, vol. 8, no. 1, March 1972, p. 19.

21. Ingrid Palmer and Lance Castles, "The Textile Industry," in Bruce Glassburner, ed., *The Economy of Indonesia* (Ithaca and London: Cornell University Press, 1971), pp. 333–34.

22. *BIES*, [vol. 4], no. 11, October 1968, p. 23.

23. Sumitro Djojohadikusumo, *Trade and Aid in Southeast Asia,* vol. 1: *Malaysia and Singapore* (Melbourne: F. W. Cheshire, 1967), p. 110.

24. *BIES*, vol. 8, no. 1, March 1972, pp. 5, 29.

25. *BIES*, vol. 7, no. 1, March 1971, pp. 25–26; David Cole, "New Directions in the Banking System," *BIES*, vol. 5, no. 2 (July 1, 1969), p. 69.

26. Figures (approximate) taken from *BIES*, vol. 6, no. 2 (July 1970), p. 17; and table prepared by the Arbeitskollektiv Köln-Bonn in *Südostasien Korrespondenz*, no. 2 (July 1971), p. 16.

THE ASIAN DEVELOPMENT BANK:
An Imperial Thrust into the Pacific

RICHARD DE CAMP

Until World War II, the American empire was largely confined to the Western hemisphere. But after the war, the United States —the only major power whose territory had not been a battlefield —emerged as the unquestioned hegemon of the "Free World." Only the Soviet Union appeared capable of challenging American supremacy, and Soviet industrial and military capabilities were clearly inferior. Nonetheless, America's empire soon faced an unexpected threat. First in China and then in Vietnam, Asian peasant revolutionaries challenged and defeated American-supported elites. Since 1965, the Indochina War has disastrously undermined American military and economic might. The Nixon Doctrine, designed to defend America's world hegemony with fewer American dollars and fewer American bodies, is a response to the decline of American power in Asia.

American participation in the Asian Development Bank (ADB) is a part of this emerging policy. As its leading American exponent, international banker Eugene Black, has pointed out, the ADB was initially designed to "change our policy image" at a time and in a part of the world where that image is dominated by war and wanton destruction.[1]

The United States did not, however, create the ADB alone. By the mid-1960s, Japan had begun to assume a major economic role in Asia, a role reflected and enhanced by its position in the ADB. In helping to create the bank, Japan provided not only an initial capital subscription of $200 million, an amount equal to that of the United States, but also the bank's first president—Takeshi Watanabe. As America's role in the bank has declined, Japan has become its leading contributor and dominant force.

The ADB is but one link in the complex chain of capitalist financial institutions created by the United States and its partners since World War II. Central to this structure are the World Bank and the International Monetary Fund (IMF). In the immediate postwar period, the World Bank provided loans to the war-devastated European countries and to Japan. When the Marshall Plan took over the task of reconstruction, the Bank began to extend loans to Third World countries, especially for the development of those power and transportation facilities which served the needs of private investors.[2] The World Bank was explicitly created to promote capitalist development and to keep the door open to private foreign investment. Countries which nationalize foreign investments without compensation or fail to repay their international debts do not receive loans.[3]

In its operations, the World Bank cooperates closely with the IMF. By lending or refusing credit to countries whose balance-of-payments accounts show a deficit, the IMF holds enormous leverage over the internal affairs of many countries. For without IMF credit, a deficit-nation will not be able to pay to import needed goods. IMF credit is available only when borrower nations agree to specific "stabilization" measures which include devaluation of the currency, encouragement of foreign investment, and domestic anti-inflation policies. A country which persists in defying the IMF generally finds that all "major sources of credit in the developed, capitalist world"—private capital, regional development banks, the World Bank, and bilateral government aid—dry up.[4]

The IMF pursues monetary stability at a heavy cost. In Indonesia, where IMF policies were imposed after the military coup of 1965, many Indonesian-owned businesses were forced to shut down; imported consumer goods flooded the market; many thousands of workers lost their jobs; prices of essential goods and services were decontrolled and rose; and the country's foreign debt burden soared. While inflation was slowed, the price paid in lost jobs, reduced social welfare, and dependence on the rich capitalist nations has been enormous.[5]

For two decades after World War II, the United States dominated the major international financial institutions just as it dominated the international finances of the capitalist world. Yet declining American economic supremacy in the late 1960s has had repercussions within the institutions of international finance. The ADB is the first component of this financial network in which Japan has assumed a dominant role. It illustrates important themes and contradictions of Japanese and American policy in Asia.

BACKGROUND

The major theme of the ADB is multilateralism. Liberals have long favored multilateral aid in order to disarm critics of American aid programs both at home and abroad. They also believe that a multilateral approach limits the American commitment to any particular regime and thus reduces the possibility of becoming involved in new "Vietnams." Joining in the advocacy of multilateral aid are representatives of the multinational corporations who feel that an international agency, presenting a united front of the rich, aid-giving nations that a single poor nation finds hard to defy, can make demands of a Third World country that would be politically repugnant to that country if made by the United States or Japan alone. Such a perspective meshes well with Nixon's notion of lowering America's foreign policy profile, and in 1970 it received the stamp of approval from a blue-ribbon Presidential Task Force on International Development.[6]

The American government was not always so enthusiastic about multilateral aid. In fact, the proposal for an ADB, first put forward by a study group of the U.N.'s Economic Commission for Asia and the Far East, was neglected for several years. At the time, both the United States and Japan saw drawbacks to an ADB. The United States was "reluctant to adopt a multilateral approach that would limit American influence," while Japan "did not want to lend its resources to an institution that seemed destined, like the World Bank, to become primarily an instrument of American policy."[7]

As late as March 17, 1965, the most the United States would offer was the possibility of American support for the proposed bank at some future date. This position was reversed less than a month later in Lyndon Johnson's speech at Johns Hopkins University. Seeking to offset the image of U.S. destruction in Vietnam, he turned to the ADB as a cheap means to put the United States on the side of development in Asia.[8]

Japan, meanwhile, was registering spectacular increases in trade with Southeast Asia and preparing the way for massive foreign investment. As Eugene Black pointed out: "The bigger Japanese trade and investment in the region become, the more Japan will have to match it with a coherent political policy if only to forestall a wave of expropriations of her property or restrictions on her trade."[9] With both of the major economic powers of the Pacific seeking to improve their positions through peaceful "development" programs, the ADB was born on December 4, 1965.

Its charter, explicitly modeled on that of the World Bank,[10] provided that the bank would 1) "promote investment of public and private development capital"; 2) "finance regional, subregional and national development projects in Asian developing countries"; 3) "assist in the coordination of national development policies and plans"; 4) "provide technical assistance"; and 5) "cooperate with national and international institutions and private sources investing development funds."[11] Ultimately nineteen non-Communist Asian and twelve Western countries joined.[12]

A COMMON NEED FOR STABILITY

Multilateralism is predicated on a basic identity of purpose among the developed capitalist nations. The United States and Japan are foremost among those rich nations which require stability and an Open Door in Asia so that their corporations can utilize the raw materials, markets, and investment opportunities of the region on the best possible terms.

Dominating the economic life of the Pacific Rim are the ADB's three major contributors—the United States, Japan, and Australia. Japan is America's second best customer. In 1971, she absorbed $4.1 billion (nine percent) of U.S. exports. The United States in turn is Japan's number one customer taking $7.3 billion (thirty percent) of Japanese exports in 1971. Australia is the minor partner in this network, but her interest in it is substantial. Over one-third of her trade is carried on with the United States and Japan. Particularly important are Australian mineral exports to resource-hungry Japan. As a unit, these three nations annually conduct $15.4 billion worth of trade with each other. This triangle trade grew 200 percent during the 1960s while total U.S. exports were growing only sixty-nine percent and total world exports increased eighty-seven percent.[13]

American investment in these countries is substantial. At the end of 1970, total U.S. direct investment abroad amounted to $78 billion and was growing by over $7 billion each year. Investment in Japan increased fivefold during the 1960s to a total of $1.5 billion, and under strong U.S. pressures the Japanese have recently relaxed their investment restrictions. American investment in Australia and New Zealand tripled to exceed $3 billion by the end of the decade.[14] By the end of 1971 Japanese investment in Australia had reached $200 million and is expected to at least triple in the next three years.[15]

These three developed countries dominate the economies of the poor countries of non-Communist Asia. The U.S. export trade with these countries was worth $4 billion (nine percent of total U.S. exports) in 1971, and the value of imports from them reached $3.9 billion (nine percent of the total). U.S. direct investment interests in the area, worth $2.5 billion in 1970, centered in the Philippines, in Indonesian oil and in low-wage manufacturing in Singapore, Taiwan, South Korea, and Hong Kong.[16] Australian investment in Asia totals about $100 million.[17] Her trading interests are also substantial. In 1971, Australians sold $525 million of goods (twelve percent of total exports) to the poor nations of the region and bought $242 million (six percent of total imports).

While the American economic interest is substantial, Japan's rapidly growing economic interests in the region have raised a significant challenge to America's political and economic dominance of Asia. Her economy relies overwhelmingly on imported raw materials. In 1968, for instance, she depended on imports for ninety-eight percent or more of her consumption of crude oil, iron ore, phosphate, bauxite, cotton, wool, and crude rubber.[18] Japanese business leaders worry if it will be "possible to secure stable overseas supply sources commensurate with the growing scale of the nation's demand for resources," estimated at $30 billion for industrial raw materials in 1975.[19] In 1971, $3.4 billion (seventeen percent) of Japan's imports came from the non-Communist countries of Asia. Particularly important is Indonesia, from whom Japan hopes to take increasing amounts of oil in order to end her costly reliance on the Middle East and on American-owned international oil companies. Rich in untapped resources, Southeast Asia may hold the key to Japan's raw material needs.

To pay for these imports and to sustain her rapid economic growth, Japan needs foreign markets. In 1971 the poor nations of the region absorbed $5.8 billion (twenty-four percent) of her exports and provided Japan with a $2.4 billion trade surplus. This trade is particularly profitable because Japan controls it so completely. Japanese corporations ship their products on Japanese ships; market them through Japanese-owned trading firms; and frequently consume them on Japanese investment projects. In the future, the Japanese expect to do even better. As Chikara Makino of the Planning Office, Minister's Secretariat, has put it:

> When the various Southeast Asian nations can acquire as great
> an economic buoyancy as the ROK and Taiwan, the economic
> market of the Pacific region will become the biggest and deep-
> est in the whole world and it will become the most suitable
> place for the activities of the leviathan named Japan.[20]

The China market is also of concern to Japanese businessmen. Some major Japanese firms are transferring their main efforts from the Taiwan market to the mainland. These include such giants as Nippon Steel, Mitsubishi Corporation, Sanwa Bank, and Fuji Bank.[21] But, in their scramble for the China market, it is unlikely that even these firms will withdraw from Taiwan and South Korea. Trade with both Taiwan and South Korea substantially exceeded that with China in 1971, and Japan has investments of more than $200 million in South Korea and $100 million in Taiwan.[22] While trade with the People's Republic of China will undoubtedly grow, Derek Davies, editor of the *Far Eastern Economic Review,* is certainly correct to assert that the most powerful groups in Japan see their economic future as lying at

> the centre of an Asian common market or customs union
> (much along the lines of the old co-prosperity sphere) in which

the countries of East Asia, plus possibly South Asia and Australasia, are gradually tied in to the Japanese market by trade and tariff agreements and by a planned programme of regional investment.[23]

Stripped of her foreign investments after World War II, Japan required the next twenty years to rehabilitate her domestic economy. By the end of 1966, Japan's overseas investments had reached $1 billion, of which only twenty-two percent was direct investment.[24] Since 1966, Japan's enormous trade surplus has provided the capital to more than triple overseas investments to an estimated $3.6 billion in early 1971.[25]

While still short of American totals, Japan's investment in Asia is growing rapidly in importance. Her investment in Thailand ($41 million) is already estimated to be sixty percent of all foreign investment.[26] She is the largest provider of private credit grants in South Korea and is the second largest investor behind the United States in both South Korea ($200 million) and Taiwan ($100 million).[27] In the Philippines, sixty percent ($260 million) of all new foreign investment in 1971 was Japanese, though total Japanese investments lag far behind those of the United States.[28] In Singapore, Japan is now the third largest foreign investor with $61 million.[29] Perhaps the greatest potential lies in resource-rich Indonesia. Japanese investment there is already a substantial and rapidly growing $268 million, second only to that of the United States.[30] The Japanese investment boom is only beginning. By 1980 it is estimated that Japanese corporate investment abroad will exceed $25 billion, a rate of increase far above that predicted for the United States.[31]

Japan's interest in non-Communist Asia, when combined with strong American interests in the region and in Japan itself, add up to an overwhelming pressure to protect the Open Door. Since 1945, the United States has fought two major wars and threatened several others to protect these interests. It has extended $14.7 billion in aid to ADB member states Taiwan, South Korea, Thailand, South Vietnam, Indonesia, and the Philippines.[32] Now that economic and military reverses require U.S. retrenchment, Japan is taking up the economic burdens of empire. The ADB is one element in the American and Japanese strategy for developing and controlling the resources of Asia.

POWER IN THE ADB

One of the favorite myths of ADB publicists is that the ADB was created and is run by and for Asians. The evidence in support of this notion is scanty. The bank has its headquarters in Manila. Its president is an Asian. And, most important, more than sixty percent of its initial capital came from Asian members. As Black argues: "This unique combination of a big voice for the lenders and a big voice for the Asians is what distinguishes the ADB."[33]

Unfortunately for the Asian people, however, the ADB fosters the interests of the developed capitalist nations—particularly the United States and Japan. The crucial division in the ADB is not between Asian and non-Asian members, but rather between the rich member nations and the poor. At the ADB's inaugural meeting the representatives of Sihanouk's Cambodia expressed the concrete demands of the poor nations. They wanted "quick progress," long-term credits "at very low interest rates," and greater power for the small recipient nations within the bank's administration.[34] U.S. Treasury Secretary Fowler spoke for the rich nations. He insisted that the bank should "concentrate its energies and skills first and foremost on becoming a banking institution . . . [with] prudent management of funds, high standards of loan appraisals . . . [and] policies that permit accumulation of adequate reserves. . . ."[35] The U.S. vision prevailed.

It is striking that of the three major regional development banks (Asian, African and Latin American), only the ADB was warmly greeted by the rich capitalist nations.[36] The ADB was graciously accepted by the rich because power within it lies with them. Of the capital put up by "Asian" nations, half has been donated by Japan, Australia, and New Zealand. In combination with other rich nations, they put up $657 million, over two-thirds of the bank's initial capital.

Voting power is heavily dependent on donations of capital. Eugene Black, representing the U.S. government, originally fought for ninety-five percent of voting strength to be based on contributions. He reluctantly accepted eighty percent.[37] This left the United States with about 17 percent of the vote in the bank, a fact which some U.S. Senators were quick to decry. But the lack of absolute American control is not a high price for the

United States to pay. It is unlikely that any important decision could be taken against American interests. Important questions require a two-thirds majority; so the United States, Japan and any other member could block any major decision. Rich countries hold 64.5 percent of the total voting power. To give an initiative the two-thirds or three-fourths majority that the charter requires, they must only exert pressure on such heavily dependent nations as Taiwan, South Korea, Laos, Thailand, South Vietnam, West Samoa, and the Philippines. As Black has testified: "the majority of the votes are from the capital exporting countries, which is very important. In other words, the borrowers can't run the Bank."[38]

ADB OPERATIONS

The heart of the ADB is its lending program. By October 1, 1971, it had announced over $470 million in loans.[39] President Watanabe once argued that his bank "should be a bank with a heart," not simply a "money lending machine."[40] But, if there is a heart, it is not a warm one. Eighty-five percent of all bank loans have been ordinary loans with terms of ten to twenty-five years at rates of 6 $\frac{7}{8}$ percent, and these interest rates rose in mid-1970 to 7 $\frac{1}{2}$ percent. On these terms, the bank's loans can hardly be called aid. They are scarcely distinguishable from commercial bank loans. Typically, the ADB's first loan went to the Industrial Finance Corporation of Thailand, an institution that could easily have gotten the money elsewhere.[41]

ADB loans add to the debt burden of the poor nations of the area, already staggering under service payments on existing foreign debt of about $1.2 billion per year.[42] Less than $80 million, seventeen percent of all ADB loans, have been "soft" (low-interest) ones. These come from the bank's "special funds." They are donated by individual countries and are not part of the bank's ordinary capital.

The ideological foundations for ADB policy are elucidated in the ADB-sponsored study, *Southeast Asia's Economy in the 1970s*, which efficiently fits non-Communist Asia into the economy of the capitalist world. The study bluntly describes the role of the "developing countries" as one of producing raw materials. "To exploit this, effective links must be forged to connect the region's abundant natural resources with the expanding world market demand for their exports." It recommends "the introduction of private foreign capital into primary production," argues against self-sufficiency and strategies of import substitution, and stresses that adequate power and transportation facilities as well as cheap but skilled labor and adequate government administrative and fiscal systems will draw needed foreign capital.[43] It is in short a recipe which calls for heavy dependence upon American and Japanese capital and techniques for the foreseeable future.

The ADB seeks to stimulate private investment and capitalist development. Investment in infrastructure is costly and often unprofitable at first. But because the potential for private investment is limited in a country lacking an adequate "infrastructure," it is logical that $214 million, forty-five percent of all ADB loans, has gone to help create infrastructure—roads in Taiwan, South Korea, and the Philippines; ports in Ceylon, Taiwan, Malaysia, and Thailand; power grids in Taiwan, South Korea, Indonesia, Singapore, and Laos; and airports in Singapore, Nepal, and West Samoa. For domestic and foreign capitalists, the benefits are notable. Public funds are used to build an infrastructure which will enable private industries to profit.

The next largest category of loans, $112 million which is nearly twenty-five percent of the total, has gone to the national development banks of South Korea, Taiwan, Pakistan, Singapore, Thailand, and the Philippines. This money is then re-loaned to small- and medium-sized businesses in these nations. It can be used not only by local capitalists but also by foreign investors.[44] These loans stimulate domestic private enterprise, aid foreign investors, and help to build a small bourgeoisie with a stake in the stability of a capitalist society and in continued good relations with the rich capitalist nations.

The bank has supported modern industry with $46 million in loans to two of its favorite clients. Of this relatively small sum, $25 million has gone to a single enterprise, the Hankook Caprolactum Corporation. The Hankook project is a "key component" of the Ulsan Petrochemical Complex which in turn is crucial to South Korea's second five-year plan.[45] First supported by American interests, the Ulsan project is now dominated by Japanese capital.[46] There have been four other loans for modern industry, all of which are quite small. In addition, the bank has loaned

$34 million to such traditional processing industries as tea, palm oil, jute, cotton, rice, and rubber in Ceylon, Malaysia, Nepal, Pakistan, and Indonesia.

The ADB has made much of its concern for Asian agriculture. It has published a regional agricultural survey, devoted two-thirds of its technical assistance grants ($4.5 million by the end of 1970) to agriculture, and made $50 million worth of loans—largely "soft" loans—in the agricultural sector. In general the ADB's loans have concentrated on providing those inputs of fertilizer and irrigation necessary to realize the promise of the "green revolution."

But the "green revolution" has had certain profoundly destructive social consequences. Only rich peasants and landlords can afford the capital investment necessary to make dramatic increases in production. For the poor peasant, the result has been falling crop prices, lowered income, increased tenancy, and rural unemployment.[47]

Even in its own terms, the "green revolution" is faltering. The Philippines, where "miracle rice" was first developed, has been unable to achieve self-sufficiency and was forced to import 458,000 tons of rice in 1971. Further imports are projected for 1972.[48]

The ADB has shown "no evidence of any sense of social priorities." Instead it emphasizes "sound banking principles."[49] One loan for education has been made—$3 million on concessional terms to Singapore to expand a technical college. As the *Far Eastern Economic Review* points out, Singapore is by Asian standards no longer a truly low-wage economy. But it does offer a tough Employment Act and a highly skilled labor force. "To maintain the overseas investor's technological standards, Singapore must ensure there is adequate trained fodder for his plants."[50] The ADB loan will help more with the "development of human capital resources"[51] than with the development of human beings.

Three nations have received over half of all ADB loans. They are South Korea ($111 million), Singapore ($74 million), and Taiwan ($64 million). Five others have received more than $30 million apiece: Pakistan, the Philippines, Thailand, Indonesia, and Malaysia. Seven others—Ceylon, Nepal, Afghanistan, Laos, Western Samoa, South Vietnam, and Cambodia—have together received less than $50 million (about nine percent of the total).

The distribution of loans has both political and economic motivation. It is a banker's choice. All three countries provide iron-clad assurances for the foreign investor and have received large influxes of foreign capital in recent years. Singapore, by far the largest per capita recipient of ADB loans, is also the most prosperous of the poor ADB nations. Taiwan and South Korea are the two which have shown the most rapid growth of GNP, and both of them are slowly passing from a role as American military bastions in the Cold War. While the American economic position is firm in both, Japanese economic interests are crucial and growing rapidly.

Korean economic growth has been described as "the growth not of 'the ROK itself' but of the country integrated into the Japanese economic bloc."[52] Thirty-nine percent of South Korea's imports come from Japan and twenty-five percent of her exports go there. In the 1970s, as American aid and military procurement purchases dry up and repayments on her huge foreign debts increase (to $452 million in 1976), South Korea will become increasingly dependent on Japanese capital. The Pohang Integrated Steel Works and the Ulsan Petrochemical Complex, both essential to South Korea's development plans, are dependent on Japanese capital. South Korea's recent economic growth, symbolized by such projects, has blinded some to the fact that few of the benefits go to the Korean people. With unemployment in Seoul as high as twenty-three percent, the government, like the ADB, continues to ignore the need for housing, urban planning, health, and education programs.

Like South Korea, Taiwan is a former Japanese colony and now a profitable appendage of the Japanese economy. Between 1965 and 1970 Japan's surplus in trade with Taiwan totaled $1.6 billion.[53] At the same time, investment skyrocketed. Such a profitable business arrangement will not be abandoned, but growth in the Japanese interest in Taiwan has slowed recently—not only in private investment but also in government aid. The ADB has reflected this reappraisal of Taiwan's value. New loans declined sharply in the first three-quarters of 1971. With the seating of the People's Republic of China at the U.N., even Taiwan's right to ADB membership was questioned; but ADB President Watanabe has publicly stated that the bank would continue to aid Taiwan and not ask Peking to join "at present."[54]

Singapore has a "potential position as the new commercial

center for the multinational corporations of Europe, America and Japan."[55] Japanese investment is third behind the United States and Britain, but it too is rising rapidly. In mid-1971, Singapore's investment promotion center was processing $1 billion worth of Japanese investment proposals. Japan also makes huge profits in trade with Singapore. In 1971 Japan sold $1.5 billion worth of goods to Singapore while buying only $400 million worth—a favorable balance of $1.1 billion.[56] Reflecting these interests, the ADB has poured $74 million worth of loans—almost entirely to create infrastructure—into this tiny nation of two million with the highest per capita income in Southeast Asia.

Indonesia has been the seventh largest recipient of ADB loans, but the $31.5 million she has received has all come out of the bank's special funds. In fact, Indonesia has received forty percent of all ADB "soft" loans. Since the 1965 coup that brought Indonesia back into the "Free World," Indonesia's trade with Japan has nearly tripled.[57] Japanese investment has poured into Indonesia; and, while the Japanese total remains a distant second to the United States, it is gaining rapidly, and Japan has already outstripped the United States in total number of projects. ADB interest in Indonesia reflects not only the intrinsic economic importance of that nation, but also the Japanese and American desire to keep its resources within their control.

The ADB claims that it "is bound by no political considerations when it examines the merits of a project proposal."[58] In fact this is not so. The ADB refused to make loans to Cambodia while Sihanouk was in power. Its single loan to Cambodia was approved two weeks after the coup which overthrew him.[59] The ADB moved into South Korea and Taiwan just when substantial U.S. aid was cut back. More than half of all ADB loans have gone to six member states with large U.S. bases and direct involvement in the Indochina War—South Korea, Taiwan, the Philippines, Thailand, Laos, and South Vietnam. The loans to South Vietnam and Laos were the first that those two states had ever received from an international development bank.[60]

A small program in actual investment but one with profound political implications is the ADB's work in the Mekong area. The projects envisioned for the Mekong involve billions of dollars and at least four countries: Cambodia, Laos, Thailand, and South Vietnam. They are designed to provide food, water, and power to transform these states from centers of conflict to models of capitalist development. While the Indochina War has prevented large-scale construction, the ADB has been closely involved in planning for the Mekong project, has made over $6 million worth of "soft" loans for power and agriculture, and has granted over $1 million in technical assistance. In Northeast Thailand, a center of Thai revolutionary activity, the ADB is supporting "Accelerated Rural Development" and irrigation projects in at least six localities. Similar programs for agricultural development are being carried out in war-torn Laos. The ADB has even gone so far as to allocate $95,000 for an evaluation study of a bridge that may someday be used to ferry Thai troops into Laos for a last-ditch defense of Vientiane.[61]

In sum, I wish to emphasize four points. First, the ADB functions as a bank, making profitable loans on "sound banking principles." Second, bank loans have gone predominantly to those member states with large U.S. and Japanese investments: South Korea, Taiwan, Singapore, Indonesia, Thailand, and the Philippines; and they have centered in such sectors as infrastructure and light industry to complement the economies of the rich nations and aid their investors. Third, the political thrust of the bank is clear. It excludes the revolutionary nations of Asia and supports client elites in the non-Communist ones. Finally, it provides financial props and external pressure to perpetuate capitalism within the recipient nations. The bank's strategy for stability, like that of other "aid" donors, involves the creation of an urban middle class with capitalist interests to protect and the strengthening of the rural upper class with a "green revolution," whose primary social effect is to benefit landlords and rich peasants and to force the poor off the land.

CONTRADICTIONS

The ADB was created to provide "development" assistance in countries with a total population of one billion. It is to do this with only $500 million of capital (not including its special funds resources which currently are about $130 million and what it can borrow by floating bonds in Japanese, European, and American money markets) ; and nearly one-third of this total capital has been contributed by the poor nations themselves. Such figures, combined with the results of ADB-funded projects, make a mockery of the words of "liberal" Congressman Henry Reuss:

> Usually the founding of a financial institution does not normally give vent to the expression of the hopes of mankind in a better tomorrow. Yet the establishment of this Bank augurs hope for the beggar children born on the streets of Calcutta and Bangkok, for the rice paddy peasants of Vietnam and Malaysia. . . .[62]

For all the rhetoric about "aid" and "development," the ADB is merely a bank. It operates largely at the prevailing rate of 7½ percent to benefit its stockholders, the developed capitalist nations. Its customers, the client states of Asia, take what they can get; and in the process they become ever more deeply entangled in the workings of international capitalism and ever more dependent on the United States and Japan.

Why do the poor nations accept such "aid"? Part of the answer lies in the fact that they have no place else to turn. The socialist nations are themselves relatively poor and the limitations of their aid programs reflect this poverty. But more important is the fact that the tiny elites which rule the client states of Asia have a stake in the current system. Third World elites complain of the dominance of foreign corporations and attack unequal trade relations, but for the most part they only complain. They fear direct retaliation since any country that nationalizes foreign investments or defies the "advice" of the multilateral financial institutions faces formidable economic and possible military sanctions. To break out of the imperialist system requires that the elite be popularly based and prepared to substitute austerity for the luxury of Western-style consumption patterns. Still more threatening to the elite than retaliation is the fact that breaking out of the system might lead to revolutionary changes. The perpetuation of their power and of their inflated standard of living depends directly on the military and financial support of the imperialist powers.

The crisis of the American economy is mirrored in the continuing debate over the ADB. As American financial troubles deepen, spokesmen for major corporate economic interests such as the National Association of Manufacturers and the International Economic Policy Association insist that the ADB plays an important function for U.S. business interests in Asia. Others disagree. Representative Otto E. Passman of Louisiana has complained that, with the ADB, "foreigners are getting preferred treatment."[63] The substance of his complaint is absurd, but in this time of economic difficulty those outside the strongholds of corporate power tend to be strongly critical of any kind of spending which takes from their constituents but does not come back to support the locally based interests (local banks, small and medium industries, etc.) upon which their power depends.[64]

Consequently, although Congress passed the initial request for a contribution of $200 million to the bank, it has time and again turned down Administration requests for additional money for the ADB's special funds. American reluctance to contribute to the ADB has led to increasing Japanese power within the bank. By the end of 1970, the Japanese had solidified their leading role in the bank by contributing $71 million (fifty-six percent of the total) to the bank's special funds.[65] The ADB today is an integral part of Japan's economic thrust into Asia as it is "the sole international organization of significance in which Japan is the most influential member."[66]

The ADB is an *Asian* bank only in the sense that it is one more institution that has been created within the region to unite the anti-Communist states against revolutionary change and in mutual dependence on the imperialist nations, particularly Japan. From Eugene Black's point of view, it provides one prop against formidable "divisive and destructive forces in Asia. . . . The nations of the area," he notes, "are showing a growing desire to establish close ties among themselves. . . ." So American investment in the ADB "represents precisely the sort of investment we can make today which we hope will prevent future Vietnams."[67]

But neither the ADB nor the system it so closely reflects can ever really aid the overwhelming majority of the Asian people. Its beneficiaries are limited to those Asian political and economic leaders who presently benefit from the status quo. The imperialist powers are trying to prop up a socioeconomic order that does not meet popular needs. Since the "development" policies of a Eugene Black cannot assuage the popular revolution that neither Johnson's nor Nixon's wars could destroy, liberation struggles must continue on to victory.

NOTES

1. Eugene R. Black, *Alternative in Southeast Asia.* New York: Praeger Publishers, 1969, p. 150.

2. Bruce Nissen, "The World Bank: A Political Institution," *Pacific Research and World Empire Telegram,* vol. 2, no. 6, September–October 1971, pp. 18–19.

3. Teresa Hayter, *Aid as Imperialism.* Middlesex, England: Penguin Books, 1971, p. 15.

4. Cheryl Payer, "The Perpetuation of Dependence: The IMF and the Third World," *Monthly Review,* vol. 23, no. 4, September 1971, p. 38.

5. *Ibid.,* pp. 39, 42.

6. Report to the President from the Task Force on International Development, *United States Foreign Assistance in the 1970s: A New Approach,* Washington, D.C., March 4, 1970, pp. 3, 23. On the ability of the multilateral finance institution to exercise leverage, see: Hayter, *Aid as Imperialism,* especially p. 94.

7. *Far Eastern Economic Review (FEER)* , April 14, 1966, p. 59.

8. Philip Geyelin, *Lyndon B. Johnson and the World.* New York: Praeger Publishers, 1966, pp. 276–83.

9. Black, *op. cit.,* p. 155.

10. Dominick Puccio, "The Asian Development Bank" (unpublished) , p. 4.

11. *FEER,* April 14, 1966, p. 59.

12. Of the major Western powers, only France refused to participate because of her conviction that the bank was a tool of U.S. policy. However, she has since reversed this stand in the interest of doing better business with the poor nations of Asia. (*FEER Yearbook* [Hong Kong, 1971], p. 95.) Other European contributions have generally been small, reflecting the fact that their major interests lie in other regions.

13. Unless otherwise noted, trade figures all come from: International Monetary Fund & International Bank for Reconstruction and Development, *Direction of Trade,* March 1972, pp. 3, 5, 49, 51, 67. The trade figures for Australia reflect not a full year, but the period January–October 1971. American investment figures, unless otherwise noted, have been drawn from: R. David Belli & Julius N. Freidlin, "U.S. Direct Investments Abroad in 1970," *Survey of Current Business,* vol. 51, no. 10, October 1971, p. 32.

14. *FEER,* August 28, 1971, p. 27.

15. *FEER,* March 4, 1972, p. 53.

16. *FEER,* August 28, 1971, p. 27.

17. *FEER,* August 27, 1970, p. 37.

18. Minoru Genda, "Japan's National Defense," *Pacific Community,* vol. 2, no. 1, October 1970, p. 43.

19. Masakazu Echigo, President of C. Itoh & Co. Ltd., *Japan Times,* January 18, 1971, p. B-5.

20. Chikara Makino, "Japan–United States Relations," *Summaries of Selected Japanese Magazines.* Tokyo: U.S. Embassy, September 1970, p. 30.

21. *FEER,* March 4, 1972, p. 44.

22. *Ibid.,* pp. 44, 66, 67.

23. *FEER,* March 27, 1971, p. 30.

24. "Advance of Japanese Enterprises Overseas," *Oriental Economist,* vol. 35, no. 679, May 1967, p. 295.

25. *FEER,* August 28, 1971, p. 29.

26. *Ibid.,* pp. 30, 59.

27. *FEER,* March 4, 1972, pp. 66–67; Seiya Yano, "Overseas Business Age Has Dawned," *Oriental Economist,* vol. 38, no. 714, April 1971, pp. 24–25.

28. *FEER,* August 28, 1971, p. 30.

29. *FEER,* March 4, 1972, p. 65.

30. *Ibid.,* p. 39.

31. *FEER,* August 28, 1971, p. 29.

32. U.S. Department of Commerce, *Statistical Abstract of the United States, 1971,* Washington, D.C., p. 722.

33. Black, *ibid.,* p. 99.

34. Liaison Committee for the Inaugural Meeting of the ADB, *Inaugural Meeting Asian Development Bank.* Tokyo: 1966, pp. 226–31.

35. *Ibid.,* p. 314.

36. John White, "The Asian Development Bank: A Question of Style," *International Affairs.* vol. 44, no. 4, October 1968, p. 678.

37. *FEER,* April 14, 1966, p. 59.

38. Puccio, "The Asian Development Bank," p. 14. Black was testifying before the House Subcommittee on International Finance of the Committee on Banking and Currency (February 27, 1968, p. 80).

39. Loan data is derived from: ADB, "Quarterly Newsletter" (January 1971), pp. 8–10; April 1971, p. 8; July 1971, p. 3; and October 1971, pp. 4–5.

40. Takeshi Watanabe, "The Asian Development Bank," *U.N. Monthly Chronicle,* vol. 4, February 1967, p. 35.

41. White, *ibid.,* p. 685.

42. ADB, *Annual Report, 1970.* Manila: Asian Development Bank, February 4, 1971, p. 9.

43. ADB, "Quarterly Newsletter," January 1971, pp. 11–12.

44. Takeshi Watanabe, *Paths to Progress.* Manila: ADB, March 1971, p. 63. In this speech, delivered to the Chase Manhattan International

Advisory Committee in Tokyo, Watanabe is quite explicit in advertising the benefits of the ADB to foreign investors.

45. ADB, "News Release No. 55/70," December 22, 1970.

46. *FEER*, March 4, 1972, p. 66. Because of the limited availability of coastal land and because of Japanese antipollution measures, some Japanese business leaders have called for "Japanese–Korean cooperation" in certain industries "in which in particular Japan expects great development in the future—steel, aluminum, oil, petrochemicals . . ." (Jon Halliday & Gavan McCormick, *Japanese Imperialism Today.* London: Association for Radical East Asian Studies, 1971, p. 72.)

47. Bruce Nussbaum, "Green for Danger," *FEER*, October 31, 1970, pp. 29–30. Also Thomas B. Wiens, "Seeds of Revolution," *Bulletin of Concerned Asian Scholars,* vol. 2, no. 3, April–July 1970, pp. 104–108; and the discussion of India's abortive "green revolution" in Thomas Weisskopf's essay in this volume.

48. *FEER*, January 29, 1972, p. 24.

49. White, *ibid.*, pp. 684–85. White claims to have heard the phrase "sound banking principles" twenty times a day on his visit to ADB headquarters in Manila.

50. *FEER*, August 28, 1971, p. 39.

51. ADB, *Annual Report, 1970,* p. 3.

52. Kaoru Murakami, "Korean Peninsula and Japanese Munitions Industry," in *Summaries of Selected Japanese Magazines,* December 1970, p. 17.

53. *FEER*, October 16, 1971, p. 51.

54. *Japan Times,* October 29, 1971, p. 10. The legality of Watanabe's position is questionable. The ADB Charter restricts membership to "any member of the United Nations or its specialized agencies."

55. Peter F. Bell and Stephan A. Resnick, "The Contradictions of Postwar Development in Southeast Asia," *Journal of Contemporary Asia,* vol. 1, no. 1, Autumn 1970, p. 43.

56. *FEER*, March 4, 1972, p. 65.

57. *Ibid.*, p. 59.

58. ADB, "Quarterly Newsletter," April 1971, p. 4.

59. Puccio, "The Asian Development Bank," p. 20.

60. ADB, "Quarterly Newsletter," April 1971, p. 3.

61. ADB, "Quarterly Newsletter" (October 1971), pp. 1–3, 6. See also: Tony Fels, "The Mekong River Project and Imperialist Interests in Southeast Asia," *Perspectives,* vol. 1, no. 1 (published by the Socialist Labor Committees, May–June 1971), pp. 18–36.

62. House Banking and Currency Committee, Subcommittee on International Finance, *ADB Act Hearings,* 89th Congress, 2nd Session, 1966, p. 3.

63. House Appropriations Committee, *Foreign Relations and Re-*

lated Agencies Appropriations for 1970, Hearings before Subcommittee, 91st Congress, 1st Session, 1969, p. 274; House Banking and Currency Committee, *ADB Act Hearings,* pp. 135, 137.

64. This analysis is developed in "Thoughts on the American System," *Monthly Review,* vol. 20, no. 9, February 1969, pp. 1–13.

65. ADB, *Annual Report, 1970,* p. 88. The only other substantial contributors by this date were Canada ($25 million), Great Britain ($14.5 million), and Australia ($10 million).

66. *FEER,* May 1, 1971, p. 61.

67. Committee on Foreign Relations, U.S. Senate, *ADB Special Funds Hearings,* 90th Congress, 2nd Session, part 2, 1968, pp. 60, 63.

THE VIETNAM WAR AND THE CIA-FINANCIAL ESTABLISHMENT

PETER DALE SCOTT

The effects of intervention in Vietnam have not been confined to its Asian victims; increasingly they have meant lasting changes for the economy and polity of the persecutors as well. The concomitant expansion of U.S. defense industries, overseas investment, money supply, and foreign exchange deficits has led to a weakening of the domestic U.S. economy and of its domestic political institutions, in much the same way that gold from the Western Hemisphere weakened Spanish industry and parliaments in the sixteenth century and the illicit profits from the First Indochina War immobilized the French Fourth Republic.

This essay will attempt to study the workings of the intervention process as it was formulated in Washington, rather than as it was executed in Vietnam. In so doing it will draw heavily on "insiders'" accounts, and above all on the evidence of the Pentagon Papers. The latter are like Ribbentrop's memoirs: precisely where they are inaccurate as to the facts, they tell us something about the minds and concerns of their authors. I shall dwell particularly on what they tell us about periods of changes and contradictions in U.S. policy, partly because such moments outline most clearly the forces underlying U.S. decision-making, and partly because they are the key to further change.

One such period is March 1968, when Wall Street "advisers"

and the CIA, faced with the imminent disappearance of U.S. gold reserves, dictated an end to further U.S. troop escalations in Vietnam. The other, much more obscure, is the 1963–1965 period, when the same CIA financial alliance, faced in late 1963 with President Kennedy's plans for a withdrawal of U.S. forces from Vietnam, emerged in support of Lyndon Johnson's program of escalation. This new program, which involved the explicit co-operation of banks to prevent a payments crisis, annulled the Kennedy withdrawal plan, and made a "decisive commitment" to Vietnam.

From an external or Asian perspective such moments of change may seem less important than the continuity of U.S. policy which underlies them. Most Asians can see only too clearly that Washington supported a French war until the defeat at Dienbienphu; then, when nuclear intervention was rejected as too dangerous, developed a conventional capability in Southeast Asia under the guise of SEATO and intervened directly after the infrastructure for an American war had been completed.

Many sophisticated radical studies of American foreign policy, developed also from an external perspective, point out that the planning for the new "limited war" defense posture of the 1960s, associated with Kissinger, Maxwell Taylor, and the pivotal 1957 Rockefeller Brothers Fund Panel II Report, was explicitly addressed to the limitations in a nuclear posture which Indochina had made obvious in 1954. Some of these stress the coherency and what Harry Magdoff calls "the logic of imperialism"; they believe that the cure must be total: "the elimination of imperialism requires the overthrow of capitalism."[1] One problem for Americans with such an apocalyptic external perspective is that it may take action out of our hands. Still, Harry Magdoff's analysis of U.S. economic interests in Southeast Asia is closer to the point than Richard Barnet's confident assurance that "neither territory nor economic advantage has been pursued in Vietnam."[2]

Barnet's pragmatic and potentially optimistic perspective is that of an ex-insider. It is also one in which there are so many trees that the forest risks becoming invisible. Where Magdoff writes of economic "logic," Barnet writes of bureaucratic "illusion" and "fantasy":

> The bureaucratic model had completely displaced reality; the hard and stubborn facts, which so many intelligence analysts were paid so much to collect, were ignored.[3]

Not that Barnet ignores economic interests: he argues rather that they do not inspire but *follow* bureaucratic decisions, "once a commitment is made."[4]

While Magdoff's logic does not account for certain untidy anomalies of history, as in the case of Cuba, so the hesitancies of U.S. intervention in Vietnam made less imperialist sense than the brutal scenarios offered up by the Joint Chiefs of Staff. In like manner Barnet ignores the hard-headed economic planning that preceded escalations, the recurrent influence on bureaucratic decision-making by privately interested institutions like Socony-Mobil and the First National City Bank of New York, and the way in which the war, which he rightly labels a disaster, has worked throughout to these institutions' direct profit. I shall argue that there is truth in both positions. *Economic interest, increasingly at odds with the irrational bureaucratic over-expansion of the war, has always been a prevailing concern at the civilian center of decision-making, particularly in the civilian "intelligence community" and the CIA.* The overall prevalence of perceived economic interest in moments of crisis has led policy to determine "intelligence estimates," rather than the other way round.

This thesis does not imply a rigid economic "dictation" or "predetermination" of specific policy matters. On the contrary, we shall see both dissensions between economic and bureaucratic interests and flexibility in perceiving the optimum models or paradigms for maximizing military and economic advantage. This was particularly true between the Kennedy administration, whose paradigm gave priority to balance-of-payments equilibrium and military retrenchment, and the Johnson administration, whose paradigm in 1965 gave priority to international expansion and direction of investment. Thus Kennedy's announced plans for the withdrawal of troops from Vietnam were only one move in plans for a revised posture vis-à-vis the Soviet Union, and for reducing the foreign military expenditures which he acknowledged to be a critical factor in U.S. balance-of-payments deficits. The serious entertainment of this withdrawal program, which was reversed within hours of Kennedy's assassination, shows that the continuity of economic interests did not lead to a single-minded and rigidly inflexible U.S. policy. On the contrary the economic restraints on the exercise of U.S. power, overwhelming in the 1968 U.S. dollar crisis and already apparent in 1963, created moments in which the reformulation of U.S. policy was not only possible but necessary.

There has, however, been continuous economic subordination in the sense regretted by Matthew Arnold or J. A. Hobson in nineteenth-century imperial Britain: private affluence at the cost of public indigence. The economic advantages pursued by a central CIA-financial establishment were not truly national interests but private distortions of them: the advantages of a socially-restricted elite class who were as over-represented in government (particularly the CIA) as they were in the economically-concentrated areas of oil, international banking, and multinational enterprise. The disastrous success of this socially-restricted establishment in furthering their own version of national priorities is now forcing America to a serious questioning of its status quo: can this body politic afford a restricted system of elite decision-making which in the last decade has (while furthering private interests) almost literally bankrupted the international exchange account and public sector of the national economy?

In formulating the thesis that economic interest has prevailed in civilian decision-making and intelligence reporting concerning Indochina, we must carefully qualify two widely-held misperceptions of the 1960s, both of which are reinforced by systematic distortions, which in my view are probably deliberate, in the Pentagon Papers themselves. The first misperception (which I shall call the Blueprint Fallacy or the Fallacy of Foreknowledge) is that U.S. policy is a logical deduction from unswerving strategic premises and incapable of reformulation in response to specific crises. This is reinforced by an overemphasis in the Pentagon Papers (based on the self-protecting rhetoric of the original documents) on the fixity and unbroken continuity of U.S. policy, thus diminishing the responsibility of the Johnson–McNamara team for the violent escalations of 1964–1965. The second and related misperception (which I shall call the Fallacy of Neglected Intelligence) depicts the CIA and other civilians in the intelligence community as "skeptical" of, or even opposed to, escalations of bombing and other tactics which they actually supported. This is reinforced, as will be demonstrated, by sustained distortion and censorship in both the Bantam and Government editions of the Pentagon Papers. Such a widespread effort to vindicate the CIA testifies more to its hidden power than to its alleged lack of influence.

THE BLUEPRINT FALLACY: CLAIMS OF U.S. FOREKNOWLEDGE

Kennedy's move in 1961 toward "limited partnership" in the Vietnam War is rightly criticized by Robert Scheer, but wrongly understood:

> Kennedy was obsessed with a global strategy for stopping wars of national liberation from Cuba to Vietnam. It was a political view of guerrilla warfare concentrating on logistics. . . . Lansdale had sent a memo that Diem did not want U.S. combat units—"Afraid of losing control"—smart man, given what was to happen to him later. How to fool both Diem and the American public? The Kennedy team was in a quandary.

The answer, according to Scheer, was General Maxwell Taylor's stratagem of sending 6000 to 8000 troops, mostly logistics forces but including "some combat troops," under cover of dealing with the serious floods in the Mekong Delta.

> Taylor's answer: "What will be lost is not merely a crucial piece of real estate . . . the United States must decide how it will cope with Khrushchev's 'wars of liberation' . . . it is clear to me that the time may come in our relations to Southeast Asia when we must declare our intentions to attack the source of guerrilla aggression in North Vietnam and impose on the Hanoi government a price for participating in the current war." This shows that the Kennedy government realized that it was committing the U.S. to the path of escalation. The "Rostow Plan" of bombing the north and Johnson's later use of large-scale American troops were both foreseen.[5]

But Kennedy did not accept Taylor's view; he *turned down* the Taylor proposal, which in turn was explicitly motivated in part by Diem's recent request (in marked contrast to his earlier reluctance) for a bilateral defense treaty, tactical air combat squadron, and ground "combat-trainer units" (PP Bantam, pp. 100–107; Beacon, II, 81). Taylor's proposal was supported strongly by the American mission in Saigon, which reported "the Vietnamese people's 'virtually unanimous desire' for the introduction of American troops";[6] but its prospects were apparently warned against by the CIA's Special National Intelligence Estimate (SNIE) of November 5.[7] Taylor himself was a moderate compared to the Joint Chiefs of Staff, who were being rebuffed by the new president in their proposals for "allied intervention to seize and hold major portions of Laos" (PP Bantam, p. 97; cf. PP Beacon, II, 12, 74). Leslie Gelb, the director and editor of the Pentagon Papers project, rightly reminds us that Kennedy's concurrent efforts to de-escalate the U.S. commitment in Laos exercised pressure for a countervailing commitment in Vietnam: "U.S. policy was driven by the unthinkability of avoidably risking another defeat in Southeast Asia hard on the heels of the Laos retreat" (PP Beacon, II, 5).

This pressure arose not only from the generals and those (to quote Daniel Ellsberg) "usually characterized as right-wing—and sometimes ... 'Asia-first'—non-Eastern Republicans."[8] It also arose from the concern, and capacity for blackmail, of America's allies and/or puppets in Southeast Asia. One of these, Diem's Secretary Nguyen Dinh Thuan, responded on November 20 to Kennedy's rejection of the Diem-Taylor request for combat troops, with the statement that Diem now wondered "whether U.S. was getting ready to back out on Vietnam ... as we had done in Laos" (PP Beacon, II, 121, cf. 651).[9]

Despite his own rhetoric about stopping communist wars of liberation, Kennedy did not initiate the immediate pressure to intervene in Vietnam, and responded to it with a significantly smaller effort than was proposed. In the end the Taylor proposal for 8000 troops was not passed upward by Rusk and McNamara for approval. Instead they drafted a substitute memorandum—"one obviously more to the President's liking (and ... quite possibly drawn up to the President's specifications)"—which "contained stronger rhetoric ... but milder recommendations" (PP Bantam, p. 106). The substitute memo called only for helicopter and other support units now, with plans for possible other units later.

At the same time the secretaries recommended that "we now take the decision to commit ourselves to the objective of preventing the fall of South Vietnam to Communism" (PP Bantam, 152; Beacon, II, 113). Three days earlier McNamara had warned that, without this clear verbal commitment, "major units of U.S. forces should not be introduced in South Vietnam." Yet Kennedy specifically declined to make this programmatic commitment, and declined again as late as October 1963.[10]

This whole episode shows very clearly that (as on other occasions) the decision to upgrade U.S. intervention came in response not to a presidential blueprint or "program," but to immediate and special pressures generated or transmitted through the bureaucracy.[11]

Why Kennedy yielded as much as he did to these pressures (and he did yield much) is another question. Joe Alsop claims "that Kennedy had told Harriman to get whatever settlement he could on Laos, but that the U.S. really intended to make its stand in Vietnam" (PP Beacon, II, 76). But why then did Kennedy rebuff not only Taylor but even McNamara's urgent arguments for a "clear commitment," as the only way "the other side can be convinced we mean business" (PP Beacon, II, 108)? Kennedy's reluctance suggests that he was still keeping options open with respect to Vietnam.

The piecemeal escalation on which he embarked may in fact have been the necessary price for keeping subordinates and puppet-allies aboard ship as he steered toward peace in Laos. It is certain that Kennedy, in rejecting the Taylor proposal, noted that introducing U.S. troops "before Laotian settlement might wreck chances for agreement, lead to break up of Geneva conference" (PP Beacon, II, 119). It is certain also that the *Times* story of the first new support-troop arrivals in Saigon was printed opposite a story that on the same day (December 11) the Geneva Conference on Laos had resolved two of the three chief issues (the future French military presence and the timetable for withdrawal) obstructing a Laotian settlement.[12] Kennedy's first troop commitments to South Vietnam, like those to Thailand five months later, have the earmarks of a *quid pro quo,* to buy off recalcitrant pro-Western forces in Indochina and their influential backers in Thailand.

Daniel Ellsberg, discounting the importance of these Laotian negotiations, has used his in-depth analysis of the 1961 escalation to provide what he calls a "decision model" for all of the major presidential escalations in Vietnam, including the dramatic Johnson–McNamara escalations of 1965.[13] The resulting stress on what he calls the "sameness" of presidential decision-making reinforces an impression of continuity which was carefully laid by the relevant Johnson–McNamara documents themselves, and progressively strengthened in turn by the Pentagon Studies which McNamara commissioned, Leslie Gelb's "summaries" of these studies, and selected quotes from these "summaries" in the Bantam–*New York Times* Pentagon Papers.

As a result, as perceptive a critic as Richard DuBoff can write that

> during the Kennedy-Johnson years . . . the NSAMs show total programmatic continuity . . . NSAM 273, November 26, 1963, and NSAM 288, March 17, 1964, reaffirmed "the central object[ive] of the United States in South Vietnam . . . to win the contest against the externally directed and supported Communist conspiracy.[14]

But there was no such "total programmatic continuity." Kennedy's last-known National Security Action Memorandum on Vietnam, NSAM 263 of October 11, 1963 (not mentioned in the Pentagon Studies),[15] had implemented a token 1000-man withdrawal of U.S. troops as the first stage of a program to Vietnamize the war "by the end of 1965" (PP Beacon, II, 770; cf. 752). And though NSAM 273 of November 26, 1963, the first Johnson NSAM, "reaffirms" a commitment "to win," the word (as its authors knew very well) was misleading. In October 1963, as in November 1961, McNamara and Taylor had proposed an affirmation of this objective, and Kennedy had rejected it.[16]

One original Pentagon Study notes the need in NSAM 273 "that the U.S. reaffirm its commitment to GVN in a credible way" (PP Beacon, II, 457), while failing to note that in NSAM 111 of November 11, 1961 (and subsequently) Kennedy had declined to affirm it. The same study adds that NSAM 288, of March 17, 1964, "went considerably further." Leslie Gelb, in his "Summary and Analysis" of this study, makes a strange and unjustifiable deduction:

> If there had been doubt that the limited risk gamble undertaken by Eisenhower had been transformed into *an unlimited commitment under Kennedy,* that doubt should have been dispelled internally by NSAM 288's statement of objectives [PP Beacon, II, 412, emphasis added].

Finally the Bantam–*New York Times* section on Kennedy, in its opening paragraph, distorts still further, by transferring the responsibility to Kennedy himself:

> The Pentagon's [i.e., Gelb's] study of the Vietnam war concludes that President John F. Kennedy transformed the "lim-

ited-risk gamble" of the Eisenhower Administration into a "broad commitment" to prevent Communist domination of South Vietnam [PP Bantam, p. 79].

One example of such progressive distortion could be accidental. We shall see that there are many, particularly with the thrust of improving the image of CIA intelligence.

In fact Kennedy refused, despite his own rhetoric, to articulate an explicit commitment to Vietnam: This refusal (which contributed significantly to the chaos in Saigon two years later) should warn us against drawing too specific a conclusion from the rhetoric of speeches and memoranda. It is in this spirit that I would take issue with the thesis of the recent essay by Noam Chomsky, one of the most intelligent and courageous of the war's critics:

> Never has there been the slightest deviation from the principle that a noncommunist regime must be imposed and defended, regardless of popular sentiment. . . . Given this principle . . . one can deduce with precision the strategy of annihilation that was gradually undertaken.[17]

The hidden premise in this aprioristic argument for fixity and inflexibility is that U.S. governments always live up to their anticommunist principles, an assumption which, though generally correct, has fortunately been disproven in Cuba, and was also called very much into question by Kennedy's 1962 shift of U.S. policy in Laos.

And when Chomsky suggests that U.S. administrations were always mindful of their policy's risk of war, he quotes (like Scheer) from language which the administration actually rejected:

> Successive administrations were compelled to widen and intensify the conflict. The risks were always appreciated. In November, 1964, a National Security Council (NSC) working group argued that the commitment to maintain a noncommunist South Vietnam "would involve high risks of a major conflict in Asia," leading almost inevitably to "a Korean-scale ground action and possibly even the use of nuclear weapons at some point" [p. 24, quoting PP Beacon, III, 217].

In fact the Pentagon Papers show considerable and frequent disagreement (at least on paper) as to the particular risks involved. Intelligence on this matter, like intelligence generally, had the power to shape policy, so that bureaucratic debates over policy were frequently carried on in the guise of intelligence estimates. Taylor, for example, backed up his 1961 proposal for introducing U.S. ground combat troops with his estimate that "there is no case for fearing a mass onslaught of Communist manpower into South Vietnam and its neighboring states" (PP Bantam, p. 143); but this estimate was strongly disputed four days later by the CIA's SNIE (Special National Intelligence Estimate) of November 5, 1961 (PP Beacon, II, 107). Such intelligence disputes were characteristic of many of the critical escalation periods of the Vietnam War.[18]

More specifically, the November 1964 intelligence estimate of risk, quoted by Chomsky, was submitted in an early draft by William Bundy to the NSC Vietnam Working Group, *but deleted by it in its final assessment*.[19] Policy considerations urged (and perhaps dictated) this deletion. The warning of "a Korean-scale ground action" had come from civilian members anxious to articulate the case for "a fall-back position" (one since articulated by spokesmen like Clark Clifford and Edwin Reischauer) in which the United States would aim at strengthening its position in Southeast Asia while accepting a "failure in South Vietnam ... due to special local factors" (PP Beacon, III, 216–17).

Both the fall-back position and the accompanying risk estimate were strongly opposed by Vice Admiral Lloyd Mustin, the sole JCS representative facing six influential civilians.[20] In the final version of the Working Group Paper Mustin's solitary influence had prevailed: "missing was the earlier draft's reference to potential costs and risks" (PP Beacon, III, 219). Later, on February 18, 1965, in the midst of the U.S. bombing, the allegedly "realistic" William Bundy had changed his tune: "the most likely prospect is for a prolonged period without major risks of escalation" (PP Beacon, III, 328).

This bureaucratic victory for the bullheaded Admiral Mustin (for whom the "best hope for minimizing risks, costs, and losses" was a "resolute course of action") shows that by November 1964 the supposedly more sophisticated civilians like CIA veteran Bill Bundy could no longer ride herd over the Joint Chiefs as Kennedy had done in 1961. This change in the military–civilian balance of bureaucratic power can be safely attributed to the replacement of Kennedy by Johnson. In refusing to make the explicit commitment about which the Joint Chiefs felt strongly,

Kennedy had precisely been preserving for himself Bundy's option of a fall-back position. Johnson's Vietnam commitment on November 24, 1963, was made in the context of his admitted "serious misgivings" about "Congressional demands for our withdrawal from Vietnam."[21]

But the shift was clearly not so violent or discontinuous as to silence debate, as this contest one year later between Bundy and Mustin confirms. The intelligence disputes of this period were real ones. By late 1964 there was a bureaucratic consensus for the application of pressure, but not yet for war. By April 1965 the bureaucracy had agreed to a "victory strategy" despite a consensus that fighting might last as long as two years (PP Bantam, p. 407). Decisions to go to war are like important decisions in private life, not easy to pinpoint. For example, a man bent on marriage might decide to visit an agency or matchmaker, pick out a photograph, write rhetorical love letters, and ultimately propose. Experience tells us that such a chain of decisions (including the proposal or "commitment") usually leads to the words "I do"—but not always. The strategic rhetoric of the 1950s, the long-delayed commitment in NSAM 273 of November 26, 1963, did not protect the lethal bridegroom from worrisome indecisions, debates, and second thoughts, as late as 1964–1965.

THE FALLACY OF NEGLECTED INTELLIGENCE: CLAIMS OF GOVERNMENTAL STUPIDITY AND CIA DISSENT

Chomsky's emphasis on the coherency and continuity of U.S. expansion into Asia is certainly closer to the truth than the Barnet model of an irrational leviathan which "ignored" the advice of its own intelligence analysts. Hannah Arendt goes so far as to claim that "the fact-finding branches of the intelligence services," which "were largely separated from whatever covert operations were still [!] going on in the field ... told the truth, year in, year out":

> The mistaken decisions and lying statements consistently violated the astoundingly accurate factual reports of the intelligence community, at least the reports quoted in the Bantam

edition [of the Pentagon Papers].... The relation, or rather non-relation, between facts and decision, between the intelligence community and the civilian and military services, is perhaps the momentous, and certainly was the best guarded, secret that the Pentagon Papers revealed ... those who were responsible for intelligence estimates were miles away from the problem-solvers, their disdain for facts, and the accidental character of those facts. The price they paid for these objective advantages was that their reports remained without any influence.[22]

When in 1971 I wrote that the Pentagon Papers had been systematically distorted in their editing to create just this illusion, I little anticipated that it would soon be marketed by sources as learned as Miss Arendt and *The New York Review of Books*.[23] Covert operations are of course "still going on" (at an estimated annual cost of some $300 million in Laos when Miss Arendt wrote) ; and are also intimately linked to fact-finding. Indeed, fact-finding operations, like the ELINT (electronic intelligence) missions of the destroyer *Maddox* in August 1964, and of the *Pueblo* in 1970, have not infrequently, perhaps even regularly, been the covert trigger in a strategy of provocation and escalation. The most sustained example of this has been the Air Force's use of "low-level reconnaissance" in Laos and North Vietnam: the pilots knew that they could obtain as good photo-intelligence from higher levels; but then the enemy might not shoot at them and incur retaliation.[24]

Those selected for Miss Arendt's accolade are the civilian writers of National Intelligence Estimates in the CIA's Directorate of Intelligence; yet they share prominently in the blame for the general drift and occasional scramble toward escalation. Those "responsible for intelligence estimates" were not "miles away," either literally or metaphorically, from those in the NSC. In 1964 they included CIA Inspector-General Lyman Kirkpatrick, who forwarded approvingly a special CIA report from the Saigon CIA station chief (Peer de Silva) that "military victories were needed to nourish the popular attitudes conducive to political stability" (PP Beacon, III, 2; cf. 41–42) , and added his own comment that, "with the Laos and Cambodian borders opened, this entire pacification effort is like trying to mop the floor before turning off the faucet."[25] The policy thrust of these pessimistic reports was for escalation, not against it. And in fact the U.S. war effort in Laos was sharply escalated two months later, in the wake of the CIA-linked right-wing coup of Siho Lamphoutacoul.

Another CIA fact-finder was Chester Cooper, perhaps the top CIA liaison in the White House, who "had put together a major report on Hanoi's support and direction of the guerrillas," based on "evidence" from the "intelligence community" about infiltration.[26] This report, consciously compiled as "a public account" (PP Beacon, III, 255), was that infamous collection of distortions released in February 1965 as the State Department White Paper on Vietnam. Cooper's acceptance of newly escalated intelligence estimates on infiltration dating from October[27] may have been important for Johnson's decision in February to bomb North Vietnam. For the State Department in August

> had made "clear evidence of greatly increased infiltration from the North" an explicit condition for any policy judgement that "systematic military action against DRV" was required . . . And leading officials from several agencies were beginning to feel that such action might be inevitable [PP Beacon, III, 192].[28]

One could hardly ask for a clearer example of the way in which shifts of policy anticipated shifts of "intelligence" (rather than vice-versa). On November 5 and 6, 1964, we find William Bundy and William Sullivan of the State Department working together on "materials" about North Vietnamese control and infiltration, for release through "all our information media" and "CIA's outlets"—and even the draft of "a possible article to be issued with authoritative anonymity in some mass circulation medium, such as the *New York Times* Magazine." Yet at this point the United States was still only "on the verge of intelligence agreement that infiltration has in fact mounted"; and Sullivan foresaw that a number of the statements in his "possible article . . . would probably give trouble to our 'specialists' " (PP Beacon, III, 593–96).[29]

Internal intelligence documents did not, however, differ greatly in tone, not even those quoted so misleadingly by Miss Arendt. The much-cited CIA estimate that "the primary sources of Communist strength in Vietnam are indigenous" might appear to take issue with the impression, gathered from Army Security Agency "interceptions of radio traffic . . . that Hanoi controlled and directed the Vietcong."[30] Yet in May 1964 the

CIA's Board of National Estimates, conceding that "the primary sources of Communist strength are indigenous," prepared a National Intelligence Estimate in support of the faucet theory:

> Hanoi "would order the Viet Cong and Pathet Lao to refrain from dramatic new attacks, and might reduce the level of the insurrections for the moment" in response to U.S. force deployments or . . . attacks.[31]

The thrust of the May 1964 NIE, as reported in the study, was that (in Leslie Gelb's accurate Summary) "only *relatively heavy* levels of attack on the DRV would be likely to have any significant compelling effect" (III, 107), an estimate concurred in at that time by most members of Johnson's Executive Committee. In the Bantam-*Times* Pentagon Papers (p. 242) Mr. Sheehan nonetheless says of this May 1964 NIE:

> The study shows that President Johnson and most of his key advisers would not accept this intelligence analysis that bombing would have no lasting effect on the situation in the South.

The CIA's point, as it would be for the next two years, was that because the sources of Viet Cong strength were indigenous, bombing the North "would not seriously affect communist *capabilities*"; but could affect "Hanoi's *will*":

> The DRV "must understand that although the U.S. is not seeking the destruction of the DRV regime, the U.S. is fully prepared to bring ascending pressures to bear to persuade Hanoi to reduce the insurrections" [III, 169].

Miss Arendt is not alone in promoting the thesis of a "non-relation" between intelligence and policy through selective quotation. Take, for example, a recent history of OSS by a young and normally perspicacious CIA veteran, R. Harris Smith:

> CIA reports questioned the economic or psychological value of U.S. bombing of North Vietnam. CIA reports questioned the wisdom of committing American ground troops to battle in South Vietnam. The Agency warned: "We will find ourselves mired down in combat in the jungle in a military effort that we cannot win and from which we will have extreme difficulty [in] extracting ourselves."[32]

This warning on April 2, 1965, by CIA Director McCone was against a compromise escalation program which he found "not sufficiently severe," because of his belief in the Kirkpatrick faucet ("forcing submission of the VC can only be brought about by a decision in Hanoi"). The duplicity of Mr. Smith's half-quotation is amply revealed by quoting from McCone's next sentences:

> Therefore it is my judgment that if we are to change the mission of the ground forces, we must also change the ground rules of the strikes against North Vietnam. *We must hit them harder, more frequently, and inflict greater damage.* Instead of avoiding the MIG's, we must go in and take them out. A bridge here and there will not do the job. We must strike their airfields, their petroleum resources, power stations and their military compounds. This, in my opinion, must be done promptly and with minimum restraint [PP Bantam, p. 441, emphasis added; cf. p. 386; PP Beacon, III, 353].[33]

This had been McCone's position in March 1964, when he criticized the McNamara proposals in NSAM 288 as "too little, too late"; and recommended "intensive air and naval action against the North."[34] McCone's recommendation in 1965 to intensify the air war was supported by his successor Admiral Raborn, who in turn was able to cite an earlier professional opinion (reinforcing the faucet theory) from the "intelligence community":

> I thus concur with the USIB [U.S. Intelligence Board]'s judgment of 18 February 1965, that, given such US punishment, the enemy would be "somewhat more likely" to decide to make some effort to secure a respite, rather than to intensify the struggle further [PP Beacon, III, 365].[35]

There seems also to have been support in the CIA for the modified fall-back position outlined in late 1964, which might be crudely summarized as a sharply limited war effort designed to make the rest of Southeast Asia conducive to "economic development" (i.e., investment). And from February 1966 there was undoubtedly a stream of CIA assessments that the bombing program against North Vietnam was not achieving its stated objectives. The CIA negative bombing assessments date from the time of McNamara's effort in 1966 to "Vietnamize" and to stabilize U.S. troop levels:

> This important war must be fought and won by the Vietnamese themselves . . . we must improve our position by getting ourselves into a military posture that we credibly would maintain indefinitely . . . the solution lies in girding, openly, for a longer war [PP Bantam, pp. 543, 549].

Although the CIA shared McNamara's interest in stabilizing the costs of the war, its 1966 memoranda are consistently ahead of McNamara in advocating an escalation of the level of "pain" administered within these financial restrictions:

> We concur in Secretary McNamara's [October 1966] analysis of the effects of the ROLLING THUNDER program [against North Vietnam]. . . . We endorse his argument on stabilizing the level of sorties. We do not agree however with the implied judgment that changes in the bombing program could not be effective. We continue to judge that a bombing program directed both against closing the port of Haiphong and continuously cutting the rail lines to China could have a significant impact [PP Beacon, IV, 129].

So wrote George Carver of the CIA in 1966, showing yet again the CIA's consistent success in advocating the policies of the future—in this case, both Johnson's stabilization of 1968 and Nixon's escalations of 1972.

CIA memoranda from this period belie the same Pentagon Study's earlier reference to

> The steady stream of memoranda from the intelligence community ["throughout the autumn and winter of 1965–66"] consistently expressing skepticism that bombing of any conceivable sort (that is, any except bombing aimed primarily at the destruction of North Vietnam's population) could either persuade Hanoi to negotiate . . . or effectively limit Hanoi's ability to infiltrate men and supplies into the South [PP Beacon, IV, 38].

This claim (reprinted in the Bantam Pentagon Papers) is not borne out. The same study notes that, in 1965,

> The idea that destroying, or threatening to destroy, NVN's industry would pressure Hanoi into calling it quits . . . was based on a plausible assumption . . . which the U.S. intelligence community as a whole seemed to share . . . that the value of what little industrial plant NVN possessed was disproportionately great [PP Beacon, IV, 57].

The CIA shifted its emphasis in March 1966, when bankers and economic planners had begun publicly to express concern about the pressures exerted by U.S. troop levels on both the Saigon piaster and the U.S. dollar. In marked contrast to the tone of its February 1966 SNIE, the CIA expressed renewed preference for the less inflationary and payments-costly option of bombing:

> A study by CIA . . . made a strong case for almost unlimited bombing such as CINCPAC and the JCS had steadily advocated . . . such measures as mining harbors, maintaining steady pressure on LOC's [lines of communication] with China, and destroying militarily insignificant but "highly prized" industrial plants would not only reduce North Vietnam's capacity to support the insurgency in the South but would influence her leaders' willingness to continue doing so . . . One point stressed was the importance of taking out all remaining POL [petroleum] storage facilities simultaneously and at an early date [PP Beacon, IV, 77].

The last sentence (along with others like it) amply refutes the claim in the Bantam Pentagon Papers that

> From the outset of the debate over bombing North Vietnam's oil tanks, the study discloses, the intelligence community had been skeptical that such bombing would have much effect on Hanoi [PP Bantam, p. 476].[36]

On the contrary, we learn from the study itself, a

> March CIA report, with its obvious bid to turn ROLLING THUNDER into a punitive bombing campaign and its nearly obvious promise of real payoff . . . gave a substantial boost to the proposal to hit the POL targets. The POL system appeared to be the one target system in NVN to which what the report called "the principle of concentration" might be applied [i.e., to maximize "pain" by concentrating target attacks rather than increasing sortie levels; PP Beacon, IV, 74].

This section of the study, headed "The CIA Recommends Escalation," was later censored in the U.S. government edition (the only censorship in this study volume's 180 pages) ; one concludes that the Nixon administration has a stake in the elaborately contrived image of the CIA as a lonely foe of escalation.

THE CIA, THE BANKS, AND THE BALANCE OF PAYMENTS

The turning point of Johnson's decision to stabilize, it is generally agreed, was a special meeting on March 25–26, 1968, of the President's Senior Advisory Group, a collection of veteran government officials and in-and-outers who were now mostly Wall Street bankers and lawyers. At this meeting the pessimistic civilian intelligence briefings, one of them by recently-converted CIA hawk Carver, prevailed over the more optimistic military intelligence briefing by Major William DePuy, who during the Korean War had been part of the CIA's operations directorate.[37]

Congress was totally excluded from this important meeting, as from others like it. The representatives of those who had paid for the war (with lives as well as taxes) were less important at this crucial juncture than the representatives of those who would shortly pay for the election campaigns of both political parties.[38] That the Pentagon studies could only describe this meeting by falling back on published newspaper accounts (which got the dates wrong) is an important reminder that the true locus of vital decision-making lay in silent upper altitudes, beyond the reach of busy interoffice memoranda. What is most important is to see that the CIA-supported decision to stabilize, and to gird (in McNamara's words of 1966) "for a longer war," represented a change neither of fundamental objectives nor of fundamental policy. For that policy had always been the maximization, within acceptable limits, of U.S. power in Southeast Asia.

The closing Pentagon studies try to represent Johnson's March 1968 speech as "the decision that turned American policy toward a peaceful settlement of the war" (IV, 275), as "the first step on ... a long and tortuous road to peace" (IV, 603). These echoes of old White House escalation announcements fully deserve Fred Branfman's dismissal of them as "incredible":

> The authors of the Pentagon Papers ... had just completed months of reading ... records of an Indochina War already more than two decades long ... There was that final State Department ... "Cable to Envoys in Asia on Day of Johnson's De-Escalation Speech" ... "... air power now used north of 20th can probably be used in Laos (where no policy change planned) and in SVN. ...[39]

The truth is put candidly in the last two sentences of the Pentagon Papers: The March 1968 retrenchment

> made it possible to limit the American military commitment to South Vietnam to achieve the objectives for which this force had originally been deployed. American forces would remain in South Vietnam to prevent defeat of the Government by

Communist forces and to provide a shield behind which that
Government could rally, become effective, and win the support
of the people [PP Beacon, IV, 604].

The retrenchment, in other words, represents the final adoption
of McNamara's 1966 "longer war" strategy, for achieving the
"objectives" of Johnson's NSAMs 273 and 288. A key event in
achieving this retrenchment was the "startlingly accurate" leak-
age of an important Defense memorandum (one of the few to
mention the U.S. balance-of-payments problem) in the *New
York Times* of March 10, 1968. It should come as no surprise that
the memorandum ("strengthened by intelligence estimates from
the CIA") was drafted under the direction of Morton Halperin
and Leslie Gelb, who were simultaneously overseeing the like-
minded Pentagon Papers project; and leaked by Neal Sheehan
and Hedrick Smith, who three years later would leak the Pentagon Papers (PP Bantam, 598–99, 607; Beacon, IV, 550, 564, 585).

Fred Branfman notes that "the authors of these papers are . . .
in a word, still inside the machine." I suspect that the unedited
papers should be seen as a contribution to the bureaucratic
process and that the edited papers as published by the *Times*
served the careful management of public opinion. A more important point is that the CIA-supported stabilization in 1968, dictated in large part by the impact of troop increases on the
rapidly weakening dollar, was entirely consistent with the CIA-
supported escalation ("concentration") of the air war in 1966.
In both cases the context rationalizing the CIA's shifts of emphasis was the same: the prospects for the U.S. economy and polity as
perceived on Wall Street.

It may of course be coincidental that the CIA's 1966 shift from
troop deployments to "a strong case for almost unlimited bombing" (IV, 77) came just as the *First National City Bank Monthly
Economic Letter* began to worry about the rise in the money
supply ("since the Korean War, there has not been such a sharp
increase") and "apprehensions of an inflationary outbreak":
"The scale of the fighting and *any further troop buildup* will
determine the pressure placed on the economy in coming
months."[40] But thanks to New York banker Townsend Hoopes,
who was then in the government, we know that, in 1968, it was a
worried consensus of New York bankers and lawyers which
prevailed in bringing Johnson around by siding with the CIA
intelligence estimates over the military one.

Of the eleven outsiders in the Senior Advisory Group, four represented New York financial circles, two were Wall Street lawyers, three were retired generals on industrial boards of directors in New York and Pittsburgh, one was the Ford Foundation president, and one—Dean Acheson—was a Washington lawyer.[41] To be sure the "Senior Advisory Group" could only "advise." But when two days later Defense Secretary Clifford came to Rusk's office and read Johnson's draft speech, which "was still essentially a defiant, bellicose speech" and "did not reflect the majority view of the Senior Advisory Group," Clifford single-handedly vetoed it: "The President cannot give that speech!"[42]

The sanction behind Clifford's veto is quite obvious: the United States could no longer significantly escalate the ground war in Vietnam, *because it could no longer afford to.* The costs of the war, aggravated by Congressional delay (despite Dillon's lobbying) in the enactment of taxes to pay for them, and inflamed finally by press leaks about Westmoreland's new troop requests, had led to the imminent collapse in March of the dollar-based international monetary system established in 1944 at Bretton Woods.[43] On March 14, 1968, following the failure of Dillon to win immediate Congressional action on the proposed war tax surcharge, the United States had arranged to close the London gold market, lifted the twenty-five percent gold cover for the U.S. dollar, and moved to secure tentative international agreement of a "two-tier system" of gold prices, and a monetary system based not on gold but on so-called "Special Drawing Rights."[44] This new system, announced on March 17 and finalized at Stockholm on March 29, marked the end of the international gold pool; it also meant recognizing (as Tom Wicker foresaw) [45] the "economic impossibility" of Westmoreland's victory strategy: the banks of Europe and Japan were no longer willing to pay for it.

The very real and bitter confrontation between U.S. bankers and generals in early 1968 is a reminder that there is much truth to *both* of the competing models of U.S. involvement—the "rational" or economic versus the "irrational" or bureaucratic—which I have taken such lengths to qualify in this essay. Scheer and Chomsky, on the one hand, are quite right to stress the continuity and inexorability of U.S. expansion into Southeast Asia, though we must add that this expansion could (as in 1954 and in 1961) be deflected from immediate combat strategies into compensatory structural "fall-backs" and buildups.[46]

Even William Bundy's so-called "fall-back position" of late 1964, supported by the suppressed intelligence estimate which Chomsky quotes, was explicitly designed "to hold the situation together as long as possible so that *we have time to strengthen other areas of Asia*" (PP Beacon, III, 216, emphasis added). It was, in short, very much like the holding and Vietnamizing operation proposed by McNamara in 1966 and carried on for four years by Richard Nixon. Many Congressional antiwar measures have been aimed at hastening such a deflection, not at reversing the trend of U.S. involvement.

In perceiving this underlying continuity of U.S. policy, it is important also to see that there have been real divisions within the U.S. bureaucracy, and that these divisions have been reflected in real changes of emphasis—with caution prevailing in 1961, rampant escalation in 1965, and renewed caution in 1968. The very memoranda we have been citing suggest that bureaucratic competition may have accelerated and multiplied the forces for expansion, with the CIA arguing for "limited" programs like "pacification" and covert action, and the Joint Chiefs for bombing as a more efficient alternative.[47]

Again, Scheer and Chomsky are right to stress the contemptuous lack of concern for Asians, other than Asian rulers and businessmen. But this did not preclude the numerous occasions when (as in 1961 and 1964) the United States was embarrassed by pressures for escalation from its allies and not-wholly-manipulable puppets. These pressures could be very significant when they were strongly reinforced if not indeed inspired by the bureaucratic splits to which we have referred.

In like manner, Barnet and Arendt are quite right to stress the irrationality, the self-deception and auto-intoxication, of a closed circle of bureaucrats in contact only with their own restricted elites. It would take an essay much longer than this one to analyze the mental sickness of those in power, as laid bare by their own metaphors. That sickness was a matter of sex, prose, and economics, the fundamentals of life itself. For example, when President Johnson "explained to friends and critics one day that the slow escalation of the air war in the North and the increasing pressure on Ho Chi Minh was seduction, not rape," this is reported deadpan in the Pentagon Papers as "a vivid sexual analogy."[48]

Compared to those who were "seducing" Hanoi, the intelligence analysts on the team have no doubt been relatively objective. But there is plenty of evidence in the Pentagon Papers that even the "best" intelligence faction consistently supported the bureaucratic consensus objective of maximizing U.S. power in Southeast Asia (or, in their words, of "strengthening" the region against Communist penetration); they dissented only in doubting that a local victory in Vietnam was either attainable or necessary to this end, and it may even be that Nixon's new military operations against Cambodia and North Vietnam were undertaken against civilian CIA advice.[49] But Nixon's fluctuating and half-hearted pursuit of these military operations (which the CIA may have opposed) can be contrasted with his relentless escalation of a much more lethal bombing campaign in South Vietnam. As Leslie Gelb has noted, there is no evidence that the CIA ever opposed *this* bombing: the published negative assessments on which the CIA's current apologists rely so heavily all relate specifically to the bombing of *North* Vietnam. The CIA is neither omnipotent nor undivided, but time after time, both in the long term and in the short, the CIA intelligence assessments have proved to be on the winning side.

Barnet and Arendt argue that, in registering its dissents, the intelligence community was objective ("astoundingly accurate") but "without any influence"; this "irrationality" model of U.S. involvement is linked to their larger theses that "neither territory nor economic advantage has been pursued in Vietnam."[50] But their own evidence, when looked at more closely, suggests that the intelligence community was consistently influential, in support of policies that were destined to prevail, and that this influence was maintained at the expense of factual objectivity. For example, the "intelligence community" argued against the introduction of U.S. combat troops in 1961 (when they were refused) but was for them in 1965 (when they were sent). In like manner it argued successfully for the faucet theory and the bombing of North Vietnam in 1964–1965, for intensifying the bombing in 1966, and for retrenchment in 1968.

One could of course defend the "objectivity" of these shifts by referring to changes of situation or of knowledge; frequently the objective thing to do is to change one's mind. Alternatively one might jettison the hypothesis of the CIA's objectivity by falling back upon the "irrationality" model. One could, for example, refer the differing moods of 1961, 1965, and 1968 to the differing personalities of the scholarly Dulles, the hawkish McCone, and the professional Helms. To some extent both explanations may be true. But if one studies all the comparable shifts and adjustments of the 1940s and 1950s (particularly the shifts under Dulles' long and stable tenure) there is evidence for a third and more disturbing explanation: *these shifts in "intelligence" and related policy occurred because they were consistent with, encouraged by, and at times even dictated by shifts in perception of the overall U.S. economic posture.*

Marxist critiques of the Vietnam War have documented their case by reference to general statements and facts about the international posture of the United States. Efforts to relate the immediate dynamics of the war to the immediate dynamics of the economy are doomed to failure; for since about 1966 the chilling effects on the stock market of each new escalation (and conversely the buoyant effects of Kissinger's "secret" peace trips) have been obvious to all. The response of Marxist critics (rightly) has been that the continued expansion of the war, while a disaster to the economy as a whole, has been immediately profitable to the special corporate interests (banks, petroleum, electronics, aerospace, munitions) which have helped wage the war, and ultimately so to the specific corporations (banks, petroleum, electronics) with overseas interests in the Far East and elsewhere. If banks had grown cool to escalation by 1968, munitions companies had not, and it is a striking feature of Nixon's "Vietnamization" program that under it the total quadrennial consumption of munitions has actually increased.[51]

In crises of economic constraint, such as the collapse of the Gold Pool in March 1968, one can see a conflict between two divergent sets of economic interests in government policy. On the one hand are the firms of the Central Establishment (typified by the New York international banks and their lawyers—such as those in the Senior Advisory Group), which identify their well-being with the overall and long-term development of the U.S. economy. At the other extreme are the Marginals (typified by *ad hoc* munitions or contract airlift firms, often with ex-military men as their Washington lobbyists), whose interest in government policy is defined by the specific short-term profits to be reaped thereby. One can see that, in 1968 as in other periods, the CIA has reflected its special links to the Central Financial Establishment, while the Joint Chiefs and other military personnel have reflected their special links to the Marginals.

The latter group—often distinguished as the\ military-industrial complex—have frequently been focused on by antiwar critics. And it is indeed true that much of the noisiest lobbying for the Vietnam War came from a Chicago-based marginal group called the American Security Council, whose links are to the military (including a former CINCPAC admiral), and to the oil and defense firms of the Southwest. The frequent suspicion and occasional hostility between the CIA–Council of Foreign Relations Establishment in the Northeast and the military–ASC have encouraged Carl Oglesby and others to distinguish geographically between them—as "Yankees" and "Cowboys" respectively.

The difference, however, is not so much geographic as functional. In times of unchallenged economic expansion, as through the 1950s, the Center and the Marginals (like the CIA and military) have collaborated, with much of the finance capital for the latter coming from the former.[52] And in times of retrenchment, when Marginals have been cut back or sacrificed to preserve the long-term interests of the Center, geography has not been a factor.[53]

There are two complications to this (or any) effort to analyze the divergent interests in the 1968 U.S. military–economic crisis. The first is the ambiguous status of the oil industry in general (ranging from central Majors to marginal Independents, yet mobilized into one of the most powerful and independent lobbies) and of five so-called Majors in particular. The latter (Exxon, Mobil, Texaco, Gulf, and Standard of California) are clearly central to U.S. long-range economic planning, and have their visible close links to Wall Street banks (like Chase Manhattan) law firms (like Sullivan and Cromwell), and the CIA, particularly CIA Operations.[54] Thus a top CIA veteran like Robert Amory, later with the oil-linked law firm of Corcoran, Foley, Youngman and Rowe, still had privileged access to CIA information as well as frequent intercourse with CIA personnel.

But the interests of oil majors like Mobil, Exxon, and Standard of California are not as flexible as those of the First National City Bank of New York (with which they have all interlocked recently). Mobil's stake in, and profits from, the oil resources of

Asia are too great to allow it to think of simply redirecting its interests elsewhere. In their strategic concerns as in their participation in military operations, the oil interests find themselves in a mid-position between the long-term Center banks and the short-term Marginals. An analogous mid-position in the government, between the civilian intelligence analysts and the military, is occupied by the more militant activists of the CIA Operations (formerly Plans) Directorate. In noting the special links between oil and CIA operations, one can observe also that the CIA's links to business overseas have led it or its members into positions more reactionary (particularly in the Far East) than those of the U.S. government as a whole.

A second problem is that the CIA milieu or mentality is not restricted in government to the Central Intelligence Agency. Just as there is at the center a considerable interlock and mutuality of interest between banks, war industries, and multinational corporations,[55] so there is considerable movement and exchange of personnel between the various branches of the national security bureaucracy, particularly from the CIA into Intelligence and Research (INR) at State, and International Security Affairs (ISA) at Defense, which generated the Pentagon Papers.

Thus one's office is less important than one's background and formation: aristocrat William Bundy did not change views when he moved from CIA to Defense (ISA) to State. Again, former CIA Director Richard McGarrah Helms is a grandson of the prewar World Bank's first president, Richard McGarrah; a CIA moderate, he has shown less obvious sympathy for the oil companies than his predecessors Allen Dulles (a lawyer for oil companies) and John McCone (an oilman). But Helms' CIA career has been in the Plans (Operations) rather than the Intelligence Directorate. The wealthy families of the oil industry and old China trade (with their in-laws) have been heavily represented in all branches of the postwar security establishment, including those with a prominent interest in or responsibility for Indochina.[56] But such genealogical links are of course not deterministic or predictive. They are cited only to show the survival, at least into the 1960s, of a hereditarily privileged "Ivy League" milieu (one relatively open to recruitment from outside), which by all accounts is more overrepresented in the CIA than anywhere else.

Remarks about the "CIA" in this essay should perhaps more

accurately be referred to the states of mind prevalent in this privileged milieu, which in the 1960s included senior positions both in the State and Defense departments, particularly in the International Security Affairs Division of Defense. As late as 1968 men in these various positions were linked not only by schooling, clubs, and secret societies, but by genealogy.[57] It is this milieu (part public and part private, and hence more powerful than either a government agency or financial consortium) that we should think of when speaking of a CIA-financial complex, able at times to separate from and restrain the so-called military–industrial complex.[58]

That finance prevailed over the military in 1968 does not of itself prove that banks always have their own way in America, for in that crisis the veto of the Senior Advisory Group was backed by an unusually harsh set of economic necessities. If, however, we turn to a historic survey of the CIA's positions on Vietnam since 1959, we shall see that when the CIA and the financial center have reached a consensus, they have generally prevailed, whether on behalf of diminishing the war-level or of escalating it. The same bankers and lawyers who vetoed the troop-increases of 1968 supported those of 1965, and in both cases were backed by the CIA intelligence "experts." It is my thesis that fluctuations in perceptions of the U.S. economy, which correlate so crudely with the actual conduct of the war, show a much more sensitive correlation with the fluctuating "intelligence" estimates of the CIA. That this says little for the CIA's "objectivity" and "skepticism" is not particularly important. But an effort to illustrate some of these correlations may be more useful in suggesting (it can do no more than that) the economic pressures for the escalation of the Vietnam War.

There is a double difficulty in arguing this thesis from the Pentagon Papers: the distortions (as we have seen) with respect to CIA estimates; and a virtual silence of the Pentagon Papers after 1961 (in marked contrast to the candor of the previous decade) with respect to economic considerations. But this silence, also, testifies to the importance of the absent material and the possibility of censorship.

Let us begin with the obvious example of Indonesia, a country very much on the mind of U.S. planners in 1964–1965, when Sukarno made increasingly noisy threats against Malaysia ("tying up substantial British military forces," as the Council on Foreign

Relations historian noted, "which were thus made unavailable for service in Vietnam or elsewhere") [59] and threatened also to nationalize the U.S. oil companies in his country.[60] No less an authority than Richard Nixon has noted the obvious fact that the U.S. commitment and presence in Vietnam

> was a vital factor in the turnaround in Indonesia . . . It provided a shield behind which the anti-communist forces found the courage and the capacity to stage their counter-coup [of October 1965].[61]

Nixon's point is echoed by Lyndon Johnson in his memoirs, *The Vantage Point* (p. 357), while his language echoes that of Johnson's Vietnam statement just before the Indonesia coup:

> There are great stakes in the balance. Most of the non-Communist nations of Asia cannot, by themselves and alone, resist growing might and the grasping ambition of Asian communism. Our power, therefore, is a very *vital shield*.[62]

One recalls that Nixon himself was perhaps the most active lobbyist in 1965 for bombing North Vietnam and blockading its ports, citing the "immense mineral potential" of Indonesia, "the region's richest hoard of natural resources," which must not be allowed to fall into Communist hands.[63] One month before the Indonesian coup Nixon made one of his "private business trips" to the Far East (the third in eighteen months), telling at least one audience in Australia that the free nations "cannot allow Indonesia to go Communist any more than Vietnam."[64]

The Pentagon Papers, however, give the impression that in this critical period Indonesia had somehow slipped from the Vietnam planners' minds. Earlier Indonesia was relevant: McNamara's urgent memo to Kennedy of November 8, 1961, notes his agreement with the Joint Chiefs that

> 1. The fall of South Vietnam to Communism would lead to the fairly rapid extension of Communist control, or complete accommodation to Communism, in the rest of mainland Southeast Asia *and in Indonesia* [PP Beacon, II, 108, emphasis added].

But when the CIA–DIA–INR Panel Draft of November 6, 1964 (already referred to) surveyed "probable reactions" to proposed courses of U.S. escalation among "the Asian states," it catalogued the responses of South Korea, Nationalist China, the Philippines,

Thailand, Japan, India, and Cambodia (PP Beacon, III, 598 cf. p. 658). Apparently omitted at the time of a heightening Indonesian crisis is any reference to Indonesia, by far the largest non-Communist country in the area and (along with Malaysia, also omitted) the major focus of U.S. investment.

It is not clear if this striking lacuna is due to bureaucratic decorum at the time, skillful editing in the Pentagon Papers, or a combination of the two. But any of these explanations would suggest that Indonesia (like other matters of direct financial interest) was much more prominent in the minds of U.S. planners than the Pentagon Papers let on.[65]

THE KENNEDY MILITARY–
ECONOMIC PARADIGM:
EQUILIBRIUM BY RETRENCHMENT

It is clear that repeatedly, in the 1960s, changes in NIEs followed changes in policy. The rapid shifts in CIA National Intelligence Estimates between 1959 and 1961 reflected, on the one hand, a real increase in the level of anti-Diem activity.[66] But they also reflected (rather than inspired) the Kennedy decision to "sink or swim with Diem." An NIE of March 28, 1961 "echoed the themes and even some of the language of Ambassador Durbrow's cablegrams" in support of "abandoning President Diem" through a coup.[67] Five months later, an NIE of August 15, 1961, echoing the Lansdale–Gilpatric recommendations of April against a coup, reversed this thrust: "Although collapse of the Saigon regime might come by a coup or from Diem's death, its fall because of a 'prolonged and difficult' struggle was not predicted."[68]

All of Kennedy's Vietnam decisions and indecisions, like all of Johnson's, were made with an eye fixed on the crisis since about 1957 in the U.S. balance of payments and loss of gold reserves. The August NIE, like those two months later which helped block Taylor's request for combat troops (II, 15, 77),[69] reflected the new President's intention to stabilize overseas defense expenditures, which he had named as the first cause of the crisis in his February 6, 1961, Special Message on the Balance of Payments. As he would tell the U.S. Chamber of Commerce in May 1962:

It costs the United States $3 billion a year to maintain our troops and our defense establishment and security commitments abroad. If the balance of trade is not sufficiently in our favor to finance this burden, we have two alternatives: one, to lose gold, as we have been doing; and two, to begin to withdraw our security commitments.[70]

As I have argued elsewhere, this concern about gold moved Kennedy in 1962 to begin to impose "gold budgets" limiting the gold drain in government departments, and apparently helped inspire his decision in late 1963 to "begin to withdraw" from Vietnam.[71]

But Kennedy's efforts to limit overseas security commitments cannot be labeled "anti-imperialist." On the contrary, they were designed to reduce mounting pressures for an obvious but unmentioned third option: establishing restraints on U.S. investments overseas.[72] All in all, they were part of what we might call a "Kennedy paradigm" for boosting the sluggish U.S. economy, a paradigm which differed in three major respects from the Eisenhower paradigm of Treasury Secretary Robert B. Anderson (a Texas oil lawyer) :

a) vastly increased *domestic* government spending on "defense" (as recommended by the Rockefeller Brothers Panel Two Report)
b) stricter measures to cope with U.S. balance-of-payments deficit (including limitations of government spending overseas)
c) government encouragement of investment at home and in developing countries, at the expense of U.S. investment in other advanced countries.[73]

Kennedy hoped that he could simultaneously reduce the costs of the U.S. military presence in the Third World (partly through cheap innovations such as increased use of Special Forces) and at the same time make the prospects for U.S. investment more favorable there. In its overseas aspects this Kennedy paradigm, like those which have succeeded it, may well have been unworkable. Like Eisenhower's, however, it was only covertly murderous; and unlike Eisenhower's it saw relative prosperity inside the United States throughout the few years it was tried.

In 1961 the Kennedy administration announced its plan for a "Decade of Development," a carefully formulated program which called for assistance planned and financed on a long-term basis, a foreign aid administration reorganized at home and abroad, and more correlated help by other industrial nations.[74]

At the same time, Kennedy found it necessary in his April 1961 tax package proposals to introduce a so-called tax equalization measure to make overseas investment in *advanced* countries less attractive to U.S. industry. This measure was promptly attacked by the First National City Bank of New York as "a new concept of public policy," challenging the traditionally accepted belief that investment abroad helped both other countries and the United States

> by expanding markets for U.S. products, building U.S. assets abroad, and providing a flow of income back to the U.S. investor.[75]

Arguments as to the profitability of U.S. direct overseas investment were challenged in the early 1960s, on the grounds that *incremental* investment since 1957 had run in excess of the increment in repatriated profits.[76] A careful study for the Joint Economic Committee of Congress in 1962 concluded in fact that

> the recorded increase in the outflow of long-term capital over the period [1952–1962], offset in part by the increased inflows related to the increase in outflow, has contributed substantially to the deterioration of our balance-of-payments deficits. . . . There has been, net, an adverse effect.[77]

Interestingly, however, this argument is only persuasive if low-risk–low-yield investments to the "advanced" countries are included, the investments which the Kennedy measures discouraged. Investments in the "developing" countries of the Third World, particularly in Asia and Africa, show high rates of return on new investment in addition to a persistent net outflow of wealth from the poor countries into the United States. *Business Week* of January 24, 1970, reported a study finding that profit returns in Asia averaged thirty-eight percent in the 1960s; versus 12.7 percent in Latin America and 16.3 percent in Africa.[78] In the ten years 1960–1969, the United States withdrew $10,755 million in profits from Asia, while directly investing only $2984 million, for a net dollar outflow (on the direct investment account) of $7071 million from Asia to the world's richest continent.[79]

This was an income account of particular interest to the U.S. oil companies, which in 1968 accounted for 42.2 percent of U.S. investments in low-income countries, and for seventy-one percent of the U.S. investment income from these countries.[80] Overseas direct investment has been dominated not only by petroleum but by big business: 45 U.S. firms accounted for fifty-seven percent of the total in 1957, and 15 oil companies for thirty percent (out of 2812 firms reporting).[81] It should not surprise us that these oil giants should supply a powerful input into U.S. foreign policy, facilitated by their intimate links with relevant branches of the bureaucracy, particularly the CIA.

So far as the petroleum industry is concerned, the Chase Manhattan Bank has itself documented that

> In the post-war period the earnings remitted to U.S. parent petroleum companies have been larger, and have tended to grow more rapidly, than outflows for new overseas direct investments. Thus the yearly average net inflow of $65 million in 1948–50 grew to about $1.2 billion in 1964 [an *eighteen-fold* increase]. Our projections indicate further growth of this surplus to roughly $2.3 billion by 1975.[82]

Net balances of this order are far too large to be ignored by national planners (the total U.S. balance of payments in 1964, as a point of comparison, was minus $2.8 billion). Small wonder that Washington had intervened so vigorously in countries (like Cuba or the Dominican Republic) where Standard Oil and its sister companies have encountered difficulties with local leaders. The displeasure of the big oil companies has also preceded a number of internal coups, from Iran in 1953 (where it is now known the CIA was implicated) to Brazil (1964), Indonesia (1965), Ghana (1966), and Greece (1967).[83]

All these figures are an argument for imperialism, but not for war. U.S. decision-makers at this time, already concerned at recurring balance-of-payments deficits, faced a choice (as was then perceived) between overseas investments and overseas military expenditures.[84] It is clear that Kennedy attached great importance to reducing these deficits, and there are many signs that, especially during the last months of 1963, his administration had determined on what Defense Undersecretary Gilpatric (in October 1963) called "useful reductions in its heavy overseas military expenditures."[85] In part these measures were to be achieved by unilateral consolidation and modernization of the U.S. defense establishment; but Kennedy hoped also to trim his defense budget and gold drain by rapprochement with the Soviet Union.

The Laotian Accords of 1962, his American University speech, and the Test Ban Treaty of a year later were all calculated moves in a diplomatic chess game with the Soviet Union. The game had begun in Kennedy's first year of office, when his NATO Ambassador, Thomas K. Finletter, had shocked Bonn by asking how it would react to U.S. support for the so-called "Rapacki Plan" for the de-nuclearization (i.e., de-NATO-ization) of West Germany and the rest of Central Europe.[86] The last public move in this interrupted chess game was McNamara's important speech of November 18, 1963, in which he hinted at a U.S.–Soviet strategic parity, "perhaps even at a lower level than today."[87] *Business Week,* in its last issue before Kennedy's assassination, found the message "loud and clear. . . : A major cut in defense spending [as suggested by Khrushchev in July] is in the works."[88]

There seems to have been CIA support for these Kennedy steps towards peace and a sounder dollar: the same intelligence establishment which had sounded the alarm of a U.S.–Soviet "missile gap" in 1960 admitted by 1963 that in fact the U.S. had the lead.[89] But Kennedy's moves in Southeast Asia were much more controversial, fiercely dividing the whole of the Washington bureaucracy, and with it the CIA itself.

Kennedy's plan to withdraw 1000 troops from Vietnam, for example, is rightly understood by the Pentagon Papers as a "signal" to North Vietnam, and as

> an opportunity for a démarche—exploiting withdrawal of U.S. forces from South Vietnam by a specified date [late 1965] in exchange for North Vietnam's abandoning its aggression against South Vietnam [PP Beacon, II, 189].

Ambassador Galbraith had proposed in April 1962 that Harriman explore this formula with the Soviets at the Geneva Conference on Laos.[90] In January 1963 he had discussed the *quid pro quo* informally with Polish Foreign Minister Rapacki, whose reply was that "North Vietnam could not get peace in the south so long as Diem was in charge."[91] As late as December 8, 1963, an informed *New York Times* editorial, noting that "there have been a number of peace feelers in the last year from North Vietnam" proposed a return to the core of the 1954 Geneva settlement, which post-poned the difficult reunification issue and brought about the evacuation *both of Communist guerrillas and foreign troops* (then French) from South Vietnam.[92]

Kennedy's discreet but insistent signals about withdrawal, and even Ngo Dinh Nhu's own belated signals toward rapproche-ment with Hanoi, must be seen in the light of Kennedy's larger strategic–economic concern of payments equilibrium and an understanding with the Soviet Union.

So indeed must the growing interest in neutralism which in 1963 the Council on Foreign Relations Historian correctly dis-cerned in Thailand. The reasons had been summarized suc-cinctly a year earlier:

> Since, by chance, the American reaction to the drain of gold and the worsening of the U.S. balance of payments position was threatening to reduce, more than had been earlier envisaged, the global U.S. hand-out, it was no wonder that the Thais sought to introduce a little competition, on the Indian pattern, into their foreign aid requirements. There were similar devel-opments in Pakistan and Laos—and neutralism as a philosophy to lean on in the modern world took firmer root in such strong-holds as Japan and South Korea.[93]

As the Kennedy administration was sharply divided over the wisdom of the withdrawal signals, so apparently was the CIA. On the one hand the fiction of the nearly completed task was sup-ported by the specious "optimism" (PP Beacon, II, 180) of National Intelligence Estimate 53–63 of April 17, 1963 (PP Beacon, II, 725), despite the fact that the highest weekly in-surgency rate of the year (1034) had occurred in February 1963.[94] (This exceeded the highest weekly figure, 1021, in the Novem-ber 1963 crisis which allegedly provoked Johnson's new escala-tion plans in late 1963).[95]

On the other hand, high-level CIA official Chester Cooper records that there was "more anxiety" in Washington than official statements indicated, and that he himself was "surprised and outraged" (as was William Sullivan of State) by the October 2 announcement that the U.S. military task would be essentially completed by the end of 1965. His memoirs draw attention to the deliberateness and symbolic importance of the passage:

> This sentence . . . was loaded with booby traps . . . Both Bundys
> agreed, but Bill had little elbow room. Finally, in utter exas-
> peration Bill said, "Look, I'm under instructions!" . . . Mac
> called Secretary McNamara, but was unable to persuade him
> to change his mind. McNamara seemed to have been trapped
> too; the sentence may have been worked out privately with
> Kennedy and therefore imbedded in concrete.[96]

It was widely believed at the time that the CIA was opposed to
Kennedy's dramatic but enigmatic moves against Diem and Nhu
in late 1963. The public recall on October 5 of Saigon CIA
Station Chief John Richardson (a friend not only of Nhu but
of his Whittier classmate Richard Nixon) came in the midst of
press speculations, leaked from high levels in the State Department, that the CIA was in revolt (or, as one headline put it:
"Arrogant CIA Disobeys Orders in Vietnam").[97] Kennedy himself
spoke for Richardson's loyalty, which appears to be corroborated
by Richardson's only cable in the Pentagon Papers (PP Beacon,
II, 736). But this does not explain why Senate Majority Leader
Mansfield, two weeks before the fact, should have publicly called
for the removal of those in the Embassy opposing the anti-Nhu
policy ("if . . . certain individuals are removed, then the sooner
they are removed the better").[98]

It is not clear who in the Washington bureaucracy led the
opposition to Kennedy's Vietnam policy; it is however clear that
that opposition was vehement, based in more than one agency,
and at a high level. It appears to have coalesced at the Honolulu
Conference of November 20, 1963, where "a decision was made"
to develop a joint CIA–military covert operations program
against North Vietnam (PP Beacon, III, 150). This plan for
increasingly overt escalation, clearly incompatible with Kennedy's troop withdrawal plan, had no presidential blessing or
authorization until Johnson's first NSAM (NSAM 273) of six
days later. Yet top spokesmen for Defense and State in Honolulu
(Sylvester and Manning) were, if correctly quoted, already twist-
ing the words of the Honolulu Conference Report, which spoke
optimistically of "an encouraging outlook for . . . the war
against the Viet Cong communists" into something new and
ominous: "the war against the *North Vietnam* Communists."[99]

These men appeared to know of plans about which the Kennedy brothers were ignorant. President Kennedy thought of the

Honolulu Conference as one ratifying his withdrawal plans—not only the symbolic 1000-man reduction of NSAM 263 (which was first officially announced on November 20) but a much more substantial Accelerated Plan for withdrawal (PP Beacon, II, 170). The latter plan was officially approved on November 20, with McNamara himself making it clear "that he felt that the proposed CINCPAC MAP [Military Assistance Program] could be cut back" (PP Beacon, II, 190). Three days later, under a new President, McNamara wrote "that the U.S. must be prepared to raise planned MAP levels" (PP Beacon, II, 191). This was the first sign of the end of the Kennedy program of Vietnamization and withdrawal, and hence ultimately of the Kennedy paradigm of equilibrium for the U.S. balance of payments.

1963: FINANCE AND
OIL COMPANIES DISSENT

In late 1963, while storm clouds gathered over his Vietnam policies, Kennedy appeared to be successful in his general efforts to stabilize government spending and balance of payments, in order to achieve his prime economic reform of a tax cut for the strengthening of the *domestic* economy. A tax cut was also his intended cure for the balance-of-payments crisis, since it would encourage both U.S. and international capital to invest in the stimulated United States market rather than overseas.[100] Yet even without it the United States was able to announce, one week before Kennedy's assassination, that there had been no gold loss for thirteen consecutive weeks, "probably the longest stable period in the history of the United States."[101]

There appear to have been two chief factors in this stabilization. One was unprecedented assistance from the Soviet Union after the signing of the Test Ban Treaty in August, in the form of Soviet bullion sales in the European market and a related $250 million purchase of U.S. wheat.[102] The other was an unprecedented drop-off of almost $1000 million in total U.S. investments abroad (both direct and portfolio) in the preceding quarter. U.S. portfolio investments abroad had been radically inhibited by Kennedy's Balance of Payments Message to Congress on July 18, 1963, announcing that Treasury Secretary Dillon would introduce legislation to tax future purchases of foreign securities, retroactively to July 18.

In retrospect Kennedy's proposed legislation (like subsequent measures in this field) seems to testify to the power of the Center financial lobby in Washington, since it specifically exempted not only direct investment but commercial bank loans (which in 1964 would thus expand, as was predicted, to restore the investment capital outflow). Nevertheless the proposal drew much protest from New York securities dealers, foreign investment consultants, and above all Japan, where the anticipated loss of vital U.S. capital would depress the Tokyo stock market by twenty-five percent in the second half of 1963.[103]

Significantly, however, the message drew explicit approval from the finance minister of France, which at that time was attempting to discourage the direct take-over of French industries by American firms (notably IBM). Though the Kennedy Message failed to propose taxing such direct investment (as the French would have wished), French sources later suggested that "the Kennedy Administration had tried and had run into insuperable opposition from the country's big overseas enterprises."[104]

On this issue (as in the related Soviet détente) Kennedy was leaning toward Paris, and away from Bonn. On other related issues (Britain, the Test Ban Treaty) Kennedy and de Gaulle were still clearly at odds, as to all outward appearances they would soon be on Vietnam, following de Gaulle's August 29 offer to help Vietnam shake off foreign [i.e., U.S.] influence. The fact remains that Kennedy's NSAM 263, with its 1000-man withdrawal plan, was authorized after Kennedy discussions with France's foreign minister, resulting also in agreement for de Gaulle to visit America in early 1964. (That visit was annulled by the assassination, and West Germany's Chancellor Erhard came instead.)

Criticism of Kennedy's balance-of-payments proposals in the New York financial community, though clearly discernible, was relatively low-key and scattered. Though Kennedy's July 1963 message was in advance of what Wall Street wanted (as Johnson's message of February 1965 would not be) it was not in advance by much. Vietnam however would be in the critical period 1963–1965 a subject of much more intensive lobbying from New York. Some of this, such as Marvin Liebman's success-ful ad campaign in 1964 for the use of more modern aircraft, was military rather than investment-oriented: it does not concern us here. What does concern us is the sustained if subtle campaign for Vietnam involvement, dating back to the first years of the Diem regime, waged by individuals connected to the Rockefeller-linked Socony Mobil Corporation and Chase Manhattan Bank.

The anxiety of 1963 within the Kennedy administration about Vietnam and Southeast Asia found its way into a paper delivered publicly in May 1963 by William Henderson, an old "American Friend of Vietnam" who was now a Socony Mobil "Advisor on International Affairs." Henderson made a strong claim for the "final commitment" which Kennedy had declined in November 1961, and which Johnson finally made on November 24, 1963:

> ... we shall ultimately fail to secure the basic objectives of policy in Southeast Asia until our commitment to the region becomes unlimited, and it has not been up till now. This does not mean simply that we must be prepared to fight for South-east Asia, if necessary, although it certainly means that at a minimum. Beyond this is involved a much greater commitment of our resources, our knowledge, and our whole national effort than we have hitherto been prepared to make, in order effec-tively to influence the political, economic, and social develop-ment of these countries along fruitful paths. Such a commit-ment will come, if at all, only in response to sustained and persuasive governmental, that is to say presidential, leader-ship and guidance.... All three [postwar] administrations ... [have shown] an unwillingness to go the whole way, *to make the final commitment* and to carry the public with them. And this has probably been because, by and large, senior for-eign policy officials have themselves, like the general public, remained unconvinced that the region is a truly *vital* interest of the United States.[105]

Henderson delivered this paper at an Asia Society Conference of May 10–11, 1963, "to reappraise the whole pattern of United States policy in Southeast Asia."[106]

In thus arguing for a much greater commitment to an inte-grated military–economic development program, Henderson was overtly attacking the policies of Kennedy's "senior foreign policy officials." Perhaps the most noted spokesman for the Henderson concept was Kenneth Todd Young, who resigned his Ambassadorship to Thailand in 1964 and became president of the same Asia Society.[107] Young is the man named in the Pentagon Papers as an inspirer of Johnson's 1965 proposals for "massive regional development" in Asia (PP Beacon, III, 355) ; and also as the first to speak of Vietnam's "crisis of confidence" (PP Beacon, II, 20). Apparently Young used these words to his friend Ngo Dinh Diem in October 1960, when he was not a U.S. official but (according to *Who's Who*) "with Standard Vacuum Oil Co.," the Socony-Jersey Standard subsidiary in Asia. Young's business with Diem in 1960 as a Stanvac employee may well have involved more than oil, especially since Young was in air combat intelligence during World War II. Employment with large overseas companies is a traditional cover for CIA activity, as for the intelligence organizations of Britain, West Germany, and other capitalist countries.[108]

But neither Stanvac, Socony, nor the Asia Society, Inc., was a neutral conduit for the fostering of CIA "objectivity." The Asia Society was largely the creature of its 1963 president, John D. Rockefeller III, who with his father and brothers owned one-sixth of Socony's stock in 1939. (President Grayson Kirk of Columbia, the chairman of the Asia Society Board of Trustees, was himself a director of Socony Mobil.) Socony Mobil, one of the four U.S. petroleum giants in Asia, derived fifty-eight percent of its profits after taxes from foreign operations in 1959 (including the Far East). Moreover, the company interlocked with others having a prominent Far Eastern stake—notably IBM and the First National City Bank of New York. In 1951 Citibank's vice-president, Walter Reid Wolf, went briefly into the CIA to set up Air America, Inc. (then known as CAT, Inc.), for the CIA.[109]

It is worth recalling that when Ngo Dinh Diem visited America in 1957 he began with a luncheon given in his honor by John D. Rockefeller (other guests included the board chairmen of Chase Manhattan and First National City Bank) and ended with a demonstration of oil production in Los Angeles at the plant of General Petroleum, a Socony Mobil subsidiary. The CIA–New York Social Register genealogical milieu also found Socony well represented. In the late 1950s, for example, a cousin of Socony's president (B. Brewster Jennings) was perhaps the most notorious CIA operative in Laos (R. Campbell James, also a Rockefeller cousin) ; and a cousin of Socony's Secretary (Arthur

Sherwood) was president of the American Friends of Vietnam (Christopher Emmet) .[110]

Both Stanvac and Caltex were represented at a 1958 AFV Conference on "Investment Conditions in Vietnam," along with the Asia Society, the C. V. Starr insurance interests in Vietnam,[111] some of the drug and trading companies who would later pay compensation to the U.S. government for their manipulation of the U.S. aid program in Vietnam,[112] and some of the banks which would later figure prominently in the currency black-market scandals.[113] In 1958 the oil companies were probably more concerned about Indonesia than Vietnam; but the presence at this conference of a small engineering firm, Off Shore Service, suggests that there may already have been more interest in the prospects for offshore oil in the South China Sea near Vietnam (following a U.S. Navy survey in 1956) than the oil companies were letting on.

Beyond any doubt these oil companies were prominent among the special interests that made up the Vietnam lobby between 1956 and 1963. And it is clear that between 1960 and late 1963 their special interests were not (in their view) adequately reflected in U.S. policy. Socony employee Henderson noted that the U.S. had "intervened in the internal affairs of Southeast Asian countries ever since the end of World War II," and appealed that henceforth we do so "frankly" rather than "surreptitiously."[114] This, like his corresponding appeal for an "unlimited . . . final commitment," represented an informed intervention into the secret bureaucratic debate over Vietnam between Kennedy and some of his military advisers, with the CIA apparently split down the middle.

For example, the idea that South Vietnam was (in Henderson's word) "vital" to the United States, was explicitly proposed to Kennedy for public announcement in October 1963 by McNamara and Taylor (PP Beacon, II, 753) : Kennedy deleted the word "vital" and substituted his usual equivocal language (PP Beacon, II, 188) . A close reading of the Pentagon Papers suggests that Henderson's demands, rebuffed by Kennedy in late 1963, were answered, at least on paper, by Johnson's NSAM 273 of November 26, 1963.[115] For the first time an NSAM had articulated a U.S. commitment "to win" and had authorized planning for a graduated program of covert operations which would become increasingly overt.

More important, Henderson (like Young afterwards) had stressed not only security but development, with a "much greater commitment of our resources." Kennedy in contrast had gone ahead with an "Accelerated Plan" for U.S. withdrawal, beginning in 1963, which would have reduced both the U.S. troop commitment (beginning in 1963) and its military assistance (beginning in 1964).[116]

THE JOHNSON MILITARY–ECONOMIC PARADIGM: EXPANSION BY CONTROLS

On April 7, 1965, President Johnson (as Henderson had counseled) linked overt intervention in Vietnam to a vision of strengthening "world order" and containing China, with "a billion-dollar American investment in . . . a greatly expanded cooperative effort for development" in Southeast Asia.[117] The Pentagon Papers rightly name Kenneth Todd Young as an inspirer of this "massive regional development effort for the area" (PP Beacon, III, 356). They do not, predictably, point out that Young had once worked for Stanvac, nor that Eugene Black, whom Johnson named in his speech to head up the development program, was a director of Royal Dutch Shell and the (Rockefeller) Chase Manhattan Bank. The Chase Manhattan vice-president who supervised Far Eastern operations envisaged in 1965 that the new U.S. military–economic intensification in Asia would produce results comparable to Truman's Greek intervention and Marshall Plan in Europe:

> In the past foreign investors have been somewhat wary of the overall political prospect for the [Southeast Asia] region. I must say, though, that U.S. actions in Vietnam this year [i.e., 1965] —which have demonstrated that the U.S. will continue to give effective protection to the free nations of the region—have considerably reassured both Asian and Western investors. In fact, I see some reason to hope that the same sort of economic growth may take place in the free economies of Asia that took place in Europe after the Truman Doctrine and after NATO provided a protective shield. The same thing also took place in Japan after the U.S. intervention in Korea removed investor doubts.[118]

This prediction represented a sharp change of mood from that made a year earlier, in a $40.00 anthology published by *Business International,* "that much of Southeast Asia, including India, will go communist."[119] Thanks in large measure to the economic impacts of the war itself, and the not unrelated anti-Communist coup of October 1965 in Indonesia, Mr. Wentworth's vision soon appeared to be being fulfilled. The Chase Manhattan Bank reported enthusiastically in September 1966:

> A heartening pattern of rapid and sustained economic growth has emerged in the Far East economies of Japan, Hong Kong, Taiwan, the Philippines, Thailand, Malaysia and, most recently, Korea . . . with real GNP expanding between 5% and 9% a year, compared to a world average of about 4% . . . a valuable example for sound development elsewhere . . . many of the countries have put out the welcome mat for investment, both domestic and foreign, with a wide range of incentives.[120]

By 1969 U.S. trade with Asia and Oceania ($16.7 billion) was almost double the figure for Latin America ($9.1 billion), while *Business Week* was predicting "a boom in U.S. export and import trade with East and South Asia, excluding Japan."[121] The same journal predicted an oil bonanza and investment boom based in Singapore, "to back up the offshore oil search . . . from New Guinea to the Gulf of Thailand—and ultimately, perhaps, to South Vietnam."[122] David Rockefeller of the Chase Manhattan Bank was reported in 1970 as predicting that in the 1970s oil companies would spend $35 billion in capital investment along the western rim of the Pacific.[123]

By late 1964, moreover, as *Fortune* reported in the month of the Tonkin Gulf incidents, the defense industries were confronted with the need for new outlets: The five-year Kennedy–McNamara program for the acquisition of strategic missile systems was now largely completed.[124] It was thus predictable that aerospace journals like *Aviation Week* would in 1964 campaign against the limited and old-fashioned air war then being waged by the United States in Vietnam. This escalatory campaign of oil and defense interests, both of which had particularly influential lobbies in Washington, was one which no president could easily resist.

But, as we have seen, Johnson's sudden expansion in 1965 of dollar outflow to Asia in both the economic and military spheres could not (it was believed) be undertaken by the United States *without some measures to protect its balance of payments.* For the balance of payments crisis had worsened again in 1964, with a return to new highs of the investment outflow which had been checked under Kennedy.[125] In January 1965 alone, a gold outflow of $262 million, aggravated by French attacks on the dollar, exceeded America's gold loss for the whole of 1964.[126] Before the "victory strategy" of 1965 could be undertaken, in other words, compensatory restrictions on the dollar outflow had to be introduced.

These were announced in the form of President Johnson's "Voluntary Program" of February 10, 1965, three days after the bombing of North Vietnam began. Under the Voluntary Program, banks and corporations would agree to reduce their direct outflow by fifteen to twenty percent, while banks, receiving antitrust immunity for their planning in this regard, would limit their future foreign lending to 105 percent of loans outstanding.[127] Significantly, the model for this voluntary program was the "voluntary credit restraint" of the 1950 Korean War, along with the enabling sections of the 1950 Defense Production Act. The success of the 1965 program was measured in a dramatic drop of investment outflow to under $400 million in the second quarter, followed by a redirection of investment from Europe to the less gold-sensitive countries of Asia and Africa.

The paradox of these two interrelated programs—expansion and retrenchment of the overseas dollar outflow—has not been generally noted. In announcing his Voluntary Program, President Johnson "made clear that of all the drains that needed calking, the outflows of private funds were most serious"[128]—he thus apparently took issue with the major banks and multinational corporations in the Committee for Economic Development and similar lobbies, who continued to maintain that "to sustain the dollar as the key international currency . . . freedom for private capital transactions is necessary."[129]

Yet in 1965 this powerful CED, and with it the other organs of the New York financial center, accepted and implemented the policy of restraints on capital outflow (including direct investment) which Kennedy, under pressure, had called unthinkable in 1963. The commercial banks in particular, instead of protesting, spoke in support of the Voluntary Program, which they had helped design.[130] There are two related reasons for this apparent paradox. The first is that, with the passage of eighteen months and the freezing at December 1964 levels, the sluice gates of the commercial bank outflows were now being locked open rather than shut. U.S. bank claims on foreigners had risen $2.5 billion in 1964, compared to $1.5 billion in 1963 and only $.5 billion in 1962. Of the total $9.5 billion in foreign claims of 150 U.S. banks on December 31, 1964 (the new base level), $5 billion (or fifty-three percent) was held by the five largest banks, seventy-five percent ($7.1 billion) was held by ten banks, and eighty-seven percent by the top 25 banks.[131] This high concentration of foreign commercial lending had increased in 1964, when only nine U.S. banks had accounted for eighty-three percent of short-term (1–3 year) capital commitments abroad.[132] It is thus hardly surprising that the program was formally proposed by Alfred Hayes, the president of the Federal Reserve Bank of New York, after supporting advice from such bankers as Alfred W. Barth (an OSS veteran) of Chase Manhattan and John M. Meyer, Jr., of Morgan Guaranty Trust.[133] Through the Voluntary Program, these banks secured a guaranteed position of dominance (which in 1968 would receive governmental sanction) in the lucrative field of foreign loans where returns were highest.

The second reason for their acceptance of previously unpalatable restraints is that by 1965 their eyes were very much focused on the investment possibilities of a militarily secured Asia. Alfred Hayes' speech of January 25, 1965, in which he first proposed the Voluntary Program to the New York State Bankers Association, is indicative of the new consensus in the banking milieu. Two years earlier, in a similar speech on balance of payments, he had reflected the Kennedy paradigm. On April 22, 1963, he had discerned three problem areas: exports, government commitments, and capital movements. Noting the need to cut government financial commitments abroad, he had raised "the hard question whether we can afford all the commitments we have taken on." As for capital outflow, he was glad that the Kennedy administration had rejected "direct controls."[134] But on January 25, 1965, two weeks before the delayed war against North Vietnam began, controls and expansion. Although overseas government commitments were now a far larger and more controversial issue than in 1963, Mr. Hayes concluded that "the spotlight of the moment would seem to be on capital movements," where a "more direct approach" was needed.[135]

With the rapid escalation in Vietnam and Johnson's speech of April 7 the apparent paradoxes in the new paradigm became understandable: the restraints on investment outflow had made it possible for the United States, with government planning and massive overseas pump-priming through its war and aid budgets (aided by massive corruption), to embark upon a concerted investment program in Asia. At the same time that the CIA supplied new intelligence figures to justify war, so the banks and international investors supplied their necessary financial consent and support to controls they had previously rejected.

The resulting new Johnson paradigm for the U.S. economy has been called a program of "guns and butter"—plus planned development. It might also be called a paradigm of massive payments deficits, at the cost of domestic inflation and the ultimate replacement of Kennedy's tax cut by Johnson's tax surcharge. The new paradigm would climax in the Nixon administration with devaluation, the imposition of domestic economic controls, a major flight of capital abroad, and a massive transference of the war's huge tax burden from corporations to the individual taxpayer. Even though the staggering costs of the war were certainly not foreseen, the new stress on overseas development (which pleased Japan) at the cost of equilibrium (which displeased France) would probably in itself have increased international liquidity to the point of bankrupting the gold pool (as happened in 1968).

The new paradigm which saw the rapid establishment of the Asian Development Bank in December 1965 cannot be said, like Topsy, to have "just growed." It took intensive cooperation and planning among the New York financial community, the U.S. government, and other nations, to throw their weight behind proposals which had languished for years in the U.N.'s Economic Commission for Asia and the Far East. It was not, however, a matter of equal concern to all U.S. investment circles, but chiefly (as we have seen) to a handful of major banks, oil companies, and other multinational firms such as IBM. Ultimately the failure of this nation to evolve a democratic and peaceful foreign policy can be explained by this economic concentration, which could plan for escalation with the support of relatively few financial institutions. And this economic concentration, I need hardly add, has been greatly intensified by the very war which it helped to bring about.

Eliot Janeway, a longtime personal economic adviser to Johnson who in 1965 threw his weight to "dove" Senator Hartke, has summarized the course of Johnson's program as follows:

> The official calculation assumed a normal emergency-time prosperity in an economy big enough to provide both guns and butter. The official calculators expected the escalation of 1965 to stabilize the boom of 1964. They were astounded when, instead, it brought crisis to the money markets in 1966 and crisis to earning power in 1967. Surprise gave way to shock when the failure of earning power in 1967 threatened the Treasury with a crisis of war finance such as the government of the United States had not faced since the days of the Continental Congress.[136]

The pump-priming impact of the war on economic expansion was felt in Asia, not in America. At home the costs of this "small" but "very expensive war" exceeded, for the first time in U.S. wartime history, the rate of domestic economic expansion—thus threatening disaster for that important "strategic asset," the dollar itself.[137]

The failure of the Pentagon Papers to show any trace of this "official calculation" is matched by the systematic and unrelenting distortion of CIA intelligence estimates in the period 1964–1967: As we have seen, the CIA's repeated recommendations in the crucial period of February–April 1965, in support of punishing U.S. air attacks and a "victory strategy" (PP Beacon, III, 353, 365), have since been misrepresented as the opposite of what they were. We can only guess that one reason for the shift in CIA estimates, including the dramatic rewriting of infiltration estimates in late 1964, was economic: the emergence of consensus for the new strategic economic paradigm.

There is, however, no doubt that the New York financial community threw its support behind the President's escalations of 1965. An ad in the September 9 *New York Times,* signed by forty-seven members of the "Committee for an Effective and Durable Peace in Asia," explained the President's aim:

> To bring about a viable peace in Vietnam and, once peace is brought about, *to enlist economic aid for the entire area* and to assure to the people of South Vietnam the right to choose a government of their own, free from assassination [!], threats of violence, or other forms of intimidation.[138]

This statement appears to have envisaged support, not only for the Johnson program, but for its evolution into the Nixon–Kissinger phase of "Vietnamization" as well:

> We support unequivocally the withdrawal of [U.S.] forces from South Vietnam as soon as the South Vietnamese are in a position to determine their future without external interference, infiltration, intimidation or threat.

The statement itself however is less interesting than the list of those who signed it. These included the chief known economic planners of the Johnson paradigm (Eugene R. Black and Kenneth Todd Young), civilians frequently associated with CIA activities (Oveta Culp Hobby, James R. Killian, Franklin Lindsay, and Lucian Pye), Council on Foreign Relations directors (Arthur Dean, Joseph E. Johnson), CED Planners (Douglas Dillon, Gabriel Hauge, John A. Perkins), and men who after 1968 would become associated with the Nixon administration (future Ambassadress Mrs. Walter Annenberg, future Defense Deputy Secretary David Packard, David Rockefeller of Chase Manhattan, future U.S. Attorney Whitney North Seymour, and future Supreme Court Justice Lewis F. Powell).

Most striking is the presence of *all five civilians* of the influential Senior Advisory Group (Committee Chairman Arthur H. Dean, Dean Acheson, C. Douglas Dillon, John J. McCloy, and Robert D. Murphy) who were not at that time (September 1965) inside the Johnson administration. Of these five, Acheson at least had been an adviser to Johnson since late 1963; and we learn from Hoopes that the Senior Advisory Group as such had regularly "counseled with the President once or twice since 1965" (when Clark Clifford, then as later a "pessimist," was their spokesman).[139]

CONCLUSIONS

The war itself cannot be rationalized by an overall economic calculus. Like the French Indochina War before it, it has strengthened a nexus of special interests in the bureaucracy, defense industries, overseas investors, and organized crime, which have struggled for some time to resist its de-escalation. These special interests, unfortunately, enjoy far more than their share of political influence in a system which has been so largely corrupted by the influence of *la guerre pourrie,* the corrupt war itself.

And, just as in the First Indochina War French interests were largely replaced by American, so in the second American overall interests in and profits from Asian development have been largely overtaken by Japanese:

> In 1964–65 the Japanese economy was cooling off; it was rekindled by the Vietnam war boom plus sudden economic access to Korea and Taiwan; and in fact, in anticipation of its escalation in Vietnam the United States appears to have worked behind the scenes to help Japan drive the opening wedge into the economies of its two former colonies. . . . William Bundy, Dean Rusk, and Walt Rostow visited Japan in quick succession during the crucial period in late 1964 and early 1965 when the massive escalation of the Vietnam war was on the U.S. drawing boards. . . . Figures are inadequate when it comes to understanding how America's wars in Asia have benefited Japan *by default,* as ruinous military outlays drained the U.S. economy and in the process created new global markets for Japan.[140]

Today one can write of East and Southeast Asia as a new "co-prosperity sphere," in which the capital will be largely American, but the trade largely Japanese.[141]

Weakness of the dollar in the 1970s, like weakness of the franc two decades earlier, may indeed have delayed the de-escalation of the Indochina War. The U.S. payments deficit has soared from a seven-year high of $3544 million in 1967, to $6958 million in 1969, to $23,977 million in 1971.[142] This staggering indebtedness to Japan and Europe has weakened America's capacity to end a war for domestic considerations. But of the 1971 deficit $10,878 million, or almost half, was in unrecorded transactions ("Errors and Omissions") , an elevenfold increase over 1967. A major flight of capital from the United States, much of it covert, was under way—into areas made more secure by America's powerful (if nearly bankrupt) military hegemony.

In this crisis, the cynical economic rationalists have not been the generals with their pet doomsday projects, but the investment and trade interests represented in the Senior Advisory Group. Since 1968 the latter have moved increasingly towards stabilization, and de-escalation in Indochina, just as Clark Clifford himself has become a spokesman for unconditional U.S.

withdrawal. This is quite consistent with a worried recommendation from the American Bankers Association in 1968 *"that some parts of our present Government programs abroad including military forces be reduced consistent with our obligations to our allies."*[143] The logic of such analysis is partly but not completely answered by Vietnamization. It may yet move the New York establishment to accept instead the imperialist logic of the "fall-back position" which its spokesmen discarded in late 1964.

One recent opponent of the war, for example, is Thomas F. McCoy, a former Laos operative who resigned from the CIA in 1968 after seventeen years' service, "to become a top campaign aide to peace candidate Eugene McCarthy."[144] Yet McCoy has not the same aversion for the CIA's covert warfare. In 1972 he wrote a letter to the *Washington Post,* claiming that the job done by the CIA in Laos, "based on any comparison with the U.S. military effort in Vietnam, would have to be: *A spectacular success."*[145]

The military who carried out the Vietnam escalation of 1965 appear now to have been losers; not so the civilian national security managers who planned it. While Sharp and Westmoreland have retired to obscurity, men like McNamara and the Bundy brothers continue to shape future American paradigms from the World Bank, the Ford Foundation, and the Council on Foreign Relations. Indeed the Nixon–Kissinger paradigm of "low-profile" U.S. involvement, through increased use of Third World mercenary forces, is as we have seen an updated version of low-level and fall-back options put forward by these very men in the 1964–1966 period.[146]

Both the strength and the contradictions of the U.S. global hegemony have been greatly increased by the Vietnam escalations of 1963–1965. On the one hand client states like Indonesia, Iran, and Brazil have emerged (thanks to coups) as willing candidates for the strategy of militarized economic development, renewing the short-term hopes for capitalist investment (from the flight of U.S. capital) in them and their neighbors. But in the process the U.S. dollar has gone through the once unthinkable crisis of devaluation, shattering the international monetary system laid down at Bretton Woods and threatening the dollar's future as the chief international reserve currency. It is of course possible that the capitalist world will continue to be held together in trade and aid by the unfettered printing presses of the U.S. mint.[147] But an alternative possibility is the accelerated demoralization of capitalist institutions, domestic as well as multinational, as uncertainty about the future leads short-term profit considerations to prevail over more rational long-term economic planning.

As I see it, one task for antiwar critics is to strip away the false propaganda veiling the CIA's performance in the Vietnam War, and to see how its intelligence estimates, issued formally as NIE's, reflected not disinterested objectivity but the policy concerns of a relatively small and economically powerful CIA financial establishment. Consciousness of this function is essential if we are to understand the process of U.S. military expansion. Insofar as (in Leslie Gelb's phrase) "the system worked," however, such consciousness is not likely to change the process.

Thus, a second important task is to expose the dysfunctions of the American system that led to the Indochina War: the scandals and irregularities, the private usurpations of the nation's political processes, the repeated distortion of decision-making by contaminated "intelligence," the draining of a weakened domestic economy for ruthless profit-making abroad.

N O T E S

1. Harry Magdoff, "The Logic of Imperialism," *Social Policy* (September–October 1970), p. 29. Cf. David Horowitz, *Empire and Revolution* (New York: Random House, 1969), p. 38: "There can be no end to imperialism without an end to capitalism."

2. Ralph Stavins, Richard J. Barnet, and Marcus G. Raskin, *Washington Plans an Aggressive War* (New York: Vintage, 1971), p. 209.

3. Stavins, *et al.*, p. 212; cf. pp. 206, 214.

4. Stavins, *et al.*, p. 214.

5. Robert Scheer, "The Language of Torturers," *SunDance* (August–September 1972), p. 36; cf. Pentagon Papers (New York: Bantam, 1971, henceforth cited as PP Bantam), p. 101; (Boston: Beacon, 1971, henceforth cited as PP Beacon), II, 87–93.

6. PP Bantam, p. 102; cf. Beacon, II, 105.

7. PP Bantam, p. 105.

8. Daniel Ellsberg, *Papers on the War* (New York: Simon and Schuster, 1972), p. 103; cf. pp. 91–94.

9. It is quite likely that the lies at this time to the U.S. press, denying that Taylor had requested combat troops, were prompted, as the

Pentagon Study suggests, by Kennedy's wish "to put a quick stop" to Diem's expectations (PP Beacon, II, 76).

10. PP Bantam, pp. 107, 148–49; Beacon, II, 108–10; cf. my essay in PP Beacon, V, 214–16, for a fuller discussion of Kennedy's frequently misrepresented "commitment."

11. Taylor's optimistic predictions for his own proposals may well have contained an element of what Ellsberg calls bureaucratic "self-deception" (p. 118) ; but in terms of his special interest they seem less irrational. Like other escalation proposals in periods of crisis, they were nakedly linked to Taylor's desire to see a "permanent increase" for his own service—the Army—"in current considerations of the FY 1963 budget" (PP Bantam, p. 143; Beacon, II, 92). One is reminded that 1964 proposals for an expanded air war arose in a context of Pentagon anxieties about long-term aircraft procurement, and that the Tonkin Gulf incidents gave a timely boost to a concurrent Navy campaign for new aircraft carriers.

12. *NYT*, December 12, 1961, pp. 20–21. The same pages also announced Souvanna Phouma's December 11 proposal for a tripartite meeting of the three opposing Laotian princes, a proposal which led ultimately to the final breaking of the Laotian deadlock in June 1962.

13. Ellsberg, pp. 100–01.

14. Richard B. DuBoff, "Business Ideology and Foreign Policy: The National Security Council and Vietnam," PP Beacon, V, 26–27, quoting PP Beacon, III, 50.

15. Not even in Pentagon Study IV.B.4, "Phased Withdrawal of U.S. Forces, 1962–1964" (cf. PP Beacon, II, 173–200). NSAM 263 is however listed in the chronology preceding this study (II, 169). Frequently one finds traces in the chronologies of important facts not in the studies themselves—suggesting that the studies were clumsily edited and censored for public consumption before their dramatic release to *The New York Times*.

16. Scott, PP Beacon, V, 214–16.

17. Noam Chomsky, "Vietnam: How Government Became Wolves," *New York Review of Books* (June 15, 1972), p. 23, reprinted (with slight changes) in Noam Chomsky, *For Reasons of State* (New York: Pantheon Books, 1973), p. 28.

18. Scott, *The War Conspiracy*, pp. 64n, 94, 118, 163–64; PP Beacon, V, 217.

19. PP Beacon, III, 219: "Missing was the earlier draft's reference to potential costs and risks involved in pursuing current objectives." The compromise final document said only that "strong military action necessarily involves some risks of an enlarged and even conceivably major conflict in Asia."

20. PP Beacon, III, 218. The six civilian members of the NSC Working Group were Chairman William P. Bundy (State), Marshall Green

(State), Michael Forrestal (White House), Robert Johnson (State), Harold Ford (CIA), and John McNaughton (Defense).

21. Lyndon B. Johnson, *The Vantage Point* (New York: Holt, Rinehart and Winston, 1971), pp. 43–44; Scott, PP Beacon, V, 221–22.

22. Hannah Arendt, "Lying in Politics: Reflections on the Pentagon Papers," *New York Review of Books,* November 18, 1971, pp. 32, 34.

23. Scott, *The War Conspiracy,* pp. 222–23.

24. Joseph Goulden, *Truth is the First Casualty* (New York: Rand McNally, 1969), p. 97.

25. PP Beacon, III, 42. Richard Barnet had presumably not had access to this CIA document when in 1971 he too attempted to divorce policy-makers from "the intelligence community," and to depict the latter as "most skeptical" of "the faucet theory of how to end the war" (Stavins, *et al.,* pp. 213–14).

26. PP Bantam, 338; Beacon III, 244, 681. The Pentagon Papers merely describe Cooper as "a former intelligence specialist" (III, 255), but they inadvertently reveal that the elite members of Cooper's "Special CAS Group" despatched to Vietnam in February 1964 were "all drawn from CIA" (PP Beacon, II, 194; III, 33; cf. Chester Cooper, *The Lost Crusade: America in Vietnam,* New York: Dodd Mead, 1970, p. 229). *Former* CIA men who advocated some form of escalation in 1964 included William Bundy and Roger Hilsman.

27. PP Beacon, III, 673; cf. Scott, *The War Conspiracy,* p. 46. The Pentagon Studies defend the White Paper's correctness, explaining that "the most persuasive evidence on DRV infiltration was derived from Special Intelligence sources which could not be revealed" (PP Beacon, III, 330; censored in U.S. Government edition, IV.C.3, p. 59). Later Cooper would return the compliment: "Although it probably did not cross Ellsberg's mind when he released the Pentagon Papers... he made the CIA 'look good'.... The CIA's estimators and analysts... remained impeccably objective, and they [sic] have been right" (*Foreign Affairs,* January 1972, pp. 228, 233).

28. Cf. PP Beacon, III, 595.

29. In the *New York Times* Magazine of November 22, 1964 (pp. 32–33) duly appeared photographs by James H. Pickerell of a CIA-sponsored CIDG mission against the Ho Chi Minh trail, "down which the Communists send men and material to the Vietcong guerrillas." An article by Peter Grose in the January 24, 1965, issue (pp. 10–11, 64–67) contains the fiirst reference I have seen in print to the so-called COSVN—"what American intelligence bureaus have named the Central Office South ... connected by an elaborate system of underground tunnels neatly outfitted with timbered supports and sophisticated telephone and radio facilities" (p. 67). This resembles the description of COSVN in an April 1965 memo from General Westmoreland ("collected ... during recent months" by "firm intelligence"), as the

heart of his successful argument for the first use in Vietnam of SAC B-52's (PP Beacon, III, 383–84). A similar description of a static COSVN in Cambodia was used by the Joint Chiefs and President Nixon as the case for the 1970 Cambodian invasion: based on alleged "intercepted radio messages" from Army Intelligence, ASA's picture of reinforced concrete bunkers "to house some 5,000 men" was challenged by other intelligence analysts before the invasion, and soon proved to be a complete delusion (Scott, *The War Conspiracy*, pp. 163–64). That did not stop Grose (or Sullivan?) from using COSVN in 1965 to make the necessary case for going North: "There is no doubt . . . that overall strategy is determined at a higher level, in the confidential councils of the Government of North Vietnam. The chain of command from the hamlet cells to Hanoi has been forged and hardened over more than a decade" (Bundy's November 5 memo points out that Grose had just published in the *Times* the escalated infiltration figures which he and Saigon wanted to "surface"; PP Beacon, III, 593).

30. PP Bantam, p. 242; Arendt, p. 35. For an extended study of the role of radio intercepts in inducing U.S. escalations, cf. *The War Conspiracy*, pp. 3, 5, 6; Scott, PP Beacon, V, 217.

31. PP Beacon, III, 169. This was a consensus estimate, "prepared by the Board of National Estimates, CIA, with State and DIA assistance, and concurred in by the U.S. Intelligence Board" (III, 168).

32. R. Harris Smith, *OSS: The Secret History of America's First Central Intelligence Agency* (Berkeley and Los Angeles: University of California Press, 1972), p. 382.

33. Cf. Scott, *The War Conspiracy*, pp. 222–23.

34. Johnson, *Vantage Point*, p. 119.

35. As cited by Raborn, this USIB opinion appears to refute Barnet's undocumented claim that at about this time "the CIA deduced that North Vietnam could not be bombed into submission" (*Roots of War*, p. 7).

36. Recall McCone's already cited memo of April 1965: "We must strike . . . their petroleum resources" (III, 353).

37. PP Beacon, IV, 266–67, 591–92; Townsend Hoopes, *The Limits of Intervention* (New York: David McKay, 1969), pp. 207–08, 214–17; Lyndon Baines Johnson, *The Vantage Point* (New York: Holt, Rinehart & Winston, 1971), p. 416; Cooper, *The Lost Crusade*, p. 393.

38. The 90th Congress, like others before it, was imperfectly representative, and still largely dominated by the munitions, oil, and aerospace lobbies. Their exclusion may be due to administration fears of the hawks in Congress, as revealed in a March 14, 1968, memo to Clifford from Townsend Hoopes: "Extremists in Congress would probably demand, as the price of their support [for escalation], elimination of all restriction on bombing of the North, and some might advocate measures designed to provoke a U.S. confrontation with China or the U.S.S.R.

There would also be pressures to expand the war into Laos and Cambodia [!], which, if yielded to, would only serve to spread thinner the U.S. forces in SVN" (Hoopes, p. 192).

39. Frederick Branfman, "Beyond the Pentagon Papers: The Pathology of Power," PP Beacon, V, 296.

40. First National City Bank of New York, *Monthly Economic Letter*, March 1966, pp. 26, 32; April 1966, p. 38, emphasis added.

41. The others were George Ball of Lehman Brothers International; Douglas Dillon of Dillon, Read; John J. McCloy of Chase Manhattan; Robert Murphy of Morgan Guaranty Trust (finance); Cyrus Vance of Simpson, Thacher and Bartlett; Arthur Dean of Sullivan and Cromwell (lawyers); Generals Omar Bradley, Matthew B. Ridgway, and Maxwell Taylor; and McGeorge Bundy. Three members were still in government: Justice Abe Fortas and Ambassadors Henry Cabot Lodge and Arthur Goldberg. Of the eight civilian outsiders, at least five (Acheson, Dillon, Vance, Dean, McCloy) were members of New York's elite Century Club.

42. Hoopes, p. 219.

43. *NYT*, March 13, 1968, p. 20; March 29, 1968, p. 9; and *passim*. More specifically, the U.S. gold reserves not tied to the twenty-five percent legal backing for Federal Reserve currency had dwindled on March 14, 1968, to the point where they were insufficient for the next day's foreign exchange transactions.

44. Johnson, pp. 318–19; *NYT*, March 15, 1968, p. 1.

45. *NYT*, March 17, 1968, p. 13.

46. Scott, *The War Conspiracy*, pp. xiii–xiv.

47. Even the CIA's support for bombing in 1965–1969 saw it as a means not of victory but of making limited programs more viable.

48. PP Beacon, III, 354, quoting Rowland Evans and Robert Novak, *Lyndon B. Johnson: The Exercise of Power* (New York: New American Library, 1968), p. 564.

49. Scott, *The War Conspiracy*, pp. 163–66.

50. Barnet, in Stavins, *et al.*, p. 209; cf. Arendt, p. 33: "The ultimate aim was neither power nor profit. Nor was it even influence in the world in order to serve particular, tangible interests." Barnet explains his position much more plausibly in his *Roots of War* (p. 190): "The massive intervention in Vietnam has also opened up commercial opportunities for American business. Construction firms such as President Johnson's political mentors Brown & Root, shipping and transport companies, oil companies, banks, even MGM, have profited directly from operations in Vietnam even while the American economy as a whole and business in general suffered from its consequences."

51. Ralph Littauer and Norman Uphoff, eds., *The Air War in Indochina*, rev. ed. (Boston: Beacon Press, 1972), p. 279.

52. Thus in the 1960s one of the more aggressive "Cowboy" Mar-

ginals was Union Oil Company of California, a firm supporting the American Security Council and interested in exploring for oil in Southeast Asia. Its president, A. C. Rubel, was a prominent right-wing financial backer of Ronald Reagan, while other directors included Charles B. Thornton of Litton Industries, Dwight Whiting of Douglas Aircraft, Francis S. Baer of the RMK–BRJ Vietnam construction combine, and Daniel B. Ludwig, who put much of his profits from oil tankers into developing Bahamas casinos before being cut into Vietnam war contracts. A "Cowboy" firm to all outward appearances—yet in the 1960s there were also two "Yankees" on the board: F. H. Brandi of Dillon Read (which marketed Union Oil's stock and debenture offerings in the 1950s) and Horace Flanigan of Manufacturers Hanover Trust in New York (whose son Peter was a vice-president of Dillon Read). There are similar "Yankee" capital links to the other ASC–"Cowboy" Marginals. True "Cowboys" like H. L. Hunt, who spurned the Yankee capital markets, do not appear to have figured prominently in defense or other U.S. government contracts.

53. Thus, when the Kennedy and Johnson administrations accepted the survival of the Castro regime in Cuba, rather than risk another major confrontation with the Soviet Union, major losers included what we might call Old Marginals: like IT&T and American and Foreign Power Company, both based in New York.

54. One such link is Kermit Roosevelt of the CIA's Plans Directorate, where he helped overthrow Premier Mossadegh of Iran and thus open up Anglo-Iranian Oil to a consortium including Gulf Oil. In 1957 Roosevelt resigned to become the top Washington lobbyist for Gulf; in 1960 his friend C. L. Sulzberger could write of him that "Kim is now vice president of Gulf Oil Company in charge of government relations, *but he is still linked with the CIA*" (C. L. Sulzberger, *The Last of the Giants,* New York, Macmillan, 1970, p. 742, emphasis added).

55. Relevant examples in Scott, *The War Conspiracy,* Introduction, pp. xvii–xxi.

56. The in-laws of one such family, the Pratts of Standard Oil, have included CIA Paris Station Chief Robert Thayer, Secretary of State Christian Herter, and Deputy Secretary of Defense Paul Nitze (former Assistant Secretary of Defense for International Security Affairs). Christian Herter, Jr., left the State Department to become a director of the Council on Foreign Relations and general manager for government relations of Socony Mobil (see below).

57. Cf. G. William Domhoff, *The Higher Circles* (New York: Vintage, 1971). Some of the non-CIA principals in this essay who were relatives or in-laws of CIA Social Register members include Acheson, Nitze, Vance, McGeorge Bundy, and no doubt many more.

58. To translate our oversimplified model into a Freudian analogy, CIA intelligence personnel and their allies of the Center have tended

to represent the "ego" of a neurotic (or psychotic) corporate capitalist society. Extending this analogy, one can compare the Marginals interested only in immediate special profits to a capitalistic id, and the "win-at-any-cost" anti-Communists to an ideological superego. Bureaucratic fixation upon the distorted perceptions of NSAM paradigms (like the "externally directed and supported conspiracy") can then be compared to the inflexibility of the ego-structure in the neurotic personality. Freud himself, for different reasons, drew attention to the functioning of what he called *Gemeinschaftsneurosen* or "communal neuroses" in society; though he criticized the "cultural superego" for excessive severity, leading to an unbalanced distribution of libido between ego and objects, rather than for inherent ideological perverseness (as in Cold War anti-Communism). Cf. *Civilization and Its Discontents* (New York: W. W. Norton, 1962), pp. 86–92.

59. Richard P. Stebbins, for the Council on Foreign Relations, *The United States in World Affairs, 1965* (New York: Harper and Row, 1966), p. 236.

60. Michael Tanzer, *The Political Economy of International Oil and the Underdeveloped Countries* (Boston: Beacon, 1969), pp. 363–64. (CIA Director McCone, a leading hawk in these years, held $1 million worth of stock in Standard Oil of California, whose subsidiary Caltex accounted for seventy percent of Sumatran oil production.) Cf. David Wise and Thomas B. Ross, *The Invisible Government* (New York: Bantam, 1965), p. 207; citing U.S. Congress, Senate, Committee on Armed Services, Hearings on the nomination of John A. McCone, January 1962.

61. Richard Nixon, "Asia After Viet Nam," *Foreign Affairs* (October 1967), p. 111. Cf. Lyndon Johnson, *The Vantage Point*, p. 357: "A number of Asian statesmen who had good reason for their opinions told me that the Indonesian turnaround would probably never have occurred if . . . the United States and others had not taken a stand in Vietnam."

62. Presidential Statement of July 28, 1965, PP Beacon, IV, 632.

63. *NYT*, February 27, 1965, p. 1; September 15, 1965, p. 5; Richard M. Nixon, "Facing the Facts in Vietnam," Speech to the Executives Club of New York, January 26, 1965. *Vital Speeches of the Day* (March 15, 1965), p. 338; quoted in Virginia Brodine and Mark Selden (eds.), *Open Secret: The Kissinger-Nixon Doctrine in Asia* (New York: Harper and Row, 1972), p. 42.

64. *NYT*, September 10, 1965, p. 13.

65. If the Beacon Index can be trusted, then the chief reference to Indonesia in the Pentagon Papers after 1961 is an undocumented statement that in 1964–65 "some U.S. officials voiced concern over the development of a 'Peking-Jakarta axis' to promote revolution in Asia" (III, 267). Interestingly, this suggestive hint is censored from the U.S. Government edition. It may have been important: on January 9, 1965 a

New York Times editorial alluded to a "Jakarta-Peking axis" arousing "apprehension and displeasure ... in the rest of the world" (p. 29). Two other passing references suggest that in 1964, before the U.S. decision to go to war, Washington tended to write off Indonesia as "not now explicitly Communist but likely ... to become so" (PP Beacon, III, 500, cf. III, 220, 601).

66. "In contrast to the May 1959 NIE's confident statement that Diem 'almost certainly' would remain president 'for many years,' we find the August 1960 NIE predicting that the recent 'adverse trends,' if continued, would 'almost certainly in time cause the collapse of Diem's regime'" (PP Beacon, II, 20).

67. PP Bantam, pp. 86–87.

68. PP Beacon, II, 11–12; 30–31. The 1961 collapse of pressures on Diem for reform corresponds to the U.S. shift of 1950 with respect to Chiang Kai-shek; and like it has been attributed to the long shadow of pressures from McCarran, McCarthy, and the China Lobby: "The President, after all, could remember the charges that the Truman Administration had given away China by holding back on aid to Chiang to try to pressure him toward reform. As a young Congressman, he had even joined the chorus" (II, 30; cf. Ellsberg, pp. 80–81).

69. We have only one complete intelligence estimate summary from this period (that of SNIE 53–2–61 of October 5, 1961), and its opening sentences should be read by those who (like Daniel Ellsberg, p. 73n) eulogize the "persistent, realistic skepticism" of NIE's: "The Communist subversive and guerrilla apparatus in South Vietnam, known as the Viet Cong, is an integral part of the North Vietnamese Communist Party and it looks to Hanoi for political and military guidance and various forms of support. Hanoi is the implementing agency for [Communist] Bloc activity in South Vietnam, and the Hanoi authorities are allowed considerable local freedom in conducting Viet Cong guerrilla and subversive activity" (Pentagon Papers, U.S. Govt. edition, V.B.4, p. 291). Ellsberg himself in his own Pentagon Study IV.B.1 described the next SNIE of November 5, 1961 as "the *only* staff paper found in the available record which treats communist reactions primarily in terms of the separate national interests of Hanoi, Moscow, and Peiping [Peking], rather than primarily in terms of an overall Communist strategy for which Hanoi is acting as an agent" (PP Beacon, II, 107, emphasis added).

70. Quoted in Benjamin Graham, "The Case Against Foreign Investment," in Bela Balassa (ed.), *Changing Patterns in Foreign Trade and Payments* (New York: W. W. Norton, 1964), p. 54.

71. PP Beacon, V, 226–27.

72. Graham, p. 54.

73. Stabilization of the defense budget had of course been an increasing concern of the Eisenhower administration after 1957. His Treasury

Secretary, Robert B. Anderson, wrote in 1960: "... as a great power with far-flung responsibilities and with world-wide financial and economic interests, both public and private, the United States to a surprising extent must depend on a reasonable equilibrium in its balance of payments to carry out its responsibilities and to accomplish its political and economic aims. We make military expenditures abroad, we carry on private investment in foreign countries, and we extend grants and loans with public funds, not as a matter of chance and relative indifference but because these activities are important to us and to the rest of the free world. We can carry out these activities on a large and continuing scale only if we have a reasonable equilibrium in our balance of payments" (*Foreign Affairs*, April 1960, p. 425). Kennedy's successful electoral campaign to increase *domestic* defense spending, in response to the mythical "missile gap" that was created for him in large part by a cooperative intelligence community, did not reflect any dissent on this need to stabilize the U.S. balance of payments.

74. Russell H. Fifield, *Southeast Asia in United States Policy* (New York: Praeger, for the Council on Foreign Relations, 1965), p. 265.

75. First National City Bank of New York, *Monthly Letter*, June 1961, p. 67.

76. Graham, p. 52.

77. Philip W. Bell, *Private Capital Movement and the U.S. Balance-of-Payments Position,* Study Paper prepared for the U.S. Congress, Joint Economic Committee, 87th Congress, 2nd Session, Joint Committee Print, *Factors Affecting the United States Balance of Payments*, Part 6 (Washington: G.P.O., 1962), p. 466.

78. *Business Week,* January 24, 1970, p. 48. The study was prepared by Herbert K. May on behalf of the Council for Latin America.

79. U.S. Department of Commerce, *Statistical Abstract of the United States, passim.* These profit figures are of course swollen by the grotesque earnings on Middle East petroleum: in the one year of 1969, for example, Middle East petroleum showed interest, dividends, and branch earnings of $1181 million against a total book value of only $1805 million. For the Far East alone the net balance runs slightly in Asia's favor: $1684 million in profits against $2392 million in new investment. But the Vietnam War has been explicitly fought in defense of a global U.S. system; and the recent rapid development of petroleum reserves in the Far East, which has accompanied the war, has clearly strengthened the bargaining hand of the U.S. oil companies against the demands of Middle Eastern nations for a bigger share of profits.

80. U.S. Dept. of Commerce, *Survey of Current Business* (October 1969), p. 28.

81. U.S. Dept. of Commerce, *U.S. Business Investments in Foreign Countries* (Washington: G.P.O., 1960), p. 144.

82. The Chase Manhattan Bank, *Balance of Payments for the Pe-*

troleum Industry (New York, October 1966), p. 14; quoted in Michael Tanzer, *The Political Economy of International Oil and the Underdeveloped Countries,* p. 47.

83. Details in David Wise and Thomas B. Ross, *The Invisible Government* (New York: Bantam Books, 1965), pp. 116–21; Tanzer, pp. 357–66.

84. An article by C. L. Sulzberger on the editorial page of *The New York Times* (November 28, 1960, p. 30) perceived the same choice, even while preferring security to profits: "We must enact new laws to make American investments in these countries distinctively less attractive. Our outmoded tax system still induces U.S. firms to fabricate goods in branches overseas which are then sold at cheaper prices in world markets. The corporate owners make profits in the end. And Uncle Sam loses exports. This is the real problem. It won't be settled by pulling home soldiers' wives or, for that matter, soldiers."

85. *NYT,* October 20, 1963, p. 66.

86. Julius Epstein, "President Kennedy, Détente, and the Rapacki Plan," *Central Europe Journal* (February 1970), reprinted in *Congressional Record,* March 10, 1970, p. 6772.

87. *NYT,* November 19, 1963, p. 11.

88. *Business Week,* November 23, 1963, p. 41; for further discussion, cf. Scott, PP Beacon, V, 227, 238.

89. Ralph Lapp, *The Weapons Culture* (Baltimore: Penguin Books, 1969), pp. 38, 55.

90. Pentagon Study V.B. 4, p. 461; J. K. Galbraith, *Ambassador's Journal: A Personal Account of the Kennedy Years* (Boston: Houghton Mifflin, 1969), pp. 340–44.

91. Galbraith, *Ambassador's Journal,* pp. 537–538.

92. *NYT,* December 8, 1963, IV, 8. The editorial proposed specifically that the U.S. accept a proposal by Prince Sihanouk (with French backing) for a conference (like that on Laos) to achieve the neutralization of Cambodia. Later the Soviet Union and China both accepted the proposal for a Cambodian conference, but the Johnson administration, rightly fearing that it might lead to a discussion of Vietnamese neutralization as well, never did. Nevertheless the idea of a Cambodian conference did not die finally until the U.S. bombings of 1965.

93. Far Eastern Economic Review, *Yearbook 1961,* p. 24.

94. Bernard Fall, *The Two Viet Nams* (New York: Praeger, 1964), p. 397.

95. Speech of March 26, 1964 by R. S. McNamara, U.S. Dept. of State, *Bulletin,* April 13, 1964, p. 568.

96. Cooper, *The Lost Crusade,* pp. 215–16. William Sullivan of Harriman's staff who accompanied the McNamara–Taylor mission also registered a "strong dissent" (Schlesinger, p. 996).

97. *Washington Daily News* (Richard Starnes), October 2, 1963.

Earlier the *Washington Post* had charged that "In Saigon the CIA . . . was unable to provide a detached intelligence corrective because its own agents were enmeshed in the regime" (September 10, 1963). The *Washington Star* had referred to "incredible and garish blunders committed in a sickening sequence by the CIA" (September 23, 1963). James Reston reported that McCone "has convinced himself that there is a conspiracy inside the government and in the press to destroy his Agency" (*NYT*, October 8, 1963).

98. *Congressional Record*, September 20, 1963, pp. 17595–96. Mansfield's remarks were supported by Republican senators Carlson and Kuchel.

99. *Washington Post*, November 21, 1963, A19; discussed in Scott, PP Beacon, V, 230.

100. Kennedy made this clear in his July 18, 1963, Message to Congress on the United States Balance of Payments: "improving this nation's over-all long-range economic performance . . . is the key to . . . reducing our capital outflows" (*NYT*, July 19, 1963, p. 30; reprinted in Balassa, p. 166). Kennedy explicitly rejected direct capital controls to limit direct U.S. investment abroad: "The initiation of direct capital controls, which are in use in most countries, is inappropriate to our circumstances. It is contrary to our basic concept of free markets. We cannot take this route" (Balassa, p. 173).

101. *NYT*, November 15, 1963, pp. 1, 47.

102. *NYT*, November 29, 1963, p. 59.

103. *NYT*, July 20, 1963, p. 23; January 6, 1964, p. 119; January 13, 1964, p. 42; July 1, 1964, p. 45. Cf. the CFR historian (Stebbins, *The United States in World Affairs, 1963*, p. 35): "This expedient appealed neither to the American financial community nor to prospective foreign borrowers in the U.S. capital market. It was particularly alarming to Canada, which was granted a partial exemption in view of its heavy dependence on U.S. capital, and to Japan."

104. *NYT*, February 11, 1965, p. 57.

105. William Henderson, "Some Reflections on United States Policy in Southeast Asia," in William Henderson (ed.), *Southeast Asia: Problems of United States Policy* (Cambridge, Mass.: M.I.T. Press, 1963), pp. 253–54; emphasis added.

106. Henderson, p. x. Of the thirteen contributors at least half had intelligence backgrounds, two (Henderson and Frank Trager) were veteran excom members of the American Friends of Vietnam lobby, and six participated in a Council on Foreign Relations Southeast Asia project published in the same year. Cf. Fifield, *Southeast Asia in United States Policy*, p. ix: the six were Russell Fifield, William Henderson, Colonel Amos Jordan, Paul M. A. Linebarger, Frank Trager, and Charles Wolf, Jr.

107. Kenneth T. Young, Jr., *The Southeast Asia Crisis: Law, Power*

and Policy in Search for Regional Order (New York: Association of the Bar of the City of New York, Eighth Hammarskjold Forum, 1965), p. 122: "The outcome in Vietnam is directly linked to the region as a whole and cannot be treated separately, even though Vietnam has become the arena of decision. The resolution of conflict and new approaches to regional order will require a skillful meshing of political and military actions and the use of diplomacy and force in tandem. Military containment alone is not enough. Only a mixture of political, social, economic and defensive measures, particularly in Vietnam, can give us any hope for some stabilization. Vietnam is the crux of this challenge and the keystone for peace or war."

108. Known fronts for U.S. intelligence operations include oil companies, insurance companies, airlines, and hotels.

109. Scott, *The War Conspiracy*, pp. 196–97. I have since read that Wolf negotiated the financial arrangements for U.S. subsidy of the German espionage apparatus headed by Reinhard Gehlen, whose agents operated also in Taiwan and Japan (E. H. Cookridge, *Gehlen: Spy of the Century*, New York: Random House, 1971, p. 135).

110. The first OSS contacts with Ho Chi Minh were established in early 1945 by Major Austin Glass, a former Socony official. He was followed by an OSS "official of the Chase Manhattan Bank" (Smith, *OSS*, pp. 326, 330).

111. C. V. Starr's insurance firm was used as a front to put China lobbyists like Freda Utley on the OSS payroll, and had close links through Washington lawyer Tommy Corcoran with the CIA as well (Freda Utley, *Odyssey of a Liberal: Memoirs*, Washington: Washington National Press, 1970, p. 298; Scott, *The War Conspiracy*, xvii–xix, 209–10).

112. Sterling Products International, Merck, Sharp and Dohme, Pfizer Corp., American Trading Co., Brownell, Lane International. Cf. U.S. Cong., Senate, Committee on Government Operations, *Improper Practices, Commodity Import Program, U.S. Foreign Aid, Vietnam, Hearings*, 90th Congress, 1st Session (August 1, 1967), pp. 315–20; Hamilton-Paterson, *The Greedy War*, p. 266. Pfizer named as director J. Lawton Collins, former U.S. Ambassador in Vietnam, 1954–1955.

113. Manufacturers Trust, Chase Manhattan Bank, First National City Bank of New York. Tristan Beplat, vice-president of Manufacturers Trust and a trustee of Rockefeller's Japan Society, attended the 1958 conference; in 1969 he was called by a Congressional Committee to explain how one single account in his International Division ("Prysumeen") had been allowed to handle over $51 million in lateral transfers for Vietnam black market operations. His fellow vice-president Peter White also attended; by 1968 he was president of a Swiss–Lebanese-owned bank (Republic National Bank of New York) with $72 million in deposits. Just one of this bank's accounts handled $43 million of

black-market deposits in 1968 (*Illegal Currency Manipulations, Hearings*, pp. 612, 645).

114. Henderson, p. 263.

115. For more discussion see Scott, PP Beacon, V, 215–16; 228–30.

116. PP Beacon, III, 18; cf. II, 276, III, 304, Cooper, p. 224; discussion in Scott, PP Beacon, V, 224–25.

117. Address by President Johnson, Johns Hopkins University, April 7, 1965, in U.S. Department of State, *Bulletin*, April 26, 1965, pp. 606–10.

118. "Economic Considerations in Foreign Relations—An Interview with Alfred Wentworth," *Political*, I, 1 (July 1965), pp. 45–46; quoted in Magdoff, p. 176.

119. *International Executive*, Fall 1964, p. 16; reviewing Wilbert E. Moore *et al., Corporate Planning Today for Tomorrow's World Market* (New York: Business International, 1964).

120. Chase Manhattan Bank, *World Business*, September 1966, p. 14. *World Business* itself, like the two journals from 1965 just cited, may have been a by-product of the new vision. Its first issue was in July 1966, replacing the Chase Manhattan's former regional newsletters for Europe and Latin America.

121. International Monetary Fund, *Direction of Trade* (March 1970), pp. 87–88, cited in Michael T. Klare, *War Without End* (New York: Knopf, 1972), p. 316; *Business Week*, December 6, 1969, p. 206.

122. *Business Week*, December 6, 1969, p. 67.

123. Klare, p. 317; Scott, *War Conspiracy*, pp. 154–56. In 1972 Rockefeller's senior oil specialist, John Winger, predicted that oil investments in the Far East between 1970 and 1985 would reach $65 billion, and that much of this new capital would be raised outside the industry (*San Francisco Chronicle*, June 15, 1972, p. 58).

124. Charles J. V. Murphy, "The Defense Industry Is Facing Trouble," *Fortune* (August 1964), p. 141: "The great buy in the strategic nuclear systems—the investment that profoundly changed the character of the defense business—seems to have come to an end."

125. The investment outflow, under $700 million in the third quarter of 1963, had risen steadily to over $2200 million in the last quarter of 1964 (First National City Bank of New York, *Monthly Economic Letter*, February 1966, p. 21). Capital outflows in all of 1964, according to a Commerce Department Report, were up more than $2 billion from 1963 (*NYT*, February 11, 1965, p. 57).

126. Richard P. Stebbins, for Council on Foreign Relations, *The United States in World Affairs 1965*, p. 20. It is often suggested that France's exchanges of dollars for U.S. gold had to do with de Gaulle's opposition to U.S. policy in Vietnam.

127. *NYT*, February 11, 1965, p. 1; Stebbins, p. 22.

128. *NYT*, February 11, 1965, p. 57.

129. Committee for Economic Development, *The Dollar and the World Monetary System,* December 1966, p. 19; cf. p. 48: "A policy of restricting private capital outflow may have had some temporary benefits for the balance of payments but at substantial cost to our future payments position. For private capital transactions, notably United States direct investment, make an indispensable contribution to the plus side of our international ledger through the income they earn and the exports they induce. Freedom of capital movement not only maximizes our foreign exchange earnings but helps speed world economic development." This was also the position of *Business International,* whose editor Elliot Haynes had written in 1961: "The meaning to the U.S. balance of payments is clear. If we wish to remain a viable nation, we must help, not hinder, manufacturers to become world corporations . . . proposals to restrict investment in Europe represent a threat to the national interest" (Balassa, p. 62). For a critique of these claims, see Benjamin Graham, in Balassa, pp. 45–55; Philip Bell, *passim.*

130. Cf. Rudolph Peterson, Bank of America president, Thomas S. Gates, Morgan Guaranty Trust president; *NYT,* January 31, 1965, III, 7; February 11, 1965, p. 57.

131. U.S. Congress, Committee on Judiciary, *Anti-Trust Exemptions —Balance of Payments, Hearings,* 89th Congress, 1st Session (Washington: G.P.O., 1965), pp. 6, 49, 98 (henceforth cited as Balance of Payments Hearings).

132. *NYT,* February 11, 1965, p. 57.

133. *NYT,* January 26, 1965, p. 49, Balance of Payments Hearings, p. 127.

134. Federal Reserve Bank of New York, *Monthly Review* (May 1963), pp. 71–73.

135. Federal Reserve Bank of New York, *Monthly Review* (February 1965), pp. 19–21.

136. Eliot Janeway, *The Economics of Crisis* (New York: Weybright and Talley, 1968), pp. 294–95.

137. Janeway, pp. 280, 300–01. Janeway attributes this loss of control to the surprising decision of Donald Cook to refuse the Treasury Secretaryship where he might have exercised restraints on McNamara's budget requests. For other bleak estimates by bankers of the war's impact on the economy see U.S. Cong., Senate, Committee on Foreign Relations, *Impact of the War in Southeast Asia on the U.S. Economy, Hearings* (91st Congress, 2nd Session), April 15–16, 1970.

138. *NYT,* September 9, 1965, p. 30, emphasis added. The Committee gave as its address that of the law firm, Sullivan and Cromwell, of its chairman Arthur H. Dean. Other prominent members of Sullivan and Cromwell have of course included CIA Director Allen Dulles and Secretary of State John Foster Dulles.

139. Hoopes, p. 207. Lyndon Johnson tells us that before the July

28, 1965, escalation he held a meeting with "Rusk, McNamara, Ball, General Wheeler, Bundy, and several civilian advisers, including Clark Clifford, John McCloy, and Arthur Dean." Clifford at least was as "pessimistic" in 1965 as he was later in 1968: " 'I don't believe we can win in South Vietnam,' he said. 'If we send in 100,000 more men, the North Vietnamese will meet us. If North Vietnam runs out of men, the Chinese will send in volunteers' " (Johnson, *The Vantage Point*, p. 148). As Chairman of the Foreign Intelligence Advisory Board (the CIA's civilian "watchdog"), Clifford sat in on NSC meetings. Morton Halperin, then in the Pentagon, informs me that the Senior Advisory Group, as such, met with Johnson only twice: in July 1965 and in March 1968.

140. Dower, PP Beacon, V, 121. I agree with Dower that the war evolved in response to a cooling economy rather than to an expanding one. Elsewhere in this book Richard de Camp, speaking of Johnson's pivotal speech of April 7, 1965, claims that "Japan, meanwhile, was registering spectacular increases in trade with Southeast Asia and preparing the way for massive foreign investment" (p. 74). U.N. Statistical Yearbooks show that Japanese exports to Southeast Asia, like the Japanese economy, increased in the period 1964–1965, as in all other years between 1961 and 1968. But the Japanese economy was expanding more slowly in 1964–1965, and the percentage of Japanese exports to Southeast Asia was dropping steadily, from 14.9 percent in 1961 to a low of 10.8 percent in 1965 (when the trend was reversed).

141. Far Eastern Economic Review, *Yearbook 1972*, p. 40: "The strength of the Japanese economy has been the main factor in pulling the region together and providing the shadowy outlines of a future "coprosperity sphere. . . . Japanese economists have projected that by the end of the 1970s Japan might account for almost half of the rest of Asia's import."

142. Department of Commerce, *Statistical Abstract of the United States, 1972*, p. 764.

143. American Bankers Association, Department of Economic Research, *The Cost of World Leadership: An Analysis of the United States Balance-of-Payments Problem,* New York, 1968, pp. 12, 291, emphasis in original.

144. Smith, *OSS*, p. 381. McCoy was recruited by Tom Finney, another ex-CIA McCarthy worker, who was a member of Clark Clifford's law firm and campaigned for Johnson in 1964.

145. *Washington Post*, January 11, 1972, A15; quoted in Walt Haney, "The Pentagon Papers and United States Involvement in Laos," PP Beacon, V, 293. Haney also cites Senator Javits' description of the Laos conflict as "one war that is a success" and Senator Symington's question, "Why do we publish our military failures . . . in Vietnam, but do not tell the people about our successes in Laos?" McCoy in his

letter conceded that the decision to intervene in Laos "was wrong, just as I think almost every other decision with regard to our involvement in Indochina has been and continues to be wrong." But he predicted that "a long hard look at the CIA operation with the Meo" would produce "general approval."

146. For discussion see Brodine and Selden, *Open Secret;* Michael T. Klare, *War Without End* (New York: Knopf, 1972).

147. For this view, read Michael Hudson, *Super Imperialism* (New York: Holt, Rinehart, and Winston, 1973).

PART II

THE PHILIPPINES:
A Case History of Neocolonialism*

WILLIAM J. POMEROY

I

As the only country in Asia that has been an American colony, the Philippines provides a unique portrait of the aims and policies of American imperialism in that vast region. Seizure of the Philippines from Spain in 1898 was proclaimed by the frank exponents of an imperialist policy who then commanded the levers of foreign affairs as the acquisition of a base from which to capture a large share in the great China market, whose sheer size fascinated the expanding manufacturing and commercial interests in the United States. Only to a far lesser extent were the market and raw material advantages of a Philippine colony itself appreciated; these evolved slowly after American possession became a fact.

Throughout the forty-eight years of American colonial rule in the Philippines, the problems and contradictions that flowed from this territorial venture were never fully resolved. For one thing, China market hopes did not materialize significantly. This was not due to any withering of the American expansionist drive but to two interconnected realities: rival imperialist powers, especially Japan, were able to thwart American ambitions, while the increasing American export of manufactured goods and capital went instead to other, less disputed areas in Canada,

---

* This essay was completed prior to the Marcos coup in the Philippines.

Latin America, and Europe. In the overall pattern of world power, the Philippines remained as more of an outpost than a cornerstone of empire.

Secondly, possession of the island colony proved to be a major cause of dissension in American society itself. The "anti-imperialists," who opposed colonial possessions on strategic, tactical, moral, and constitutional grounds, were highly vocal; but the really influential opposition came from domestic agricultural producers of sugar beets, sugar cane, tobacco, and dairy and other products who were concerned that the main Philippine products would be serious competition if allowed the free entry to the United States that territorial possession implied. This domestic opposition, augmented by pressures from American investors in Cuban and Puerto Rican sugar, caused significant limitations to be placed on exploitation of the Philippine colony.

From early in the American occupation, rivalry with Japan made the Philippines a sensitive subject of U.S. diplomacy. The Taft-Katsura agreement of 1905 and the Root-Takahira agreement of 1908 stemmed from the United States' fear that a rising Japan might move south and seize the Philippines: Japanese dominance in Korea and Southern Manchuria were recognized in exchange for a pledge to recognize American control of the Philippines.

After long dispute in U.S. military circles, it was concluded by 1908 that major forward naval and other military bases should not be constructed in the islands because they could not be defended due both to distance from the continental United States and to a lack of support base structure in Asia. Accompanying this controversy, bills were introduced in the U.S. Congress from 1906 for neutralization of the Philippines by "an agreement between the United States and the great nations of Europe and Asia."[1] In its election platforms of 1908 and 1912 the Democratic party put forward the idea of neutralization—i.e., after U.S. withdrawal a hands-off agreement among the colonial powers in regard to occupation or use of the Philippines as a base—an idea that continued to rise in the minds of American policy-makers right up to the adoption of the Tydings-McDuffie Independence Act of 1934. This act contained a provision urging international negotiations for "perpetual neutralization of the Philippine Islands" after independence.

One of the factors behind the Tydings-McDuffie Act was

heightening Japanese aggression in Asia, which American military planners felt could be met with no more than a holding action in the Philippines. Independence for the colony, it was believed, along with neutralization, might reduce it as a target of conquest for the rival Japanese imperialism.

If this problem of retaining a colony made it at times appear a liability, controversy over its exploitation undermined its retention even further. The nature and extent of American investment were curtailed by the opposition of U.S. domestic producers, whose influence caused the basic legislative act of American rule (the Organic Act of 1902) to rebuff the more aggressive imperialists who advocated corporate ownership of Philippine lands of up to 60,000 hectares. The act limited disposition of Philippine public lands to 144 hectares for individuals and 1024 hectares for corporations, thus inhibiting development of a foreign-owned plantation system such as emerged in Indonesia, Malaya, and Indochina.

These American domestic agricultural groups, which favored aggressive expansion of an overseas market in developed countries for U.S. agricultural products but which fought for protection from foreign competition at home, had much to do with shaping the evolution of the Philippines. They hampered the setting up and operation in the islands of agricultural banks, fought against free trade that would enable Philippine products to enter the United States preferentially and, when free trade was enacted in principle, initially compelled the imposition of quotas on the main Philippine exports to the United States (sugar, coconut products, and tobacco). When the Great Depression of the 1930s severely hit the American economy, including its agriculture, the U.S. domestic agrarian producers threw their full weight behind an independence act and constituted the decisive influence in its passage. The Tydings-McDuffie Act, under their influence, provided for the gradual phasing out of free trade between 1940 and 1946 and for its full termination upon independence.

On two major counts, military bases and investment advantages, the U.S. arrangements for independence tended to downgrade Philippine importance.

The United States was prepared to give up most military bases in the islands. The first piece of legislation for independence adopted by the U.S. Congress, the Hare-Hawes-Cutting Act of

1933, did contain a provision for the permanent retention of military bases. It was rejected by the Philippines due to a power fight between the two leading Filipino politicians, Sergio Osmeña and Manuel Quezon y Molina. Osmeña had negotiated the Hare-Hawes-Cutting Act; Quezon used the military bases provision to defeat it on grounds of infringement of Philippine sovereignty. The Tydings-McDuffie Act, which Quezon then negotiated in one-upmanship fashion, changed the bases provision, its Section 10 (a) declaring that

> the President of the United States shall by proclamation withdraw and surrender all rights of possession, supervision, jurisdiction, control, or sovereignty then existing and exercised by the United States in and over the territory and people of the Philippine Islands, including all military and other reservations of the Government of the United States in the Philippines (except such naval reservations and fueling stations as are reserved under Section 5).

(The latter were impliedly minor.)

Furthermore, the constitution of the Philippines adopted in 1935 in accordance with the Tydings-McDuffie Act curtailed future U.S. economic exploitation. Its Article XIII, Section 1, states:

> All agricultural, timber, and mineral lands of the public domain, waters, minerals, coal, petroleum and other mineral oils, all forces of potential energy, and other natural resources of the Philippines belong to the State, and their disposition, exploitation, development or utilization *shall be limited to citizens of the Philippines, or to corporations or associations at least sixty per centum of the capital of which is owned by such citizens,* subject to any existing right, grant, lease, or concession at the time of the inauguration of the Government established under this Constitution. [Italics by the author.]

In other words, American corporations were to be limited to a maximum of only forty percent share in future investments, although wholly owned mining, public utilities, and other exploitation of natural resources had up to then absorbed the main American investments.

As independence approached, set, prior to World War II, for July 4, 1946, some American firms even began to liquidate their interests. In the middle of 1941 the Pacific Commercial Company, one of the oldest and largest American companies in the islands, with extensive import–export operations and with hold-ings in transportation and sugar milling, was liquidated, a step interpreted by some in the American community in Manila as the "handwriting on the wall."[2] Trepidation about the long-term prospects for American interests took another form in an attempted "reexaminationist" move toward the whole idea of independence on the part of some American and Filipino *com-prador* interests from 1939 onwards, one of the chief spokesmen being U.S. High Commissioner Paul V. McNutt.

American interests, at the outbreak of World War II, had direct investments of around $268 million, which amounted to about one-half of all foreign investments in the Philippines. Chinese investments of around $268 million, which amounted to about followed by Japanese ($50 million), Spanish ($35 million), and British (nearly $30 million). The bulk of Filipino capital was of the *comprador* variety, tied in with foreign investment and trade activities and located in the extraction, planting and processing operations that served them: e.g., sugar and coconut industries alone absorbed about $350 million of Filipino capital, while barely $60 million was scattered in very small manufacturing enterprises. The United States in the 1936–1940 period ac-counted for 72.6 percent of Philippine trade, Japan in second place taking only 7.9 percent. After forty-two years of colonial rule, the United States held the dominant position in an unde-veloped, unbalanced, colonial-style Philippine economy.[3]

II

World War II radically altered the position of the United States in Asia. The elimination for the time being of a Japanese rival and the weakening of British, French, and Dutch imperialisms, coupled with the enormous military and economic power that the victorious war effort had given to the United States, left the Pacific literally as "an American lake," and revived the imperial-ist thrust into Asia that had been pressed and then blunted at the beginning of the century.

These renewed ambitions forced heavy modifications upon the original design of Philippine independence. For the ebullient policy-makers of American dominance, the Philippines had ac-quired a heightened significance, both as a secure established base for an expansionist drive in all Asia and as a market for the overflow of the vast production machine and capital accumulation that the war had fostered. It was not feasible, however, to reverse the independent course that had been set for the Philippines without generating strong Filipino nationalist sentiments. Filipino expectations that the United States would keep its word had been increased by a national liberation struggle against Japanese occupation. Therefore, a series of American measures was prepared and pushed through to secure full American control of the independent Philippines.

A key measure toward guaranteeing this was the passage by the U.S. Congress of the Philippine Trade Act of 1946, known as the Bell Act, signed barely two months prior to the July 4 independence date. Its basic aim was to revive and continue the free trade arrangement that was to have terminated at independence: duty-free trade between the two countries was to last for eight years, until 1954 (except that U.S. domestic interests again compelled the imposition of quotas on Philippine products entering the United States), and the gradual imposition of mutual tariffs was to be stretched over the following twenty years until 1974. Thus, for its first twenty-eight years of independence, the Philippines was to be tied to the old colonial trade pattern of being a supplier of raw agricultural products and mineral ores to the United States in exchange for U.S. manufactured goods, with possible independent industrial development frustrated.

Other provisions of the Bell Act made this pattern rigid and deepened the frustration immeasurably. Most onerous was the so-called "parity" provision that made it obligatory for the Philippines to grant American citizens and corporations equal rights with Filipinos in the exploitation of Philippine natural resources. The pertinent Section 19 read:

> Notwithstanding any existing provision of the constitution and statutes of the Philippine government, citizens and corporations of the United States shall enjoy in the Philippine Islands during the period of the validity of this Act, or any extension thereof by statute or treaty, the same rights as to property, residence, and occupation as citizens of the Philippine Islands. Such rights shall include rights to acquire land of the public domain, to acquire grazing, fishing and mineral rights, and to engage in the ownership and operation of public utilities. . . .

For "parity" to be made law, the Philippines was obliged to amend the Constitution of 1935 which provided for a sixty percent share in all corporations to be held in Filipino hands, a provision that had never had a chance of implementation. This alteration was literally imposed upon the newly independent Philippines: a provision in the Rehabilitation Act that was passed in the U.S. Congress and signed into law at the same time as the Trade Act, designed to pay war damages to the devastated Philippines, made all payments in excess of $500 conditional upon acceptance of the Bell Act and of "parity." A war-stricken population was thus coerced into agreeing to continued American domination of its economy.

On American insistence, the Bell Act had to be approved by the Philippine Congress before the day of handing over independence. Congressional agreement, particularly in regard to the "parity" amendment of the Constitution, required, however, a three-fourths majority vote and then a national plebiscite for the amendment. An outstanding Filipino nationalist, Senator Claro M. Recto, later described how the majority was obtained:

> It will be recalled that the Parity Amendment was not adopted by our Congress in 1946 without a truly heroic resistance on the part of those who were bent upon rejecting the Trade Agreement and Parity... Actually the parity amendment resolution obtained an affirmative vote of only 68 representatives and 16 senators. Because the expected affirmative vote would not reach the required minimum (72 representatives and 18 senators), it became necessary, for the passage of the parity amendment resolution, to oust eight (8) Coalition Minority representatives and three (3) Coalition Minority senators for alleged frauds and terrorism in certain provinces of Central Luzon. Only in this shameful manner was the required number of votes secured to amend the Constitution.[4]

Ouster of the representatives, who were all elected from the Central Luzon provinces mainly by the votes of Communist-led mass peasant organizations, set the new nation on a path of ruthless suppression of popular dissent, and was a primary cause of the armed struggle that broke out in this region a few months later, generally known as the Huk Rebellion. The Bell Act and "parity" thus had a disastrous effect on Philippine democratic hopes as well as on hopes for economic development.

Three days after the "parity" plebiscite, held on March 11,

1947, the Philippines signed a Military Bases Agreement with the United States. Although the United States had prepared the way for this during World War II with a Joint Resolution of Congress on June 29, 1944, for obtaining military bases in the independent Philippines (the course of the war by that time was revealing the postwar power pattern in Asia), the step was not pushed through in treaty form until American economic interests in the Philippines had been secured.

The Military Bases Agreement gave the United States twenty-three base sites in the Philippines, sixteen of them active and seven held in reserve. In addition, the Philippines agreed "to enter into negotiations with the United States at the latter's request, to permit the United States to expand such bases, to exchange such bases for other bases, to acquire additional bases, or to relinquish rights to bases, as any of such exigencies may be required by military necessity."[5] Among the sixteen active bases were the huge air base complex at Clark Field, Pampanga, and the enormous U.S. Seventh Fleet base in the Subic Bay–Olongapo area, Zambales.[6]

On March 21, 1947, the bases agreement was complemented by a Military Assistance Agreement. This provided for furnishing U.S. arms, ammunition, and supplies for all Philippine armed forces, the training of Philippine military personnel (particularly officers to be trained in the United States), and the stationing in the Philippines of a Joint U.S. Military Advisory Group (JUSMAG) drawn from all branches of the service "to assist and advise the Republic of the Philippines on military and naval matters."

The twenty-three military base sites were provided to the United States on a ninety-nine-year lease, renewable on expiration. The Philippine public land laws, constitutionally defined, permit lease periods of only twenty-five years, but no amendment of these was made to accommodate the bases. In 1954 the then U.S. Attorney General, Herbert Brownell, Jr., made a legal claim of U.S. proprietory rights over the bases—i.e., U.S. sovereignty over large areas of the Philippines. The Brownell opinion provoked protest from nationalists in both major Filipino ruling parties, leading to a dropping of the claim and to an agreement in 1958 for reduction of the lease period from ninety-nine to twenty-five years. This, however, was an agreement only at ambassadorial level; it was not until 1966 that the Johnson administration, as part of maneuverings to obtain a Philippine contingent to participate in U.S. operations in Vietnam, ratified the twenty-five-year lease period. Since the reduced time did not include the nineteen years the United States had already held the bases, this actually meant a forty-four-year retention all told, eight of them gained by stalling on lease reduction.

Under the Military Bases Agreement the American military authorities have jurisdiction within the bases over all offenses or crimes committed by American personnel. Eventually this became a major source of protest from Filipinos, due to the innumerable cases of Filipinos being shot or abused by American troops who could not be tried in Philippine courts. By the end of 1971 at least thirty-seven Filipinos had been killed as "trespassers" on U.S. bases. American troops committing crimes both on and off the bases have been transferred out of the Philippines to place them beyond the reach of the Republic's courts. Despite the many and prolonged demands for renegotiation of the bases agreement to remove this cause of irritation, the United States has dragged its feet on such a step.

As for the Military Assistance Agreement, its effect was summarized in April 1967 by Filipino Congressman Carmelo Barbero, chairman of the Committee on National Defense in the Philippine House of Representatives:

> In the final analysis, JUSMAG controls our armed forces. If the organization of our armed forces is determined by foreigners, the political decisions based on our military capabilities are, in effect, determined by foreigners. It's the Americans who control our armed forces and their JUSMAG may be expected to predicate decisions on what is best for their country.[7]

U.S. military bases, as part of the complex of American bases in Asia, have acted as a strong factor in aligning the Philippines with U.S. Cold War policies. They provided the basis for two other treaties that followed: a Mutual Defense Treaty signed on August 30, 1951, pledging the Philippines to recognize that "an armed attack *in the Pacific area* on *either* of the Parties would be dangerous to its own peace and safety," and the Southeast Asia Treaty Organization (SEATO) Collective Defense Treaty, signed in Manila on September 8, 1954, Article IV of which states that "each Party recognizes that aggression by means of armed attack in the treaty area against any of the Parties or *against any State or territory which the Parties by unanimous agreement may here-after designate,* would endanger its own peace and safety." Article II of the SEATO treaty provides that the parties "separately and jointly" will act "to prevent and counter *subversive activities directed from without* against their political integrity and political stability." (All italics by the author.)

Philippine foreign affairs, as a consequence of a set of treaties drawn up to serve American aims in Asia, became predicated on the narrowest possible form of anti-Communism, on opposition to national liberation movements, and on isolation from non-alignment or "Third World" trends among countries similar to it in development needs. Neutralism and even nationalism in the Philippines in the 1940s and 1950s were equated with Communism. Pursuing a Cold War attitude "more Popish than the Pope" (as Filipino nationalists have termed it), the Philippines, in striving to please its American advisers and investors, from 1946 to the end of 1971 formed no diplomatic, trade, or cultural relations with any socialist country. (A trend toward such relations began in 1965 and received official endorsement at the start of 1972, for proposed implementation within two years, that is, by the end of the 1946 Trade Act. In part this is in comformity with U.S. foreign policy changes, in part it is due to pressure from both traditional and new Filipino export interests seeking diversified markets.)

In Asia, the treaty obligations of the Philippines have repeatedly involved it in aggressive American adventures against Asian peoples: a Philippine battalion was sent at U.S. insistence to Korea in 1950–1953 and suffered heavy casualties; a Philippine battalion and other counterinsurgency units were sent to Vietnam, Laos, and Cambodia (paid for, mercenary fashion, by the United States) ; American planes and naval vessels have operated from their Philippine bases against Vietnam; American planes connected with the CIA raided Indonesia from Philippine bases in 1958 to aid a "colonel's revolt" against the Sukarno government.

In the Republic's domestic affairs, the Philippine armed forces, directed by the JUSMAG under the Military Assistance Agreement, have been organized, equipped, and trained entirely as a counterinsurgency establishment, for the internal suppression of popular unrest. With its heavy U.S.-supplied anti-Communist indoctrination, the Philippine military organization naturally has played an extreme reactionary role in the country's politics.

It was the JUSMAG-directed Philippine army legal office that formulated the charge, not contained in Philippine laws or statutes, of "rebellion complexed with murder, arson, robbery, and kidnaping" and used it to imprison thousands of supporters of the Huk movement in the 1950s for excessively long terms, intervening to prevent the Supreme Court from acting on cases appealed for twenty years. JUSMAG advisers drew up and pushed through Congress in 1957 the Anti-Subversion Law, which formally outlawed the Communist party and "all similar organizations," with penalties up to the death sentence provided for membership. A constant threat of military intervention in political affairs to insure pro-American governments is illustrated by the election of Ramon Magsaysay to the presidency in 1953. Magsaysay was handpicked by the JUSMAG and the CIA as a compliant Secretary of National Defense and was boosted from this key post of control over the armed forces to the presidency.

Being tied to American military policy has had a disastrous effect on the nation's development. It has caused heavy arms expenditures for the type of military establishment recommended by the JUSMAG, consuming an overall average of fifteen percent of the Philippine budget since independence, and substantially more in some years. From 1946 to 1971 over six billion pesos was spent on the Philippine armed forces, to maintain an army of 54,000, plus 10,000 in the paramilitary national police force, the Philippine Constabulary (also under JUSMAG. This sum, vast by Philippine standards, has gravely detracted from economic development programs that could have gone infinitely further to remove basic internal causes of discontent.

The Republic of the Philippines, launched with these neo-colonial economic and military arrangements weighing it down in thoroughgoing dependency, has never really gotten off the ground. Over a quarter of a century later it is still as far as ever from reaching an independent course.

III

The relative ease with which the United States refashioned Philippine independence to fit its aims after World War II cannot be ascribed merely to the bullying and coercion of a ruthless imperialist power. Popular movements that opposed the neo-colonial agreements *were* brutally suppressed, but, of greater pertinence, there were willing Filipino groups that supported and acquiesced to the American demands and that have readily implemented the agreements.

There is, indeed, another side to the imperialist coin, without which colonial or neocolonial systems could not function: the collaboration of native ruling groups with the imperialist power. In the Philippines this tendency has had a long history, reaching far back into the Spanish colonial period that preceded American conquest.

The wealthy groups of Filipino large landowners, urban real-estate owners, and moneylenders supported the Spanish colonial regime and, during the revolutionary upsurge that developed in the Philippines in the latter part of the nineteenth century, either refused to support or opposed both the middle-class movement for reforms known as the "Propaganda Campaign" and the proletarian-based movement for revolutionary change and independence known as the Katipunan.

Middle-class demands in this period were merely for provincial status for the Philippines under Spain, for representation in the Spanish Cortes, and for political and social position in a colonial society in which the friars of the Spanish religious orders played the dominant role. It was not until the Katipunan raised the banner of revolt and independence in the Revolution of 1896 that the middle-class sectors swung to a revolutionary position, their ambitions aroused by the mass movement, and took control of the Katipunan. The wealthy Filipino groups opposed the Revolution of 1896 and did everything possible to press compromise and surrender upon the revolutionists.

The Spanish-American War of 1898, which brought U.S. defeat of the Spanish forces in the islands, first stimulated and then caused disaster to the Philippine revolution. In hopes of independence, a Philippine Republic was established and a semblance of national unity of all Filipino classes formed around it. The peasantry and working classes in general were solidly behind the revolution and the new Republic and expected that the confiscation and breaking up of the big Spanish feudal estates would follow. The middle-class and *ilustrado* (educated and propertied) elements took over the reins of government, including the army command, and looked toward landlord status, political careers, the professions, and commercial ventures. Even the wealthy landlord and moneylender aristocracy, which had adhered to Spanish rule to the last, shifted hastily to the new Philippine government set up in Malolos, Bulacan, in November 1898 in order to protect its interests.

Such unity was short-lived. When it became clear that the Americans intended to remain, to take possession of the colony from Spain, and to refuse to recognize the authority of a Philippine government, the wealthy Filipino landlords and aristocrats immediately abandoned the Republic, sought accommodation with the new foreign ruler, and actively supported the suppression and subjugation of their own people. A collaborationist Federalista party which they created set up local governments loyal to the Americans in territory conquered by the invading army and worked for the surrender and cooperation of those middle-class leaders who continued to resist.

In essential respects, Filipino class behavior in the rise and fall of the First Philippine Republic was a parallel of the events in the independent Philippines after 1946. The wealthy groups collaborated with American power without hesitation, the intermediate groups eventually struck a bargain and accommodated themselves with the new colonialism, and the poor peasants and workers resisted long and determinedly, conducting armed struggle for many years after the official termination of the Fil-American War in 1902.

U.S. colonial policy-makers like Jacob Schurman and William Howard Taft were shrewd enough to see that the middle-class revolutionaries could be won over to a great extent on the basis of the reformist demands that they had made of Spain. Without diminishing tight American control, the ambitions of the restive middle class were partially appeased by ending the role of the friars in political life and in extensive land ownership, and by staffing the colonial administrative system at all levels with Filipinos, with a minimum of American officials.

One of the enticements used to encourage submission was the promise to establish a National Assembly of elected Filipino representatives whose acts would be subject to the approval of the American-controlled Philippine Commission. In accepting this (it was embodied in the 1902 Organic Act), wealthy and middle-class Filipino groups agreed to the proviso laid down by

American authorities that political activity must be based on complete acceptance of American sovereignty and on peaceful participation in an indefinite period of "education for self-rule." The former middle-class revolutionaries thus agreed to foreswear all forms of struggle for independence except a peaceful parliamentary one with guidelines laid down by the colonial ruler. They shifted to the setting up of rival political parties and to the fight for position and patronage, a corrupting process that was to feature the entire period of American rule and to intensify following the neocolonial independence.

Within the first decade of American rule the class lines of collaboration had been drawn and were fully in operation. Wealthy Filipino landlord and *comprador* groups, first and foremost allies of American rule, were made the chief beneficiaries of colonial relations with the United States, profiting greatly from the preferential export of sugar, abaca, coconut products, and tobacco to the American market.

The Filipino middle class was also able to realize its ambitions to a great extent within the American colonial system, in which office-holding and attendant corruption were a path to enrichment. In its stunted and distorted form, this class played a reformist collaborationist role throughout American rule. The political party its leaders founded to win seats in the Assembly, the Nacionalista party, soon eliminated the Federalistas and related parties, but inevitably, by the relentless process of bourgeois power politics, it came under the control of the big land-lord–*comprador* groups; the fortunes of the middle class and its politicians as they evolved were linked in a subsidiary relationship with those of the producer-exporters and of the American investment interests.

In contrast, living conditions of Filipino peasants and workers scarcely changed. Statistics indicate that conditions actually worsened for the peasantry: in 1903 the rate of farm tenancy was nineteen percent but it was thirty-six percent by 1938.[8] Farm laborers were reported by the U.S. Census of 1903 as receiving fifty-five centavos a day; a 1940 survey revealed farm workers to be earning only fifty centavos a day.[9] The average daily wage of urban workers was forty to fifty cents in 1916; according to the Philippine Department of Labor in 1939 the average worker's daily wage was forty-five cents.[10]

A new wave of peasant organization and of trade unions came

into being at the end of the second decade of American rule as a consequence of mass impoverishment. These movements, which were climaxed in 1930 by the foundation of the Communist party of the Philippines, condemned the wealthy and governing Filipino groups as allies of American imperialism. When the Tydings-McDuffie Act was passed in 1934 it was denounced as a fraud by these left-wing nationalist forces, which asserted that it would change nothing and would leave the colonial relationship unaltered.

Involvement of the *ilustrados,* middle-class sectors in the system and mechanics of colonial rule, was one of the main methods by which the United States developed a collaborationist ruling class of Filipinos. The question of independence itself was predicated on "educating" these groups toward a "capacity for stable government"—i.e., one that would protect American interests and put down popular revolutionary forces.

Related to this aim, the American regime implanted a system of education that was most effective in developing a colonial mentality among Filipinos. The native Philippine languages and culture were literally purged from schools and media, and everything Filipino was by bald statement or inference made to seem inferior to the "superior" American political system, society, culture and way of life in general. A *pensionado* system of training government employees and technical personnel in universities in the United States augmented the devotion to "America." The colonial education system was the more effective by its contrasts with the restrictive education under the old Spanish regime, an effect shrewdly assessed by the early U.S. Philippine Commissions in working out their policies.[11]

More important and basic in the collaborationist process was the "free trade" arrangement devised for the Philippines. After much controversy, Philippine agricultural products were given preferential entry to the United States in 1909 (in a section of the Payne-Aldrich Tariff Act of that year). "Free trade" firmly tied the interests of the Filipino landlord—*comprador* groups to the American market and to perpetuation of American domination, and it smothered the possibility of an industrial manufacturing class arising in the Philippines to compete with American manufactured products, given free and unrestricted entry to the colony. A bourgeois nationalist movement in the Philippines was thus deprived of a real economic base.

By the time the Tydings-McDuffie Independence Act was passed in 1934 the development of a subservient Filipino ruling class was virtually complete, with the bulk of the Filipino ruling groups and the educated elite conditioned for collaboration.

World War II, far from stimulating national liberation tendencies from these groups as occurred in Indonesia, Burma, and elsewhere in Asia, actually augmented the collaborationist trend. The majority of Filipino politicians actively collaborated with the Japanese occupation and served in the puppet "Philippine Republic" and other governmental instruments set up by the Japanese. When the American army reconquered the Philippines in 1944–1945, its commander-in-chief, General Douglas MacArthur (who had been head of the combined American–Filipino armed forces in the Philippines from 1935 to 1941 and had an intimate association with Filipino ruling circles), and the "re-examinationist" Paul McNutt, who was restored to the post of High Commissioner in 1945, chose some of the leading collaborators to form a new political party, the Liberal party, and guided it undisguisedly to victory in the pre-independence day election that determined who would hold the reins of power in the new republic. The Liberal party President thus placed in power, Manuel Roxas, had been a cabinet member in the Japanese puppet government. Roxas and his associates were protected from prosecution by the People's Court set up to try collaboration cases, and their undoubted gratitude provided an ideal basis for their readiness to engineer approval of the neocolonial agreements pressed upon them by the United States.

IV

In 1946 the United States had several clearly evident aims in the independent Philippines: to retain a secure base, militarily and politically, for overall U.S. Asian policy; to maintain a protected, privileged Philippine market and investment area for American interests; and to perpetuate in the Philippines an agrarian, non-industrialized economy best fitted to the U.S. trade and investment pattern. Reinforcing these objectives were the necessary strategic policies of suppressing and eliminating popular revolutionary nationalist or anti-imperialist movements, and thwarting or repressing the development of an independent, nationalist Filipino industrial bourgeoisie.

The pushing through of the neocolonial economic and military agreements generated deeper opposition from both left-wing and bourgeois nationalist sectors than had been anticipated. When President Manuel Roxas, in August 1946, at American bidding, began military suppression of the left, he boasted that he would eliminate the Huk movement in sixty days. The unexpected consequence of the suppression attempt was the provoking of an armed struggle on a national scale, begun defensively by Huk adherents and developing into a revolutionary offensive. Armed struggle lasted full-fledged for a decade, until 1956, with features of it persisting to the present day. It brought political crisis to the neocolonial government that American policy had carefully set up, and has caused a degree of political instability ever since. Although the Huk movement was set back militarily, the Communist party that led it and the party's roots were not destroyed.

Economic crisis also developed with equal rapidity, undermining the neocolonial regime further. The United States has attempted to evade responsibility for economic crisis in the Philippines in this period by pointing to the large amounts of "aid" that it poured into the country and by claiming that it was mishandled by Filipino leaders. Only a tiny portion of the $3,526,252,904 in grants, loans, credits, transfers and expenditures made in the fifteen-year period of 1946–1961 could be classified in any way as "development aid," the vast bulk being in the form of piecemeal payments for war damage—much of which went to American firms—and for veterans' benefits, construction of military bases, and similar purposes.

However, as a consequence of "free trade," the Philippines was overwhelmed with duty-free, nonessential American commodities, causing these "dollar reserves" of the new republic to be dissipated at an incredible rate. Within four years, 1946–1949, the Philippines suffered a balance of payments deficit of $1,088,-000,000, of which $1,067,000,000 derived from trade with the United States (including eighty-four percent of imports). By the beginning of 1950 dollar reserves had fallen so low as a result of this trade raiding that the bottom was dropping out of the peso which could not be adjusted in value since the Bell Act officially pegged it to the dollar at a two-to-one rate. As fast as American "assistance" arrived in the Philippines it was drained back to American hands: "aid" was nothing more than a gigantic priming operation to benefit American export interests.

By 1950 the Philippines was thus in a state of grave economic and political crisis, with armed struggle lapping at the outskirts of Manila, with fantastic government corruption battening off the "aid" funds and budget appropriations alike, and with the people as a whole bearing the brunt of nondevelopment and terroristic suppression. In these circumstances, with the Chinese Revolution and national liberation struggles echoing in Asia, the United States was compelled to adjust its Philippine policies with emergency measures.

Beginning in the latter part of 1949, the operations of the trade act and of "parity" had to be curtailed by the adoption of import and exchange controls to check the drain on the economy. Nonessential consumer commodity imports were sharply cut, and the remittance of profits by U.S. corporations was largely suspended. Exchange controls were recommended by an International Monetary Fund team that visited the Philippines in 1949 as reserves began to slip. Both import and exchange controls were imposed through the Philippine Central Bank that had been established in 1947 on recommendation of a Joint Philippine-American Finance Commission; it was recognized that a managed monetary system might be detrimental to short-range operations of American interests but beneficial in the long range.

These controls, which lasted for over a decade, temporarily checked the more serious features of deterioration, but they had an effect unwished for by American interests: they gave for the first time a modicum of protection to Filipino entrepreneurs, who soon seized on the opportunity to try to break from the neocolonial straitjacket by setting up light industries to produce commodities now barred from importation. A base of sorts began to take shape for an infant industrial group that soon raised serious nationalist slogans, including demands for an end to "parity."

American interests, reluctantly agreeing to controls, thus found themselves having to contend with both a left-wing national liberation struggle and rising bourgeois nationalist pressure for industrialization. In 1950 two official U.S. missions journeyed to the Philippines, both ostensibly to deal with the left-wing threat.

One of these, the Melby Mission, from the Pentagon, set up the program of revitalizing the Philippine armed forces for counter-insurgency and of supplying U.S. military assistance. (Between 1946 and 1967, a minimally stated sum of $512 million of military assistance was provided to the Philippines for internal suppression.) The other mission, the Bell Mission, had a more sophisticated aim of contending with both left-wing and na-tionalist groupings.

The Bell Report that this mission produced blamed the Philippine government for the nation's plight, listing "misdi-rected investment and excessive imports for consumption," "in-efficiency," "graft and corruption," "strained relationship be-tween the landlords and their tenants," and similar causes,[12] all of them traceable to the U.S. colonial and neocolonial policies. It was much like a father upbraiding an offspring for habits with which he had deliberately imbued it. The Bell Report then made a number of emergency recommendations, later embodied in the Quirino-Foster Agreement of November 14, 1950, and the U.S.–Philippine Economic and Technical Cooperation Agree-ment of April 27, 1951. Of these, the main items were the provi-sion of $250 million in U.S. economic aid, and the dispatch of a Special Technical and Economic Mission to disburse the funds.

Economic aid had for its primary purpose not basic develop-ment programs that could strike at the root of Philippine prob-lems but scattered palliative measures of a counterinsurgency nature for dealing with the Huk movement. Outlays of only $233 million were ever actually made, spread between 1951 and 1967, and the great bulk of these went to rural projects in the areas of Huk strength, including military roads for army operations in remote areas.

The aid program, however, had more subtle and more complex features. Allocation of projects and of funds was not left to Filipinos but was put in the hands of the U.S. Special Mission, in accordance with a Bell Report recommendation that any aid "will be more effective if the United States retains control of the funds and of their use for development purposes."[13] This safe-guard was extended even further, to the soaking up of Philippine means, the agreement binding the Philippines to appropriate counterpart funds to take care of the "peso costs" of aid projects, a technique by which Philippine resources were harnessed to projects of American choice. On top of this, the Technical

Cooperation aspect of the agreement placed American "advisers" in all key departments of the Philippine government, controlling in particular military, economic, and educational matters, literally a reversal to colonial practice.

There was still the factor of embryonic Filipino industry, springing up in the protection of economic controls, to be dealt with. Methods were devised to cope with this as well. American "advisers," working all the levers of command in the government, in the Philippine Central Bank and in other agencies, managed to distort this trend toward manufacturing by encouraging the development of industries of a "packaging and assembly" nature, forced to rely not only on the importation of American capital goods, but on American raw materials, manufactured parts, and half-finished products, including licensed American processes and brand names.

Much of the distortion was brought about by the import controls operated under Central Bank directives. Licenses that were issued to importers for allocation of foreign exchange went mainly to foreign companies that were established, large, and well-capitalized; these were chiefly American and resident Chinese. The use to which "essential imports" were put by these firms was, of course, the erection of "packaging and assembly" plants. These were augmented further by the operation of U.S. Public Law 480 for disposal of U.S. agricultural surplus commodities: the Philippines purchased these commodities with pesos, thus saving foreign exchange, but the result was the creation of a whole range of packaging plants set up around such imports, many of them having ties with American corporations, such as General Foods.

An Import Control Board established to issue import licenses had a three-way representation: the Central Bank, businessmen and consumers. The ties of both businessmen and consumers on the Board could be traced to foreign interests. As for the Central Bank itself, its governors and department heads invariably owed their allegiance to the "sugar bloc," to other *comprador* interests, or to foreign corporations on which they had served as corporation lawyers or executive board members. This same choice of men occurred in such key government posts as Secretary of Finance or Chairmen of Senate and House of Representatives finance, commerce, and industry committees.

When the "Filipino First" campaign arose in the late 1950s, it started as a struggle to win a greater share of import licenses for Filipino entrepreneurs, a fact that speaks volumes about the working of the import control system.

In essence, a hopeful trend toward the beginning of Philippine industrialization was warped into a continued reliance on American trade policies, the American export pattern merely shifting from nonessential to "essential" commodities. This character forced on Philippine industry has persisted to the present. By 1968, ninety percent of local manufacture was "import-oriented," with forty-seven percent of all imports comprising the raw or half-finished materials of this limited semi-industry.

Both the Huk and the bourgeois nationalist movements called for industrialization as the key to Philippine development, and the most cursory survey of Philippine resources has indicated the basis for a self-sufficient industrial economy: abundant coal, iron ore, alloy metals, hydroelectric power, agricultural raw materials, food crops, and labor force. Even American consultant agencies hired by the Philippine government at the beginning of independence could not avoid pointing to industrial possibilities. The 1947 Hibben Plan recommended "domestic production, where quantities warrant, of all goods now imported for the manufacture of which the principal raw materials are now or can be made locally."[14] The Beyster Plan, also in 1947, stressed the possible creation of machine-tool industries, nonferrous foundries, and an extensive chemical industry.[15] Under American persuasion, only agricultural recommendations of these plans were given attention.

The thwarting of genuine industrialization has been one of the main features of American neocolonial policy in the Philippines. It had its most marked and open expression during the administration of Ramon Magsaysay, put in office in 1953 as the undisguised instrument of American interests to suppress the Huk movement and the nationalist industrial trend alike. Magsaysay, in public debate with the proponents of industrialization, openly proclaimed his policy to be "agriculture first." The perfect puppet, played up as an ideal modern Asian political leader by U.S. propagandists, he rejected even the term "Philippine nationalism," insisting on qualifying it as "positive nationalism," based on a "special relationship" with the United States.

"Agriculture first," which serves the raw material demands of the U.S. economy, has continued to be the main line of the American-designed development course in the Philippines, not only checking the industrial trend but reversing it. In 1950 manufacturing accounted for 7.3 percent of Philippine gross national product; the initial impetus given by economic controls had boosted it to nearly eighteen percent in 1960. Since then, under the impact of American pressures, there has been first stagnation and then retrogression in manufacturing's share of the economy: it had dropped to 17.3 percent in 1969, and at the end of the 1971–1974 development plan it is planned to be cut to 16.8 percent.[16]

This stifling of economic development did not occur without a fight on the part of Filipino nationalist groups. It was particularly sharp during the Magsaysay period and the Carlos García Nacionalista administration that took office in 1957 on the death of Magsaysay. So blatant was the direction given to the 1951 aid agreement, for example, that in 1954 the Philippine Congress overrode Magsaysay by adopting a resolution criticizing the fact that "undue emphasis has been placed on agricultural development" and calling for "the shifting of direction ... to that segment of the economy requiring the promotion of industrial development so as to achieve a viable and balanced economy for the Philippines."[17] Out of $68 million of American-targeted funds for 1951–1954, only $1.4 million had gone to "industry and mining" combined. Despite nationalist protest, between 1951–1968, out of a total of $157,836,000 of American "project-type assistance," only $7,269,000 went to "industry and mining" combined.[18]

During Magsaysay's regime the United States increased its hold over any tendency to industrialize. In 1955 the U.S.–Philippine Trade Act was replaced by the Laurel-Langley Agreement. This bolstered the agricultural sector of the economy and the land-lord–*comprador* allies of the United States, by slowing the application of graduated U.S. tariffs on Philippine products entering the United States. In exchange for this concession, however, *"parity" privileges for Americans in the Philippines, originally limited to exploitation of natural resources, were extended to cover all forms of business activity,* an immeasurably greater boon to American interests and one designed to enable them to dominate any industrial or manufacturing trend.

With the subjugation of economic nationalism, since the 1950s there has been a change in the pattern of American investments. Prior to Philippine independence, 23.2 percent of these were in mining, the largest percentage, while manufacturing accounted for a negligible amount. At the end of 1970 American mining investments, although they had more than doubled in quantity, were only 14.6 percent of the total, while manufacturing accounted for 51.6 percent.[19] Stimulus to industrialization, however, was minimal, the bulk of these investments being in "packaging and assembly," oil refining of imported crude oil, and other ventures aiding U.S. trade in Asia as a whole.

The main struggle as the 1950s ended came over the retention of economic controls. American interests, chafing in particular over the restriction of remittance of profits, agitated for their abolition. Filipino manufacturing sectors raised the slogan of "Filipino First," and fought for controls that gave them some protection from foreign competition. However, the powerful American Chamber of Commerce in the Philippines, in concert with Filipino *comprador* allies, helped defeat García, who endorsed "Filipino First," in the election of 1961, and secured the abolition of economic controls early in 1962 in exchange for backing the Liberal party victor, Diosdado Macapagal.

With their victory over controls, which, however poorly implemented, represented a degree of independent management of the Philippine economy, American interests literally strangled the nationalist economic trend in its cradle. In place of economic controls, the United States persuaded its Filipino subordinates to handle balance-of-payments deficits by basing themselves on "stabilization" loans from Western banking agencies. Abdication from controls in 1962 was, in fact, literally bought by a stabilization loan of over $300 million, urged on the Philippines by the U.S. Treasury in collusion with the International Monetary Fund. One of the terms of the loan was the devaluation of the peso, from two pesos to one dollar, to 3.9 pesos to one dollar, done allegedly to encourage exports.

The results of the 1962 decontrol and devaluation were disastrous for Philippine development. Under the theory that balance-of-payments deficits could be offset by loans to "aid the peso," an unbalanced neocolonial trade pattern has worsened. For only two years out of the twenty-five-year independence period to 1971 did the Philippines show a slightly favorable trade balance, in 1959 and 1963. By the latter 1960s the heavy deficits reappeared, reaching $301 million in 1968. All told, the Philippine balance-of-payments deficit during a quarter of a century of independence has topped $3000 million and has shown no sign of being reversed.

Devaluation of the peso in 1962 dealt a severe blow to the infant Filipino industries. Their debts contracted at two pesos to one dollar for the importation of capital goods and materials, mainly for U.S. suppliers on credit terms, now had to be paid off at the rate of 3.9 pesos to one dollar. A number of promising local enterprises were consequently forced to the wall and into the arms of waiting American corporations.

One of the saddest of the victims was the Filoil Corporation, set up in 1959 by Filipino entrepreneurs with the hope of breaking the hold of the imperialist oil companies on refining and marketing. It was launched with the allowance of only a minority share to a U.S. firm, Gulf Oil, to ensure a supply of crude oil imports and of technical aid. By 1964, decontrol and a tight government credit policy that was one of the terms of the 1962 IMF stabilization loan, coupled, as Filoil officials bitterly commented, with "relentless competitive efforts of international oil companies to get a larger share of the market with the support of unlimited resources," had driven Filoil to bankruptcy debt and had led to a takeover by Gulf Oil of a sixty-seven percent share in the company.[20]

At this time, American interests, with "parity" rights expanded, launched a campaign for "joint venture" arrangements with Filipino capital, to take advantage of debt-burdened and credit-starved Filipino enterprises. Today the American joint-venture takeover has been carried to a point where a nationalist-inclined Filipino bourgeoisie has almost ceased to exist as a factor in the politico-economic perspective. At the end of 1970 the plight of Filipino enterprises, forced to rely on loans and credits of foreign suppliers, was reflected in the total foreign debt of the private sector, which stood at over $1200 million, leaving local industry at the mercy of foreign creditors.

Reliance of the Philippine government itself on foreign loans to offset the balance-of-payments deficit and to carry out "infrastructure" programs demanded by foreign investors has driven the nation into almost unmanageable debt. In 1962 the Philippine public external debt was $275 million; by 1970 this had risen to over $1 billion (from 8.7 percent to 13.3 percent of the

gross national product). This required annual repayment of
$120 million in interest alone. "Debt servicing" amounted to
payments of $387 million in 1971, with repayment of $475
million scheduled for 1975. The financial problem was made
graver by an enormous internal debt of over eight billion pesos.
By the beginning of 1970 the Philippines was unable to meet its
international obligations. A return to economic controls advocated by nationalist circles was logical, but U.S. pressure against
such a step prevailed. The government of President Marcos
yielded to American advice and negotiated fresh "stabilization"
loans from the United States and Japan and a *tranche* loan from
the IMF just to "roll over" interest payment on debts.

The price exacted for these loans and for "restructuring"
repayment of existing debts was heavy. Along with the usual IMF
terms of no restriction on remittance of profits by foreign companies, of tight credit, and of cuts in public services, the Philippines was again forced to devalue the peso, taking the form of a
"floating peso" policy in February 1970. Value of the peso
promptly dropped precipitously to 6.5 pesos to one dollar. Prom-
ulgated ostensibly as a means of boosting export earnings, it
merely facilitated the cheaper buying up of the Philippine economy. For example, the Filipino private foreign debt that had
formerly stood at the peso equivalent of 4,680,000,000 pesos now
had been raised overnight to over eight billion pesos, greatly
increasing the vulnerability of Filipino enterprises to foreign
penetration.

A Filipino economist, Alejandro Lichauco, assessed the process
in this way:

> The devaluation of the peso operated to cheapen consid-
> erably the cost of Filipino labor and services in terms of the
> dollar. Before devaluation, one dollar could purchase and ac-
> quire only 3.90 pesos' worth of Filipino labor and services.
> After devaluation, the same dollar can acquire 6.50 pesos'
> worth of Filipino labor and services. No wonder, for example,
> that the Philippines has now become one of the cheapest places
> to live in, in terms of the dollar. And, if one may add, one of
> the cheapest places to do business in, in terms of the dollar.
>
> The devaluation of our peso was imposed on us by the
> American-controlled IMF in obvious anticipation of America's
> new economic policy toward Communist China and of its trade
> offensive in Asia. Our economy is being set up for the export
> operations of American companies, such as GM, whose com-

petitiveness in the Asian market will be based and will depend on their capacity to exploit cheap Filipino labor—labor which the peso devaluation last year made sure will be cheap in terms of the dollar.[21]

By 1971 the Philippines was even more thoroughly hog-tied a neocolonial victim than when it stepped forth to "independence" a quarter of a century earlier.

V

The trade–loan–devaluation cycle is only one neocolonial process that has sapped the vitality of the Philippine economy and severely retarded its development. A more significant adverse effect has come from the operation of "parity" that has enormously augmented the dominance of American corporations.

At independence, total American investments in the Philippines, resident and nonresident, stood at $268 million, located almost wholly in raw material extractive operations, public utilities, and the import–export trade.[22] "Parity" rights were not taken advantage of immediately under the twenty-eight-year Trade Act: significantly, they were not resorted to on a sizable scale until after the crushing of the Huk military struggle in the mid-1950s and the demolition of economic controls in 1962, that is, after the smothering of the left-wing and other nationalist movements. By that time, too, the revived competitiveness of Western Europe and Japan and the growth of nationalism in the Third World had made more attractive the exploitation of areas of privilege like the Philippines.

By 1968, the U.S. Department of Commerce estimated that the direct American investment in the Philippines was $700 million, while the U.S. Embassy in Manila shortly afterward published reports of a real figure reaching $1 billion, or nearly four times the amount during the colonial period. This does not include loans or portfolio investments but represents the book value of 187 American companies with an investment of $1 million or over in the Philippines (their market value would be roughly $2,500,000,000). Total assets of American companies on December 31, 1970 were 7,767,000,000 pesos (or $1,200,000,000), and they held 77.62 percent of the net worth of all foreign investments in the Philippines.[23]

These 187 American firms accounted in 1968 for 40.9 percent of the gross receipts of all business operations in the Philippines, for 43.8 percent of the total import of materials, supplies, and services, and for 37.3 percent of the total production of nonagricultural goods and services. They paid 500 million pesos in taxes in 1968 or twenty percent of all taxes paid that year to the Philippine government.[24]

In 1970, thirty of the fifty largest corporations in the Philippines from the standpoint of sales were American-owned, and a number of the others had the participation of American capital or were heavily indebted to American financial agencies.[25]

Impressive as these figures may be, they do not fully indicate the salient role of the American investment stake, which is located in the strategic sectors of the economy, as follows:

• The petroleum industry. Five of the six oil companies in the country are American (Caltex, Mobil, Esso, Getty Tidewater, and Gulf-Filoil) , the remaining one being British-Dutch (Shell) . With a value (prior to the 1970 devaluation) of 1,500,000,000 pesos, the petroleum industry, both refining and distribution, is eighty-seven percent foreign owned. In 1969 it earned over 100 million pesos in clear profit, or 12.69 percent of stockholders' equity.[26] Oil exploration rights in the Philippines and its offshore areas, believed to lie over the extensive Southeast Asia oil deposits, are mostly American-held.

• The chemical industry. This is controlled by some of the largest international corporations in the field: Union Carbide, Esso Standard, Borden Chemicals, American Cyanamid, Dow Chemicals, Sherwin-Williams, Dodge and Seymour. Chemicals and chemical products realize an 18.45 percent return on investment.

• The tire and rubber industry. It is wholly in the hands of Goodyear and Firestone. Rubber products yield a return of over thirty percent in the Philippines.

• The drug industry. Dominated by Abbott Laboratories, Merck, Sharp and Dohme, Parke Davis, Pfizer Laboratories, Mead Johnson, Winthrop Stearns, Vick International. Return in 1970: 16.19 percent.

• The metal fabrication or manufacture industry. Controlled by Reynolds, Phelps Dodge, General Electric, Westinghouse, Singer, Rheem, Atlantic, Gulf and Pacific Company, Earnshaw Docks, and Honolulu Iron Works.

• The communications industry. International communications are in the hands of Mackay Radio Telegraph Co., Globe Wireless, RCA Communications, and Eastern—all American. Domestically, General Telephone and Electronics Corporation holds the second largest block of shares in the telephone system, with a ten-year option to buy control.

• Heavy equipment industry. There is none in the Philippines, so this sector is dominated by foreign suppliers, mainly American, acting through local branches and distributors. No machine-tool industry, except for small simple machines, exists; all capital goods have to be purchased abroad, relying on foreign creditors. International Harvester dominates in farm machinery supply.

• Mining. A sector dominated by American investment for seventy years. Benguet Consolidated is the major gold mining firm. The largest iron ore producer, Philippine Iron Mines, Incorporated, is controlled by two American firms, Atlantic, Gulf and Pacific, and Soriano y Cia. A new American-Canadian copper company, Marcopper, has quickly become foremost in that field. Mining has an extremely high return of forty-four percent.

• Agro-industries. Canned pineapple, among the ten principal Philippine exports, is an industry owned from plantation to packing plant to export by Dole Pineapple and Del Monte Corporations. The expanding banana industry has been taken over by United Fruit and Dole.

• Soap and cosmetics. Dominated by Proctor and Gamble, Colgate-Palmolive, and the British Unilever. This is part of the coconut products sector. Desiccated coconut is controlled by the American Franklin Baker Co., a branch of General Foods. Coconut products have a 24.66 percent return on invested capital.

• Insurance. Seventeen American insurance companies, headed by the giant Philippine-American Life Insurance Co., dominate the field, accounting for thirty million pesos in premiums in 1968. Over two billion pesos of Filipino savings are tied up in the American-controlled business.

• Banking. Two of the biggest banks in the country are American, the National City Bank of New York, and Bank of America. Their 1970 assets exceeded 969 million pesos.[27] Foreign loan operations have mostly been handled by the American-controlled World Bank, the Asian Development Bank, the U.S. Export-Import Bank, and a range of U.S. commercial banks. Significant has been the increased role of finance capital in the Philippines. Besides loan operations that have placed the country in debt bondage, American banks have moved in to control the mobilization and investment of Filipino capital. One of the chief means of doing this is to assume a share in or even to promote investment banks and "development corporations" to absorb Filipino capital and savings that can be drawn upon by American firms. An intensifying of this soaking up of local capital can be seen in a request early in 1972 by the World Bank for the Philippine National Economic Council to undertake a thorough survey of Philippine savings. The National City Bank of New York has also been setting up finance corporations to extend loans for the purchase of American-made appliances like refrigerators, television sets, and air conditioners.

• Paper industry. In the latter part of 1971 the Paper Industries Corporation of the Philippines, a subsidiary of the U.S. Soriano y Cia (which has a monopoly spread in beer, mining, textiles, and steel products), inaugurated a $72 million pulp and paper making complex that will exert influence over the entire newspaper and publishing field.

These American holdings, with others of lesser importance, represent 77.6 percent of the net worth of all foreign investments in the Philippines (as contrasted with fifty percent before independence); these obviously have a stranglehold on the key sectors of the economy. British investments, the largest of which are Royal Dutch Shell and Unilever, run a poor second, with only 7.4 percent of the total. In third place, Japanese investments, with a 6.2 percent share, are, however, the fastest growing: they have been pouring in just since 1967, their main individual holdings being in ore extraction, electronics, and synthetic fibers. In trade, however, the Japanese have climbed rapidly, in 1971 displacing the United States as the foremost trading partner of the Philippines, with over forty percent of overall trade.[28] As elsewhere in Asia, Japan has once again become the major competitor of the United States in the Philippines.*

A key industry that has felt the hampering effect of American

---

* The percentage decline of the U.S. trade position, which fell to twenty-six percent of Philippine imports in 1971, needs to be considered, however, beside the fact that many U.S. commodities formerly exported to the Philippines are now manufactured, assembled, or packaged there, while a growing share of Philippine exports is attributable to these American Philippine-based firms.

influence is steel, basic to an industrialization program. In 1955 the Philippine government passed a law authorizing a government corporation, the National Shipyards and Steel Corporation (NASSCO), to establish, finance, and operate a steel industry. Approached for an implementing loan, the U.S. Export-Import Bank insisted that steel must be a joint private–government venture, with forty-nine percent private stockholding. The Philippine government yielded on this in 1960, and a Filipino group headed by the Jacinto interests subscribed the private capital. After the 1962 decontrol, however, further pressure by the U.S. bank compelled a complete turnover of the industry to private hands in 1963, the Iligan Integrated Steel Mills, Incorporated, being established. The Export-Import Bank loan of an initial $62.3 million did not come through until it was fully a private venture, in January 1964 (although with a Philippine government credit guarantee), and actual construction did not begin until May 1965. American loan machinery had been used not only to thwart the building of a public sector steel industry, but had delayed such an industry for over a decade, during which steel and steel products have comprised the third or fourth leading imports, from the United States and Japan. By the end of 1970 the IISMI was in a bankrupt state due to inability to repay a foreign debt of over $200 million that had become swollen abnormally by the February 1970 peso devaluation, and the debt-ridden Philippine government, as guarantor, had to assume this additional repayment burden. The underlying defect in the American-influenced conception of the IISMI has been the fact that it is not really "integrated" but has a halfway character: it was set up without a blast furnace and has relied on imported raw materials for its cold and hot rolling mills.

A saturation campaign of propaganda, pressure and economic "advice" from American interests has been kept up in favor of a private enterprise capitalist economy and against development by public sector industrial efforts. This campaign achieved a major goal with the adoption by the Marcos administration of an Investment Incentives Law that enormously enhances "parity" by pledging never to nationalize foreign firms, by granting extensive tax concessions, by giving guarantees against government competition and of noninterference in remittance of profits, and by designating foreign companies with up to forty percent ownership as "Philippine nationals."

Extensive in size and control as the American investment is, it actually does not represent a very considerable flow of capital to the Philippines. To a much greater extent it has been built up through a soaking up of Philippine savings and of painfully accumulated Filipino capital. Philippine domestic savings that could be drawn upon for genuine development—in government and private insurance agencies, savings banks, mutual funds, and other forms of personal as well as corporate savings—have been sizable. The assets of banking institutions alone jumped from 3,889,000,000 pesos in 1957 to 16,779,000,000 pesos in 1967.[29] These, however, have been heavily milked by American firms, utilizing their "parity" privileges and their "risk" power based on size and backing. They borrowed from Philippine banks and savings institutions over eight billion pesos between 1962 and 1968.[30] The Government Service Insurance System, for example, provided the funds to build the Hilton Hotel in Manila. In this fashion, Philippine local capital has been drained by dominant foreign corporations. Coupled with this has been the spread since the early 1960s of stock exchanges, which did not exist previously; there are now four stock exchanges in the Philippines, in Manila, Makati, Quezon City, and Cebu, which serve to draw Filipino savings into foreign firms.

A survey of 108 American companies in 1969 by the Office of Statistical Coordination of the Philippine National Economic Council discovered that they had remitted to the United States $386 million in profits from 1956 to 1965, compared with a total inflow of $79 million in American investments in the same period. The high rate of remittance was made possible by heavy borrowings of Philippine savings.

These sums are declared earnings. Further investigation has shown that total outward remittance of all kinds from the Philippines from 1962 to 1968 reached $2,216,850,000, an average of $316,690,000 per year. In addition, dollar payments outward for "miscellaneous invisibles" from 1962 to 1969 were $2,133,-750,000, an average of $304,820,000 more per year.[31] This fantastic drainage of the Philippine economy, going mainly to American companies and banks, includes loan repayments with interest, royalty payments, licensing fees, freight charges, insurance, misdeclared values of imports and exports, other forms of earnings and profits, outflow by corrupt politicians salting away funds in foreign banks, and losses through smuggling operations carried on on a grand scale (one smuggling–black market leak is the duty-free American military bases).

The fact that the American investment stake in the Philippines today is three or four times as large as it was prior to independence and carries proportionately larger influence is but one aspect of its present power. Much of the investment in the colonial period was built up by resident companies. Today, however, many of the major American monopoly interests, operating through subsidiaries of the nonresident parent, have an international character much more difficult to dislodge. These monopoly branches, or multinational firms, have unrivaled competitive power in the Philippine economy, with access to virtually unlimited capital and loan facilities. If need be, they can afford to open up to dispersed Filipino shareholding, which looks like yielding to "Filipinization" but is a form of drawing on local capital sources while retaining essential control of operations and policy.

To a greater extent than ever before, the Philippines in the 1970s is a neocolonial base for American penetration of Asia. A large number of the present American firms in the country, engaged in manufacturing, packaging and assembly, and agro-industry, have been set up with a view to export operations in Asia, made considerably more competitive through the use of cheap Filipino labor.

Since August 1971 the Ford Motor Company, which already had assembly plants in the Philippines, began a $100-million investment program to produce auto bodies and other components to supply assembly plants all over Asia.[32] General Motors has followed suit. These investments, the forerunners of others, have entered the Philippines under the new Investment Incentives Law and the plants are located in a special Free Trade Zone in Bataan that enables the bypassing of taxes and other charges. Choice of the Philippines for these operations was related to the 1970 devaluation of the peso, which literally cut the cost of Filipino labor in half in relation to the U.S. investment dollar.

The big American agro-industries have been developed along similar lines. In July 1971 Alfred Eames, Jr., chairman of the board of Del Monte Corporation, which has large banana and pineapple plantations and packing plants on the island of

Mindanao, said: "The Philippine operations are taking on new significance as a strategic base for supplying fast-growing Japanese and other Far Eastern markets."[33] (Del Monte and its companion corporations, United Fruit and Dole Pineapple, have been engaged in recent years in highly questionable transactions to acquire large tracts of land in the Philippines, amounting to 8000 to 10,000 hectares, although the Philippine Constitution permits corporations to acquire only 1024 hectares. The Dole deal involving 7605.7 hectares was actually done through a Philippine government agency, the National Development Corporation.)

As the 1974 termination of the Laurel-Langley Agreement and "parity" draws near, the entrenched American corporations have engaged in complex maneuvers to retain their privileged position indefinitely. One of the main issues in the Constitutional Convention that began year-long sessions in June 1971 for writing a new Philippine Constitution was the question of granting U.S. corporations "national treatment," a euphemism for "parity."

An ending of "parity" would mean a reversion to the condition under the 1935 Constitution that stipulates a sixty percent Filipino share in all corporations. American interests and their Filipino allies have claimed that neither the private nor the public sector has the means to implement such a shift of ownership, which would involve buying out a great part of the huge American investment. In some nationalist quarters the belief was voiced that the 1970 peso devaluation was designed to impede American "divestment," since the peso value of American investments jumped from around 3,900,000,000 pesos to about 6,500,-000,000 pesos. One "divestment" solution that has been advanced is for American banks to extend loans to the Philippines to buy the sixty percent share in American firms; this would require a loan in the neighborhood of $500 million, the repayment of which would exacerbate the present Philippine debt bondage while guaranteeing a prolonged period of profit-taking to American financial interests.

Yet even were "divestment" carried out to the constitutional limit, American companies that retained a forty percent shareholding could see to it that the Filipino share would be fragmented into many hands, leaving the Americans with the controlling interest. It is readily apparent that the long fight for economic independence in the Philippines is very far from its goal.

VI

It has been a common belief that independence for a former colony embodies political freedom, and that neocolonialism persists because of the nonattainment of economic freedom. This is an inadequate picture of the continued American domination which thwarts Philippine political freedom as well. The fact is, Philippine political parties, politics, and governmental policy have from the outset of independence been shaped and controlled by American imperialism.

In collaborationist political circles, power has alternated between the two main parties, Liberal and Nacionalista. The Liberal party was literally created by the General MacArthur–Commissioner McNutt team in 1945 as the reliable body to which independence could be handed. The Nacionalista party at that time took a stand of moderate opposition to the extremes of neocolonial arrangements desired by the United States. The first Liberal administrations, those of Manuel Roxas and Elpidio Quirino, quickly became discredited for corruption, electoral fraud, and terroristic suppression, making them liabilities to American interests. A "reform" administration was needed, and the Nacionalistas filled the bill.

For a short period after independence and the outbreak of civil war, the Nacionalista leaders wavered between a rough alliance with the Huk movement and accommodation with American imperialism. In 1953 the Nacionalistas came to terms with the Americans and accepted the ex-Liberal ultra–pro-American Ramon Magsaysay as their leader and presidential candidate. This event marked the success of American tactics in splitting the left forces from the potential bourgeois nationalist grouping. American imperialism, able to deal with each in turn, isolated and crushed the Huk armed struggle, and then suffocated and mastered the nationalist industrial trend that emerged from the emergency measures needed to deal with the Huks.

Today there is no ideological difference between the two main parties, both being aggrupations of landlord, *comprador,* and new commercial and industrial interests, all of which maneuver within these parties to advance their interests, with pro-American sectors dominant in both. American interests have skillfully manipulated the two-party system, fostering continual changes in administration and bitter political in-fighting of rival politicians, conveniently preventing the entrenchment of any grouping that might acquire an independent outlook.

Aside from political maneuvers by the Catholic Church to maintain its powerful propertied position in Philippine society, there has been only one significant effort to break from the pattern of neocolonial politics. That was the Nationalist-Citizens party, led by Senator Claro M. Recto, created in the latter phase of the econonic controls period and in existence from 1957 to 1961. Recto, a Nacionalista who could not stomach the capitulation to Magsaysay and his American mentors, became the spokesman of the new industrial elements that were struggling for a foothold in the economy. His untimely death in 1960 beheaded his party, which had the weakness of being built around his personality and of having failed to build a grass roots base. The NCP took a fairly strong nationalist, anti-imperialist stand for an end to neocolonial agreements with the United States, for all-out industrialization, for an independent foreign policy including relations with socialist countries, and for national-democratic freedoms at home. With Recto's death it began to subside, and its base of support was literally destroyed by decontrol in 1962, after which the NCP's industrialist backers tried to accommodate themselves within the two main parties. Since then, the possibilities for an independent national bourgeois political grouping to arise have been steadily eroded by American policies that subordinate these elements to junior partnership.

American control of Philippine political life is not merely a matter of bribery or of other crude forms of persuasion. As in the colonial period, large strata of influential Filipino educated and intellectual elements, the modern *ilustrados,* have been tied in a variety of ways to the neocolonial structure. These include not only the mass of politicians bought and paid for by the bribes, kickbacks, and campaign donations of foreign corporations. They include the lawyers who handle the affairs of foreign and *comprador* corporations (and who incidentally graduate to political activity and provide the majority of politicians devoted to the status quo) ; they include the Filipino junior executives, managerial personnel, technicians, clerks, advertising agents, etc., of the foreign enterprises, and the bankers, consultants, salespeople, and retailers who also serve them; they include the army and police officers trained in the United States and totally dependent on American arms and equipment; they include the university professors, administrators, editors, writers, economists, scholarship recipients, government bureau heads and others educated in American universities or receivers of grants from American foundations. These strata have become enormously enlarged since independence.

A case in point is the key government-run University of the Philippines, which has been literally "Americanized" by large string-tied grants from the Ford and Rockefeller foundations which determine what colleges and institutes are to be built, what is to be taught in them, how it is to be taught, and who teaches.

Throughout Philippine institutions of higher education, American textbooks on economics, sociology, political science, public administration, and other subjects still predominate. At lower school levels, the Peace Corps, employed on a large scale, has distributed American teachers and "advisers" down to the villages. American books, movies, news services, TV programs, music, comic book art, and fashions, dominate all media, smothering Philippine culture and expression.

Trade unions have been subverted by institutes set up and financed by U.S. aid funds, such as the Asian-American Free Labor Institute established in 1969 by the U.S. Agency for International Development. In 1970 this had fifty-two Filipinos, "trainees," on its payroll while they still held office in their unions; it was exposed in 1971 by Filipino trade unionists as a CIA front.

Continued nurturing of the colonial mentality in Filipinos has led to a further sapping of the nation's vitality and means in the "brain drain" of educated, trained Filipinos to the United States. Filipino doctors have been drawn to staff hospitals in the United States despite the fact that in 1968 there were only 1423 rural doctors in the Philippines, a ratio of one doctor to every 25,216 inhabitants.[34] As the *New York Times* reported on March 5, 1971, immigration of Filipinos jumped from 2545 in fiscal 1965 to 25,417 in fiscal 1970, and "the Filipinos coming here now are neither poor, nor illiterate, nor unaccustomed to American ways, in contrast to former immigrants" but "today a majority of

Filipino immigrants are doctors, lawyers, engineers, teachers, nurses, and other professionally trained persons."

These trends and signs of retrogression, which have enlarged the base of neocolonial collaboration, have been offset to a large extent by the rise of revolutionary, anti-imperialist consciousness. Suppression of the Huk movement by the mid-1950s and smothering of the impulse toward nationalist industrialization by the early 1960s were no more than temporary retardations of the revolutionary nationalist movement, which, within a decade, emerged in new and even broader forms. Although the Communist party of the Philippines has continued to be outlawed, the new peasant, trade union, youth, and left-wing nationalist organizations profess Marxism and have a definite hereditary link with the national liberation struggle of the immediate post-independence period.

In many ways, the revolutionary forces that arose in the mid-1960s have a deeper and more solid foundation than did the Huk movement; although termed the *Hukbong Mapagpalaya ng Bayan,* or "Army of National Liberation," that earlier movement drew its followers mainly from the victims of agrarian abuses and of the fraud, corruption, and terror practiced by the newly installed collaborationist government; anti-imperialism was not so pronounced a factor in the struggle because most Filipinos had not yet actually experienced the nature of the independence they had received, which took time to reveal itself. The movement that developed in the latter 1960s, however, embracing peasant and worker as well as middle-class sectors, has been strongly nationalist in character and is primarily directed against imperialism and neocolonialism. A many-faceted movement, it employs the term "national-democratic revolution" rather than simply "national liberation" to define its objectives.

Youth have played a prominent part in this movement. By 1969 about sixty percent of Filipinos were aged twenty or under and seventy percent had been born after independence, growing up without the direct experience of colonial masters. Generations born in the years of independence that are coming to maturity can see more vividly the gap between the ideal and the reality of independence than older generations that grew up under American rule, and were more directly imbued with a colonial mentality. In the latter 1960s and early 1970s the Filipino left has been winning substantial numbers of youth to the national-democratic cause, while the only answer of those in power has been the negative one of suppression.

The all-pervading political corruption, the blatant use of public office for personal enrichment, the vote-buying and terrorism in elections (over 200 were killed in the election campaign of 1971), the outlawing of left-wing movements, the smothering of liberal or nationalist alternative parties, the failure of economic development, and the obvious subservience of successive administrations to American dictation have brought an increasingly disillusioned and cynical rejection of both main parties by Filipinos.

An impression has grown in ruling circles, including American, that the neocolonial political system that has prevailed since independence, with its façade of democratic processes, is becoming unsuited to hold in check the revolutionary pressures building up in Philippine society. Ideas of dictatorial rule, by a civilian strong man or by the military, have been voiced with increasing frequency.

It is significant that these ideas have come to the fore after the Nixon administration's advocacy of "Asianization" as an American policy in Asia. The re-negotiation of all economic and military agreements with the Philippines was put forward as a companion step. Seen as an adjustment to nationalist demands in the Philippines, such a policy would amount to a pretended partial "low profile" withdrawal of the American presence. A greater reliance on neocolonial collaboration is the complement of this. The shape of collaborationist policy to come was forecast in part in the proposal made by the Marcos administration in November 1971 to increase the size of the Philippine army by 30,000 men, a move associated with the Association of South East Asian Nations' proposal to "neutralize" Southeast Asia that would be unrealizable without the removal of U.S. bases. Since "neutralization" implies the diminishing of an external threat, a large military establishment would be chiefly designed for internal uses. This would boost to approximately 100,000 an army-constabulary force organized for internal suppression of national-democratic movements and would bring military expenditures to nearly one-third of the Philippine budget.

A casting aside of the remnants of democratic pretense and a resort to open authoritarian rule thus appears to be the next neocolonial stage.

VII

The condition of the Philippines a quarter of a century after a neocolonial independence may be read in the circumstances of life known by the Filipino people today. In few countries does there exist such an enormous gap between a small percentage of extremely wealthy landlords, monopolist businessmen, and corrupt politicians and the vast majority of the extremely poor.

A visitor to Manila is struck more than anything else by the glaring and vulgar contrast between the palatial, well-guarded homes of the rich in the Bel-Air and Forbes Park subdivisions and the sea of rusty huts in the crowded working-class districts of Tondo, Sampaloc, or Pandacan. Bel-Air is the exclusive district for wealthy American businessmen, and Forbes Park, checkpointed and patrolled by armed security guards, houses the ostentatious residences of the Filipino super-rich; both have sprung up since the 1950s and are symbols of unbalanced neocolonial development.

In 1948, ten percent of Filipino families received thirty percent of the country's income; by 1956 the top ten percent were receiving 39.5 percent of income; by 1965 the share of the top ten percent was nearly 42 percent. Indications are that this trend has accelerated since that time. In 1956 the bottom one-fifth of families accounted for 4.5 percent of family income; by 1965 the share of the bottom one-fifth had shrunk to 3.5 percent. By 1965 the top five percent had as much as the sixty-five percent on the bottom.[35]

When translated into actual incomes, the gap becomes more visible. An inaccurate picture is given by attempts at per capita income figures. A United Nations estimate placed Philippine per capita income at $231 in 1966, contrasted with $3153 in the United States in that year.[36] However, in 1969 over fifty percent of all Filipino *families* had incomes of less than 1500 pesos per year (by official exchange rates at the time, the equivalent of $380); the average Filipino family has six members, which means that over one-half of the population had annual average per capita incomes of around 250 pesos, or about $63.[37] A *New York Times* report in 1970 claimed the median income in the whole country as only $50 per year.[38] The difficulties in estimating the actual degree of poverty may be seen in the fact that in the lower income grouping there has been an estimated one million families, or six million people (nearly one-sixth of the population), with literally no cash income at all. Of these, the leading Philippine periodical has said that "they are doomed to lead an animal-like existence for the rest of their lives."[39]

At the other end of the scale in 1969 were 2.6 percent of families earning 10,000 pesos per year or over, i.e., $2560 or more. Those in the "or over" category, numbering a mere handful with incomes ranging up to one million pesos or above, are the real power sector of wealth. It is estimated that 400 families control ninety percent of the Filipino share of the economy, and that 500 millionaires, 200 of them sugar barons, are embraced by this small family complex.[40]

Of the twenty-five highest individual income taxpayers in the Philippines in 1967, whose taxes range from 420,000 to 1,582,978 pesos, only eight were Filipino; twelve were American, three Spaniards, one British, one Swiss.[41]

Philippine living conditions become more painfully clear with figures on unemployment, a phenomenon that has grown into a major problem since independence. One congressional report states that the number of totally unemployed rose from 859,000 in 1956 to 1,067,000 in 1968 (out of a labor force of 12,213,000, or an unemployment rate of 8.7 percent).[42] For the same period, a leading Filipino economist and former head of the statistical bureau of the Philippine Central Bank, estimated the completely unemployed at 2,428,000 or nineteen percent of the labor force.[43] The Philippine National Economic Council estimated in 1970 that the underemployed—those who are idle for twenty-three to fifty-one weeks out of the year, at 2.2 million.[44] A consensus of government reports indicates that fifty to sixty percent of the labor force is either totally unemployed, partially unemployed, or seriously underemployed.

In the rural areas, where sixty-five to seventy percent of the Filipinos live, the levels of income are much lower than the national average. In 1968, the average yearly income of a rural family of six was 400 pesos, about $100, or a rural per capita income of less than $17.[45] Since independence, rural conditions have greatly worsened. The rate of farm tenancy, which stood at thirty-five percent before independence and had become thirty-seven percent in 1948, had jumped to nearly fifty-two percent by 1970, embracing nine million peasants. This has occurred despite the passage of repeated and much-publicized laws on "land re-form" that have been mainly propaganda exercises to quiet agrarian revolt.

Mass poverty and mounting population pressure (a birth rate of 3.5 percent, one of the highest in the world) have combined to drive millions to the cities from the countryside, where they endure unemployment and misery. In the swollen city of Manila two out of every five families (1,102,000 people) lived in patch-work shacks as "squatters" in 1968, without toilets, running water, electricity, drainage, or other household amenities.[46]

Concluded a 1969 Philippine Senate report on "levels of living":

> Our economy has grown, but its basic structure is changing very slowly. It remains essentially a colonial economy based on agriculture and trade oriented, in a society characterized by in-equality, dependence, and foreign dominance. This is why our median family income remains low and income and wealth are not equitably distributed among our people ... Filipino control of the economy must be asserted, and at the same time a greater share of the income must be apportioned to the laborer and the peasant ... changes in the structure of our economy must be matched by equally far-reaching changes in the institutions of education, of government, and of other social forces. At the rate our population is growing, these changes must come fast.[47]

The changes urged by this and by similar warning reports that have emanated from concerned Philippine quarters have not only failed to materialize, but all signs point to a worsening of inequalities and of growing foreign dominance. As in any other part of Asia where imperialist influence is pervasive, the neo-colonial Philippines can be said to be sitting on a volcano.

NOTES

1. *Committee on Insular Affairs, House of Representatives: Committee Reports, Hearings and Acts of Congress (59th Congress)*, 1905–1907, p. 216.

2. A. V. H. Hartendorp, *History of Industry and Trade of the Philippines From Pre-Spanish Times to the End of the Quirino Administration.* Manila: American Chamber of Commerce, 1958, p. 58.

3. *Ibid.,* pp. 54–55; Shirley Jenkins, *American Economic Policy Toward the Philippines* (Stanford University, 1954), p. 39.

4. Renato Constantino, *The Making of a Filipino.* Manila: Malaya Books, 1969, p. 204.

5. *Agreement Between the Republic of the Philippines and the United States of America Concerning Military Bases,* 1947.

6. During the Vietnam War, the United States utilized its rights under the agreement to activate one of the reserve bases, the large army and naval air base on Mactan Island, near Cebu. This became a key staging base for air attacks on North Vietnam, as did Clark Field.

7. *Philippines Free Press* (Manila, April 22, 1967).

8. *Census of the Philippines Islands, 1903* (Washington, Government Printing Office, 1905), vol. 4; *Census of the Philippines* (Manila, Bureau of Printing, 1940).

9. *Ibid.,* p. 432; Jenkins, *op. cit.,* p. 41.

10. Charles B. Elliott, *The Philippines to the End of the Commission Government* (Indianapolis, Bobbs-Merrill, 1917), p. 266; Jenkins, *op. cit.,* p. 41.

11. *Report of the Philippine Commission to the President.* Washington: Government Printing Office, 1900, vol. 1, pp. 30–36.

12. *Report to the President of the United States by the Economic Survey Mission to the Philippines.* Washington: 1950, pp. 1, 2, 55.

13. *Ibid.,* p. 105.

14. Thomas Hibben, *Philippine Economic Development: A Technical Memorandum Prepared for the Joint Philippine-American Finance Commission.* Manila: 1947, p. 2.

15. *Proposed Program for Industrial Rehabilitation and Development.* Manila: 1947.

16. *Four Year Development Plan (FY 1971–74).* Manila: National Economic Council, 1970, p. 20.

17. "Concurrent Resolution No. 13, May 18, 1954," *Laws and Resolutions, Republic of the Philippines* (Manila, 1955), vol. 9.

18. "Compilation of Statistics on the Philippine Economy," *Committee Report No. 2513, Senate Committee on Economic Affairs, 6th Congress, 4th Session* (Manila, 1969), Table 11.02.

19. Hartendorp, *op. cit.,* p. 54.

20. "Filoil Turns Ten," *Graphic* (Manila, December 10, 1969).

21. Alejandro Lichauco, "Dollar Devaluation: New Design on the Philippines," *Graphic,* Manila, September 8, 1971.

22. Hartendorp, *op. cit.,* p. 730.

23. *Graphic,* Manila, November 11, 1970; *Manila Chronicle,* November 22, 1971.

24. *Graphic,* Manila, October 28, 1970.

25. "200 Top Philippine Corporations," *Manila Chronicle Special Report,* August 31, 1971.

26. *Memorandum on Oil Prices Controversy.* Submitted to Philippine Price Control Council by Senator Jose W. Diokno, February 1971.

27. *Manila Chronicle,* November 23, 1971.

28. *Manila Chronicle,* November 22, 1971.

29. "Compilation of Statistics on the Philippine Economy," Table 7.07.

30. "Foreign Economic Policy for the Philippines," *Political Review* (Organ of Movement for the Advancement of Nationalism) , Manila, April–May 1971.

31. *Philippines Free Press,* June 20, 1971. (Quoting Constitutional Revision Report of University of the Philippines Law Center.)

32. Patrick J. Killen, UPI "Business Today" report from Manila, August 20, 1971.

33. *Financial Times,* London, July 28, 1971.

34. "Compilation of Statistics on the Philippine Economy," Table 5.022.

35. *Ibid.,* Tables 2.03 and 2.06.

36. *United Nations Statistical Yearbook,* 1967.

37. "Compilation of Statistics on the Philippine Economy," Table 2.03.

38. *New York Times,* March 12, 1970.

39. *Philippines Free Press,* August 7, 1965.

40. "Compilation of Statistics on the Philippine Economy," Table 2.03.

41. *Ibid.,* Table 12.02.

42. *Ibid.,* Table 3.03.

43. Dr. Horacio Lava, "The Economics of Underdevelopment," *Movement for the Advancement of Nationalism* (Basic Documents and Speeches of the Founding Congress) , Manila, 1967.

44. *Four Year Plan,* p. 70.

45. *Graphic,* Manila, February 26, 1969.

46. *Government Survey of Households,* Manila, 1968.

47. "Compilation of Statistics on the Philippine Economy," pp. 13–14.

DEPENDENCE AND IMPERIALISM
IN INDIA*

THOMAS E. WEISSKOPF

INTRODUCTION

Of all the excolonial nations that gained political independence in the aftermath of World War II, India appeared the most likely to escape foreign economic domination and pursue an independent path of economic development. First, with a large and varied endowment of natural resources and a huge population, India was not bound to depend heavily on external resources or external markets. And, even though India emerged from colonial rule as one of the poorest countries of the world, its continental size offered a vast potential for mobilizing domestic resources.

Second, India at independence had already experienced some degree of industrialization, and a substantial share of modern business enterprise had come under the control of indigenous capitalists. Although factory establishments and mines accounted for only 6.5 percent of the national product and employed only

* In preparing and revising this paper, I have benefited greatly from the assistance of Larry Lifschultz and from the comments of many friends and colleagues. I would like to acknowledge particularly the helpful suggestions of Peter Bell, Noam Chomsky, Edward Friedman, Michael Meeropol, Mark Selden, and the participants of the Harvard seminar of the Union for Radical Political Economics.

2.6 percent of the labor force in 1950,[1] modern industry was, in absolute terms, quite important. Furthermore, since the early nineteenth century, Indian capitalists had gradually improved their position vis-à-vis foreign (predominantly British) capital. A good deal of British capital followed the retreat of the colonial government to London, and by the early 1950s only a third of corporate business in India was still financially controlled by foreigners (mostly British).[2] Thus, India attained independence with a significant indigenous capitalist class that had a history of considerable antagonism towards foreign capitalist competitors. Unlike most other excolonial nations, India was not completely dependent on foreign business enterprise or managerial expertise.

Third, at independence there already existed a significant class of indigenous professionals and administrators. This British educated elite had assumed increasingly important—though always subordinate—positions in the professions and in the colonial administration. Such educated and Westernized Indians naturally came to resent their enforced subordination and figured prominently among the leaders of the Indian nationalist movement. Their own professional competence, combined with their anticolonial perspective, contributed both to the feasibility and to the desirability of limiting the role of foreign personnel and technical assistance in independent India.

Finally, the pronouncements of the leaders of the nationalist movement, who subsequently became the rulers of independent India, emphasized the restriction of foreign economic interests. Jawaharlal Nehru, the leading spokesman on economic matters and, as Prime Minister, India's most powerful political leader, set the tone for Indian economic policy by committing the ruling Congress party to a "socialistic pattern of society."[3] Nehru's concept of socialism involved a strong emphasis on economic self-reliance to be achieved by centralized economic planning and a foreign policy of nonalignment. The government was clearly on record in favor of a path of economic development in which foreign aid, foreign private capital, and foreign personnel would play at most a minor and subordinate role.

Yet, in spite of the seemingly favorable conditions at the time of independence, the Indian economy soon became heavily dependent upon the capitalist powers. By the 1960s, foreign aid and investment had become critical to India's development plans, and foreign officials, businessmen, and advisers had come to play important roles in India's strategy of development. While this Western influence was less blatant and comprehensive than the earlier British colonial control, it constituted nonetheless a significant new form of Western economic imperialism.[4] How did all of this come about? In this paper I propose to examine and to explain the process whereby India's initial commitment to self-reliant development yielded, as in so many other Third World countries, to a strategy of growth dependent upon the major capitalist powers.

I. TOWARD SELF-RELIANT DEVELOPMENT?

Few people were under any illusions about the magnitude of the task of economic development facing India at the time of its independence in 1947. Two centuries of colonial rule had brought about little, if any, growth in India's per capita income, which was lower than in almost any other part of the world. The colonial government had invested some resources in railroad construction, irrigation canals, and related infrastructural facilities, and a limited amount of modern industry had developed. The economy and the society, however, remained overwhelmingly agricultural, and the great majority of Indians eked out a precarious living by cultivating land under exploitative conditions with very inefficient techniques.[5]

Under such circumstances, a self-reliant strategy of economic development called for organized effort on an unprecedented scale. Clearly the national government—now finally in Indian hands—would have to spearhead economic growth. Jawaharlal Nehru was particularly keen on establishing a framework for systematic centralized planning, to be implemented by means of a strong public sector encompassing many key industries as well as a private sector subject to careful government control. In rural areas, the government was to initiate an agrarian revolution which would free the cultivator from his innumerable social and economic burdens and release his energy for productive agriculture.[6]

It was not only India's political leadership that recognized the need for a strong state to promote economic growth. The Indian business class, having suffered through decades of discrimination at the hands of the colonial government, looked to the new Indian government for protection and stimulation. Business leaders were well aware that Indian private enterprise was not strong enough to promote economic growth without substantial aid and public investment, and they generally supported the kind of mixed capitalist economy in which a strong public sector would be complementary to a growing private sector.[7] Both business and government leaders were determined at the outset to rely largely on India's own resources and to limit the role of foreign capital; in this endeavor the state would necessarily play a critical role.[8]

In the early years following independence, however, the role of the state in the economy was quite limited. The disruptive effects of the partition of the subcontinent, and the inherent difficulties of establishing a new system of rule, placed a premium on stability and consolidation in the minds of the political leadership. Far from formulating a long-range policy geared to self-reliant development, the government concentrated on restoring production levels as rapidly as possible. Earlier pronouncements about nationalizing key industries in the private sector were set aside as the government relied on existing private enterprise to boost production. With the publication of the first Industrial Policy Resolution (defining the respective roles of the public and private sectors) in 1948, and subsequent government actions designed to stimulate private enterprise, it became clear that Indian private capital had little to fear from the kind of "socialism" practiced by the political leadership.[9]

Government policy with respect to foreign capital followed a similar pattern of retreat from initially strong positions. Although existing foreign enterprise (mostly British, and much of it in plantations and services[10]) was never threatened with expropriation, the government of India at first did not encourage new foreign investment. The Industrial Policy Resolution of 1948 promised strict regulation of foreign capital "in the national interest," and India was generally unwilling to accord foreign investors the kind of conditions they expected. Only a year later, however, Nehru announced a new more liberal policy in a Statement to Parliament, and by 1953 a London business weekly affirmed that "the terms on which capital can be invested in India now match almost exactly the conditions laid down in the 'Code' [of the U.S. International Chamber of Commerce]."[11]

In spite of the progressive relaxation of restrictions, foreign investors remained suspicious of the Indian investment climate. During the first decade after independence there was little net inflow of foreign private capital, with the significant exception of the oil industry. In the early 1950s, the Indian government negotiated agreements with three major Western oil companies (Esso, Burmah-Shell, and Caltex) to set up branch refineries on terms extremely favorable to the investors.[12]

While the official attitude toward foreign private capital mellowed quite rapidly, the attitude toward foreign public aid remained much firmer throughout the first decade. The urge to avoid reliance on external aid was strengthened by American efforts to use a wheat loan in 1950 to pressure India into modifying its neutral stance in the Korean War.[13] In public statements Indian leaders extolled the virtues of self-sufficiency, and sought to minimize the role of foreign aid in financing development programs.

With the establishment of the National Planning Commission in 1950, and the inauguration of the First Five-Year Plan (1951–1956) a year later, the government moved to implement its long-heralded policy of systematic planning for self-reliant development. The First Plan proved to be very modest in scope, consisting essentially of a set of projects most of which were already slated to be carried out by various governmental agencies.[14] It was only in the mid-fifties, as the process of formulating the Second Five-Year Plan (1956–1961) got under way, that a concerted effort was made to define a new strategy of economic development.

Several circumstances combined to favor a new strategy.[15] First of all, the overall economic situation had improved markedly since independence; a couple of good monsoons and a boom in private business activity produced an atmosphere of optimism among economic planners. Secondly, there was a growing popular demand that the Congress party begin to fulfill its pledge to bring about a "socialistic pattern of society." This demand was reinforced after 1953 by key electoral challenges from the opposition Socialist and Communist parties. Finally, the Soviet Union began in late 1954 to demonstrate interest in developing economic relations with India. Accepting the domestic political status quo and displaying strong support for the Nehru government at the expense of the Communist party of India, the Soviet government offered technical and financial assistance for major public sector industrial projects—notably the first big public sector steel plant. This Soviet display of friendship and assistance greatly encouraged those planners—among them Nehru himself—who favored large-scale planning and rapid industrialization of the kind achieved by the Soviet Union.

The initial formulation of the Second Five-Year Plan owed much to the efforts of Professor P. C. Mahalanobis, head of the Indian Statistical Institute and principal economic adviser to Nehru, who prepared an influential "Plan Frame" outline published in March 1955.[16] Mahalanobis's Plan Frame called for the promotion of rapid growth "by increasing the scope and importance of the public sector" and through the development of heavy industries "to strengthen the foundations of economic independence."[17] Although the final version of the Second Five Year Plan involved some modification of Mahalanobis's original suggestions, it did represent a dramatic departure from the conservative economic policies of earlier years.

Planned public expenditure for the Second Plan was more than twice as great as for the First Plan; the outlay on industry increased almost fivefold, and the share of the public sector in total investment was to rise from forty-four percent to over sixty percent.[18] At the same time that this ambitious plan strategy was being formulated, the government undertook other measures to bring the economy more directly under state control. The (domestic) Imperial Bank and life insurance companies were nationalized, a major Companies Act (of 1956) was passed to permit closer government regulation of private enterprise, and a new State Trading Corporation was set up. In April 1956, the Indian Parliament adopted a new Industrial Policy Resolution that was somewhat more emphatic about the role of the public sector than the first Resolution of 1948.[19] More than at any time since independence, it appeared that the government might take decisive control of the direction of the economy.

Formulating elaborate development plans and promising large government expenditures are relatively easy tasks under any circumstances, and this was especially true in the optimistic Indian climate of the mid-fifties. The more difficult and more crucial question, however, was whether the necessary financial resources could be raised. In 1955 a Taxation Enquiry Commission issued a report calling for major fiscal reforms to increase tax revenues.[20] But it soon became clear that the major increases in planned government expenditures would outstrip the anticipated rise in tax revenues. It was expected that additional financial resources could be generated from the profits of public enterprises, from a moderate dose of deficit financing, and from foreign aid. However, estimates of foreign assistance remained fairly low, and the Minister of Commerce and Industry, T. T. Krishnamachari, reflected the prevailing spirit of self-sufficiency by categorically opposing foreign aid.[21] Even under optimistic assumptions about various sources of finance, there remained a significant gap between anticipated outlays and resources for the Plan—yet it was hoped that taxation could be further stepped up to meet any need as it arose.

Related to the problem of financing the large Second Plan was the problem of covering its foreign exchange requirements. The strategy of rapid industrialization with emphasis on large-scale projects in heavy industry was bound to generate rapidly increasing demands for imported raw materials and capital equipment. It was hoped that the foreign exchange to pay for these could be obtained from increased export earnings, from the curtailment of nonessential imports and from the use of some of India's sizable stock of accumulated sterling balances. Another potential source of foreign exchange was, of course, foreign capital, but the planners did not want to rely excessively on foreign aid and the current inflow of foreign private capital was too limited to warrant much optimism.

Not surprisingly, the Western capitalist powers severely criticized the Indian planning effort. A 1956 World Bank Mission condemned the Second Plan as overambitious.[22] Subsequently the chairman of the Bank, Eugene Black, addressed a letter to T. T. Krishnamachari berating the Indian planners for failing to accord a sufficient role to private enterprise and urging especially more positive measures to facilitate foreign private investment. Black went on to issue a stern warning: "We feel that we would have to consider the pace and the scale of our further loan operation in India from time to time in the light of economic conditions and prospects and taking into consideration the economic policies pursued by your Government."[23] This letter did not shake the confidence of the government in its policies; it was in effect rejected by Krishnamachari. For the time being, at least, Indian decision-makers were in no mood to accommodate themselves to the wishes of the World Bank.

II. THE DRIFT TO DEPENDENCE

Unfortunately for the proponents of the new strategy, the big plans and the bold rhetoric of the mid-fifties came crashing down to earth within a year after the Second Five Year Plan was initiated. The clearest symptom of the problem was an unprecedented foreign exchange crisis. The deficit on India's balance of trade, which had averaged about $200 million a year during the First Plan period, suddenly rocketed to almost $1 billion in 1956–1957 and reached a level of more than $1.3 billion in 1957–1958.[24] A large part of these deficits had to be paid out of India's sterling balances, which dwindled from $1.9 billion to $900 million within two years.

The dramatic increases in India's trade deficit were due to corresponding increases in imports at a time when export earnings remained static. The surge of imports can be attributed in considerable part to the failure of the Indian government to exercise the control over the private sector necessary for the fulfillment of the Second Plan.[25] In the beginning of the Plan period the booming private sector had run into supply shortages, especially in the domestic provision of basic industrial goods. Anxious to obtain imported goods before foreign exchange itself became limited (a likely prospect in view of the size of the new Plan), private businesses indulged in an import spree. Far from restraining this spree, the government handed out import licenses liberally and actually contributed to the problem with its own excessive use of foreign exchange. Only in 1957, when the drain of foreign exchange reserves had reached crisis proportions, did the government begin to clamp down on imports. By the end of 1957, only "essential" imports were being licensed. But the damage had already been done: before many of the projects of the Second Plan had even begun, India had squandered most of its foreign exchange reserves.

The foreign exchange crisis was matched by a crisis in financial resource mobilization for the Second Plan. Total development expenditures by the central and state governments rose from 6.9

percent to 10.2 percent of net national product (NNP) from 1955–1956 to 1957–1958, contributing heavily to an increase in total government expenditures from 14.0 percent to 17.7 percent of NNP.[26] But tax revenues increased only from 7.7 percent to 9.2 percent of NNP in the same period, and revenues from other sources barely changed at all. As a result, the overall government budgetary deficit increased from 1.6 percent to an unprecedented 4.4 percent of NNP. The initial optimism about financing the Second Plan had proved hopelessly naive.

The response of the government to these crises was to steer the economy in quite a different direction than that intended by the formulators of the Second Plan. In the first place, public expenditure on the Plan was cut back significantly.[27] Yet, even with this cutback it was clear that major efforts would have to be made to provide an adequate base of financial resources and foreign exchange for the rest of the Plan. Unable or unwilling to envisage any other course of action, the government turned its eyes toward the West.

Within a year after T. T. Krishnamachari had rejected the letter from Eugene Black and questioned the need for any foreign aid at all, the tune had changed.[28] In the summer of 1957, Krishnamachari himself (now Minister of Finance) led an official delegation on a tour of Western capitals in the first systematic effort to attract financial aid on a massive scale. This government effort was complemented in the same year by a foreign tour on the part of the Indian Industrial Mission, led by G. D. Birla (head of one of India's two wealthiest business houses) and including many of the most powerful representatives of Indian corporate business. Public officials and private businessmen alike sought to alleviate Western fears about Indian "socialism" and to affirm India's enthusiasm for an inflow of foreign capital. H. V. R. Iyengar, the Governor of the Reserve Bank of India, explained to an audience of industrialists in California that:

> The "Socialism" contemplated in India does not, by any stretch of the imagination, mean communism; it does not mean state capitalism. . . . It is a system under which private competitive enterprise has and will continue to have a vital role to play; it is a system which respects private property and provides for the

payment of compensation if such property is acquired by the state. I submit there is nothing in the system which should be repugnant to the social conscience of the U.S.A.[29]

And G. D. Birla assured an American Council for Commerce and Industry that the government of India was "favorable and indeed much more receptive than in 1948" to foreign capital.[30] This was not mere rhetoric. In specific agreements, new tax concessions and formal invitations, the government of India made clear that foreign majority ownership of joint ventures was acceptable and that foreign capital was welcome in a number of industries previously reserved for the state.

The response from the West was everything that anxious government officials and businessmen could have hoped for. The urgent appeals for help galvanized a small but influential pro-India lobby in the United States into action aimed at a massive stepup in American foreign aid.[31] The World Bank, apparently satisfied that the recent changes in economic policy were moving India in the right direction, set up a permanent mission in New Delhi in late 1957 and organized a prompt and substantial loan operation that enabled India to meet its immediate foreign exchange obligations. In August 1958, the Bank gave institutional form to Western assistance by establishing a Consortium for India (known popularly as the Aid-India Club). Comprising representatives of the major Western donor nations as well as the World Bank and its affiliate, the International Development Association, the Consortium was to meet at least once every year to assess India's development plans and to coordinate the allocation of loans and grants. Thanks largely to the efforts of the Consortium, the level of gross aid utilized by India jumped from $425 million in the First Plan period to over $3 billion in the Second Plan period.[32] This foreign aid financed roughly 25 percent of total public development expenditure and a slightly larger percentage of total imports during the Second Plan.

Although foreign public aid came much more quickly and in much larger amounts, foreign private capital also began to flow in increasing quantities to India as the Second Plan neared its end. Abandoning its earlier enthusiasm for self-sufficiency, the government from 1958 on put pressure on Indian firms to associate themselves financially and technically with foreign partners. In order to obtain investment and import licenses, Indian firms found it advantageous and often essential to seek agreements with foreign firms who could provide the foreign exchange to cover the import costs of a project. Encouraged by the growing economic links between India and the Western capitalist powers, foreign firms entered increasingly into joint ventures with their Indian counterparts. The number of government licenses for new enterprises involving foreign financial participation rose from an average of about ten per year in the period 1951–1957 to over thirty in 1958–1961 and over fifty in 1962–1963; in more than half the cases control was granted to the foreign partner.[33] This growth of foreign participation in Indian business was reflected in a rise in the average annual level of long-term foreign capital inflow and a corresponding growth of the value of long-term foreign investment assets in the private sector.[34]

India's increasing dependence on Western assistance was reflected in agriculture as well as in industry. While the agricultural sector had recorded some growth in output during the 1950s (slightly over three percent per year), more than half of the growth was due to the expansion of acreage. It was clear that an adequate rate of growth in the future would depend on more rapid improvement in agricultural productivity.[35] The possible reasons for the limited improvement in productivity are diverse and difficult to evaluate comparatively. They include the limited attention given to agriculture vis-à-vis industry in the Second Plan, the failure of the much-heralded rural Community Development Program to reach most peasants, and the widespread ineffectiveness of the land reform bills that had been passed by state legislatures to fulfill the Congress' pledge of "land to the tiller." In short, the government had neither brought about its promised agrarian revolution nor had it provided the massive infusion of agricultural inputs and credit which might have improved productivity even in the absence of significant institutional change.

Within the agricultural sector, food production was particularly disappointing. As the demand for foodgrains outstripped the domestic supply, India became increasingly dependent on imports to feed its growing population. Throughout the 1950s there was an unmistakable upward trend in food imports, which averaged 1.8 million tons annually during the First Plan period, 3.8 million tons during the Second Plan period, and reached an unprecedented level of 5.1 million tons in 1960.[36]

In the context of the overall foreign exchange shortage that developed in the Second Plan, the burden of food imports became increasingly onerous. Under these circumstances, the availability of surplus agricultural commodities from the United States under Public Law 480 proved irresistible.[37] Most of the commodities shipped under PL 480 are provided free of charge to the Indian government for subsequent sale in the domestic market. Between eighty-five and ninety percent of the rupee proceeds—known as counterpart funds—accrue to the government in the form of long-term loans (repayable in rupees to the United States) for mutually agreed upon development projects. The remainder of the counterpart funds—as well as the debt service on the loans—is held in a rupee account by the U.S. government for local administrative expenses. The PL 480 program thus channels aid to India in a manner very advantageous to the two governments involved. The U.S. government simply disposes of surplus commodities that it has already obliged taxpayers to buy from American farmers, and it accumulates and spends rupees in India while at the same time exercising some leverage over development expenditures by the Indian government. The latter, in turn, gains substantial budgetary resources from the sale of the surplus commodities while reducing the severity of food crises.

Commodity assistance to India began in 1955 but reached significant proportions only after the foreign exchange crisis in 1957. During the Second Plan period as a whole, the total value of PL 480 assistance amounted to $1.05 billion dollars, representing approximately one third of the total value of gross aid utilized.[38] PL 480 food imports accounted for about sixty percent of overall foodgrain imports during the Second Plan and contributed significantly to the stabilization of food grain prices.[39] It was clear that unless major steps were taken to increase the rate of growth of agriculture, Indian dependence on imported food would continue to exacerbate an already difficult foreign exchange problem.

As the formulation of the Third Five-Year Plan (1961–1966) got under way in the late 1950s and early 1960s, Indian planners had few illusions about the extent of their dependence on external assistance.[40] The ruling Congress party was still committed to rapid economic growth as a general objective, and to a major role for the state in achieving that objective. Thus, an ambitious target was established for the Third Plan: $21.9 billion of net investment for the economy as a whole, of which about sixty percent was to be in the public sector. Including both current outlay and capital investment, total public development expenditures were to rise from an actual figure of $9.7 billion in the Second Plan to $15.8 billion in the Third.

The financing of these expenditures was linked clearly to anticipated inflows of foreign capital. The planners recognized that existing taxation would barely cover current government expenditures already committed, and they projected additional taxation of $3.6 billion to be raised during the Plan period.[41] But even after stretching as optimistically as possible this and other sources of revenue, there remained a gap of $4.6 billion which was explicitly sought in external aid. In fact, the cumulative trade deficit had been estimated in the Draft Outline of the Third Plan to reach $6.7 billion.[42] As a scholar of Indian planning has observed, "Essentially, this was an advance bill presented to the 'consortium' and other foreign powers presumed to be interested in the Third Plan's success."[43]

Foreign powers did in fact foot most of this bill—but, as will become evident later, not without extracting a significant *quid pro quo*. Although the real value of public outlay fell somewhat below the targeted level, gross foreign aid utilized during the Third Plan period doubled from its Second Plan level to $6 billion.[44] Foreign aid financed thirty percent of total public development expenditures and nearly one half of total imports. Debt service on prior foreign loans claimed only $260 million during the Third Plan period, so that the net inflow of aid was only slightly lower than the gross inflow. Of the $6 billion in gross aid, more than ninety percent came from members of the Consortium and less than ten percent from the Soviet bloc countries. Thirty percent of the aid was accounted for by PL 480 assistance from the United States, which financed the bulk of India's growing foodgrain imports. The production of food grew very slowly during the Third Plan period, and average annual foodgrain imports rose to 6.5 million tons—about twice the level during the Second Plan.[45]

The growth in India's dependence on Western aid was matched by the rapidly growing role of foreign private enterprise in the Indian economy. The value of outstanding long-term foreign investment in the private sector, which had increased from

$930 million in December 1955 to $1.3 billion in December 1960, accelerated to $2.2 billion by March 1966.[46] This growth was marked by two significant shifts in the structure of foreign investment.[47] First, the share of manufacturing industry rose from twenty-nine percent of the total in 1955 to fifty-one percent in 1966. Second, the share of British capital declined from eighty-three percent in 1955 to fifty-one percent in 1966, while the share of American capital rose from nine percent to twenty-three percent in the same period. Foreign investors were clearly becoming much more interested in manufacturing than in the older extractive and service sectors of the economy, and American capital was gradually eroding the earlier dominance of British capital.

In the mid 1960s, foreign branches and foreign-controlled companies incorporated in India accounted for approximately twenty-five percent of India's total private nonfinancial corporate assets.[48] But the true significance of foreign private enterprise is understated by such figures which identify foreign control with ownership of at least forty percent of share capital.[49] The increasing involvement of foreign capital in manufacturing industries, typically in the form of joint ventures with Indian capital, has led to many instances of collaboration in which the Indian firm retains financial control but depends on technical assistance from its foreign partner. The number of government approvals for technical collaboration with foreign firms increased from an annual average of roughly thirty-five in the period 1948–1955 to 100 in 1956–1959 and 350 in 1960–1965.[50] Most such collaboration agreements involve little or no financial investment by the foreign partner, who is rewarded by annual payments of royalties and various technical and service fees. But the foreign role in management and decision-making is often critical even where foreign equity participation is negligible.[51]

However the significance is measured, it is clear that Western public officials and private businessmen assumed increasingly important roles in the Indian economy from the late 1950s by virtue of India's increasing dependence on Western public and private assistance. With interests of their own to defend and to promote, it is hardly surprising that these foreigners attempted to exercise the power which their critical roles conferred upon them.

III. CASE STUDIES IN ECONOMIC IMPERIALISM

A few preliminary points deserve emphasis before some specific cases are examined. Whenever there is a Western interest in a particular policy, there is bound to be a similar interest on the part of at least some Indians. Indeed, the policies promoted by Western capitalist powers are often intended precisely to create or strengthen Indian classes with similar interests. Thus policy differences rarely involve an alignment of Westerners on one side and Indians on the other side of an issue. Rather, the typical case of economic imperialism is one in which Western power is used to influence decisions in favor of one side of a domestic policy debate, bringing support to that group of Indians whose own views and/or interests are found most congenial.

In contrast to the heterogeneity of Indian interests, the Western interest in India tends to be homogeneous because the interested community is small and closely knit, consisting mainly of public officials and private businessmen. Articulated by the World Bank and the United States Agency for International Development (USAID) on behalf of the Aid-India Club, the consensus of Western officials and businessmen is that India should develop along capitalist lines by giving maximum latitude to private enterprise and opening the economy as widely as possible to trade and investment from other capitalist nations. This outlook results in an alignment of the Western powers with Indian capitalists both in urban and rural areas, especially those who are associated with foreign capital. At the same time, it brings the Western powers into conflict with the Indian government to the extent that the latter attempts to increase India's economic independence by restricting private enterprise or interfering with the operation of market forces.

Agricultural Policy

The unsatisfactory growth of Indian agriculture had led to increasing concern among Indian planners in the late 1950s. The American Ford Foundation (represented in India by one of its largest overseas missions) entered the discussion of alternative policy measures with the publication of its *Report on India's Food Crisis and Steps to Meet It*.[52] This report, prepared after a whirlwind ten-week visit to India by a dozen American agricultural experts, spoke ominously of an impending food crisis and recommended major steps to deal with it.[53] The influence of the report was profound. The foundation assigned another team of agricultural experts to draft a program of action and the resulting Intensive Agricultural Districts Programme (IADP) was adopted by the Indian government in June 1960. The principles embodied in the IADP, strongly supported by USAID, informed Indian agricultural policy throughout the next decade.[54]

The IADP selected one pilot district in each of the fifteen Indian states which was to be supplied with all of the various agricultural inputs—fertilizers, pesticides, improved seeds, water, credit, marketing facilities, technical assistance, etc.—necessary to improve significantly agricultural productivity. Districts were selected from areas already favored by a well-organized community development bureaucracy, good credit, and marketing facilities, an assured water supply, no major "farm consolidation problems," and "readily available local agrarian leadership receptive to change."[55] In other words, the new agricultural policy explicitly concentrated scarce resources in the hands of better-off farmers in favored areas in an all-out effort to increase output without regard to adverse distributional consequences. Notably absent from the initial Ford Report as well as from the IADP itself was any concern for land reform or related institutional changes.

The actual achievement of the IADP in raising output was described in disappointing terms a decade later by a sympathetic American economist, Dorris D. Brown, long associated with the Ford Foundation in India: "Only 3 of the 15 IADP districts reported significantly higher rates of change in output and yield for foodgrains during the IADP years (than) during the previous five years. Only 2 IADP districts reported significantly higher changes in outputs of foodgrains than did bordering districts."[56] Nonetheless, the principles of resource concentration and reliance on the "progressive" (i.e., wealthy) farmer to spearhead agricultural growth were further promoted in the mid-1960s by the extension of the IADP concept to the Intensive Agricultural Areas Programme (IAAP) and the introduction of a High Yielding Varieties Programme (HYVP) in selected areas with assured irrigation and rainfall. As described in glowing terms by John P. Lewis, Minister-Director of the USAID Mission to India from 1964 to 1969, the new agricultural strategy:

> relied for its drive on the Indian cultivator's appetite for gain and upon his native intelligence for much of its implementation . . . it would take bold steps, despite the heavy drain on the country's scarce foreign exchange, radically to increase the importation of fertilizers and provide the new seed supplies; ʾand follow up forthwith with swift expansion of (and recruitment of foreign private participation in) domestic production of fertilizer, seeds, pesticides and other agricultural inputs. The strategy would rely on the initial success of the seed-fertilizer combination in the hands of the more alert farmers to create effective pulls on other such potentially bottle-necking factors as agricultural credit and irrigation.[57]

Toward the late 1960s there was evidence that the increased use of fertilizers and new seeds in the so-called "green revolution" had contributed to an improvement in the agricultural performance of some crops in some areas (notably wheat in North India).[58] However, the extent of such improvement was in doubt, and it was clear that the benefits of the agricultural gains were distributed very unequally as among different regions and different classes of people.[59] The lion's share of the gains from the green revolution have accrued to large landowners, who have used government programs to concentrate land and agricultural resources in their own hands. These beneficiaries of the new agricultural policy, now commonly referred to as "kulak" farmers, have become an increasingly powerful rural class that has derived much support from Western sources in promoting its economic interests. Meanwhile, the vast majority of the rural population—small-holding cultivators and agricultural laborers—have scarcely managed to maintain their standard of living, and many have lost what little rights to land they initially held.

Oil, Drugs, and Fertilizers

The oil and chemical industries are often the focus of economic imperialism because of the immense power of the major multinational oil and chemical concerns. This was conspicuously true in India where Western influence was brought to bear upon the development of the oil, pharmaceutical, and fertilizer industries. It should be noted at the outset that the Second Industrial Policy Resolution (1956) had classified oil in the first category of industries in which all new units would be established by the state while drugs and pharmaceuticals, as well as fertilizers, were classified in the second category in which new undertakings were to be established increasingly by the state.[60]

The Indian government had attempted initially in the early 1950s to set up several public sector drug plants with help from Western firms, but it proved impossible to negotiate any agreements satisfactory to both parties.[61] In 1956 a group of Russian experts recommended an integrated multiplant industry under state ownership. Soon thereafter, private Indian and Western interests began to register their opposition to the Russian suggestion, and they managed to generate an alternative proposal from within the Indian Ministry of Commerce and Industry that called for a private sector drug industry with aid from Western firms. In spite of a new Russian offer of substantial aid for the public sector project, the Indian government concluded a major agreement with Merck and Company, Incorporated, of the United States for the production of antibiotics, and encouraged other Western firms to enter the industry with Indian partners. Merck's production costs were nearly twice those envisaged by the Russians, and the cost to India in royalty payments, service fees and technical secrecy was far higher than in the Russian proposals. The Indian decision was clearly influenced by the exercise of Western power. As one American trade-journal reported it:

> Drug officials started looking at India about two years ago, just as the Russians began a big push to have India freed from the dependence on Western chemicals and pharmaceuticals. Soviet engineers, loans, and all else needed would be provided if the Indians would take USSR help and build the state-owned industry.
>
> Fortunately for the Free World, Merck and other U.S. and Western drug and chemical firms have not been idle since.
>
> Merck's efforts have helped in part to stall this Soviet offensive . . . the original Soviet offer . . . is shelved, and the Indian pharmaceutical industry will not be a government monopoly.[62]

Since that time, the rapidly growing and highly profitable pharmaceutical industry has been dominated by foreign firms, whose patent rights and remittances have priced many important medicinal products out of the reach of the average Indian consumer.

The Indian oil industry was completely dominated through the 1950s by the three foreign private oil companies, Burmah-Shell, Esso, and Caltex.[63] The monopolistic position of these companies has only gradually and incompletely been undermined in the 1960s by the development of a domestic public sector capacity for oil extraction, refining and distribution. The development of India's state-run oil operations depended crucially upon Soviet bloc assistance, and it has gradually improved India's bargaining position vis-à-vis the Western oil companies. However, the bargaining is almost continual, always hard, and often influenced by the power of the World Bank and its partners in the Aid-India Club.

A decisive point in the conflict between the Indian government and the oil companies was reached in 1960, when the Soviet Union offered to supply India with large quantities of crude oil at a price well below that charged by the Western-controlled refineries.[64] Because a large part of the profitability of the major oil companies stemmed from the use of their own crude oil, they adamantly refused to process Soviet oil. The oil companies did offer to lower the prices charged for their own crude, but the Indian government remained dissatisfied and there were calls from various quarters for nationalization of the refineries.

The actual response of the government, however, was necessarily conditioned by India's economic dependence on the West. At the time of the debate over the Soviet offer of crude oil, the Third Five-Year Plan was being prepared and the World Bank was carrying out one of the periodic assessments of the Indian situation on which it based its recommendations to the Aid-India Club. The Bank would clearly not stand for the forced introduction of Soviet crude oil, much less the nationalization of Western refineries.[65] In the event, the Indian government stopped well short of nationalization or of any attempt to force the use of Soviet crude. Instead, it responded by setting up a new Oil Price Enquiry Committee, reasserting lamely the priority of state over private refineries, and refusing to allow the expansion of existing refineries or building of new refineries by the three major Western companies. As one close observer put it: "Western pressure, whether explicit or implicit, undoubtedly played a major role in the Indian government decision."[66] Even this mild response, however, was subsequently moderated. Under pressure from the Aid-India Club, the general scarcity of foreign exchange, and the steady rise in domestic demand for oil products, the government soon permitted substantial increases in oil processing by the three major Western refineries, and it dropped its earlier policy of confining new refineries wholly to the public sector by agreeing to joint state refining ventures with foreign private firms.[67]

In spite of significant concessions to Western oil companies over the years, the development of an Indian national oil industry and the use of Soviet bloc assistance has freed India from total dependence on foreign private oil interests. At present India can meet approximately half of its oil requirements from domestic sources and the government continues to bargain with Western firms over the other half. During the 1960s, however, Indian dependence and Western imperialist influence has become increasingly evident in the rapidly growing petrochemical fertilizer industry.

As noted earlier, one of the key elements of the new agricultural policy in India was a massive increase in the supply and use of fertilizers. At the end of the Second Five-Year Plan, Indian fertilizer consumption was extremely low by comparison with most other countries.[68] To step up rapidly the supply of fertilizers, the Third Plan aimed at almost a tenfold expansion of domestic production, and—the Industrial Policy Resolution of 1956 notwithstanding—the private sector was licensed to provide the major share of the increased capacity. But Indian businessmen found it difficult to interest foreign chemical companies—on whose technical assistance they depended—in joint fertlizer ventures largely because the foreign companies rejected the Indian policy of domestic majority ownership in the fertilizer industry. As a result of both public and private sector short-falls, fertilizer production lagged well behind its targeted level during the Third Plan, fertilizer imports increased rapidly, and the government found itself increasingly desperate for a solution to the food and fertilizer problem.

Under pressure from all sides, government officials met in 1964 with executives of major United States corporations interested in foreign investment in an attempt to improve the Indian investment climate, particularly for fertilizers. Soon thereafter a major proposal for building five new plants to produce one million tons of fertilizer (close to the actual target of the Third Plan) was put forward by the Bechtel Corporation. Negotiations with Bechtel were marked by disagreements over acceptable rates of return, control of marketing and distribution, and the extent of ownership and control by the Indian government. Although the government had by then agreed in principle to sanction new fertilizer ventures with majority foreign capital, the Bechtel proposal was ultimately rejected.

But in late 1965 and early 1966, the crisis in India deepened and the pressure from the West increased. On top of the mounting food problem of the early 1960s, India was struck by the worst drought of the century and in 1966 faced an enormous deficit of foodgrains. At the same time, India had incurred the displeasure of the United States and a temporary suspension of Western aid because of her involvement in the Indo-Pakistan War which broke out in August and September 1965. Under these circumstances President Johnson, as reported in the *New York Times,* "declined to sign a new year-long Food-for-Peace program, insisting that India must first take some hard decisions about food policy."[69] Moreover, "The United States government and the International Bank for Reconstruction and Development have insisted that India provide easier terms for foreign private investment in fertilizer plants as one condition of resumed economic aid."[70] It should come as no surprise that in December 1965 the Indian government announced a reversal in policy that gave private fertilizer plants full control over their own pricing and distribution for seven years; and in May 1966, the government signed a collaboration agreement with the American International Oil Company in which management control was to be split 50–50, although the government retained fifty-one percent of equity in the joint venture.

Liberalization and Devaluation

The pressure brought upon Indian fertilizer policy was part of a more wide-ranging effort by the Western powers to change the whole tenor of Indian economic policy.[71] World Bank missions to India had long complained about the extent of government controls over both domestic and foreign private enterprise. Beginning with the Bell Mission Report of 1964, increasing pressure was brought to relax these controls, to simplify licensing procedures, to allow greater freedom in the use of foreign exchange, and—as a key element and striking symbol of the whole strategy of economic "liberalization"—to devalue the rupee.

The nature of the pressure applied by the Western powers was blatant enough to offend almost all segments of Indian opinion and to produce a vocal, if impotent, nationalist reaction. First of all, most of the Western aid suspended during the Indo-Pakistan War was not resumed until April 1966—long after the fighting had ceased. Secondly, President Johnson held up PL 480 shipments and eventually authorized them only on a month-to-month basis under near-famine conditions. Finally, the World Bank made it unmistakably clear that future Consortium aid was contingent upon economic liberalization and the devaluation of the rupee.[72]

The inevitable outcome was announced in early June 1966 when the Indian government devalued the rupee from 4.75 to 7.50 rupees per dollar and simultaneously liberalized its import licensing policies. The economic impact of these measures is a matter of some controversy. There can be no doubt that economic conditions in India failed to improve, but this failure is sometimes attributed to exogenous factors such as the second successive year of drought in 1966–1967.[73] Nonetheless, the World Bank, on behalf of its consortium partners, continued in subsequent years to promote policies of liberalization and to "load its advice with the promise of aid."[74] As explained in a *New York Times* dispatch (under the significant heading: "Drift from Socialism to Pragmatism") :

> Much of what is happening now is the result of steady pressure from the United States and the International Bank for Reconstruction and Development, which for the last year have been urging a substantial freeing of the Indian economy and a greater scope for private enterprise.
>
> The United States pressure, in particular, has been highly effective here because the United States provides by far the largest part of the foreign exchange needed to finance India's development and keep the wheels of industry turning.
>
> Call them "strings," call them "conditions," or whatever one likes, India has little choice now but to agree to many of the terms that the United States, through the World Bank, is putting on its aid. For India simply has nowhere else to turn.[75]

IV. THE POLITICAL ECONOMY
OF INDIAN DEVELOPMENT

The pattern of economic development in India since independence poses a number of important questions. Why did Nehru's conception of a self-reliant "socialist" development strategy not prevail? Why did India turn to the West to bail out the economy in the late 1950s, rather than impose a domestic austerity program, or seek greater assistance from socialist countries? Why was the government unable or unwilling to bring about significant agrarian reform, and why did it turn instead to an agrarian strategy based on strengthening the rich farmer? To answer such questions, one must examine the class structure of independent India as it emerged from the history of British colonial rule and the nationalist movement.[76]

Two centuries of British hegemony on the subcontinent had a significant impact on the traditional pattern of social stratification based upon the hierarchical Hindu caste system. The introduction of new property rights and new forms of taxation, as well as an increasingly rapid growth of population, led to an increasingly *economic* stratification of agrarian society. At the apex of a multilayered pyramid was an elite group of native princes, absentee landlords, and moneylenders who owed their comfortable position entirely to the British, with whom they jointly maintained order in the countryside. Below this parasitic elite were many intermediate layers of cultivators with varying rights to land, ranging from a very small percentage of farmers with large holdings to a mass of peasants with some (usually tenuous) claim to a plot of land barely sufficient to provide for one family. At the bottom, representing roughly a quarter of the rural population, was a class of landless and often serflike agricultural laborers. This structure of economic classes was correlated with, but not identical to, the traditional caste hierarchy.

In contrast to the precapitalist relations of production that characterized almost all of Indian agriculture, a limited amount of modern capitalist industry had emerged under British rule. Although the colonial government consistently favored British capital, an indigenous Indian capitalist class began to develop slowly in the second half of the nineteenth century from among earlier trading classes which had collaborated with the British.

Because of the obstacles faced by Indian capital, the indigenous capitalist class remained highly concentrated among particular families and regions of India. Furthermore, its relations with British capital were highly ambivalent; the Indians generally depended upon the British for technical and managerial assistance, but they became increasingly competitive with the British in marketing their output. In the last decades of British rule Indian capitalists gained financial control of an increasing number of industries formerly dominated by the British, and by the beginning of the Second World War they had become a wealthy and powerful national bourgeoisie.

With the growth of modern industry and related services (e.g., railways and communication) India developed an organized industrial working class. Because of the limited spread of industry, however, it represented only a small fraction of non-agricultural workers. A larger number of wage earners were employed as white-collar workers in government services. Together, these blue-collar and white-collar workers constituted a relatively privileged labor aristocracy. The great majority of the nonagricultural working force belonged neither to the capitalist nor to the organized working class. Instead, they were either self-employed persons in services and household industry or part of the unorganized *Lumpenproletariat* irregularly employed by small enterprises of one kind or another.

Finally, a very important class to emerge from the British colonial period was the elite, highly educated class of professionals and administrators. Like the Indian capitalist class, its relations with the British were highly ambivalent. As recipients of an English education, they were very much oriented to Western culture and very much at home with their British counterparts. On the other hand, in spite of the British policy of gradual "Indianization" of public administration, they grew more and more resentful of their subordinate status in the colonial hierarchy.

The Indian nationalist movement had its origins in a moderate group of professionals—both English and Indian—who formed the Indian National Congress in 1885 to press for reforms that would improve the position of the Indian upper class within the framework of continued British rule. Leading Indian capitalists soon supported and participated in the organization as their interest in promoting Indian industry coalesced with the aims of the Indian intelligentsia. But only after the First World War, when the nationalists began to press seriously for independence from British rule, did the Congress become a mass movement. By the Second World War the Congress had gained support among the urban middle and lower classes as well as many strata of the peasantry. Although the most downtrodden and the most isolated groups were largely unaware of or indifferent to the Congress, only a few groups that were very closely linked to the British (e.g., native princes, large absentee landlords, and a few members of the urban upper class) actually opposed independence.

From the point of view of subsequent developments, the most important aspects of the nationalist movement were 1) that the Indian bourgeoisie and intelligentsia remained in firm command of the struggle for independence, and 2) that the attainment of independence involved no revolutionary social upheaval, but simply a transfer of power from the retreating colonial rulers to the dominant Indian classes. Indian independence left the indigenous class structure and distribution of political and economic power basically unchanged, with the exception of the few pro-British groups who lost some of their power and privilege.

The Congress party that took power in independent India was controlled by a narrow elite of businessmen and professionals which enjoyed widespread support from other classes. The Western orientation of the new leadership, and the natural desire of dominant classes to limit the threat of radical upheavals, contributed to the establishment in India of a framework of parliamentary democracy in which persuasion rather than coercion was expected to bring about social and economic change. In the absence of any social and economic revolution, this framework served in fact to maintain an extremely inegalitarian class structure as the stronger classes fairly easily dominated the weaker classes in the political arena.

The strongest urban class was clearly the big bourgeoisie, with substantial financial power. To some extent the highly educated professionals exercised independent power through their control of government administration, but their strength ultimately depended on political support from outside the government. The most important new development in the class structure was the emergence of a new landed elite in the rural areas. The old elite of princes and large absentee landowners was discredited by its association with the British and became early victims of Congress legislation. In its stead rose the next layer of agrarian society, the relatively wealthy large landholding farmers who dominated the villages. Their ability to deliver the rural vote (which constitutes eighty percent of the total) gave them a strong base of political power.

Against this background, it becomes clear that socialism in any meaningful form was out of the question for India in the period following independence. The political base of Congress party rule precluded serious challenges to the sanctity of private property. The exigencies of electoral politics did demand, however, that the Congress party raise the banner of social and economic change as well as that of nationalism. To this end the rhetoric of a "socialistic pattern of society" as well as "self-reliant development," as propounded by Jawaharlal Nehru, proved very useful.

However, the effort to carry out self-reliant development in India appears in retrospect to have been doomed by the basically capitalist economic framework to which the Indian leadership was committed. To achieve self-reliant development in India, it would be necessary 1) to mobilize sufficient financial resources from domestic sources to finance massive development expenditures; 2) to shape the structure of the economy in such a way as to limit the demand for foreign goods and services; and 3) to mobilize the full productive potential of the rural population so as to make constructive use of the vast reservoir of idle and underutilized labor. The history of Indian economic policy-making since independence brings out clearly how the capitalist framework of the economy—and the class structure upon which it was based—inhibited the achievement of any of the above measures essential to self-reliant development.

In the two decades since the inauguration of economic planning in India, the rate of net domestic savings as a proportion of net national income has rarely exceeded ten percent.[77] Why were higher rates of saving not achieved? In part this was due to the continual difficulty of raising taxes from the powerful upper-income groups who control a substantial share of the taxable surplus. To this day there is almost no taxation of agricultural income in India, even though it is recognized that great fortunes have been made by large landholding farmers. While wage and salary earners cannot escape the income tax net, much business and professional income goes undeclared and untaxed. Incentives for private saving have been limited by the operation of a consumption "demonstration effect" propagated by the opulent standard of living of foreigners and many indigenous elites. In the context of limited private saving and limited public ability to raise tax revenues, the government soon found it much easier to seek foreign financial resources than to take serious steps against domestic surplus-holding classes in order to promote development.[78]

The failure of Indian economic decision-makers to limit effectively the demand for foreign goods and services is closely related to the failure to raise adequate domestic savings. For the limitation of such demand would require curtailing the purchasing power of the richer classes whose expenditure involves goods and services with a relatively high foreign input content.[79] But the political and economic power of the rich has prevented sufficiently stringent control of their luxury expenditure and thereby contributed to the so-called "foreign exchange problem."

Finally, the economic history of independent India points to an enormously costly failure to mobilize the full productive potential of the rural population. On the one hand, much of the cultivating population has too small or too uncertain a stake in land to be motivated to work efficiently; thus the spread of modern farming techniques has been limited to the wealthier landholders.[80] On the other hand, in spite of much talk about the desirability of employing idle labor on large-scale rural development works, such programs have in fact been extremely limited in scope.[81] The attainment of equity and cooperation in rural areas has been blocked by the power and influence of large landholding farmers, who have prevented the implementation of most of the land reform bills enacted by various state legislatures.[82] Large-scale labor-intensive public works programs have run up against the obstacles of inadequate resource mobilization and a lack of collective spirit, both of which were due in considerable part to the persistence of a grossly inegalitarian rural society. After the failure of initial efforts to bring about agricultural improvement on a new foundation of equity and cooperation, the government—with a strong push from the Western capitalist powers—turned instead to a strategy of "kulakization" involving heavy foreign involvement in the supply of chemical fertilizers, tractors, etc.

In sum, the political economic base that characterized India at independence offered a choice between virtual economic stagnation or an incomplete, inegalitarian, and dependent form of economic growth. The government recognized this partially in its early moves to attract foreign private capital and came to understand it fully in its later drive for foreign aid. Indian business leaders, at first distrustful of foreign competition, soon came to realize that their own interests would be served far better by collaboration with foreign firms in industrial ventures than by the more difficult effort to develop indigenous technological capability. Given this logic of dependent growth, it made sense for the government and for private capital to seek help wherever they could find it. But it remains to be explained why India became so heavily dependent on the Western capitalist powers and did not at least balance its dependence between East and West so as to improve its bargaining position.

In the first place, it should be noted that some five to ten percent of the total aid received by India has come from the socialist countries.[83] This aid has helped India to set up some important public sector projects, and in some cases (notably the oil industry) it has enabled the government to bargain for better terms from Western firms. Yet on the whole the flow of financial aid and other forms of assistance from the East has been too small to reduce significantly India's dependence on the West.

The major reason for India's Western orientation appears to be the predominance of Western-oriented class forces within India. Both the urban bourgeoisie and the urban intelligentsia are culturally inclined to the West. More important, the basic economic interests of the Indian propertied classes—both in urban and rural areas—are much closer to those of Western capitalists than Soviet officials. While differences may well arise over issues such as tariff protection and import restrictions, the Indian propertied classes share with their Western counterparts a common stake in the sanctity of private property and related rules of the capitalist game. The only significant force in India operating to promote closer relations with Soviet bloc countries is the desire of the government bureaucracy to extend state control over economic activity. The history of Indian economic policy demonstrates clearly, however, that the government bureaucracy does not have the power to impose its will on private groups when the interests of the two come into serious conflict.

In sum, India's economic dependence on the Western capitalist powers has arisen as the natural consequence of the class structure that characterized India at the time of independence. The class basis of the dominant Congress party led to a commitment by the leadership to a fundamentally capitalist path of development, which in turn precluded a self-reliant strategy and led inexorably to dependence on Western capital. Moreover, once such channels of dependence are established they tend to become self-perpetuating. As the links between Indian and Western interests (both in the private and the public sector) grow stronger, there is a corresponding growth in the number and significance of those Indians with a stake in continued links to the West. Thus the domestic balance of power in India has shifted more strongly in favor of those classes—e.g., urban capitalists and rural "kulaks"—who share the desire of the Western capitalist powers to promote a path of dependent capitalist growth.

V. CONCLUSIONS

The main conclusion to be drawn from the experience of independent India is that, in the absence of a revolutionary transformation of the domestic class structure, an excolonial underdeveloped country faces a choice between economic stagnation or economic dependence on the major capitalist powers. The latter course opens the country to Western imperialist influence, which in turn reinforces the dependency relationship by strengthening those domestic classes most interested in a Western-oriented capitalist path of economic growth. Thus, dependence and imperialism are closely woven together in the fabric of international capitalism.

The overall strategy of economic growth promoted by the Western powers and their Indian allies calls for a basically capitalist economy, closely linked through trade and investment with the world capitalist system; it relies on domestic and foreign private enterprise, aided by sympathetic public agencies, to bring about economic growth. This strategy must be condemned both for the inadequacy of the rate of growth that it yields and for the character of the economic and social conditions that it fosters.

From 1948–1949 through 1969–1970 the average annual rate of growth of real national product in India was approximately 3.3

percent, and the corresponding rate of growth of per capita income was just over one percent.[84] The rates of growth were actually lower in the 1960s than in the 1950s. While this performance represents an improvement upon the economic stagnation that characterized the colonial period, it falls far short of the objectives of the Indian leadership as well as the aspirations and needs of the Indian people.

Many of the obstacles to more rapid economic growth in India stem from the capitalist framework of development.[85] The strength of private upper income groups in India has limited the ability of the government to finance its development plans, and the propensity of the rich to consume luxury goods has limited their own private saving. The inconsistency of appeals to collective social effort with the dominant capitalist ethos has contributed to the widely recognized failure to mobilize idle labor. And many institutional changes that could motivate a much greater application of human resources to production (e.g., land reform) have been inhibited by powerful propertied interests. The foreign aid received by India since independence has scarcely compensated for such obstacles. At its peak, the net inflow of foreign capital averaged little more than three percent of India's national product.[86] With a rapidly mounting burden of foreign debt repayment cutting into a steadily diminishing supply of new aid from foreign donor countries, it has become clear that India cannot expect the inflow of foreign resources to make up for the grossly inadequate level of domestic resource mobilization.[87]

But even if such obstacles to economic growth are somehow overcome, what kind of growth does capitalism offer a country like India? Many of its characteristics are visibly associated with the limited growth that has occurred since independence. In the first place, it is growth that is based upon steadily widening inequalities of income and wealth. Reliance on urban capitalists (domestic and foreign) and on kulak farmers to bring about growth can only succeed to the extent that those groups are rewarded with high income and consumption levels. Most of the economic gains that India has realized in the past two decades have been enjoyed by a limited set of middle- and upper-income classes.[88]

Secondly, the capitalist strategy of growth does not provide adequate employment opportunities in a labor-surplus economy. The purchasing power of the rich, and the influence of foreign practice on the choice of production techniques, tend to generate excessive demands for such scarce resources as capital, skilled labor and foreign exchange, and insufficient demand for un-skilled labor.[89] Moreover, a capitalist government is typically incapable of putting idle labor to work. During two decades of planned development in India, the problems of underemploy-ment and unemployment appear to have grown steadily worse.[90]

Finally, capitalist growth brings many of the undesirable qual-ities that characterize the rich capitalist societies in the con-temporary world. Human values such as community, spirituality, and brotherhood are undermined by the competitive logic of the market. Traditional forms of security are replaced not by new social arrangements catering to the same basic needs, but by increasing insecurity and alienation. Cultural life is continually threatened by homogenization to the lowest world-wide common denominator, gradually losing its distinctive indigenous charac-ter under the onslaught of Coca-Cola bottles and James Bond films. There are already numerous signs of such changes in India, even though capitalism has not yet fully penetrated the country.

In sum, the most fundamental criticism of the Western role in independent India is that it helps to promote an internationally oriented capitalist development strategy whose long-run conse-quences for the great majority of the Indian people are bleak indeed.

EPILOGUE

In recent years events have taken place in India that may suggest a departure from the syndrome of dependence and imperialism described in this essay. Successive years of poor rainfall and bad harvests from 1965 to 1967, the humiliating episode of devalua-tion in 1966, a three-year postponement of the Fourth Five Year Plan (originally scheduled to start in April 1966), and generally deteriorating economic conditions had contributed to an atmo-sphere of growing unrest in the late 1960s. The ruling Congress party was increasingly attacked for its failure to achieve self-reliant growth and a "socialistic pattern of society." In effect, India's capitalist framework of development was being chal-lenged, and the Congress party had to move to meet the chal-lenge.

First of all, the Congress leadership began to adopt a more nationalistic stance on economic questions. The virtues of self-reliance, which seemed to have been gathering dust during the previous decade, were once again brought out and extolled at public forums. Since aid prospects were in any event becoming increasingly gloomy—because of dimming enthusiasm on the part of the major donors (especially the United States) and the mounting burden of debt service on past loans—the new posture may largely have reflected the making of a virtue out of necessity. But government spokesmen did seek to align themselves with the critics of aid dependence.

Secondly, Mrs. Gandhi sought to project her government as the champion of the poor by initiating a series of measures designed to display its socialist *bona fides*. These measures included the nationalization of India's fourteen largest private commercial banks in July 1969; the subsequent firing of a Finance Minister (Morarji Desai) long identified with the conservative wing of the Congress party; a continuing effort to strip the former rulers of princely states of some remaining special privileges; and, most recently, the promotion of legislation aimed at facilitating state acquisition and redistribution of private property with ample discretion over the amount of compensation due.[91] This apparent lunge to the left provoked an intraparty dispute within the Congress that led ultimately to its formal split into two distinct parties, with a substantial majority of the old party members adhering to Mrs. Gandhi's ruling "new Congress" party. Riding a new wave of popularity, but suffering from a slight minority position in the national assembly, Mrs. Gandhi abruptly called a new general election in March, 1971, and emerged with a stunning victory over all the opposition parties.[92]

The events in Bangladesh in the following year helped to reinforce the new trends. With the Soviet Union emerging as India's major political ally (although still a minor contributor of economic aid) and the United States becoming one of India's major political enemies, pro-Western forces in India suffered a serious setback. When the United States suspended part of its aid to India, the rhetoric of self-reliance became all the more insistent. The Moscow-oriented Communist party of India was welcomed by Mrs. Gandhi into domestic electoral alliances, and her Congress party gained further strength on the Left. Finally, in the elections to state assemblies in March 1972, Mrs. Gandhi rode the crest of her popularity for the liberation of Bangladesh to further electoral triumphs.[93] More than at any time since the mid-1950s, India seemed poised to launch a genuinely new economic policy.

In many ways, the current situation resembles that of the mid-1950s: a popular leader committed to socialism and self-reliance; warm political relations with the Soviet Union and coolness towards the United States; and a domestic class structure dominated by strong propertied classes. But Mrs. Gandhi in the 1970s appears to be more strongly committed to change than was Nehru in the 1950s, and less inclined to compromise with opposing interests. The prospects of aid from the Western powers are not as good as they were in the 1950s, although foreign private capital is probably more enthusiastic than before. And the Indian masses are no doubt much more politicized than they were in the early 1950s, more aware of their needs, and more capable of pressing their demands. All of these points suggest a greater likelihood now than in the past that the ruling Congress party will bring about significant change.

However, in one important respect the present situation poses a much stronger barrier to evolutionary change than was true in the past. The capitalist pattern of development that has characterized India during the last two decades had greatly strengthened those classes most committed to a Western-oriented capitalist strategy. The Indian urban bourgeoisie, the rural kulak farmers, as well as foreign investors and collaborators, are all much more firmly and powerfully entrenched in Indian society than they were two decades ago. It seems probable, therefore, that only a revolutionary redistribution of power—of a kind that has never taken place in modern India and is certainly not on the agenda of Mrs. Gandhi's government—could usher in a genuinely new pattern of economic development.

NOTES*

1. These figures are drawn from Table 28, p. 106, and Table 5, p. 23, of FRNIC (1954).

2. This estimate is based on calculations made by the author using

* Abbreviated references refer to statistical sources identified at the end of the list of bibliographical references.

data on the total assets of foreign branches and foreign-controlled rupee companies in IFLA (1950) and IFLA (1955), and data on the total assets of all public and private limited joint stock companies in FSJSCI (1967). Mazumdar (1959) arrives at a similar figure in Table 9, pp. 72–73.

3. This term has figured prominently in statements by Congress leaders, and it was declared to be an official policy objective in a resolution passed by the Congress party in its session at Avadi in 1955. See the Indian National Congress (1969), pp. 86–89.

4. Throughout this essay I shall be concerned with *economic* rather than other forms of imperialism. By economic imperialism I mean the exercise of power by nationals of one country to affect *economic* conditions within another country. Thus I shall not be concerned with the impact of foreign powers on such issues as India's international political relations.

5. For a detailed analysis of the state of the Indian economy at independence, see Bettelheim (1968), Part I.

6. The economic policies favored by the ruling Congress party were set out in numerous documents published both before and after independence. A particularly comprehensive (and ambitious) presentation of these policies is contained in the statement on "Objectives and Economic Programme," issued by the All-India Congress Committee in November 1947. See the Indian National Congress (1969), pp. 18–32.

7. For a summary of the views of Indian businessmen on the economic role of the state, see Kidron (1965), pp. 72–4. Kidron quotes a business weekly to the following effect: "The real choice before the country is not between Government versus private enterprise but it is between Government-cum-British enterprise versus Government-cum-Indian enterprise."

8. As Kidron expressed it, "the Congress Government entered Independence confident that its existence was alone sufficient to release the springs of economic growth. Pre-independence thinking in both business and political circles was agreed on this." See Kidron, p. 97, and also pp. 71–2.

9. For documentation on this paragraph, see Kidron (1965), pp. 74–97.

10. The pattern of foreign private investment in 1948 is shown in Table 5.

11. For documentation on this paragraph, see Kidron (1965), pp. 97–102; the quotation is from p. 102.

12. See Eldridge (1969), pp. 118–19.

13. See Eldridge (1969), pp. 29–31.

14. For a detailed description of the First Five-Year Plan, see Hanson (1966), Chapter 4.

15. See Kidron (1965), pp. 113–16 and 128–30.

16. This and the following paragraph draw heavily on the thorough analysis of India's Second Five-Year Plan in Hanson (1966), Chapter 3.

17. Quoted in Hanson (1966), p. 126.

18. See Hanson (1966), Table 7, p. 134; and Kidron (1965), p. 136.

19. For details, see Hanson (1966), pp. 460–62.

20. See Government of India, Ministry of Finance (1955).

21. Hanson (1966), p. 132.

22. This was the verdict reached by the McKitterick Mission of the World Bank in its report released in August 1956; see Hanson (1966), p. 152.

23. Quoted in Kidron (1965), p. 154.

24. The figures cited in this paragraph are drawn from Table 1.

25. The points made in this paragraph are suggested by Kidron (1965), pp. 123–27.

26. The figures cited in this paragraph are drawn from Table 2.

27. Although the financial outlay was to be reduced from an initial level of forty-eight billion rupees only to forty-five billion rupees, the *real* value of the new figure was much lower because of the inflation that had occurred in the first few years of the Plan. See Kidron (1965), pp. 126, 141.

28. This paragraph is based on the account given in Kidron (1965), pp. 156–59.

29. Quoted in Kidron (1965), pp. 157–58.

30. Quoted in Kidron (1965), p. 158.

31. This pro-India lobby "was spearheaded by such personalities as the former ambassadors Bowles and Cooper, Professor J. K. Galbraith . . . and Senators Kennedy, Kefauver, Humphrey, Mansfield, and Fulbright"; see Eldridge (1969), p. 32.

32. The figures cited in the paragraph are drawn from Table 3.

33. The figures are given in Kidron (1965), p. 259 and pp. 274–75.

34. See Table 4. The value of long-term foreign investment assets should be distinguished from the value of the total assets controlled by foreigners. The former includes some foreign investment in Indian-controlled companies; while the latter includes a substantial amount of Indian investment in foreign-controlled companies.

35. According to ES (1971), Table 1.5, agricultural acreage increased by 21.2 percent and yield per acre by 17.5 percent between 1950–1951 and 1960–1961.

36. These figures for the two Plan periods are given in Eldridge (1969), Table 33, p. 112; the figure for 1960 is from ES (1971), Table 1.9.

37. See Eldridge (1969), Chapter 6, for a concise discussion of American aid to India under the PL 480 program.

38. See Table 3.

39. Eldridge (1969), pp. 112–13.

40. The Third Five-Year Plan is analyzed in Hanson (1966), Chapter 6. The figures on anticipated Third Plan expenditures cited in this paragraph were drawn from Table 15, p. 204, and Table 17, p. 206, in Hanson (1966); rupee values have been converted into dollars at the official exchange rate of 4.75 rupees per dollar.

41. The figures on anticipated Third Plan revenues cited in this paragraph were drawn from Table 20, p. 212, in Hanson (1966); rupee values have again been converted into dollars at the official exchange rate.

42. Hanson (1966), p. 194.

43. Hanson (1966), p. 194.

44. The figures on foreign aid cited in this paragraph are drawn from Table 3.

45. The figures are given in Eldridge (1969), Table 33, p. 112.

46. See Table 4.

47. The structure of foreign investment in India in 1948, 1955, and 1966 is shown in Table 5.

48. This estimate is based on calculations made by the author using data on the total assets of foreign branches, foreign rupee-controlled companies, and public and private limited joint-stock companies from annual articles in the *Reserve Bank of India Bulletin* monthly (Bombay) on the finances of a large sample of these types of companies.

49. Foreign-controlled companies are defined precisely but arbitrarily by the Reserve Bank of India as all subsidiaries of foreign companies "40% or more of whose shares are owned abroad in any *one* country, or 25% or more of whose shares are owned by a foreign or foreign controlled joint stock company, or which are managed by foreign controlled managing agents"; see IFLA (1964), pp. 25–6.

50. See FCII (1968), Table 1.

51. For a discussion of the increasing significance of technical collaboration agreements as a mechanism of foreign control, see Alavi (1966).

52. The Ford-sponsored report was published by the Ministry of Food and Agriculture and Ministry of Community Development and Cooperation of the Government of India; see Government of India, Ministry of Food and Agriculture and Ministry of Community Development and Cooperation (1959).

53. For a penetrating critique of the Ford report on the food crisis, see Thorner (1962).

54. For an enthusiastic account of the new agricultural strategy by the head of the USAID mission to India from 1964 to 1969, see Lewis (1970), pp. 1212–15.

55. The quotations are from p. 13 of Brown (1971), who provides a good descriptive account of the IADP.

56. Brown (1971), p. 59. Brown goes on to note that cultivators in

IADP districts fared somewhat better with cash crops than with food crops, but that this had little to do with the IADP program itself.

57. Lewis (1969), pp. 1212–13.

58. From 1965–1966 to 1970–1971, the official index numbers of overall agricultural output as well as yield per acre recorded impressive gains (see the Indian *Eastern Economist,* Annual Number 1972, pp. 1240 and 1243). But 1965–1966 was an exceptionally bad year due to drought conditions. T. N. Srinivasan (1971) has compared trend rates of growth for the periods 1949–1950 to 1964–1965 and 1949–1950 to 1969–1970; he concludes that only in wheat has there been any dramatic improvement in the late 1960s, while in some crops there has been relative deterioration.

59. For evidence on the distributional impact of recent agricultural growth in India, see Ladejinsky (1970) and Frankel (1971).

60. See Hanson (1966), pp. 461–62.

61. The account in this paragraph is a summary of the information presented in Kidron (1965), pp. 163–65.

62. Quoted in Kidron (1965), pp. 164–5.

63. The following paragraphs are based on descriptive accounts of the development of the Indian oil industry in Eldridge (1969), Chapter 7, Kidron (1965), pp. 166–75, and Tanzer (1969), Chapters 13–18.

64. This offer was almost simultaneous with the Soviet offer to supply crude oil to Cuba, which led ultimately to the nationalization of the Western oil companies by Fidel Castro's government. On the striking contrast between the behavior of the Cuban and Indian governments, see Tanzer (1969), pp. 344–49.

65. See Tanzer (1969), p. 189.

66. Tanzer (1969), p. 192.

67. See Kidron (1965), pp. 172–75.

68. The account in the following paragraphs relies heavily on the description of the development of the Indian fertilizer industry in Tanzer (1969), Chapter 19.

69. From the *New York Times,* December 18, 1965, quoted in Tanzer (1969), p. 254.

70. From the *New York Times,* May 15, 1966, quoted in Tanzer (1969), p. 254.

71. For a well-documented account of Western aid policy in the 1960s, see Eldridge (1969), pp. 34–36.

72. According to two very well-informed Indian economists specializing in international economic relations, "That the [devaluation] measure was adopted under heavy pressure from this source [the World Bank] is indisputable"; see Bhagwati and Desai (1970), p. 487.

73. Bhagwati and Desai (1970), Chapter 22, argue that the drought, the associated industrial recession, and the lack of enthusiasm with which the government pursued the new strategy of economic liberalism

obscured the beneficial effects of the policy. This argument has been strongly contested by other Indian economists (e.g., N. K. Chandra) who view the new policy as ineffective at best and harmful at worst.

74. In the words of an editorial in the *Economic and Political Weekly* of Bombay, April 8, 1967; see also other editorials in a similar vein on the subject of aid in the issues of November 19, 1966; May 6, 1967 and July 8, 1967.

75. From the *New York Times*, April 28, 1966, quoted in Tanzer (1969), p. 255.

76. The historical account that follows is based upon a variety of sources on Indian social, political, and economic history, particularly Moore (1966), Chapter 6; Clairmonte (1960), Chapter 2; Brecher (1959); Desai (1959); Pavlov (1964); Sen (1962); and Sinha (1965).

77. See Table 6.

78. For a similar analysis of the difficulty of mobilizing domestic resources in contemporary India, see Chakravarty (1970).

79. Hazari (1967) has demonstrated statistically that the goods and services purchased by the upper classes in India have on the average a significantly higher foreign exchange content than the goods and services purchased by the lower classes.

80. See, for example, Frankel (1971).

81. See Dandekar and Rath (1971), Part VII, for an instructive discussion of the failure of the Indian plans to provide adequate rural employment opportunities.

82. The failure of Indian land reform legislation is described and analyzed in Dandekar and Rath (1971), Part V.

83. See Tables 3 and 7.

84. Data on the annual level of per capita income in India from 1948–1949 through 1969–1970 are given in ES (1971), Tables 1 and 2; the growth rates cited in this paragraph were computed from this source.

85. For a more thorough discussion of the limitations of a capitalist strategy of growth in modern underdeveloped countries, see Weisskopf (1972).

86. See Table 6.

87. The net aid (gross aid minus debt service) utilized by India declined steadily in the late 1960s and by 1969–1970 had fallen to less than half of its level in the mid-1960s; see Table 7.

88. For evidence on the worsening distribution of real income in independent India, see Mukherjee and Chatterjee (1967) and Dandekar and Rath (1971), Part I, Section II.

89. This argument is elaborated in Weisskopf (1972).

90. For statistical evidence on the worsening employment situation in India, see the note on "Growth of Employment: 1950–1951 to 1968–1969," in the *Reserve Bank of India Bulletin,* December 1969, pp. 1909–1914.

91. The first three measures are described in Lewis (1970), pp. 1211–12. The new legislation on which Mrs. Gandhi's government initiated action in the summer of 1971 involves four parliamentary bills, labeled collectively the "socialist package." These bills seek to "restore Parliament's authority to change the fundamental rights [affirmed in the Indian Constitution], do away with the concept of market-value compensation for acquired property, and abolish privy purses and privilege of Princes and ics [the pre-independence Indian Civil Service] officers." See the *Statesman* (overseas) *Weekly,* July 24, 1971.

92. After the split of the Congress party in 1969, Mrs. Gandhi's faction held only 220 of the 522 seats in the Lok Sabha (national assembly). In the national election of 1971, Mrs. Gandhi's "ruling Congress" party won 350 seats. The complete election results are reported in *Link* weekly, March 14, 1971.

93. For a report on these elections, see the *Statesman* (overseas) *Weekly,* March 18, 1972.

TABLE 1
FOREIGN TRADE AND FOREIGN EXCHANGE RESERVES
(All Figures in Millions of Dollars)

Time Period	Imports	Exports	Trade Balance	Foreign Exchange Reserves[a]
CONSECUTIVE PERIODS[b]				
1950–1951	1367	1361	−6	2161
1951–1956 (PLAN I)	1538	1309	−228	1895
1956–1961 (PLAN II)	2275	1290	−985	638
1961–1966 (PLAN III)	2577	1573	−1004	626
1966–1970	2462	1726	−736	1095
SELECTED FISCAL YEARS[c]				
1955–1956	1628	1348	−280	1895
1956–1957	2320	1338	−982	1430
1957–1958	2596	1250	−1346	885
1958–1959	2164	1212	−952	796

a. At the end of the period.
b. The trade figures are annual averages for the period.
c. The Indian fiscal year runs from April 1 to March 31.

(SOURCES: Imports, exports and trade balance: IBP (1963), Table I*; BSRIE (1969), Table 55*; ES (1971), Table 6.3. Foreign exchange reserves: ES (1971), Table 6.1.)
   * Rupee values converted to dollars at the official exchange rate.

TABLE 2
GOVERNMENT EXPENDITURES AND REVENUES[a]
(All Figures Represent Percentages of Net National Product)

Time Period	Development Expenditures	Total Expenditures	Total Tax Revenues	Budgetary Surplus
CONSECUTIVE PERIODS[b]				
1950–1951	3.8	9.4	6.6	+0.1
1951–1956 (PLAN I)	5.0	11.2	7.2	−0.7
1956–1961 (PLAN II)	9.2	17.6	9.1	−1.6
1961–1966 (PLAN III)	10.9	24.2	13.0	−1.1
1966–1968	9.5	23.8	12.8	−1.0
SELECTED FISCAL YEARS[c]				
1955–1956	6.9	14.0	7.7	−1.6
1956–1957	8.2	14.6	7.9	−2.3
1957–1958	10.2	17.7	9.2	−4.4
1958–1959	9.5	16.9	8.6	−1.1

a. Consolidated figures for central and state governments.
b. All figures represent annual averages for the period.
c. The Indian fiscal year runs from April 1 to March 31.

(SOURCES: Rupee values for all items were obtained from BSRIE (1961), Table 46; BSRIE (1963), Table 50; and BSRIE (1969), Table 68. Percentage figures were calculated by dividing rupee figures by corresponding rupee values of net national product given in ES (1971), Tables 1.1 and 1.2.)

TABLE 3
FOREIGN AID DURING THE FIRST THREE PLAN PERIODS

	PLAN I (1951–1956)[a]		PLAN II (1956–1961)		PLAN III (1961–1966)	
	$ million	%	$ million	%	$ million	%
GROSS FOREIGN AID UTILIZED	423	100.0	3009	100.0	6038	100.0
From socialist countries	—	0.0	160	5.3	516	8.6
From nonsocialist countries	423	100.0	2849	94.7	5522	91.4
From consortium members	410	96.9	2824	93.9	5477	90.7
Under PL 480	11	2.6	1145	38.0	1795	29.7
DEBT SERVICE PAYMENTS	50	11.8	250	8.3	1141	18.9
NET FOREIGN AID UTILIZED	373	88.2	2759	91.7	4897	81.1
GROSS FOREIGN AID UTILIZED as a % of						
Net national product		0.4		2.3		3.3
Government development expenditures		8.0		25.2		30.5
Total imports		5.5		26.5		46.8

a. The figures include all aid utilized up to the end of Plan I; a limited amount was utilized prior to 1951.

(SOURCES: Gross foreign aid utilized: ES (1968), Table 7.3*. Debt service payments: ES (1971), Table 7.5*; ES (1968), Table 10. Net foreign aid utilized: subtract debt service from gross aid. Net national product: see sources for Table 2. Government development expenditures: see sources for Table 2. Total imports: see sources for Table 1.)
* Rupee values converted to dollars at the official exchange rate.

TABLE 4

GROWTH OF LONG-TERM FOREIGN INVESTMENT[a]
(*All Figures in Millions of Dollars*)

Time Period	Net Capital Inflow[b]	Value of Outstanding Investment[c]
June 1948		539
Dec. 1953	48	825
Dec 1955	34	930
Dec. 1956	76	1007
Dec. 1957	114	1120
Dec. 1958	61	1186
Dec. 1959	42	1229
Dec. 1960	105	1337
Dec. 1961	95	1431
Dec. 1962	84	1550
March 1964	170	1880
March 1965	223	2104
March 1966	141	2248
March 1967	224	2580

a. Includes foreign investment in the Indian private sector only.
b. Average annual inflow since previous date of reference. These figures are exclusive of asset revaluations which also affect the value of outstanding investment.
c. At the end of the period.

(SOURCES: Net capital inflow: IBP (1963), Table X*; FII (1966), Table 2*; IIIP (1969), Table 3.6*; IIIP (1971), Table 3.6*. Value of outstanding investment: FII (1966), Statement III*; IIIP (1971), Statement XI*.)
* Rupee values converted to dollars at the official exchange rate.

TABLE 5
STRUCTURE OF LONG-TERM FOREIGN INVESTMENT[a]

	1948	*1955*	*1966*
TOTAL VALUE OF OUTSTANDING INVESTMENT ($ million)	539	930	2248
% DISTRIBUTION BY COUNTRY OF ORIGIN			
United Kingdom	80.4	82.8	51.4
United States	4.3	9.1	23.1
Others	15.2	8.1	25.5
% DISTRIBUTION BY SECTOR OF DESTINATION			
Plantations	20.3	19.7	10.5
Mining	4.7	2.0	0.9
Petroleum	8.6	23.5	16.0
Manufacturing	27.7	29.2	50.6
Services	38.7	25.6	22.0

a. Includes foreign investment in the Indian private sector only.

(SOURCES: See sources for Table 4.)

TABLE 6

SAVINGS, CAPITAL INFLOW AND INVESTMENT
(All Figures Represent Percentages of Net National Product)

Fiscal Year[a]	Net Domestic Savings	Net Foreign Capital Inflow	Net Investment
1950–1951	5.7	−0.1	5.6
PLAN I			
1951–1952	5.3	+2.2	7.6
1952–1953	4.2	−0.2	4.0
1953–1954	5.4	0.0	5.4
1954–1955	8.0	+0.4	8.4
1955–1956	9.7	+0.6	10.4
PLAN II			
1956–1957	9.5	+3.3	12.9
1957–1958	7.0	+4.3	11.3
1958–1959	7.4	+3.2	10.6
1959–1960	8.5	+2.0	10.5
1960–1961	10.3	+3.7	14.0
PLAN III			
1961–1962	9.8	+2.7	12.5
1962–1963	10.1	+3.1	13.2
1963–1964	12.1	+2.8	14.9
1964–1965	10.7	+3.2	14.0
1965–1966	10.8	+2.8	13.7
1966–1967	7.9	+2.2	10.1
1967–1968	8.1	+2.0	10.0
1968–1969	9.0	+1.1	10.1
1969–1970	8.5	+0.5	9.0

a. The Indian fiscal year runs from April 1 to March 31.

(SOURCES: Rupee values for all items were obtained from ESIIE (1965), Table VIII; Bhatt (1971), Table 5.* Percentage figures were calculated by dividing rupee figures by corresponding rupee values of net national product given in ES (1971), Tables 1.1 and 1.2.)

  * The figures for net foreign capital inflow given by Bhatt for 1966–1967 through 1969–1970 were corrected to reflect the predevaluation exchange rate so as to maintain comparability with the earlier years; this correction also affected the figures for net investment, obtained as the sum of net domestic saving and net foreign capital inflow.

TABLE 7
FOREIGN AID DURING THE 1960s
(All Figures in Millions of Dollars)

Fiscal Year[a]	Gross Foreign Aid Utilized			Debt Service Payments	Net Foreign Aid Utilized
	Total	From Socialist Countries	From Non-socialist Countries		
PLAN III					
1961–1962	714	53	661	215	499
1962–1963	934	69	865	168	766
1963–1964	1241	109	1132	242	999
1964–1965	1524	171	1353	254	1270
1965–1966	1625	113	1511	262	1363
1966–1967	1478	74	1404	366	1112
1967–1968	1595	80	1515	444	1151
1968–1969	1204	116	1088	500	704
1969–1970	1155	96	1059	550	605

a. The Indian fiscal year runs from April 1 to March 31.

(SOURCES: Gross foreign aid utilized: ES (1968), Table 7.1*; ES (1971), Table 7.3.* Debt service payments: ES (1968), Table 10; ES (1971), Table 7.5.* Net foreign aid utilized: Subtract debt service from gross aid.)
* Rupee values converted to dollars at the official exchange rate.

BIBLIOGRAPHICAL REFERENCES

1. Alavi, Hamza, "Indian Capitalism and Foreign Imperialism," *New Left Review*, No. 37 (May–June 1966).

2. Bettelheim, Charles. *India Independent* (New York: Monthly Review Press, 1968).

3. Bhagwati, Jagdish, and Padma Desai. *India: Planning for Industrialization* (London: Oxford University Press, 1970).

4. Brecher, Michael. *Nehru: A Political Biography* (London: Oxford University Press, 1959).

5. Brown, Dorris D. *Agricultural Development in India's Districts* (Cambridge, Mass.: Harvard University Press, 1971).

6. Chakravarty, Sukhamoy, "Growth or Stagnation in India," in Arthur MacEwan and Thomas Weisskopf (eds.), *Perspectives on the Economic Problem* (Englewood Cliffs, N.J.: Prentice-Hall, 1970).

7. Clairmonte, Frederick. *Economic Liberalism and Underdevelopment* (Bombay: Asia Publishing House, 1960).

8. Dandekar, V. M. and Nilakantha Rath, "Poverty in India," *Economic and Political Weekly* (January 2 and 9, 1971).

9. Desai, A. R. *Social Background of Indian Nationalism* (Bombay: The Popular Press, 1959).

10. Eldridge, P. J. *The Politics of Foreign Aid in India* (London: Weidenfeld and Nicolson, 1969).

11. Frankel, Francine R. *India's Green Revolution* (Princeton, N.J.: Princeton University Press, 1971).

12. Government of India, Ministry of Finance. *Report of the Taxation Enquiry Commission* (New Delhi: 1955).

13. Government of India, Ministry of Food and Agriculture and Ministry of Community Development and Cooperation. *Report on India's Food Crisis and Steps to Meet It* (New Delhi: 1959).

14. Hanson, A. H. *The Process of Planning: A Study of India's Five-Year Plans, 1950–1964* (London: Oxford University Press, 1966).

15. Hazari, Bharat, "Import Intensity of Consumption in India," *Indian Economic Review* (October 1967).

16. Indian National Congress. *Resolution on Economic Policy, Programme and Allied Matters (1924–1969)* (New Delhi: All-India Congress Committee, 1969).

17. Kidron, Michael. *Foreign Investments in India* (London: Oxford University Press, 1965).

18. Ladejinsky, Wolf, "Tenurial Conditions and the Package Program," *Mainstream Weekly* (March 15, 1965).

19. Ladejinsky, Wolf, "Ironies of India's Green Revolution," *Foreign Affairs,* vol. 48, no. 4 (July 1970).

20. Lewis, John, "Wanted in India: A Relevant Radicalism," *Economic and Political Weekly* (Special Number, July 1970).

21. Mazumdar, Harendrakumar. *Business Saving In India* (Groningen, Holland: J. B. Wolters, 1959).

22. Moore, Jr., Barrington. *The Social Origins of Dictatorship and Democracy* (Boston: Beacon Press, 1966).

23. Mukherjee, M. and G. S. Chatterjee, "Trends in Distribution of National Income, 1950–51 to 1965–66," *Economic and Political Weekly* (July 15, 1967).

24. Pavlov, V. I. *The Indian Capitalist Class* (New Delhi: People's Publishing House, 1964).

25. Sen, Bhowani. *Evolution of Agrarian Relations in India* (New Delhi: People's Publishing House, 1962).

26. Sinha, L. P. *The Left-Wing in India* (Muzaffarpur: New Publishers, 1965).

27. Srinivasan, T. N., "The Green Revolution or the Wheat Revolution?" Indian Statistical Institute Discussion Paper No. 66 (October 1971).

28. Tanzer, Michael. *The Political Economy of International Oil and the Underdeveloped Countries* (Boston: Beacon Press, 1969).

29. Thorner, Daniel, "Ploughing the Plan Under," in Daniel and Alice Thorner, *Land and Labour in India* (Bombay: Asia Publishing House, 1962).

30. Weisskopf, Thomas E., "Capitalism, Underdevelopment and the Future of the Poor Countries," in Jagdish Bhagwati (ed.), *Economics and World Order* (New York: Macmillan, 1972).

STATISTICAL REFERENCES

1. Bhatt, V. V., "The Economy: Current Situation and Policy Problems," *Economic and Political Weekly* (March 20, 1967).

2. BSRIE: Government of India, Planning Commission, Statistics and Surveys Division. *Basic Statistics Relating to the Indian Economy* (New Delhi: 1961, 1963, and 1969).

3. ES: Government of India, Ministry of Finance. *Economic Survey* (New Delhi: 1968 and 1971).

4. ESIIE: "Estimates of Saving and Investment in the Indian Economy," *Reserve Bank of India Bulletin* (March 1965).

5. FCII: Reserve Bank of India. *Foreign Collaboration in Indian Industry: Survey Report* (Bombay: 1968).

6. FII: "Foreign Investments in India," *Reserve Bank of India Bulletin* (April 1966).

7. FRNIC: Government of India, Ministry of Finance. *Final Report of the National Income Committee* (New Delhi: 1954).

8. FSJSCI: Reserve Bank of India. *Financial Statistics of Joint Stock Companies in India, 1950–51 to 1962–63* (Bombay: 1967).

9. IBP: Reserve Bank of India. *India's Balance of Payments: 1948–49 to 1961–62* (Bombay: 1963).

10. IFLA: Reserve Bank of India. Census (Survey) of *India's Foreign Liabilities and Assets* (Bombay: 1950, 1955, and 1964).

11. IIIP; "India's International Investment Position," *Reserve Bank of India Bulletin* (August 1969 and March 1971).

MODERNIZATION AND PEASANT
RESISTANCE IN THAILAND*

RALPH THAXTON

I. THE UNITED STATES IN THAILAND

Thailand is now the linchpin in America's Asia. As revolutionaries in Indochina continue to force a reduction of U.S. ground troops from Asia, and as Washington's commitment to Taiwan weakens, Thailand assumes increasing strategic importance for current American counterrevolutionary operations in continental Asia. This development extends a general trend which began in the early 1950s.

With the Vietminh and Pathet Lao successes in 1953–1954, culminating in a revolutionary victory at Dienbienphu, John Foster Dulles scanned Southeast Asia for a reliable ally. Thailand seemed a logical choice. Thai elites were staunchly anti-Communist. Moreover, Washington placed its hope for political stability in modernizing military regimes. The cutting edge of geopolitics was the second crucial determinant. Thailand provided an ideal location for holding the line against a hypothetical Asian Communist conspiracy. Northern Thailand did not border China or Vietnam, but its proximity to these revolutionary governments gave it a strategic position for containment. At

* I wish to express deep gratitude to Edward Friedman, James C. Scott, and Mark Selden for their scathing and helpful criticisms of an earlier version of this paper.

the same time, the scope of local level dissidence in rural Thai society was narrow and the form was traditional: protests and occasional rebellions, but no revolution. Here was an Asian arcadia, a seemingly safe location for the hub of counterinsurgency operations in mainland Southeast Asia.

This was a *quid pro quo* relationship, at least as far as Thai generals were concerned. American foreign policy, with its offers of immediate economic assistance, played to the patronage needs of key military cliques. Moreover, Washington's plans for a counterinsurgency operation in north and northeast Thailand blended nicely with the aspirations of Bangkok and other Central Plains elites for a pan-Thai state. American containment and Thai expansion were more than compatible.

The basis for such a relationship had evolved during the immediate aftermath of World War II. Dulles did not create it. He did incorporate it within the larger framework of American policy in Asia. As early as 1950 the Thai government had become a U.S. military ally. On the eve of the Korean War, Bangkok was receiving $10 million in military assistance from Washington.[1] Following the Thai entrance into the Korean conflict, an American Military Assistance Advisory Group (MAAG–THAI) was sent to Thailand. Throughout the early 1950s Washington increased its military and economic assistance to Bangkok in exchange for Thai participation in SEATO. However, the Thai government was not bound firmly to the U.S. counterrevolutionary posture in Asia until 1957.

In 1955 Chou En-lai appealed to the Thai and other Southeast Asian delegations at the Bandung Conference for mutually beneficial trade agreements and cultural exchanges. He stressed the central theme of Chinese foreign policy under Mao Tse-tung: the willingness to accept regimes of any political configuration or coloration as long as these remain independent of major foreign military presence. At this time revolutionaries were winning on their own in Laos and Vietnam. Norodom Sihanouk was saying no to Dulles and SEATO. The U.S. response to Bandung was a series of CIA-directed and/or -supported coups against potentially neutralist Southeast Asian governments. The move in Thailand came in 1957. It was led by Field Marshall Sarit Thanarat. Approximately a year later the Thai government banned trade with China.

This move was in line with past economic and cultural policies which discriminated against Chinese businesses in Bangkok. This was neither separate from nor incompatible with the second, more critical factor: the trade ban initiated by the pro-American Sarit regime undercut the economic base of competing Thai–Chinese elites who stood to benefit from trade with China.

Placed in the larger historical context of Thai conflicts over economic strategies, the significance of the Sarit coup and the trade ban can be traced to a third factor: economic benefits for Thai elites from the United States and Japan or jointly through international financial institutions such as the World Bank. Bureaucratic capitalists, with Sarit leading the way, won out over Chinese business–Thai army elites who had a stake in a Thai-controlled political economy based on local level enterprises and mutually advantageous forms of cooperation and trade with China.

By the late 1950s a series of debts owed to international financial institutions, primarily controlled by the United States and Japan, had lowered the capacity of the Thai government to resist foreign economic penetration into previously closed or protected sectors of the Thai economy. This development coupled with a marked decline in the international market prices paid for her primary exports—tin, rice, and rubber—undercut Thailand's economic independence.

One year after the Sarit government banned trade with China the Board of Investment was organized to cooperate with U.S. AID in laying the foundation for "an industrial estate to help ease major problems faced by new investors."[2] The 1962 Industrial Investment Act intensified Thailand's growing economic dependency on the United States. According to a special report prepared by Checchi & Co., the private enterprise division of AID, this act "gives investors more privileges and benefits than ever before and alters legal procedures to make them more convenient and less complicated."[3] By the late 1960s a consistent trade deficit had involved the Thai government in a sprawling network of international finance as an alternative to bankruptcy. According to Peter Bell, a student of the Thai political economy, this process had made Thailand increasingly a satellite and "more subtly but no less unimportantly limited the range of choice for domestic policy makers."[4] U.S. loans and foreign aid would not correct this imbalance. On the contrary, they increased economic integration into a capitalist world market in the long run and served the immediate patronage needs and expansionist tendencies of the Thai military.

Growing economic dependence on the United States and pan-Thai aspirations were independent but complementary reasons why Bangkok became involved in American attempts to subvert neutralist governments in Laos and Cambodia during the 1950s and 1960s. U.S. counterinsurgency policies were superimposed on a continuing history of Thai efforts to integrate the western provinces of contemporary Laos and Cambodia into a greater Thai state. Throughout the nineteenth century peasants in the northeastern Thai provinces, hill tribesmen in northern Thailand, and local people in Laos resisted Thai attempts to force-fully bring them into a Thai state. It is no accident that in the contemporary era revolutionaries in Laos and Vietnam cooperate in a common struggle against Thai expansionist policies in their Americanized, counterinsurgency form.

As early as 1961–1962, Thai combat troops had crossed the Mekong and penetrated deep into Laos to join U.S. and Philippine forces in a SEATO maneuver against the Pathet Lao. By 1964 U.S. Special Forces bases at Oudon and Lopboury, Thailand, had become the headquarters for CIA efforts to train a multi-ethnic 20,000-man mercenary army for counterrevolutionary war in Laos. Following the U.S. intensive saturation bombing of the Plain of Jars in July 1969, the core of this mercenary army was shuttled from Oudon in Thailand to the U.S. Air Force–CIA base at Long Cheng in Laos and then parachuted over the Plain of Jars where it burned and destroyed all forms of plant and animal life and terrorized peasants.[5] By the end of May 1960 there were over 5000 Thai troops fighting in Laos.

Thailand is deeply involved in the Second Indochina War. By 1970 over seventy-five percent of the air strikes against northern Vietnam were being flown out of U.S. air bases in Thailand. By spring 1972 the strategic importance of Thailand in escalating the U.S. air war in Vietnam, Laos, and Cambodia was common knowledge. The April 23, 1972, issue of the *Pacific Stars and Stripes* reported "B-52 heavy bombers make almost around the clock bombing missions in Indochina from Utapao Airbase, about 90 miles south of Bangkok on the Gulf of Siam."[6] In 1971 over 10,000 Thai troops, funded by the United States, were operating in southern Vietnam. However, it was joint Bangkok–

Saigon intervention in Laos and particularly in the Cambodian civil conflict which underscored the Thai role in the widening Second Indochina War.

Since the inception of SEATO the Thai government has cooperated with Saigon in U.S. efforts to subvert Cambodian neutrality. In 1956 Bangkok and Saigon imposed an economic blockade against Cambodia. In the same year Thai forces occupied parts of Cambodia's northern provinces and Dulles threatened to cut off U.S. aid if Sihanouk tried to counter this Thai thrust into Cambodia.[7] The clincher came on March 18, 1970, when Bangkok cooperated with Saigon in bringing Lon Nol to power in Phnom Penh. Several days after the March 18 coup, San Nogc Thanh, who had collaborated with the Japanese in World War II, led Khmer Serei forces which had operated in Thailand into Phnom Penh in support of Lon Nol.[8]

Since 1965 the scope of joint United States–Thai counterinsurgency operations has extended beyond Vietnam, Cambodia, and Laos into Thailand itself. During the past seven years the United States has squandered $100 million a year on counterinsurgency activities in Thailand.[9] From 1965 until 1968 approximately ten to twenty percent of this sum was allocated for Pentagon-sponsored research projects, carried out by researchers in universities and private "think tanks."[10] Evidently this "scientific" approach to "village security" failed. Since 1968 over $75 million, or about three-quarters of the counterinsurgency budget, has been allocated to the U.S. Military Assistance Program (MAP) to provide the Thai military with construction equipment, helicopters, tanks, machine guns, and grenade launchers.[11]

The dialectic of counterrevolution and dominoes in continental Southeast Asia is complete. America's strategy in Indochina is increasingly dependent upon crushing a rural based national liberation movement in Thailand. Prior to the implementation of counterinsurgency policies in rural Thailand there were only pockets of resistance to an expanding Thai state. Since 1965 there has been significant revolutionary growth in the northern and northeastern provinces. Hard pressed hill farmers, exploited agricultural laborers, ex-army officers, ineffectual assemblymen, and discontented rural intellectuals make up the social basis of a revolutionary political coalition known as the Thai Patriotic Front (TPF).[12]

II. THE SCOPE AND STRUCTURE
OF THAI POLITICS

Since the "revolution" of 1932 only a small number of military figures and their counterparts in the civilian bureaucracy have actively participated in Thai politics. Prior to the 1960s this political order was linked to the Thai countryside in the most tenuous way. Thai peasants, who make up close to eighty-five percent of the total population, remained politically acquiescent in their limited relationships with the Thai bureaucracy. The low level of political instability in the rural hinterland at that time could be traced more to the absence of direct foreign penetration than to any occasional side benefits of government policies. In contrast to most other Southeast Asian peasant societies, much of rural Thailand had not experienced the destabilizing, dehumanizing consequences of colonially induced commercialization. Accordingly, traditional authority patterns upon which peasant subsistence and security were dependent remained intact.[13]

Within the narrow Thai ruling elite, cliques are the basic units of political competition. Politically, cliques are created and sustained through access to and use of state office. In Thailand the source of patronage is the civilian bureaucracy or the military. In contrast to China and Vietnam, where landed wealth often was sufficient to support private paramilitary organizations, the key to mobilizing support in Thailand is government employment. This provides clique leaders with the opportunity to operate state enterprises in a way that expands the scope of their clientele. Whereas much of this wheeling and dealing is legal, cliques are sustained primarily through corrupt politics. As James C. Scott explains,

> The distribution of high posts, financial opportunities, and government-controlled privileges represents not only the major stakes of political competition but provides the adhesive agent for each competing clique. In this distributive process, political necessity frequently clashes with formal laws and regulations, and the inevitable result is corruption.[14]

Thai political elites can use their positions to accumulate wealth and enhance their status in either of two ways. They may operate as "bureaucratic capitalists" by entering both private and public enterprises directly. This permits Thai politicians to "take direct advantage of legal monopolies, state subsidies or quotas, and government contracts to amass private fortunes." On the other hand, high ranking military figures and civilian bureaucrats may operate as "bureaucratic extortionists" by intimidating, pressuring, and exploiting the existing alien commercial elite.[15]

Direct government exploitation of public enterprise is not a recent phenomenon in Thai politics. However, during the post–World War II period government activities increased considerably—to the point where the Bangkok bureaucracy has monopolies in key enterprises. The growth of government enterprise serves the Bangkok elites in two ways: It enables them to mobilize nationalist, anti-Chinese sentiments among both their urban clientele and Thai elites in the provincial towns, and it provides them with the opportunity to use government enterprises for their own benefit. The emphasis in these ventures is on the narrow, immediate political ends of clique leaders, not on commercial profitability.[16]

A brief analysis of the structure of Thai politics is necessary for understanding the results of American-induced modernization in rural Thailand. The general features of the contemporary administrative structure emerged from over two decades of Thai attempts to prevent the British and French from carving up the kingdom during the last years of the nineteenth century.

The formal administrative hierarchy which developed from the reforms of the 1890s was a regional system with the center also appointing provincial and district officials. At the lower levels there remained an informal structure of authority. Each village continued to elect a headman. The various headmen of a cluster of villages then proceeded to elect a *kaman* who would articulate village interests to the state and oversee village activities. The essential point is that these reforms shifted the location of a semi-feudal style of politics from independent landed-wealth to the Thai bureaucracy. Today *kin muang* or corruption at the expense of the peasantry is institutionalized in the Thai bureaucracy. Peasants look to the village headman and the local *kaman* to protect them against the penetration of the Thai state. At the same time, Thai district officials and provincial authorities pressure local elites to cooperate in *kin muang*. Legally, the *kaman* and headman cannot own property, assess taxes, or enforce official rules and regulations independent of state control. In practice, they do acquire property, cooperate in tax assessment, and use legal regulations to either the benefit of the village or the state. Thus they are pivotal elites. The consequences of foreign intervention can enhance, erode, or even suddenly undercut the authority of these village leaders.

Let's look at an example. Under the protection and approval of the USOM Thai officials began to compel peasants to produce for international markets. The governor of Udorn directed the provincial and district cliques within his patronage network to pressure peasants to grow sorghum and raise chickens and cattle.[17] In many villages communal farmlands, which enabled all peasants to scratch out a subsistence during agricultural crises, were converted into grasslands for cattle breeding. In general, such programs benefited only the few villagers who had the surplus cash to purchase cattle. Most peasants bitterly resented village headmen who assisted Thai authorities in these enterprises. In villages where Thai officials imposed this design without assuring basic rights to survival, peasants joined together in various self-defensive actions against the state. Thus, the attempt of a handful of Thai bureaucrats and their local clients to modernize village economies by imposing the modes, values, and choices of foreign market relationships threatened the welfare of whole villages and provoked conflict between ordinary peasants and traditional village leaders who cooperated with the state. The Thai bureaucracy is a conduit for foreign-induced modernization in all its forms—the green revolution, economic aid, and military assistance. The impact of each form on the peasantry is a critical determinant in shaping the future of politics in Thailand.

III. WRECKING RURAL THAILAND

Chiengrai: The Green Revolution in Peasant Perspective

The green revolution is now in full swing in rural Thailand. In the northern provinces commercialization and mechanization of agriculture has not yet led to the kind of naked exploitation which produces a desperate rural *Lumpenproletariat*. Nevertheless, the following microscopic view of Ban Ping, a village in Chiengkham district in Chiengrai province, will show how the onset of tractor agriculture increases social stratification.[18] The interaction of these two primary variables, commercialization and technology, tends to magnify social class differences not only in Thailand but everywhere that the green revolution has spread.[19] U.S. foreign policy and the Thai bureaucracy are both responsible for this polarization. Both governments permit Shell Oil a free hand in the Thai economy; the policy of both is to put the means of economic development in the hands of local elites over whom the ordinary peasants have minimal control.

In this village the *kaman*, who is the wealthiest man in the district, secured from district officials the sole franchise for Shell Oil. He then joined the assistant district official and his brother in dominating agriculture.[20] Not only does their ownership of three tractors permit them to determine when fields are plowed, but they also can shut off any competition by refusing to sell petroleum products. Thus Shell Oil makes its way through a corrupt bureaucracy to fuel foreign-produced tractors which accelerate the green revolution at the expense of the majority of villagers. This "revolution" threatens to tear apart the whole fabric of Thai peasant society.

The appearance of tractors is part of the green revolution which is sweeping rural Thailand. The peasants of Ban Ping own none of the eleven tractors which plow their fields. Townsmen own them all. This puts most villagers at a distinct disadvantage in the competition for scarce resources. Most peasants no longer can determine when their fields will be worked. Tractor owners do. Therefore, poorer peasants must sell their services to wealthier villagers who already have an edge in the competition for the market. In the Thai political context tractor agriculture provides rich peasants and outsiders an opportunity to squeeze the majority of villagers.

The peasants in this formerly self-sufficient, culturally insulated village are losing their land to the "townsmen who control the means of development."[21] These outsiders can manipulate laws concerning land development and restrictions on land holdings. Prior to the commercialization and mechanization of agriculture Thai peasants acquired land on a *de facto* basis, through occupation and cultivation. However, at the close of the nineteenth century the Thai monarchy initiated changes in the procedure for acquiring land and in 1954 Bangkok passed a law requiring three steps for "legal" ownership—occupation, cultivation, and the acquiring of an official land title certificate. These changes do not protect peasant claims to land. Most villagers continue to think and act as if *de facto* residency is sufficient for land rights. However, according to Bangkok, many of them are working the land "illegally." Thus, better-informed persons can use the law to dispossess peasants of their land. This is precisely what is happening in Ban Ping and other Thai villages.

The penetration of a world market economy tends to wear away the practice of cooperative agriculture. This alters traditional patterns of labor to the disadvantage of most peasants. Farming based on multi-household cooperation and reciprocity are giving way to individual household competition and impersonal, contractual transactions.

As land and labor become market commodities and as prices and profits become critical determinants in peasant economic behavior the very quality of social relations is transformed. The penetration of commercial agriculture weakens the network of traditional obligations to kin and neighbors.[22] Unable to count on relatives and neighbors for assistance in hard times, peasants turn to traditional authorities, such as village headmen, for assistance.

In Ban Ping peasants increasingly worry about the lessened capability of the village headman to protect their claims to land from outside interests, to bring together a village work force for their mutual benefit, and to avoid obligation and debts to townsmen which threaten their community and security. The district officials who administer national land title registration attempt to use the headman as their reporting agent, expecially for claims on the more commercialized paddy fields. As officials and tractor owners pressure him for more "accurate" reporting, the headman is faced with two choices: he can continue to help fellow villagers at the risk of increasing outside pressure on himself or he can assist Bangkok at the risk of undercutting his intravillage influence. How did Ban Ping's headman cope with this dilemma? Immediately prior to the filing of land claims the headman "disappeared for some ten days."[23] In the absence of the traditional protective buffer provided by village authority figures Thai peasants are exposed to the "reporting" activities of outsiders. In this context peasants are increasingly skeptical of village leaders who cannot cushion the shocks of modernization.

The intensity of peasant discontent is in large measure dependent upon the capacity of local authorities to deal fairly with villagers. Under the pressures of the green revolution the headman in Ban Ping has begun to "borrow" both the temple treasury and communal savings for a village school in order to pay personal debts to outsiders.[24] Village institutions and culture have begun to deteriorate.

Commercialization and technology, imposed on the village by a corrupt bureaucracy, undermine the moral basis of a peasant society. The majority of peasants see the accumulation of great wealth as a sign of selfishness, not success. In Ban Ping the economic pie is expanding but the size of peasant slices is dwindling. The village headman has assisted the outsiders who receive the lion's share of increasing agricultural productivity. He pressures villagers to work without pay on commercialized rice paddy fields owned by townsmen with whom he has contractual relations. Yet the headman is in debt.[25] Peasants neither respect him as a successful entrepreneur nor look to him for protection and security. Suspicion and noncooperation have replaced trust and cooperative economic activities. Modernization has begun to erode the legitimacy of traditional political authority. In Ban Ping this process has not caused protests, demonstrations, or insurrections. It has, however, alienated those villagers whose solvency and security are threatened by the transformation of traditional agriculture.[26]

The social and psychological crises attendant on the green revolution in Ban Ping are not unique to this village. In the context of Thai politics the commercialization of agriculture is primarily a social catastrophe. It is not just economic deprivation. The data on mechanization and commercialization in Ban Ping provide only a snapshot of a long-run process which wears away the very essence of communal life. Traditional village social security mechanisms eventually break down. It becomes impossible to even share poverty. It is true that in Ban Ping the economic base has not yet collapsed. There are still subsistence level choices in agriculture. Nevertheless, the growing social stratification and psychological discontent in this northern Thai village are the critical indicators of increasing mass alienation from those who have introduced and benefited from foreign ways—the local elites who are sustained by their ties to Thai district officials and Shell Oil.

The United States Agency for International Development in Sakon Nakhon

During the early 1960s the United States increased economic and technical assistance to rural Thailand. Much of this aid took the form of a rural development program administered by AID. Throughout the decade there was a marked trend away from programs designed to spur development to activities which stressed security and counterinsurgency. From 1960 to 1963 the emphasis was on a Community Development program. When the Thai bureaucracy proved ineffective in implementing this, AID backed the creation of the Mobile Development Unit, an organization which turned rural electric cooperatives into private enterprises at the expense of whole villages. In 1964–1965 USAID began shifting most of its funds to counterinsurgency programs in the northern and northeastern provinces. In line with this, an Accelerated Rural Development (ARD) program was designed to "give the Thai army's cumbersome U.S.-style armored and infantry units easy access to these areas in time of insurgency."[27] By 1968 almost four out of every five dollars were going to counterinsurgency activities.

On June 7, 1970, John A. Hannah, the director of the USAID program, publicly admitted that AID was a front for CIA operations in Southeast Asia.[28] Thailand was no exception. A 1968 AID pamphlet. *The US/AID Program in Thailand,* declared that "The U.S. AID program in Thailand is concentrated upon a single objective: supporting the Royal Thai Government in its efforts to contain, control, and eliminate the Communist Insurgency in rural areas."[29] By 1968 AID had been replaced by the CIA, which in turn gave way to the U.S. army. AID is often presented to the American public as a program designed to democratize local level politics in the Third World. Its publicly avowed political goals in Thailand are:[30]

1) To establish local self-determination through developing leadership and organization
2) To encourage participation in village development

3) To resolve peasant problems
4) To utilize village resources
5) To change the image of the government in the eyes of the peasantry.

Let's look at the empirical consequences of USAID penetration of rural Thai politics.

Establishing Local Self-Determination through Developing Leadership and Organization. The operating assumption of the AID rural development program is that local self-determination can be achieved through foreign intervention. There are glaring contradictions in this concept. First, its ideological roots are in a colonial mentality that has been under attack by nationalists throughout the twentieth century. The contradiction in imposing self-government is clear. Second, the very nature of elite–mass political linkages in Thailand precludes a genuine mass participatory politics. Corruption and intransigence in the bureaucracy is not unique to Thailand. This has been the very hallmark of other U.S.-supported regimes in Asia: the Nacionalista and Liberal parties in the Philippines; the KMT in China; Diem and Thieu in Vietnam; Lon Nol in Cambodia, and Rhee and Park in Korea.

The third ideological dimension of USAID is laid bare in the following passage:

> ..., the establishment of the principle of self-determination for every village community, as proposed here, is not based on humanitarian or idealistic grounds; it is based on hard, practical reasons related to the promotion of village security.[31]

The word *security* goes to the heart of the matter: it means political stability, that is, insuring the perpetuation of Thai elites and their American sponsors.

Political Participation in Village Development. AID development schemes provide lower rural classes neither the economic opportunities nor the practical cues and suggestions necessary to enhance their livelihood. Instead, such programs are administered in a fashion which restricts and restrains mass political participation. The most striking example of how the bureaucracy which administers CD (Community Development) discourages and blocks peasant involvement in politics is contained in an anthropologist's account of a CD meeting in Chiengkham district, Chiengrai province, northern Thailand:

The meeting of November 20, 1960, was extremely elaborate. Headmen had been told to arrive in uniform at 8:30 in the morning, so that they would have time to rehearse their welcome to the provincial governor, who was expected at 10:00. The district school teachers had made a huge banner bearing the legend, "Meeting for the Primary Demonstration of Community Development. First time! 2503 B. E. Amphur Chiengkham." This was the first indication that the headmen were given that the meeting concerned Community Development. On the stage with the district officer and other high officials were a microphone, a phonograph, a Buddha-altar, and some placards in Thai, and some in English, illustrating poverty, ignorance, malnutrition, and disease.... The governor never arrived....

The district officer read for over an hour from a mimeographed address sent him by a superior official in charge of community development.... He spent little time on the need to foster expressions of local opinion, but he elaborated upon the elimination of gambling, repairing roads, keeping villages orderly, and ... building toilets. He announced which village had been chosen for development and ordered its headman to make sure that these things were done by the time that a community development official arrived from the provincial capital next year.[32]

As to discussing politics,

> Each group was to select one of five major problems for Community Development, discuss it and report back to the entire meeting. For the most part, only the teachers [who are employees of the Thai government and often the clients of the district officials who administer CD] were active in these groups. The headmen and other villagers sat quietly and spoke only when put a direct question. When a show of hands was called for, they looked to see how the others were voting.... [Thus,] the public reports given by the teachers or spokesmen after the discussions were recapitulations of the speeches made earlier by the district officers and other officials.[33]

Most peasants who attend this and similar meetings in Sakon Nakhon experience Community Development as a symbolic display of elite wealth, education, and status. Poor people are put in their place. With only four years of education or less, banners with foreign concepts written in Thai, not to mention English, are difficult to read. To rehearse for a provincial governor who does not show up is humiliating. To be instructed to build toilets close to the roads near their villages is frustrating. Although the peasants may not be aware of it, the location of toilets enhances a district official's relationship with superior patrons who happen to be passing through the district.[34] They use AID-sponsored toilets; the peasants do not. Participation in this northern Thai village means building toilets for corrupt elites and subsequently inhaling the stench which permeates the previous purity of village air.

Five years after AID-sponsored programs such as Community Development penetrated the northeastern province of Sakon Nakhon, where peasants are desperate for water, not even one village had a sufficient number of safe artesian wells or an adequate irrigation system. In Yang Kham the government simply dropped the materials for constructing wells in the village. Consequently, "the wells were not built properly—the brink was just a heap of stones and not cemented."[35] In 1966 there was an outbreak of diarrhea in Yang Kham. Ground water had spilled back into the well. An AID interviewer reports that "the well could have contributed to the deaths of 35 children."[36]

Resolving Peasant Problems: From Community Development to Accelerated Rural Development. There are at least four sources of credit at the village level: close kinsmen, landlords, moneylenders, and cooperative societies. An integral part of the Community Development program is the revitalization of old and initiation of new credit cooperatives at the village level. A look at how these AID backed Credit Cooperatives operate in the cluster of villages which make up the subdistrict of Kusakam in Wamon-Niwat district, Sakon Nakhon province, throws some light on who gets what, when, and how from USAID in Thailand.

In Inplaeng village forty out of sixty peasant households are in debt. Approximately sixty percent of these famlies must look to moneylenders who live outside the village because they cannot use the Credit Cooperatives. The interest rate is sixty percent a year. In sharp contrast, the fifteen families which qualify to use the Credit Cooperative pay an annual interest rate of ten percent.[37] In Kok Klang and in Hadsaimoon about two out of every three peasant households are excluded from the Cooperatives.[38] Villagers do not approve of the political constraints on their use of the Credit Cooperatives.

AID INTERVIEWER: To become members of credit cooperatives, it is necessary for people to have the Non Son 3 [a legal certificate which permits acquisition of land] first. Is that right?

VILLAGER: Yes, what we need now is the Non Son 3.

VILLAGER: We don't know what is the difficulty. We have just been waiting for the Amphur action on our request.

AID INTERVIEWER: What's the nature of your request?

VILLAGER: The request was made to the effect that the Amphur officials are required to come and see how they can get people here to find a chance to clear the land for their use and manage to grant them title to the land.

VILLAGE HEADMAN: You know, I dare say that nobody in the *Tambon* (Kusakam) owns land in the sense that they have title to the land. That's why we want the Amphur to give us a Non Son 3.

AID INTERVIEWER: ... when was the request sent to the Amphur officials to settle this matter?

VILLAGER: Last August.

AID INTERVIEWER: Last August! So about 5–6 months ago, and so far nothing has been heard from the land officer.

VILLAGER: No.

AID INTERVIEWER: Is this problem applied just to this village or other villages too?

VILLAGER: It is applied to other villages too.[39]

It is possible to extract the central political effects of AID-supported Credit Cooperatives from this account.

The most chronic debtors are excluded from this village credit system. Membership is restricted to those who can show proof of land ownership. Clearly, possession of this document is dependent upon money and the whims of land officers. Throughout the AID village surveys, peasants complain about the corrupt pressures applied by the *chow nai* (officials who behave as lords) in land registration.[40]

In 1966, concomitant with ever-increasing U.S. military activities, AID implemented a new program in the north and northeast. This program is called Accelerated Rural Development (ARD). About ninety percent of the ARD budget has been funneled to highway building activities.[41] According to a USOM cost-benefit analysis, road building is the key to modernization and progress—it facilitates farming and marketing, increases the value of peasant land, and benefits distant, culturally insulated villages by integrating them into the larger society.[42] There is another reason: counterinsurgency. ARD studies are punctuated with "law and order" rationales for highway construction.[43]

The economic impact of ARD on peasant farming and marketing is subtle but profound. In contrast to modern roads, the well-traveled peasant routes to rice fields and local marketplaces are no better off than they were prior to the appearance of ARD in the days of collective village efforts in road building and repair.[44] In fact, time spent adhering to ARD work schedules often precludes collective efforts to repair constantly used roads. Thus, indirectly, ARD activities contribute to the deterioration of oxcart trails and intravillage footpaths which are very important in peasant lives.

How do new all-weather highways harm people who still use these old trails to reach market towns? The building of such roads provides townsmen the opportunity to gain even greater economic leverage over less mobile villagers. They own the tractors and trucks which roll faster than peasant carts on ARD roads. They can secure franchises for agricultural chemicals, farm implements, and foreign-supplied fuel oil. At the same time, peasants who reside in villages which are by-passed by superhighways are left in weaker competitive positions than those who reside in villages situated near ARD roads.

Modernization can help rural people escape the bonds of poverty. New highways can accelerate marketing processes and integrate isolated villages into a larger, more beneficial political economy. However, the political context is decisive in determining who wins and loses in this process. The political context of ARD works against a highway program which would provide road workers with secure jobs, equalize village wealth and income, and balance rural market economies. It precludes an egalitarian and humane transformation of Thai peasant society.

Changing the Image of the Government in the Eyes of the Peasantry. Sakon Nakhon peasants are coming to distrust, resent, and even hate local political authorities who cannot protect their economy and preserve their culture. In this sense there is a crisis of political legitimacy in northeast Thailand. The AID attempt to resolve this crisis by winning the hearts and minds of rural people is the foundation of U.S. security-oriented rural development.[45]

AID assumes that the principal sources of instability in rural Thai society lie in factors other than the policies of the political order itself. From AID's perspective, various manifestations of political disorder, e.g., grain riots, rent strikes, tax rebellions, are caused primarily by "outside agitators" and "rising aspirations." Accordingly, rural development is geared to protect the Thai political order against insurgent attacks and to enable it to cope with the rising expectations and escalating demands of unreasonable peasant masses.

In sharp contrast to this AID version of instability, the data on modernization in the northeast suggests that modernization in its foreign-induced, Central Thai form breeds instability as it breaches the rights and corrodes the experiences which give security and meaning to peasant lives.

AID also assumes that foreign aid can renovate and stabilize a worn and rickety political order by incremental tinkering. This assumption ignores that reforms are carried out by the very order which thrives on an unequal exchange with noninvolved lower rural classes and does not consider that where the state already has violated basic subsistence rights even the smallest incremental movements which further reduce peasant benefits are likely to engender mass resistance. The consequences of American attempts to renovate illegitimate, counterrevolutionary orders in China, Vietnam, and Thailand by incremental and partial structural changes illustrates this flaw in AID logic.

The credit cooperatives in southern China during the 1930s and northeast Thailand during the 1960s excluded chronically indebted villagers and made it increasingly difficult for them to gain a subsistence share of village resources in the competition with rich and solvent peasants. Chinese owner-cultivators and Thai freeholders bitterly resented these institutions. In the 1950s the Diem regime forced Vietnamese tenants who had not paid rent during the previous decade of Vietminh rule to pay a "reduced rate" of twenty-five percent on landlord lands. This "reform" provoked a burst of peasant outrage. In each of these cases American-backed regimes left the structural basis of rural poverty and discontent intact. In no case have incremental reforms fostered lasting loyalties to illegitimate orders. In several cases peasants have revolted against the structure of exclusion itself and attempted to create their own political experience. In every case where this has happened the foreign aid scale has tilted from subsistence- to security-oriented development and the tempo of state coercion and repression has increased. The politics of U.S. aid in northeast Thailand seems to fit into this general pattern.

The multiple political crisis in contemporary rural Thailand is in part inevitable with national integration and industrialization. However, the particular means of dealing with this crisis in the northeast unnecessarily exacerbates peasant problems.

The Politics of Force in Northern Thailand

In Chiengrai the commercialization and mechanization of agriculture have combined to unravel the social fabric of village life. However, at least as late as 1965, there were strategies of subsistence open to the peasantry. People felt the pinch but they could get by. In Sakon Nakhon rural development programs have been imposed by a political order which threatens the welfare of whole villages. Taxes are increasing. Incomes are declining. Lands are being lost. The trend is from solvency to debt bondage. There have been protests, demonstrations, and occasional clashes with Thai officials.

In contrast, the situation in northern Thailand is characterized by full scale rural rebellion. Actually, Meo farmers always have offered armed resistance to pan-Thai efforts to assimilate them. However, under the impact of US.–Thai penetration traditional modes of conflict resolution between the Meo and Thai political authorities are breaking down, thus precluding less violent patterns of politics at the local level. Rural people are pushed up against the wall of subsistence. Rebellion is the only alternative to annihilation. American counterinsurgency policies have encouraged a heavy-handed bureaucracy to handle local problems through a politics of force. The genesis of political violence is U.S.–Thai penetration, leading to protests and skirmishes, counterinsurgency violence, armed revolts. This sequence of events is illustrated in several rebellions in the northern provinces. Before turning to case studies, it is necessary to briefly focus on the international forces behind the escalation of local conflict.

The 1957 Sarit coup was a victory for the Thai military. General Phao, the director of the police, lost. The Thai army took command of internal security. Throughout the 1950s the military checked efforts of Thai Border Patrol Police (BPP) and Provincial Police (PP) to extend their authority deep into northern provinces. Following the Nam Tha crisis of 1962, however, the CIA pushed for the expansion of police activities and the BPP increased its reporting of "Communist terrorist" actions in the north. Meo villages were mapped. Plans for airfields were drawn up. Thai and U.S. intelligence agencies began to offer medical and agricultural assistance, local educational facilities, and paramilitary training to villagers. The Thai army–police cleavage and the post-Cuban crisis low-key posture of the Kennedy administration in Southeast Asia temporarily constrained the immediate development of full blown counterinsurgency in Thailand in the 1962–1965 period.

The 1965 U.S. military escalation in Vietnam changed this situation. The Johnson administration gave the go-ahead for the implementation of a multidimensional counterinsurgency program in Thailand. Between 1965 and 1968 the number of personnel in the BPP increased forty percent and the PP increased thirty-six percent.[46] The Office of Public Safety (OPS) of AID, which has trained military police in counterinsurgency in the Philippines, Korea, Laos, and Vietnam, provided the Thai BPP and PP with riot gear, machine guns, and helicopter service.[47] The USIS trained Thai Police Civic Action Teams and then sent them into villages as "teachers" in hamlet development projects. The CIA stepped up its efforts to recruit and train a Meo mercenary army in Thailand to cooperate with CIA-supported Meo mercenaries in Laos.

By 1968 a loose network of counterinsurgency training camps covered the northern provinces. This strategy backfired. U.S.–Thai paramilitary operations heightened the passions of Meo resistance to Thai injustices. In village after village counterinsurgency provoked insurgency.

The Meo revolts are partly a conflict between lowlanders and highlanders, partly a struggle between an expanding modern territorial state and hill farmers, and partly a clash between an expansive, profit-oriented economy and slash-and-burn agriculturalists defending their traditional subsistence rights to the forests. Most of the inhabitants of the northern highlands are Meo tribesmen. Slash-and-burn or swidden agriculture is their primary technique of survival.

During the past decade Bangkok has encouraged the migration of lowland Thai into predominantly Meo areas. These ethnic Thai farmers use modern agricultural implements to convert vast areas of forests into vegetable farms at the expense of the Meo.

Thai civilian and police administrators also complicate the Meo struggle for survival by directly interfering in the growing of opium, their main cash crop. Thai officials constitute one of the main groups which benefit from the international opium traffic in Southeast Asia. In the past the Thai extorted the Chinese merchants who peddled the commodity. More recently these officials have tried to increase their gains by dealing directly with Meo opium growers. If the Meo cannot meet their extortionist demands, Thai officials restrict growing of this product without helping them develop other crops. This is a serious threat to people who depend on one cash crop. However, it is Thai interference in slash-and-burn agriculture which is at the heart of Meo grievances.

Modern Thai law does not consider non-Thai hill farmers to be legal citizens. The Meo are denied the right to acquire title to land. The government considers the upland forests to be state preserves. These provisions make the Meo "illegal squatters." The Thai Forest Service denies Meo access to new lands. Thai officials invoke the state preserve rights to extort Meo who seek access to *de facto* held lands. If the hill farmers attempt to clear and burn the forests, they are arrested. However, Thai district officials permit Thais who possess "proper licenses" to cut down the teak forests.[48] Thai lumber magnates ship this valuable teakwood to Taiwan through Chinese merchants. Low-wage Taiwanese carpenters use it to make furniture which is shipped primarily to the United States and Japan.

The Meo experience Thai encroachment on forests, interference in opium growing, and drastic changes in land usage as a denial of their collective identity and their cultural heritage as well as economic deprivation. They cannot find recourse through the state. The civil service in this mountainous region is exclusively Thai. Thai district officials degrade Meo language, dress, and hygienic practices. Under Bangkok rule ethnicity and class combine to increase economic hardships and preclude the peaceful and equitable settling of Meo grievances.

In the past corrupt pressures and Thai cultural arrogance provoked low levels of conflict between Meo farmers and district officials. Meo were threatened and physically harassed. Thai officials were occasionally wounded by snipers. This conflict is now taking on new and ominous dimensions.

Throughout the early 1960s several thousand Meo tribesmen practiced slash-and-burn agriculture in the hills of Lom Sak in the northern province of Phetchabun. By the mid-1960s they were experiencing an ecological crisis. Their soil was nearly exhausted. Several village clusters, approximately 3000 Meo, headed south into the uninhabited upland forests southwest of Lom Sak.

Local Thai authorities tolerated this move for several years. However, in August of 1967 the BPP ordered the Meo to move back north. According to the Thai authorities, forest preserves were being destroyed. The natural watershed would be damaged. They maintained that this would create water control problems in the Thai-dominated valleys. Also, with increasing concern about rebellion in the north, the Meo move was now interpreted by the USOM and the Thai BPP as a potential insurgency threat: the villagers had in fact moved to the southern side of the U.S. financed road designed to expand and facilitate Thai–U.S. military activities in Laos. The Meo attempted to negotiate. They explained that slash-and-burn techniques, if properly practiced, making sure that rotation periods were long, would not harm the watershed. They told the authorities their previous land would not sustain them. People would starve. The BPP told the Meo to move or else. Meo economic choices had been virtually eliminated. They chose to resist.

Almost half a year passed. Then, in mid-winter 1968, the BPP forcefully removed the eight Meo villages by truck on ARD roads. A spring harvest barely got them through until November when the crops failed. The sites had been chosen by the Thai BPP from the air. Moreover, the emergency relief supplies, which the BPP had promised the Meo as a condition of their move, did not make it through the corrupt Thai bureaucracy. The BPP action had precipitated economic disaster.

The Meo rebellion in Lom Sak took several forms, each signaling a new stage in escalating political violence, each dependent upon the actions of the BPP and eventually the Thai army. Al McCoy captures the essence of the progression:

> In mid-November the Meo began to steal food from urban storage areas, and when the BPP interfered, the Meo responded predictably by attacking nearby camps at which the BPP were training Meo for counterinsurgency work. All the Meo in those camps deserted to the insurgents, and soon the local BPP were outnumbered, surrounded, and without water. The initial government response was to send in some army troops from Phitsanulok, reinforcements for the BPP and helicopters and fighters from the Police Mobile Air Reserve. However, the Meo compensated for their inferior weapons (mainly shotguns) by using the terrain to their advantage and outmaneuvering the cumbersome government troops. By December 7, a fifty-man police squad sent in to reinforce the BPP was completely wiped out, and combined ground and air attacks had failed to break through the Meo seige of the major towns in the region.[49]

The BPP had created the conditions for a violent rural uprising. The Meo attacks on CIA-sponsored BPP camps provided the spark which set it off. The Thai Third Army rushed to Lom Sak in early December. The Meo employed hit-and-run tactics in a successful three-week defense. At this point the government escalated the conflict. Three "refugee camps" were set up. The Meo were ordered out of the forests by leaflets which they couldn't read. Then the Royal Thai Air Force proceeded to bomb and napalm Lom Sak. Children, women, men, animals, houses—nothing was spared. An incident which, prior to U.S. penetration, most likely would have been averted or resolved through minimal, low level conflict with Thai authorities, had escalated into a violent pattern of politics between starving hill tribesmen and intransigent Thai authorities.

Events in Lom Sak foreshadowed the general sequence of rebellion and reaction in the far northern provinces of Nan and Chiengrai from 1968–1971. The genesis and results of counter-revolutionary violence in Meo Maw, a Meo village located in the Nan-Chiengrai foothills which skirt the Laos border, fit into a wider pattern of events throughout these two provinces. By looking at this case we can begin to grasp how outside agitators, in this case U.S. and Thai authorities, create the political conditions which impel villagers to pick up guns and join rebels in a life and death struggle for their livelihood, their families, and their humanity.[50]

Like other hill farmers, the villagers of Meo Maw live in a crisis environment. Population is increasing. Land is scarce. But the political climate presents the greatest problem as Bangkok increases its efforts to integrate the Meo into a pan-Thai state. Recently a school has been established in the village. Since its teachers are all Thai, parents have difficulty understanding what their children learn. There also is a new Hill Tribe Development and Welfare Center in the vicinity. The arrogant provincial official who is the Center's director refers to villagers as animals, as less than human.[51]

The Thai government and foreigners began to regulate Meo lives more forcefully. USIS trained and dispatched a five-man Thai Police Civic Action Team to Meo Maw. These Thai "teachers" were trained in weaponry. Then villagers learned that the Thai government had initiated a "resettlement" of Meo tribesmen into the lowlands. There were rumors that the Meo taken to these detention camps were treated harshly, that housing was poor, and that success in agriculture was very uncertain. In fact, the provincial authorities were creating "refugee centers" in Nan and Chiengrai. At least 4000 Meo and Yao tribesmen in Nan alone had been driven into these areas by saturation bombing of suspected insurgent villages. As in Lom Sak, resettlement disrupted farming schedules and left no time to clear land for the spring planting. Whole families most likely would go hungry. The political climate in Meo Maw was one of unspoken tension.

In mid-February 1968 the USIS Police Civic Action Team was shot up by machine-gun fire. Their clothes and mattresses were blood-soaked. Revolutionaries were in Meo Maw!

Who were these persons? According to the U.S. and Thai authorities, they were Meo who had been "lured" to Laos and Vietnam for training in the strategy and tactics of guerrilla subversion. From the villagers' viewpoint, Meo Maw was being pulled apart by the presence of the foreign-trained Police Civic Action Team. One outspoken villager had accused the leader of the USIS-trained hamlet development team of embezzling pay. The conflict escalated to the point where this respected village leader threatened to kill the police honcho. Apparently the message was USIS out of our village or else. The police stayed. The villager left to contact the local Meo resistance. At 2:00 A.M.

on the eighteenth of February, he returned with four insurgents and attacked the USIS trained Thai "teachers."

The villagers understood the explosive situation which was shaping up in Meo Maw. Refugees who had recently come through the village had told them that any resistance would be met with force. In fact, one group of tribesmen had told the inhabitants of the villages in the vicinity of Meo Maw that their settlement had been burned by uniformed cavalrymen. In this situation the whole village mobilized for action. People were scared. Thai officials would be coming soon. One delegation to the headman suggested that the village not go into hiding, but move to a position nearby if the Thai government would guarantee the headman that there would be no air strike. *Otherwise, their only choice would be to cooperate with the rebels.* Another delegation pushed to leave the village immediately. The headman vehemently opposed this. According to him, any move to the forest would be interpreted by the Royal Thai Air Force as a sign that the village was assisting the insurgents. Nevertheless, the women in the village had called their own meeting and proceeded to evacuate immediately. Others moved to a location halfway between Meo Maw and the nearby village. By 7:00 A.M. on the twentieth of February, only the headman and twenty other men remained.

Throughout the next two days the headman employed his radio transmitter in order to get an assurance from the local Thai authorities that the village would not be bombed. The district officer would not give it. Instead, he mobilized the Provincial Police squad and proceeded to the village. The village spokesmen wanted to explain their dilemma and to negotiate. The Thai authorities wanted to drink. The intoxicated police commander insulted the district officer and sidearms were drawn. The anthropologist in residence and the son of the village chief managed to disarm them. According to the anthropologist's journal, three hours later the drunken district officer arrived at his house and

> ... stated that all ... [villagers] are Communists; that they had deceived me into trust. I asked him if there would be any bombing. He smiled. I told him that if one bomb hit any hamlet of the village I would report his actions of that evening to high authorities. Advised him that he should use radio to recommend against bombing.

> District officer left house in a rage shouting that I had joined
> the Communists. From outside he added that the police would
> conduct me under arrest to the town at sunrise.[52]

The actions of the Thai officials had precipitated a village
rebellion.

At dawn the village chief, assisted by the anthropologist, began
to transmit frantic calls to American authorities in the USOM to
explain that the village was not Communist. The effort failed.
CIA headquarters were closed on Sunday. At midday three T-28
planes strafed and bombed the village. Meo Maw was burned to
the ground.

Almost a month after the burning of Meo Maw the anthropologist who had been in the village was hospitalized. One night
late he felt the presence of people in his room. Meo Maw villagers and the headman informed him that the strangers who
had come to the village had established a mountain camp. "If we
stay in these hills, we will be able to plant rice. Otherwise where
will we get the rice?"[53] The Thai army had burned all granaries
in the entire village cluster, including Meo Maw. The struggle
for liberation in Nan and Chiengrai had been joined by local
Meo. Indeed, as in Lom Sak, there was no alternative if the Meo
people were to survive. The *chow nai* and American-trained
police had made the choice this simple.

This study casts serious doubt on conventional explanations of
modernization and counterrevolution in Thailand and other
rural Asian societies. The green revolution has siphoned off
village capital, narrowed peasant economic choices, and contributed to discontent. In the absence of traditional elite performance of expected communal services peasants experience the
commercialization of agriculture as a social catastrophe. Where
the state makes no allowance for redistribution and relief in
response to this crisis, or where state reforms are carried out by a
corrupt bureaucracy, social immiseration can increase during a
period of agricultural development. In southern China during
the 1930s, southern Vietnam during the 1950s, and northern
Thailand during the 1960s humans, not production statistics,
suffered.

In Sakon Nakhon modernization *cum* counterinsurgency has
increased suffering among villagers. Security-oriented development adds to the arsenal of a political order which is violating
peasant rights to subsistence. In China and Vietnam the state

transgression of these rights created a situation favorable to the revolutionary mobilization of discontent among the middle and lower stratum of the peasantry. In Thailand, which is comparatively less stratified, this development has mobilized entire villages against the state. In this context U.S. anti-Communist aid is a self-fulfilling prophecy since it has provoked the resistance which is the prior justification for its existence.

The Meo rebellions in northern Thailand are explosions against an economic order which threatens to shatter the moral basis of communal life and a political order which denies a separate and unique cultural identity. A modern Thai police force has encroached on traditional subsistence rights, endangered Meo survival, and finally cooperated with the U.S.-advised and -equipped Royal Thai Army and Air Force in crushing the miserable.

IV. IMPERIALISM IN FUTURE THAI POLITICS

Prior to the 1960s the scope of antigovernment rebellion in Thailand was rather narrow. Modernization and counterinsurgency have changed this situation. The mass discontent and violent outbursts depicted in this study typify politics in hundreds of villages in the north and northeast. Since the U.S. military buildup in 1966 there has been considerable revolutionary growth. Several provinces have experienced continuous revolts. In self-defense the Meo are training for guerrilla war against Thai armies and police. Northern border areas which could be governed by small, lightly armed Thai police patrols in 1968 could not be held by heavily armed Thai army battalions in 1971. Insurgents have established several base areas with simple and self-sufficient economies. Despite these signs of growth, local and internal politics restrain the development of a full-scale national liberation movement in Thailand.

The Meo revolts in the northern highlands, where the intensity of resistance is greatest, are separatist. One of the keys to Vietminh success was their alliance with Tho mountain dwellers, an ethnic minority which was revolting against the discriminatory policies of foreigners and their native minions. Although similar support exists in northern Thailand, the TPF has not yet entered into a viable coalition with the Meo. The Meo revolts remain regional in scope and secessionist in goals.

The peasant movements in the northeast are localized insurgencies. Although these rebellions have an antiforeign ring, they are not necessarily fueled by nationalism. Peasants are slow to respond to the nationalist appeals of the TPF. Their protests are against the shattering of a world view conditioned by limited parameters of wealth and relatively local and narrow life experiences. The absence of regular revolutionary armies places the responsibility of protecting economic gains on village militia and roving guerrillas. This enables modern counterrevolutionary armies to squelch local resistance and makes peasants fear the consequences of actively supporting the insurgents. Thus, unless the Indochina War spills over into Thailand in a way that violently splits the homogeneous Thai elite and drives whole army divisions to fight with the TPF, a full-scale peasant revolution in northeast Thailand seems unlikely in the immediate future.

The post–World War II American dominance of Thai politics is underscored by the recent withdrawal of U.S. combat troops from Vietnam. Units such as the Marine Air Wing simply have been shifted to Thailand in support of an intensive buildup of U.S. air power. Thus Thai revolutionaries must defeat a far more formidable foe than the Thai army. Since the TPF has neither the organizational strength nor the rich experience in people's war which has made for NLF success, this seems an unlikely prospect in the near future.

Imperialism in future Thai politics could take any of several forms. The most likely configuration is Thai generals permitting the United States to use Thailand for a wider Southeast Asian air war in exchange for U.S. military assistance in suppressing internal revolts. However, U.S. domestic pressures for an end to American troop participation in protracted, nonwinnable wars necessitates U.S. reliance on native nonwhite counterinsurgency forces. In the immediate future U.S. air power may be used to support Thai armies staffed with Japanese advisers. This transformation would be in line with Japan's increasing edge over the United States in trade and investment in Thailand. There is a third possibility: A drastic reversal of U.S. policies toward Southeast Asia coupled with a continued Japanese economic thrust may bring Japanese special forces as well as advisers to Thailand, practicing a science they almost mastered in an earlier drive for Southeast Asian markets. None of these scenarios portends a rapid and humane alternative to modernization and counter-revolution in rural Thailand.

NOTES

1. Jonathan Mirsky and Stephen E. Stonefield, "The United States in Laos, 1945–1962," in Edward Friedman and Mark Selden, eds., *America's Asia: Dissenting Essays on Asian-American Relations* (New York, Pantheon Books, 1971), p. 263.

2. *A Program to Strengthen the Board of Investment of Thailand,* prepared by Checchi and Company, sponsored by the Private Enterprise Division Agency for International Development, United States Operations Mission, Bangkok (Washington, D.C., February 1965), pp. 5, 7, 11.

3. *Ibid.,* p. 7.

4. Peter F. Bell, "Thailand: The Political Economy of Under-Development," Discussion Paper No. 19, University of British Columbia, Department of Economics, April 1969.

5. Burchett, *Second Indochina War, Cambodia and Laos* (New York, International Publishers, 1970), pp. 161, 174–75. Cf. Fred P. Branfman, *Voices From the Plain of Jars, Life Under an Air War* (New York, Harper and Row, 1972).

6. "Report Buildup in Thailand," *Pacific Stars and Stripes,* April 23, 1972, p. 6.

7. Burchett, *Second Indochina War,* pp. 8, 40–41, 43.

8. *Ibid.,* p. 44.

9. Michael T. Klare, *War Without End: American Planning for the Next Vietnams* (New York, Alfred A. Knopf, 1972), p. 185.

10. This estimate has been culled from Klare, pp. 73–74, 81, 90–91, 142, 154–55, 179–82, esp. p. 180. Cf. U.S. Senate, Committee on Foreign Relations, *United States Security Agreements and Commitments Abroad,* Hearings, 2 vols. (Washington, D.C., U.S. Government Printing Office, 1971), pp. 629–30, 632–36.

11. Klare, *War Without End,* p. 185.

12. Adam Schesch, "The Second Indochina War," mimeographed (Madison, Wisconsin, 1970), p. 37.

13. James C. Scott, "Non-Electoral Patterns II: Thailand," unpublished paper, Madison, 1970. This section relies heavily on Scott's analytical framework and interpretation of the Thai political process.

14. *Ibid.,* p. 10.

15. Scott, "Non-Electoral Patterns," p. 23.

16. *Ibid.,* p. 26.

17. Robert Shaplen, *Time Out of Hand: Revolution and Reaction in Southeast Asia* (New York, Harper and Row, 1969) , pp. 289–90.

18. Michael Moerman, *Agricultural Change and Peasant Choice in a Thai Village* (Berkeley and Los Angeles, University of California Press, 1968) . The following discussions of events in Ban Ping is my interpretation based on Moerman's data. Especially see pp. ix, 54–56, 58, 62, 66, 71, 74–76, 80, 93, 99–100, 108–109, 129, 132, 136, 140, 183–184 192–193.

19. Compare the analyses of the green revolution in India and the Philippines in the essays by Thomas Weisskopf and William Pomeroy in this volume.

20. Moerman, pp. 70–71.

21. *Ibid.,* p. 108.

22. Eric R. Wolf, *Peasant Wars of the Twentieth Century* (New York, Harper and Row, 1969) , p. 279.

23. Moerman, p. 110.

24. *Ibid.,* pp. 139–40.

25. *Ibid.*

26. Moerman concludes that peasant world views and economic behavior facilitate a smooth integration into an expanding Thai state and spreading international capitalist markets. The emphasis is on values which "predispose Ban Ping farmers toward the changes stimulated by the nation and the market," that is, on continuity and compatibility, pp. 192–93. Thus Moerman argues that peasants experience the transformation of traditional modes of agriculture as a "change in degree, not in kind" (p. 193) . However, if the data on the impact of commercialization and technology on peasant attitudes toward authority and economic behavior is placed in the context of Thai politics, then another interpretation is more plausible: Peasants seem to be experiencing alienation from other villagers and powerful outsiders.

27. Al McCoy, "Subcontracting Counterinsurgency," *Bulletin of Concerned Asian Scholars,* Special Issue: Vietnam Center at SIU (1970) , p. 58.

28. Interview on the Metromedia Radio News Show "Profile."

29. Quoted in Klare, *War Without End,* p. 77.

30. Toshio Yatsushiro, *Village Organization and Leadership in Northeast Thailand,* Research Division USOM/Thailand (Bangkok, Thailand, May 1966) , pp. 121–35.

31. *Ibid.,* pp. 125–26.

32. Michael Moerman, "Western Culture and the Thai Way of Life," in Robert O. Tilman, ed., *Man, State and Society in Contemporary Southeast Asia* (New York, Praeger Publishers, 1969) , p. 153.

33. *Ibid.*

34. *Ibid.,* p. 150.

35. Sawai Pradit, "An Intensive Resident Study of Yang Kham Vil-

lage," in Toshio Yatsushiro, ed., *Village Attitudes and Conditions in Relation to Rural Security in Northeast Thailand,* Research Division USOM/Thailand (Bangkok, Thailand, May 1967), p. 14.

36. *Ibid.,* pp. 7, 14.

37. Bantorn Ondam, "An Intensive Resident Study of Inplaeng Village"; Yatsushiro, *Village Attitudes and Conditions.*

38. Suthep Soonhornpeusch, "An Intensive Study of Kok Klang Village"; Bamrung Traimontri, "An Intensive Resident Study of Hadsaimoon Village"; Yatsushiro, *Village Attitudes and Conditions.*

39. *Ibid.,* pp. 8, 10–11, 21.

40. For examples see summaries on politics in Hadsaimoon, p. 41; Don Du, pp. 20, 22; Kok Klang, p. 19. Yatsushiro, *Village Attitudes and Conditions.*

41. *Evaluation Report: Joint Thai-USOM Evaluation of the Accelerated Rural Development Project* (Bangkok, Thai–American Audio Visual Service, June 1966), p. 176. Cited in Edward Leigh Block, "Accelerated Rural Development: A Counter-Insurgency Program in Northeast Thailand," unpublished M.A. thesis, Northern Illinois University, Department of Political Science, 1968, p. 57.

42. United States Agency for International Development, *A Cost-Benefit Study of Roads in North and Northeast Thailand,* Research Division USOM/Thailand (Bangkok, Thailand, August 31, 1966), p. 4, cited in Block, "Accelerated Rural Development," p. 59.

43. *Accelerated Rural Development Engineering and Construction Report for November 1967.* The Rural Engineering Division Office of Field Operations USOM/Thailand (Bangkok, Thailand, 1967).

44. For an account of eighteen villages participating together in road construction and repair before USAID penetration see the intensive interviews with residents of Ban Inplaeng, Tampon Kusukam, Amphur Wanonniwart, Sakon Nakhon province, January 12, 1967. Yatsushiro, *Village Attitudes and Conditions,* pp. 1–31, esp. pp. 2–14.

45. I am indebted to James C. Scott's perceptive and persuasive empirical studies of the process whereby traditional elites achieve and lose political legitimacy in rural Southeast Asia. Also see Eqbal Ahmad's brilliant essay on American misconceptions of the nature of authority, rebellion, and legitimacy in rural Asian societies, "Revoluntionary War and Counterinsurgency," in Norman Miller and Roderick Aya, eds., *National Liberation: Revolution in the Third World* (New York, The Free Press, 1971).

46. U.S. House of Representatives, Committee on Operations and Government Information Subcommittee, Hearings on Thailand and the Philippines (Washington, D.C., June 16, 1969), pp. 102–104. Cited in McCoy, "Subcontracting Counterinsurgency."

47. Klare, *War Without End,* pp. 182, 194–95.

48. Peter Smith, "Unrest in Northern Thailand: Year of the Guerilla," Pacific News Service, 1972.

49. This description of the sequence of political violence in Lom Sak is taken directly from Al McCoy's account of the consequences of counterinsurgency programs at the local level. I have added a few analytical comments in an effort to place it in the larger framework of this section. See McCoy, "Subcontracting Counterinsurgency," p. 66.

50. The description and analysis of the origins of political violence in Meo Maw is pieced together from several sources. John R. Thompson, "Meo Maw: The Burning Mountain," *Far Eastern Economic Review* (April 25, 1968), pp. 218–20; John R. Thompson, "Kang Haw: The Mountains Are Steppes," *Far Eastern Economic Review* (March 11, 1968), pp. 139–41; John R. Thompson, "Bangkok: Mountains to Climb," *Far Eastern Economic Review* (March 7, 1968), pp. 420–21; Douglas Miles, "Australian Anthropology in Sarkhan," unpublished paper, 1971. I rely heavily on Miles' journal here, esp. pp. 33–46. However, my interpretation of the data differs from Miles' in important respects.

51. Thompson, "Meo Maw: The Burning Mountain," p. 220.

52. Miles, "Australian Anthropology in Sarkhan," p. 42.

53. *Ibid.,* p. 45.

OKINAWA AND AMERICAN
SECURITY IMPERIALISM

MARK SELDEN

On May 15, 1972, the American flag descended in the Ryukyus and the Rising Sun once again flew over the islands. Reversion to Japanese sovereignty marked the end of the American colonial era. Or did it? American troops remain entrenched on Okinawa—supplemented now by much smaller Japanese forces—and Okinawa continues to play an integral role in America's war in Indochina. "The Ryukyus, surrounded on three sides by major powers of East Asia, are the most strategic outpost of freedom in the Far East. Known as the 'Keystone of the Pacific,' Okinawa, the most important island, is 800 nautical miles southwest of Tokyo, 325 nautical miles northeast of Taipei, 750 nautical miles northeast of Manila and 700 nautical miles northeast of Hong Kong." Thus observes the 1969 official *Facts Book* of the U.S. High Commissioner of the Ryukyus.[1] Delicately left unstated is the fact that the nerve center of America's mammoth Pacific military network was also less than 1500 miles—convenient bomber- and missile-striking range—from the capitals of North Vietnam, China, and North Korea. This strategic location for the expansion of American power in East and Southeast Asia explains why the United States detached Okinawa from Japan after World War II. Of negligible economic value, Okinawa exemplifies central features of an American postwar strategy of security

279

imperialism in the Pacific. This strategy emphasized U.S. military buildups in a chain of strategic Pacific Island bases—of which Okinawa and, increasingly in the seventies, Micronesia are the most important—directly ruled by the United States. This paper traces the development of that strategy in Okinawa in terms of its implications for American power in the Pacific and evaluates the impact of American rule on Okinawan society.

A grandiose conception of American hegemony in the Pacific was stated well by one of its primary architects, General Douglas MacArthur. In 1949 he noted with satisfaction: "Now the Pacific has become an Anglo-Saxon lake and our line of defense runs through the chain of islands fringing the coast of Asia. It starts from the Philippines and continues through the Ryukyu archipelago which includes its main bastion, Okinawa. Then it bends back through Japan and the Aleutian Island chain to Alaska."[2] MacArthur's conception extended the vision of the architects of the first great era of American insular imperialism. Expansionists as early as the 1890s viewed the acquisition of Hawaii, Wake, Midway, Guam, Samoa, and the Philippines as a springboard for turning the entire Pacific into an American lake.[3] The half-century following the seizure of these colonies in 1898 was an interlude between leaps of American territorial expansion in the Pacific. By 1943 strategic planners in Washington saw clearly that the United States would emerge from World War II without challenge as the most powerful nation in the world. Nowhere would the expansion of U.S. power be more striking than in the creation of a Pax Americana in Asia. The prospect of "power vacuums" as a result of the defeat of imperial Japan and the collapse of European empires opened new possibilities to American advocates of territorial expansion. The era of classical colonialism, however, was approaching an end. In the postwar world the United States would enter the lists simultaneously as the foe of revolutionary nationalist movements and of old-style colonialists including the Japanese, the French, and the British.[4] That, at least, was the strategy for continental Asia where the United States generally supported those newly independent governments which accepted incorporation within the economic and military framework fashioned and dominated by the United States.

Yet that was not the whole story. For, even as President Truman publicly proclaimed that the United States would forgo all territorial gains, defense officials set in motion plans for an expanded security imperialism predicated on direct control of extensive island areas. "Though the United States wants no territory or profit or selfish advantage out of this war," Truman stated at Potsdam on August 9, 1945, "we are going to maintain the military bases necessary for the complete protection of our interests and of world peace. Bases which our military experts deem to be essential for our protection, and which are not now in our possession, we will acquire."[5]

In the immediate aftermath of World War II, U.S. plans for military domination of the Pacific centered on base construction on island territories which had recently fallen under *de facto* U.S. military control. Vice Admiral Forrest Sherman, Deputy Chief of Naval Operations, testified on February 14, 1946, before the Senate Naval Affairs Committee that thirty-three naval bases and airfields in twenty-two separate localities would be needed to "maintain strategic control of the Pacific Ocean Area." The bases were:

 1 Main Naval Base: Hawaii
 1 Major Operating Base: Guam–Saipan
 1 Major Operating Base, Caretaker Status: Manus
 2 Secondary Operating and Repair Bases: Adak, Philippines
 6 Secondary Operating Bases, Small: Kodiak, Dutch Harbor, Attu, Midway, Samoa, Ryukyus
 7 Air Bases: Johnston Island, Palmyra, Canton Island, Majuro, Wake, Marcus, Iwo Jima
 4 Combined Air Bases and Fleet Anchorages: Kwajalein, Eniwetok, Truk, Palau
11 Air Fields: Hawaii, Kodiak, Dutch Harbor, Adak, Attu, Midway, Samoa, Manus, Guam–Saipan, Philippines, Ryukyus.

Within months, base construction was under way in all of these areas and appropriations had been approved for bases in half a dozen other islands in addition to Japan, China and Korea.[6] In the absence of major U.S. investments in Asia, and attuned to the powerful thrust of anticolonial nationalism on the Asian mainland, the United States cencentrated on building island bases which would guarantee hegemony over the entire critical and potentially rich area. The postwar plans for the Ryukyus as a major base complex under direct U.S. military control were part of an evolving strategy of security imperialism generated before the earliest signs of alleged Soviet expansionism or Sino-American confrontation.

Okinawa quickly demonstrated its importance to U.S. strategists intent on thwarting the Chinese revolution. In October 1945, fresh from the battle for Okinawa, 10,000 U.S. Marines stationed on Okinawa were dispatched to North China. Their job: to prevent Japanese forces from surrendering to Chinese Communist armies which had fought them in the area for nearly a decade. In subsequent months the Marines and the Japanese (Japan had already officially surrendered to the United States) engaged in joint military actions while the United States airlifted Chiang Kai-shek's Kuomintang forces to North China to formally accept the Japanese surrender. Combat was sharply restricted. The episode was critical, however, in pitting the United States against Chinese revolutionary forces for the first time.[7] The victory of radical nationalist forces in China four years later and their advance in Korea and Vietnam led to the sharp upgrading of Okinawa as a U.S. military base. In October 1949 a $58 million Congressional appropriation began Okinawa's transformation into the keystone of American military ambitions in the Pacific and doomed the Okinawan people to protracted colonial rule.[8]

The eruption of the Korean War in 1950 conclusively demonstrated Okinawa's worth to American strategists. As Okinawa-based B-29 Superfortresses rained destruction over North and South Korea and the islands became a major supply and logistical base for American forces, the United States initiated a vast program of base expansion. By 1950 Okinawa had assumed a critical forward role in the American confrontation with China and the repression of national liberation movements throughout Asia.[9]

The 1951 San Francisco Treaty restored Japanese independence. Okinawa, however, remained an American colony and provided a key link in John Foster Dulles's cordon of Pacific alliances. For Japan, "independence" meant perpetuating the presence of U.S. occupying forces, acceptance of Okinawa's continued colonial status ("residual sovereignty" was Dulles's ingenious formulation), and incorporation within a network of alliances hostile to the Soviet Union and China. "If Japan should succumb to Communist aggression," Dulles sternly warned the American people six months prior to signing the San Francisco Treaty, "there would be a combination of Russian, Japanese and Chinese power in the East which would be dangerously formidable."[10] As the Pentagon Papers make abundantly clear, a major continuing focus of the U.S. economic and political strategy in Asia was to insure that Japan, the major industrial power in the area, remained securely within the U.S. economic orbit. The core of the U.S. military posture, both in terms of recently concluded collective security arrangements with Japan, Australia, and New Zealand (1951), the Philippines (1951), and the Chiang Kai-shek forces exiled to Taiwan in 1949, as well as direct U.S. domination of Micronesia and Okinawa, lay in the insular and peninsular areas spanning the Pacific and ringing mainland China.

By 1955, Kadena Air Base had become the major U.S. Air Force installation in East Asia as post–Korean War planning began to focus increasingly on Indochina. Offshore, F-84's practiced simulated A-bomb drops while the army installed its first atomic cannon in the Far East and Okinawa housed the largest U.S. Marine contingent in Asia.[11] During the Taiwan Straits crisis of 1958 the United States dispatched the 51st Fighter Wing and naval forces from Okinawa to Taiwan to confront Chinese forces.[12]

In the 1960s, as Soviet–American relations stabilized on the basis of nuclear stalemate, American strategic preoccupations shifted from nuclear war to counterinsurgency and Okinawa's role loomed still larger. As President Kennedy observed in March 1962, "Our bases in the Ryukyu Islands help us assure our allies in the great arc from Japan through Southeast Asia not only of our willingness but also of our ability to come to their assistance in case of need."[13] Okinawa soon surpassed Kennedy's highest expectations, playing a pivotal role in the Indochina War just as she had earlier in Korea. As U.S. military involvement in Vietnam accelerated sharply, the August 30, 1965 *Newsweek* described that "strategic keystone" as

> one vast supply dump, training ground and advanced staging area for U.S. forces in the Far East. Virtually every item in America's mighty arsenal—from jungle knives to nuclear weapons—is stored here. Kadena Air Force Base, just north of Naha, is one of the world's busiest airports. . . . Attack transports and other Navy vessels steam endlessly in and out of White

Beach harbor. Camps, firing ranges and supply depots are scattered the length and breadth of the island. . . . Guerrilla-warfare specialists train in the island's steamy jungles and Army and Marine units maneuver in battalion strength on the ridges, beaches and coral-encrusted flatlands.

In the course of the Indochina War the buildup accelerated, including the stockpiling of nuclear weapons. Roger Hilsman, Former Assistant Secretary of State for Far Eastern Affairs, summed up the military posture of Okinawa in a 1969 article in *The Military Review:*

- A tactical missile group armed with Mace-B nuclear missiles.
- An F-105 base, including nuclear bombs stored on the island.
- Storage for both Army and Navy tactical nuclear weapons.
- A base for KC-135 aerial tankers and for B-52 bombers including their nuclear weapons.
- A base for Polaris submarines, including their nuclear weapons.
- A base for ground forces, most recently used in Vietnam.[14]

Okinawa has been the hub of U.S. nuclear operations in the Pacific, but its primary significance has been its central role in the Indochina War. With 14,000 air operations a month logged on its 12,000-foot runways, by 1968 Kadena Air Base became the major launching site for B-52 bombing raids which laid waste North and South Vietnam.[15] The Marines Counter-Guerrilla Warfare School, set in 40,000 acres of rugged jungle in Northern Okinawa, offered training in search-and-destroy operations for leathernecks en route to Vietnam. As the stopoff point for giant C-5A air transports, the storage base for poison gas and other secret weapons, and a major intelligence gathering installation, Okinawa with its 50,000 man army assumed a pivotal role in America's military thrust into Asia. Finally, Okinawa performed a central mission in American psychological warfare operations as the site of a major Voice of America transmitter which beams messages from Okinawa to China and Southeast Asia. Many of these functions are slated for expansion in the postreversion era. ICBM and IRBM-armed nuclear submarines will be using Okinawan ports with increasing frequency; the islands are to become a major center for training Asian mercenaries; and the Voice of America transmitter continues to operate following reversion.[16]

But Okinawa is not only $4 billion worth of bases and military hardware vital to the perpetuation of America's Asian empire.[17] It is also the home of nearly one million people who have lived for a quarter of a century under American colonial rule. What has been the record of "democratization and modernization" in the major area of direct American administration in the postwar era?

> In the beginning, according to the *Omore,* Okinawa's own Book of Genesis, there was chaos. But through the intervention of Tedo-Ke, the Sun God, this chaos was resolved into land and sea, the first land being a tiny island several miles from what is now southeastern Okinawa. There two demigods performed monumental labors, carrying stone and sand and earth, hewing rock, planting trees and arresting the floods which regularly inundated the island. . . .
>
> Substitute the chaos of war which left behind a land ruined both physically and economically, and put the United States Army in the place of the pair of legendary demigods; have that Army exert monumental efforts of very much the same nature; and finally have it introduce a new democratic form of government and you have an almost literal modern-day parallel to the ancient story of creation as told in Luchuan mythology.
>
> Unlike the demigods, however, the Army is not leaving the populace to create order out of chaos with meager or inadequate resources. This time the Okinawans are being taught new skills and new ways of life as the Army works to transform the island into a veritable keystone of the Pacific while rebuilding the over-all economy of the entire archipelago.[18]

This preoccupation with the moral justification for American domination and territorial acquisition of new areas is not new. It runs in fact through the length and breadth of American history from the dispossession and annihilation of the Indians through the Indochina War. And it was articulated clearly in the earliest official contacts between the United States and Okinawa by Commodore Matthew Perry. Perry arrived in Okinawa in 1853 determined to establish control over the Ryukyus at least until Japan acceded to American demands to establish a port of call for U.S. whaling and merchant ships. Perry succinctly joined the twin themes of American power and benevolence which would run through the writings of subsequent architects of American dominance in the Pacific. "This royal dependency of Japan," he wrote, ". . . is in such a state of political vassalage and thralldom, that it would be a merit to extend over it the vivifying influence and protection of a government like our own."[19] Perry was ahead of his time. President Franklin Pierce praised his patriotism but declined to establish a military base, no less a colony on Okinawa. "If in future," Pierce observed, "resistance should be offered and threatened, it would also be rather mortifying to surrender the island, if once seized, and rather inconvenient and expensive to maintain a force there to retain it."[20]

Almost a century later, a 250,000-man U.S. force taught the Okinawan people, whose homeland had never known a major armed conflict, the meaning of modern war.[21] The battle for Okinawa, the final struggle of the Pacific War, was also the most costly in lives. It left the islands a sea of flame. Japanese and Okinawan forces resisted massive American air and sea bombardment and "human wave" attacks for more than two months. Official U.S. Army figures place the final toll at 49,151 American casualties, including 12,520 dead, against 110,071 listed as "enemy dead."[22]

American military histories of the campaign treat the Okinawan population as a minor if occasionally irritating intruder in the heroic drama. Nevertheless, glimpses emerge of the horrifying destruction of human life. "Civilians," the official army history reports,

> became a nuisance to combat units after the assault on the final enemy lines began, and remained a burden until front lines no longer existed. [Tens of thousands] tried to pass through the machine-gun and shell fire to enter American lines or attempted the even more hazardous feat of slipping through the front lines during darkness. . . .
>
> Eighty thousand Okinawa civilians, between a third and a half of whom were wounded, crawled from caves at the south tip of the island during the last two weeks of June. These were either children, the very old, or women; there were few able-bodied men among them. . . . The bodies of many thousands of other civilians lay scattered in the ditches, in the canefields, and in the rubble of the villages, or were sealed in caves.[23]

Moreover, U.S. forces drove 350,000 Okinawans from their homes and land into stockades and detention centers for the duration of the campaign.[24] In the end, an estimated 100,000 Okinawan civilians died with as many more wounded. Two-thirds of the islands' buildings were razed in combat, and many more were bulldozed to make way for the network of roads, airstrips, and installations which were constructed after the fighting.[25] Okinawan economy and society were destroyed, eventually to be resurrected in the image of the American military. Since 1945 the Okinawan people have paid a heavy price for American military ambitions: as nuclear hostages—the islands have been prime targets in the event of global conflict; as economic hostages—the economy has been lashed to the military base complex; as political hostages—Okinawans have lived under American military domination.

Okinawa provides an example of the predominance of military and strategic considerations in charting the course of colonial rule. In the bland phraseology of the *Facts Book,* "The mission of the United States Civil Administration of Ryukyu Islands is to assure that this strategic area will contribute most effectively to the peace and security of the free world."[26] For a quarter of a century Okinawa's "civil administration" was directly controlled by the Pentagon which appointed its High Commissioner, in all cases a lieutenant general who concurrently commands U.S. forces. While Okinawans were tutored in "democracy" through the ritualistic election of a legislature and executive, the American High Commissioner retained absolute control. The High Commissioner was vested with sweeping dictatorial powers. He was empowered on the basis of any threat to U.S. interests to "veto any bill . . . annul any law . . . remove any public official from office . . . and exercise full authority in the islands."[27] Okinawan democracy has been a puppet show in which a powerless people is hypocritically manipulated by its military masters. Indeed, in the entire range of institutions, from a dual system of justice which shielded Americans from punishment for crimes against Okinawans,[28] to the long-standing ban on such elementary civil liberties as the right of labor unions to strike, we find the stamp of direct military exploitation.

Nowhere has this pattern of military hegemony been more decisive than in the economy. In January 1970, *The Oriental Economist* summed it up this way: "Okinawa has for more than two decades since the war been segregated from Japan and its economy is completely subservient to the U.S. dollar because of

overwhelming dependence on United States military base operations.... Described in the simplest terms, the economy of Okinawa is a 'military-base economy.' "

The U.S. administration has developed power, water, and
transportation facilities geared to maximizing the islands' military potential. Inevitably Okinawan interests have been sacrificed in the process. As of 1970, one-sixth of the Okinawan work
force was directly employed by the U.S. military (40,000
workers) and the colonial government (34,000). And this was
but a fraction of those forced to live off the American presence,
including an estimated 15,000 to 25,000 prostitutes and bar girls,
and more than 10,000 maids employed by servicemen (all officers
and many enlisted men have servants, a luxury made possible by
the depressed Okinawan wage scale). Tens of thousands of others
work in the wide range of subsidiary industries and services
which cater to American pleasures.

Military expenditures virtually doubled from $118 million in
1964 to $197 million by 1967.[29] Despite the Indochina War
boom the Okinawan people remain locked in the grip of poverty.
Per capita income in fiscal year 1967 was officially recorded as
$588, barely sixty percent of the Japanese average. The $.17 per
hour average wage the U.S. government and military paid its
Okinawan employees in 1955 had of course risen—along with
inflation. By January 1968 these employees averaged $.71 per
hour, far below the salaries of base workers in Japan proper.[30]

The overwhelming dependence of the Okinawan economy on
U.S. military expenditures is graphically revealed in the pattern
of foreign trade.

FOREIGN TRADE, GROSS NATIONAL PRODUCT, AND EXPENDITURES OF U.S. FORCES ON OKINAWA[31]
(In thousands of U.S. $)

Fiscal Year	Imports	Exports	Trade Balance	GNP	U.S. Forces Expenditures
1955	51,200	10,682	−40,518	—	50,000
1960	116,811	24,037	−92,774	204,100	5,000
1965	210,704	79,403	−131,301	386,600	135,000
1968	373,662	87,369	−286,293	641,900	197,800
1969	371,636	87,471	−284,165	727,100	—

By fiscal year 1968 Okinawa's steadily rising trade deficit had climbed to $286 million, more than forty percent of its $641 million GNP. The total value of exports throughout the period of American rule has consistently remained at barely twenty percent of imports.[32] Indeed, since 1965, the real value of exports has actually declined as inflation has outpaced the increase in sale abroad. Okinawa's massive trade deficit could only be balanced by the influx of U.S. dollars in the form of base expenditures and salaries, simultaneously balancing accounts and completing the circle of military dependence. Following military conquest, the islanders were deprived of their richest land and only livelihood. Their power, resources and transport facilities were channeled in the service of the U.S. military. Okinawan economic life developed as a parasitic appendage of the American military. Okinawans have helped man the bases from which America wreaks destruction throughout Asia and staffed a civil administration whose *raison d'être* is the continued subordination of Okinawans to American rule. Starvation has been virtually the only alternative to degrading service in the direct employ of the American military, except of course becoming servants or prostitutes to its men in uniform.

American colonial rule carried forward the destruction of egalitarian and communal features of Okinawan society begun during the preceding Japanese era. Prior to 1871, when Okinawa came under Japanese administration, approximately seventy percent of the land belonged to the local community with much of the remainder held in perpetuity by aristocratic families. Cultivation rights were communally assigned and rotated. Land was rarely held by a single family for more than ten years. It could be neither bought nor sold; barter was the primary medium of exchange and taxes were likewise paid in kind. Systems of collective responsibility—including payment of taxes for indigent families—centered on the village. Most of Okinawa's overwhelmingly rural population lived by subsistence farming.

In 1899, Japanese "modernizers" set out to incorporate Okinawa within Japan's dynamic profit-oriented economy. The Okinawan Land Adjustment Bureau—created by the Japanese government to carry out capitalist land reform—described the problem of economic stagnation this way:

> It is not to be wondered that he satisfies himself with a suit of clothes made of *musa basjoo* and takes up a glass of the liquor

brewed from potatoes as a unique pleasure in human life. No wonder, also, that he has no idea of saving money against the future or of starting a business, only availing himself of spades and hoes. Living expenses are so low that a man can be supported with some sen a day, and even the wealthy have savings of scarcely one thousand yen. Are these not vicious results of the above-mentioned system? Every person cultivates an equal area of land, so he has no need to undertake any other business, nor to save money. Especially as the ownership of land is not confirmed, it cannot be used as a capital for any undertaking.[33]

In Okinawa, as in nineteenth-century Mexico, Vietnam, and Russia, communal rural institutions blocking private investment and international trade were destroyed in the name of progress.[34] The Japanese government proclaimed communal land ownership "feudal." Legislation provided for individual title, including the right to buy and sell land. By 1923 nearly twenty percent of land-owning families had lost all or a substantial part of their holdings. Many found themselves tenants.[35] In the early 1880s only four or five families in all Okinawa had owned as much as twelve acres of land. In subsequent decades sugar became the focus of the Okinawan economy. The sugar industry was dominated by a single corporation—the Taiwan Sugar Corporation controlled by Japan's Imperial Household and the giant Mitsui and Mitsubishi companies. Okinawa became a classical one-crop export economy (by 1930 sugar accounted for sixty percent of exports). With Mitsubishi monopolizing shipping, Okinawa's entire economy remained a weak appendage of Japanese capital. Okinawa was the poorest and most neglected of Japan's prefectures, but it was also an important stepping stone to the riches of Taiwan, China, and Southeast Asia.[36]

The destruction of the Okinawan way of life began with the islands' forced incorporation as a Japanese prefecture. During seventy-five years as an internal colony, the communal way of life yielded to domination of the agrarian sector by Japanese sugar corporations producing for export. Thousands lost their lands and in many areas the bonds of village solidarity were sharply undermined. Control of economic, political, and cultural life passed from Okinawa to Tokyo. Many of the most degrading features of Okinawan colonial life in the American era had their origins earlier.[37]

Japan undermined the communal foundations of Okinawa's agrarian society. It remained for the United States to virtually destroy the agrarian way of life. In the battle for Okinawa and its aftermath hundreds of thousands of peasants were driven from their land. A decade later a U.S. Congressional Investigating Committee found that over a quarter of a million people had been displaced by the U.S. military which had appropriated 52,000 acres, much of it prime agricultural land. As of 1955 the U.S. government was paying less than $20 a year in rent to the average dispossessed landowner for his four-fifths of an acre holding. More than twenty percent of all arable land (much higher in populous central Okinawa) had been turned into a sea of cement airstrip, training grounds, and missile installations.[38] One result was to create heavy dependence on American food imports. More significant, thousands of rural Okinawans had no option but to leave the land and go to work for the U.S. military. "Okinawans," General James Moore told *Time* Magazine with characteristic bluntness, "must learn to give up subsistence farming and adjust to an economy like Hawaii's which lives off servicing the military."[39]

Imperialism everywhere creates a hierarchy of alien rulers over native inhabitants. But perhaps nowhere, outside of the combat zones where Third World peoples have risen in armed struggle, has a foreign military presence been so overwhelming as in densely populated Okinawa. Nowhere is the old landscape so dominated by barbed-wire military bases, guarded airstrips, and barracks alternating with the new symbols of the American military life-style abroad—golf courses, swimming pools, servicemen's clubs, and sprawling dependent housing. In Koza, the site of Kadena Air Force Base, one finds a parody of Los Angeles suburbia, on the one hand, and on the other, its Watts counterpart, the Bush, the all-black ghetto steaming under the racism for which the military on Okinawa is notorious. Okinawa is the very quintessence of a brutalizing colonial presence found in varying degrees wherever large numbers of American forces are stationed throughout Asia—from South Korea and Taiwan to the Philippines, Thailand, Vietnam, and Micronesia—and the world. On Okinawa the silken glove of a "superior" colonial culture carried by administrators, businessmen, missionaries, and teachers scarcely conceals the mailed fist of the military.

For most G.I.'s, the Okinawan population exists to provide

him with pleasure. Above all this means sex. The pure power of American wealth has produced a whole subculture, utterly alien to traditional mores, in which the daughters of farming and fishing villages are forced to don scarlet dresses and smoke grass to act out the tortured fantasies of American teenagers in uniform. Perhaps the ultimate expression of imperialist power lies in forcing its victims to conform to the grotesque patterns of the repressed lusts of the conqueror. The combination of degradation and dependency is rooted in the economic order which the Americans brought to Okinawa.

The military is not the entire Okinawa story. In a quarter century of colonial rule American multinational corporations secured an iron grip on critical and lucrative sectors of the economy. The banking system has been dominated by a combination of American government and private enterprises with the U.S. dollar as the official currency. Though latecomers to Okinawa, Bank of America and American Express rapidly assumed strong positions. But by far the most important bank on Okinawa during the American era was the official Ryukyu Bank, directly controlled by the U.S. administration, which has fifty-one percent of its capital. With assets of $222.5 million on June 30, 1969, the Ryukyu Bank overshadowed all other financial institutions.[40]

As of June 30, 1969, American investment of $222 million (exclusive of banking, insurance, and airlines) constituted the lion's share—better than ninety-five percent—of a total of $233 million in approved foreign investments.[41] To be sure, these investments are dwarfed by American investments elsewhere. They nevertheless dominate key sectors of Okinawan economic life holding the keys to any future industrialization.

In two industries, oil and aluminum, American-owned multinationals waged a fierce battle for control against their Japanese counterparts. In every instance the Americans won. By early 1970 oil refinery investments by four American corporations (Gulf, Caltex, Esso, and Kaiser Cement) overshadowed the entire foreign economic stake in Okinawa, and indeed far exceeded the annual budget of the Ryukyu government ($170 million). In June 1970, the U.S. military government rejected a plan by a consortium of Japan's five leading aluminum firms in favor of Alcoa's proposal to invest $60 million in a 70,000-ton smeltery.[42]

The result in aluminum as in oil was U.S. domination of crucial investment areas. This belated rush of American capital represents a crucial feature of American economic plans for East Asia. What is at stake ultimately is the ability of major U.S. interests to gain entry into lucrative Japanese markets. By establishing refineries in Okinawa shortly before reversion, these companies sought a springboard to Japan and a means to evade Japanese restrictions on foreign investment. For its part, the Japanese government insisted that foreign firms on postreversion Okinawa must conform to Japanese investment regulations—restricting foreign control of critical economic areas. The dance of the oil and aluminum conglomerates continues as U.S. and Japanese firms in close coordination with their governments engage in intricate maneuvers to dominate the Okinawan—and Japanese—market.

Japanese and American economic strategies have meshed in recent decades in active efforts to preserve Asia as an area for foreign investment. Indeed, the United States has fought in Indochina and preserved its farflung network of Asian bases to keep Southeast Asia open to Japanese as well as American capital. Yet cooperation premised on Japanese political and economic subordination has always been accompanied by conflict over U.S. penetration of critical sectors of the Japanese economy and competition for control of lucrative Southeast Asian markets. Japan's dynamic economic spurt in the sixties coupled with American economic stagnation and mounting pressure on the dollar has changed the equation of relative U.S.–Japan power and simultaneously brought to the surface increasing economic and political tensions.

The struggle over oil lies at the center not only of the bidding for Okinawan investment rights but of the entire U.S.–Japan economic relationship. As it did prior to World War II, the United States controls the oil resources essential to Japan's industrial expansion.[43] The American embargo on oil on the eve of World War II was a critical factor precipitating Japan's decision to fight for control of resource-rich Southeast Asia. And Japan's dependence on U.S.-controlled oil is far greater today. It is scarcely surprising, therefore, to find the recent Japanese strategic preoccupation with the Malacca Straits as a "lifeline" for Middle East oil, strenuous efforts to secure drilling rights for

Southeast Asian offshore oil, and moves to seize the potentially oil-rich Tiao-yu (Senkaku) Islands from China to break this dependency.[44]

The discovery of oil in the area of the Tiao-yu Islands, located between the Ryukyu chain and Taiwan, raised Japanese hopes of diminishing oil dependency. It also brought to the boiling point long-simmering antagonisms between China and Japan. China's claim to ownership of the islands—historically, geologically, geographically, and legally—is airtight. Following the oil discoveries, however, Japan swiftly backed up its dubious claims to the territory with military force.[45] The United States directly intervened on Japan's side in this internal Chinese–Japanese dispute by explicitly defining the Tiao-yu Islands within the area of the Ryukyus returned to Japan in 1972. Japan's thirst for oil is stimulating the growth of her war machine. Once again, as in the 1930s, China stands directly in the path of expansionist dreams.[46]

Okinawa enters the new era of Japanese administration with American capital squarely in the driver's seat in key sectors of the economy. The Japanese, in control of administrative levers once again, can be expected to challenge U.S. interests. Japanese economic interest in the islands centers on three factors. First, densely populated Okinawa, with wages lower than any other part of Japan, offers the prospect of a cheap, dependable labor supply—at present 25,000–30,000 Okinawans annually migrate to Japan in search of jobs—as Japanese industry faces an acute labor shortage. Along with South Korea, Taiwan, and other areas in the Japanese economic orbit, Okinawa is a likely site for the export of pollution-ridden industry as pressures for controls mount within the main Japanese islands.[47] Just as American interests have seen Okinawa as a springboard to the Japanese market, Japanese eyes are trained on markets to the south. Japan's Ministry of International Trade and Industry (MITI) recently put it this way: "Okinawa should be thought of not as the southernmost tip of the Japanese economic zone, but rather as the beachhead to Southeast Asia."[48]

Foreign investment in Okinawa has produced classical features of colonial dependency and warped development. U.S. investment dominates the economy, particularly in critical areas attractive to the multinational giants. By contrast, Japan's present $8 million investment is centered in sugar refining, pineapple canning and hotels, areas in which Japanese capital had secured a firm foothold prior to American rule. The major Japanese flow of investment dollars has been channeled into extractive industries, agriculture, and tourism. Industrial capacity is virtually nonexistent. Okinawan enterprises invariably lack the strength to compete with foreign firms, whether Japanese or American. The political and military dependency of the colonized people is mirrored in the economy.

In contrast to the Americanization of the Philippines, and colonialism's characteristic emasculation of the language and culture of subordinate peoples, the United States has not systematically attempted to destroy the cultural hegemony of the former colonial power, Japan. While Okinawans have had to adapt their society to fit an American pattern of bars, brothels, and bases, Japanese language, educational, and cultural patterns—effectively imposed prior to 1945—remain firmly entrenched. The explanation for this lies in the nature of security imperialism, whose primary requirement from the occupied people is docility, and in the nature of the U.S.–Japan relationship. Stability and ease of administration to facilitate American military activity took precedence over molding deeper value patterns uniquely appropriate to American dominance. Moreover, Okinawans had already been deeply socialized in the colonial school of dependency and submissiveness by their Japanese rulers.

Yet even under these circumstances, we find consistent if low budget U.S. efforts to cultivate critical Okinawan elites. As early as 1950 the Department of the Army and the occupation authorities framed orientation and exchange programs for national leaders and students. This was "no adventure in altruism," the first annual report observed, "but one which has definite objectives in terms of the welfare, peace and security of the United States and Japan."[49] Of the first group of 456 Japanese and forty-five Okinawans brought to the United States, 173 were sponsored by the Federal Security Agency while the Army sponsored sixty-six more. Within Okinawa itself, propaganda inculcated the people with "democratic philosophy" and—more to the point—drew them "toward the community of freedom-loving nations so that they will be willing to stand with us in the continuing world situation of pressures against individual freedom."[50]

Okinawa for nearly a decade has remained a critical and often tense issue in the U.S.–Japan relationship and in American military planning for the Pacific. As the United States reduces troop strength in East Asia and as Japanese military involvement in the area grows, Okinawa will play a pivotal role in joint U.S.–Japan military plans. Yet the area could also become a key bone of contention in the event that U.S.–Japan tensions heighten.

The bitter irony of "reversion" for the Okinawan people is that the militarization of Okinawa is actually being intensified. The United States has returned to Japan thirty-four military installations and sites while retaining eighty-eight others. With the exception of Naha Airport, however, all those returned are of negligible importance. The U.S. military position is in fact being strengthened concurrent with reversion by the $60 million expansion of Kadena Air Force Base scheduled to be completed by 1976.[51] Moreover, reversion itself strengthened the U.S. military by reducing friction with Okinawans. The United States has ceased to be the direct employer of Okinawan base workers who are now technically employed by the Japanese government under an indirect hiring system. Likewise the end of U.S. "military justice" eliminated another deep source of antagonism.

If postreversion Okinawa remains primarily a U.S. fortress, it also figures prominently in Japan's strategic plans. The seizure of Okinawa was the first step in Japan's nineteenth-century imperial expansion. Once again Japanese planners look beyond Okinawa to East and Southeast Asia. The November 1969 Sato–Nixon joint communiqué following the agreement to return administrative rights to Okinawa publicly announced Japan's assumption of military responsibility for Taiwan and South Korea, former colonial territories which in recent years have moved toward Japanese economic domination.[52] In 1972, 6800 Japanese soldiers were dispatched to Okinawa, and the Japanese have announced the deployment of Nike and Hawk missile systems purchased from the United States to provide surface-to-air missile defense by July 1, 1972.[53] Okinawa is the forward base for Japan's rapidly expanding military force.

As in the case of America's formative colonial experience in the Philippines, the end of direct rule finds the local population locked in the grip of dependency, degradation, and poverty, and the predominance of American strategic and economic interests assured. But, just as Okinawa's historical fate has been to fall prey to the designs of its powerful neighbors, it enters a new era supporting the dual aims of Japanese and American imperial ambitions.

N O T E S

1. The High Commissioner of the Ryukyu Islands, *Facts Book FY 1969,* United States Civil Administration of the Ryukyu Islands, APO San Francisco, 5–1.

2. *New York Times,* March 2, 1949, quoted in Allen Whiting, *China Crosses the Yalu: The Decision to Enter the Korean War* (Stanford University Press, 1968) , p. 39.

3. See John Dower's superb discussion of the evolution of the concept of the American Lake in "Occupied Japan and the American Lake, 1945–50," in Edward Friedman and Mark Selden, eds., *America's Asia: Dissenting Essays on Asian-American Relations* (Pantheon, 1971) , pp. 170–73. Cf. Eleanor Lattimore, "Pacific Ocean or American Lake," *Far Eastern Survey,* vol. 14, no. 22, November 7, 1945, pp. 313–16.

4. Gabriel Kolko develops this theme at length in *The Politics of War. The World and United States Foreign Policy* (Random House: New York, 1968) . A British paper on Pacific security prepared in early 1945 correctly noted the dawn of a Pax Americana in Asia. However, its hopes that the new era would be predicated on British-American collective security enabling Britain to retain great power status in Asia were quickly dashed by realities of American power in the postwar world. "What is the twentieth century substitute for the Pax Britannica of the nineteenth century which found its main sanction in the sea power of the United Kingdom, at all events outside Europe then living in the unstable equilibrium of the Balance of Power? The substitute, whatever it be, cannot be provided by any one Power alone, though United States naval power in the Pacific is the powerful counterpart of what British sea power was in the seven seas a generation ago. So great, indeed, is American power in the Pacific that some believe that it is a *Pax Americana* that will prevail hereafter." ("Report on Pacific Security by a Chatham House Study Group for the Ninth Conference of the Institute of Pacific Relations at Hot Springs, Virginia," January 1945, p. 27.)

5. *New York Times,* August 10, 1945.

6. Dower, p. 161.

7. See David Wilson, "Leathernecks in North China, 1945," *Bulletin of Concerned Asian Scholars,* vol. 4, no. 2, Summer 1972, pp. 33–37; Joyce and Gabriel Kolko, *The Limits of Power. The World and United States Foreign Policy, 1945–1954* (Harper and Row: New York, 1972) , pp. 248–49.

8. Seizaburo Shinobu, "The Korean War as an Epoch of Contemporary History," *The Developing Economies,* vol. 4, no. 1, March 1961, p. 26.

9. Roy Macartney, "How War Came to Korea" in Norman Bartlett, *With the Australians in Korea* (Canberra: Australian War Memorial, 1954), p. 171, cited in Edward Friedman, "Problems in Dealing with an Irrational Power: America Declares War on China," *America's Asia,* p. 226.

10. John Foster Dulles, "Building Foundations for a Pacific Peace. Report on Work of Presidential Mission to Japan," pp. 504–507, *State Department Bulletin,* vol. 24, March 12, 1951, p. 403.

11. "Okinawa: Levittown-on-the-Pacific," *Time,* vol. 66, no. 7, August 15, 1955, pp. 18–20.

12. Statement of Maj. Gen. Dale O. Smith USAF (RET.), "Okinawa Reversion Treaty Hearings Before the Committee on Foreign Relations, United States Senate Ninety-Second Congress First Session on Ex.J. 92–1" (hereafter, "Okinawa Hearings"), on October 27, 28, 29, 1971, p. 81.

13. *Facts Book,* 1969, pp. 2–14.

14. Roger Hilsman, "The Problem of Okinawa, 3–11, *Military Review,* vol 49, July 1969, p. 6. The United States never officially acknowledged the presence of nuclear weapons.

15. *Okinawa Information Guide* (Inteco, Naha, 1969), pp. 48–49. In 1970 virtually all Okinawan-based B-52 raids were shifted to Thailand, reducing the cost from $50,000 to $5,000 per run. Cf. John Dower, "Asia and the Nixon Doctrine: Ten Points of Note," *Bulletin of Concerned Asian Scholars,* vol. 2, no. 4, Fall 1970; UPI dispatch of August 24 in *Asahi Evening News,* August 25, 1970.

16. *Okinawa Information Guide,* pp. 52–53.

17. The official U.S. figure on the worth of the base complex in 1971 was $2 billion. General Dale Smith's estimate of an investment of $4–5 billion seems more accurate. ("Okinawa Hearings," p. 83.)

18. Major General David Ogden, Commanding General Ryukyus Command, Deputy Governor of Ryukyu Islands, "Keystone of the Pacific," *Army Information Digest,* January 1954, pp. 42–43.

19. Perry to Secretary of the Navy James C. Dobbin, in *Correspondence Relative to the Naval Expedition to Japan,* pp. 80–81. Indeed, as the Defense Department's *Pocket Guide to Okinawa* (Washington, 1961, p. 2) enthusiastically pointed out, Perry anticipated by almost a century the technical aid program of the U.S. government. "Commodore Perry presented to the Okinawans a butter churn and cotton gin, among other gifts, in the interest of their technological development. The Okinawans," the *Guide* notes with exceptional frankness, "had no conceivable use for these articles, however, and were considerably mystified by them." Perry's suggestions for "technical aid" to the Okinawans

and the President's approval of Perry's plan are printed in *Correspondence Relative to the Naval Expedition to Japan,* pp. 12–15.

20. *Ibid.,* pp. 112–13. Secretary of the Navy J. C. Dobbin's letter to Perry of May 30, 1854. Extensive description of Perry's expedition may be found in the special Okinawa issue of *Ampo. A Report from the Japanese New Left,* nos. 7–8, February 1971. This is the most important work in English on Okinawan history, particularly its contemporary strategic role and the struggle of the Okinawan people to end the military occupation of their country. See in addition George Kerr, *Okinawa, The History of an Island People* (Tokyo: Tuttle, 1949), pp. 4, 297–341.

21. Okinawan history has been one unbroken chain of domination by successive naval powers beginning centuries ago with fluctuating demands for tribute by China and Japan. For their part, the Okinawans steadfastly refused to take up the arts of war. Captain Basil Hall who reached Okinawa in 1818 recorded Napoleon's astonishment on being told that the Okinawans had no arms. " 'Point d'armes!' he exclaimed; ... 'Mais, sans armes, comment se bat-on?' I could only reply that, as far as we have been able to discover, they had never had any war, but remained in a state of internal and external peace." (Quoted in Kerr, p. 259.)

22. Roy Appleman, James Burns, Russell Gugeler, and John Stevens, *Okinawa: The Last Battle,* Historical Division, Department of the Army, Washington, D.C., 1948, especially pp. 253–64, 384, 387, 473; cf. Major Charles S. Nichols, Jr., Henry I. Shaw, Jr., *Okinawa: Victory in the Pacific,* Historical Branch G-3 Division Headquarters U.S. Marine Corps, U.S. Government Printing Office, Washington, D.C., 1955, *passim.*

23. Appleman *et al., Okinawa: The Last Battle,* p. 468.

24. Nichols and Shaw, *Okinawa: Victory,* p. 268.

25. Commander Stanley Bennett, "The Impact of Invasion and Occupation on the Civilians of Okinawa," *U.S. Naval Institute Proceedings,* vol. 72, February 1946, pp. 263–75.

26. *Facts Book,* 3–1.

27. *Facts Book,* 2–11.

28. The dual system of courts which provided Americans with extraterritoriality is defined in *Facts Book,* 2–8, 9. A typical instance of blatant disregard for crimes committed against Okinawans is related in *Civil Administration of the Ryukyu Islands, Report for Period 1 July 1967 to 30 June 1968,* High Commissioner of the Ryukyu Islands, p. 19. "The dependent daughter of a member of the U.S. Armed Forces was indicted for homicide ... tried [by the USCAR Superior Court] without a jury, found guilty and sentenced ... to imprisonment for 1 year, suspended for 3 years. She was released to the custody of her mother and has departed the Ryukyus."

29. *Civil Administration of the Ryukyus,* 1967–1968, p. 77. The U.S.

budget allocated huge sums for base construction on Okinawa at the height of the Vietnam War: 1966, $30,000,000; 1967, $66,500,000; 1968, $45,800,000; 1969, $29,000,000. Figures cited in *Ampo*, nos. 7–8, p. 34.

30. *Facts Book,* 6–5, 12–1. Per capita income was officially reported as $745 for FY 1969. These and other official statistics presumably present the most powerful—if not necessarily the most truthful—case for Okinawan material progress under American colonial rule. A Japanese study reports Okinawan per capita income for 1967 as $497 compared to $818 on mainland Japan. (*Okinawa Henkan* ["The Return of Okinawa"] [Tokyo, Asahi Shimbun Yoron Chosa, 1968], p. 110. I am indebted to Herbert Bix for calling this source to my attention.)

31. *Facts Book,* 10–1, 3, 5, 12–1; *Civil Administration of the Ryukyu Islands,* 1967–1968, pp. 77, 81.

32. The heavy import imbalance was one of many legacies of the Japanese era, though the commodities involved differed. Exports of 1933, typical of the 1930s, were 12,945 yen compared with imports of 1,813,365 yen. (*Civil Affairs Handbook* [1944], p. 265.)

33. The Temporarily Organized Okinawa Prefecture Land Adjustment Bureau, "Summary of the Land Adjustment in the Okinawa Prefecture," Tokyo, 1904. The quoted translation has been edited slightly for clarity. The pamphlet is available in Harvard's Widener Library under the title *Japan. Rice, Tobacco, Farms, Cattle. Department of Agriculture 1900–1928.*

34. Cf. Eric Wolf, *Peasant Wars of the Twentieth Century* (New York: Harper & Row, 1969), *passim.*

35. United States Navy, *Civil Affairs Handbook of the Ryukyus* (Washington, D.C., 1944). Cf. Ralph Thaxton's analyses of the impact of similar measures in Thailand in this volume.

36. Kerr, *Okinawa,* 186–98, 401–10, 424–35; Clarence Glacken, *The Great Loochoo, A Study of Okinawan Village Life,* University of California, 1955, 123–29.

37. An excellent example is prostitution which first became rampant during the Japanese era. In 1937, the prefectural station for examining prostitutes conducted 29,372 examinations. (*Civil Affairs Handbook* [1944], p. 63.)

38. "Report of a Special Subcommittee of the Armed Services Committee, House of Representatives, Following an Inspection Tour October 14 to November 23, 1955," U.S. Government Printing Office, 1956, pp. 7651–67. USCAR has been extremely secretive about American land-holding on Okinawa. No figures are given in the *Facts Book;* private estimates place the percent of arable land held by the United States as high as forty-six percent on the main island. (Cf. Thomas Klein, "The Ryukyus on the Eve of Reversion," *Pacific Affairs,* vol. 45, no. 1, Spring 1972, p. 16.)

39. "Okinawa: Levittown-on-the-Pacific," *Time,* vol. 66, no. 7, August 15, 1955, p. 19.

40. *Facts Book,* 13–7.

41. *Facts Book,* 10–8.

42. "Okinawa Reversion—Economic Integration Problem," *Oriental Economist,* January 1970, pp. 16–21; *Facts Book,* 10–8; *Japan Times,* June 28, 1970.

43. For American domination of Japan's oil and aluminum industry see Robert Guillain, *The Japanese Challenge, The Race to the Year 2000* (New York: J. B. Lippincott, 1970), pp. 132, 169–70.

44. Malcolm Caldwell, "Oil and Imperialism in East Asia," *Journal of Contemporary Asia,* vol. 1, no. 3, 1971, p. 7; Franz Schurmann, "The Waning of the American Empire," *Journal of Contemporary Asia,* vol. 1, no. 3, p. 85. See in addition the essays by Malcolm Caldwell and Herbert Bix in this volume.

45. *The Washington Post* of June 19, 1971, reported Japanese intentions to "operate 11 patrol boats carrying three-inch guns and 40-millimeter machine guns over a 110,000-square-mile area embracing the southern defense perimeter of the Ryukyu island chain adjacent to Taiwan. . . . These boats will eventually be equipped with ship-to-ship missiles . . . these patrols will cover the disputed Senkaku Islands . . ." (Quoted in "Statement of K. Lawrence Chang," "Okinawa Hearings, Annex," p. 9.)

46. The Tiao-yu T'ai question is fully analyzed by Kung-chung Wu in "A New May Fourth Movement" (*Bulletin of Concerned Asian Scholars,* vol. 3, no. 2, pp. 61–72), and with particular reference to Okinawan reversion in testimony presented at the "Okinawa Hearings" by K. Lawrence Chang, Thomas C. Dunn, John Fincher, Shien-Biau Woo and C. N. Yang. China's position was clearly stated in a *Renmin Ribao* (People's Daily) editorial translated in full in *Peking Review* Number 19, 1971, p. 14: "The Chinese people have always maintained that U.S. imperialism should *return Okinawa,* which it has occupied by force, *to the Japanese people.* But we will *never permit* the U.S. and the Japanese reactionaries to *annex* China's sacred territory Tiaoyu and other islands by making use of the 'Okinawa Reversion' swindle."

47. "End of American Rule on Okinawa—What It Means," *U.S. News and World Report,* June 28, 1971.

48. *Ampo,* nos. 7–8, p. 37.

49. Reorientation Branch Office for Occupied Areas, Office of the Secretary of the Army, "Annual Report of Stateside Activities Supporting the Reorientation Program in Japan and the Ryukyu Islands," October 1950.

50. *Ibid.,* July 1951.

51. *New York Times,* July 5, 1970; *Asahi Evening News,* August 20, 1970.

52. "Joint Communiqué Between President Richard Nixon and His Excellency Prime Minister Sato of Japan," November 21, 1969, reprinted in "Agreement with Japan Concerning the Ryukyu Islands and the Daito Islands." Message from the President of the United States of America and Japan Concerning the Ryukyu Islands and the Daito Islands, Signed at Washington and Tokyo on June 17, 1971 (hereafter, *Agreement with Japan*) , p. 27.

53. "Arrangement Concerning Assumption by Japan of the Responsibility for the Immediate Defense of Okinawa," *Agreement with Japan*, p. 25; *Guardian*, May 24, 1972.

PART III

JAPAN:
The Roots of Militarism*

HERBERT P. BIX

INTRODUCTION

Viewed from the military angle, the dominant theme in United States–Japan relations in the 1970s seems to be continued dependency on U.S. military power, with loyal Japan preparing to fill gaps created by the ongoing consolidation of U.S. military power in Asia; when we turn to the economic side, however, an entirely different picture emerges, one in which numerous contradictions have matured to the point where they threaten to tear asunder the entire military–diplomatic framework of the U.S.–Japan treaty system. Why the military side of U.S.–Japan relations, and, by extension, the military side of the post–World War II U.S. imperial bloc, can be preserved with relative ease even while its economic side is disintegrating, and what this situation tells us about the relationship between capitalism and militarism, are the subjects of this essay.

However, its division into two parts—military and economic—is meant to reflect more than the anomaly of a specific historical

* I wish to thank John Dower, Jim Peck, and Mark Selden for the invaluable criticism they gave me in the course of writing this essay.

moment. The military dimension of U.S.–Japan relations has, to an important extent, a life of its own. By extrapolating it from other dimensions it becomes possible to highlight not only how the military functions, but also how the momentum of technological change in the field of weapons development can, under certain conditions, impinge on domestic and foreign policy affairs in ways that close off options for peace—though not, of course, before the real power-holders know what is happening.

PART ONE: THE MILITARY DIMENSION

I. The Mystification of the Military Budget

Nothing has more mystified discussion of the Japanese military than the innumerable simplistic conclusions drawn from percentage comparisons with gross national product (GNP) or with international levels of military spending. This is seriously misleading on two counts: 1) the actual size and growth of the military and 2) the key role that Japan's defense expenditures play in supporting American imperialism in Asia.

Although annual defense costs are slightly less than one percent of its GNP, since 1967 Japan has had the seventh strongest all-round military establishment in the world with the third most powerful navy and air force in the Pacific after the United States and the Soviet Union. (Japan's armed forces, though comparatively small, are heavily over-officered and hence capable of rapid expansion.) Moreover, Japan's industrial structure is both technologically prepared for nuclear weapons development and self-sufficient in the manufacture of most, though not all, conventional weapons. The Defense Agency, like its model the Pentagon, emphasizes machines over manpower but spends far less than the Pentagon on personnel.

Japan's defense spending, moreover, is increasing at an astounding rate. Whereas one could dismiss this phenomenon in the sixties by saying that the country with the world's fastest-growing economy could hardly avoid having the world's fastest-growing military budget, that argument will no longer suffice in the seventies as Japan goes on increasing its military spending at a rate far in excess of its projected annual growth rate. Projected defense outlays alone suggest that Japan is entering a new stage of militarization. Having developed its armed forces at a rapid pace through three consecutive five-year plans (1956–1971), Japan suddenly stepped up its defense spending at the end of the third plan—by 15.1 percent for 1970, 17.8 percent for 1971, and 19.3 percent for 1972.

In April 1972 Japan was to have officially launched a fourth five-year defense buildup. However, Diet opposition plus budgetary difficulties in the wake of the Nixon economic and diplomatic shocks and the upward revaluation of the yen caused a postponement of final government approval of the plan.[1] When approval was finally secured, on October 9, 1972, following Prime Minister Tanaka's return from China, the total cost of the fourth plan had been reduced from $16.7 billion to approximately $15 billion. Even after this reduction, however, the fourth plan represented a 2.2-fold cost increase over the previous five-year plan. A fifth five-year plan, scheduled to begin in fiscal 1977, is expected to climb above $33 billion—more than double the cost of the fourth.[2] Japan's defense spending increased at an average annual rate of 14.5 percent under the third plan. During the next five years, its projected annual increase may reach as high as 19 or 20 percent.[3] This would advance the absolute amount of Japanese defense spending above its current seventh place world ranking.

Although these figures suggest the tempo and magnitude of Japan's military expenditures, they mask crucial features of the military budget. Allocated annually in accordance with a five-year plan, the bulk of defense expenses are accounted for by items of predetermined cost. Consequently, defense outlays are carried over from year to year under such rubrics as "continuing expenses" and "national treasury debt liability transactions" [*kokko saimu futan kōi*], making it difficult to grasp the substance of the defense budget in any single year, and thus impeding Diet control over the military.[4] A close look at the 1971 defense budget discloses that production of components for F-4E Phantom jets and tanks scheduled under the fourth plan has already commenced. Similarly, items of sophisticated technology scheduled for the fifth plan will go into production years before that plan's official commencement.

Another reason why Japan's defense spending appears small lies in the misleading dichotomy between "defense spending" and "non-defense spending," which many nations use to de-emphasize the scale of their military spending. The Japanese military budget, which does include some of the costs of maintaining U.S. military bases in Japan and Okinawa, fails to include economic aid to other Asian nations, though such aid serves military as well as economic functions. Japan's economic "aid" for South Korea's Pohang Steel Works, for example, is designed to equip the armed forces of the Park dictatorship with an industrial capacity both for mercenary operations in other Asian theaters and for waging "limited" warfare against North Korea. Insofar as such aid integrates South Korea into Japan's military sphere, it is "defense spending." Similarly, in Cambodia and South Vietnam, Japanese "economic aid" helps keep alive the mercenary Lon Nol dictatorship and the Saigon generals, thereby furthering American control over Indochina and Japanese participation in the economic exploitation of the region. Any discussion of Japan's defense spending therefore must make clear at the onset that "defense" is usually employed in the narrowest sense, that is, as an official statistical category designed to obscure public discussion of the real state of affairs.[5] But in Japan's case the military budget is a poorer guide to military strength than it would be with most other countries. If Japan's military establishment is to be judged realistically, it must be judged in terms of its ability to achieve certain objectives, not solely in terms of its GNP.

From this perspective an understanding of the political goals of Japan's leaders in the 1970s is crucial. Politically, they hope to assume a gradually increasing share of America's policing "burdens" in Asia. Since 1969 they have not hesitated to express that hope in official statements such as the Nixon-Sato Joint Communiqué of November 21, 1969, which linked Japan's security to the defense of the oppressive dictatorships in Taiwan and South Korea. The U.S.–Japan Treaty on Okinawa, signed on June 17, 1971, incorporated a reference to the joint communiqué in its preamble, thereby giving it a treatylike status.[6] Even more light on Japan's military strategy is shed by two other documents—the October 1970 White Paper on Defense and the Fourth Defense Plan draft of April 1971. These not only provide a clearer picture of Japan's emerging militarism but also set the stage for considering the phenomenon as one internal to Japanese society.

II. The Fourth Draft Plan

On April 27, 1971, the Defense Agency formally announced to the nation its final "draft" version of the fourth five-year defense plan without having obtained prior, explicit National Defense Council approval, as was done with the first three defense plans. Never before had the Defense Agency signaled so openly its impatience with the nation's top civilian economic and military planners. Never before had it so high-handedly ignored the postwar practice of publicizing the five-year plan only after securing final approval from the cabinet's National Defense Council—the nation's highest organ for determining overall defense policy. By its April 27 announcement the Defense Agency breached an important informal mechanism of civilian control. It also exacerbated a bitter internal feud with the chief secretary of the National Defense Council, Kaihara Osamu. In the eight months following the April 27 announcement, while details of the fourth plan were being intensely debated within the bureaucracy, the Defense Agency experienced four changes in director-generals: Nakasone Yasuhiro, Masuhara Keikichi, Nishimura Naomi, and the current Ezaki Masumi.[7] But if the manner of the fourth plan's announcement and the stormy process of securing its final approval were both unprecedented, no less significant were the contents of the plan itself.

In one fundamental respect the new plan represented a qualitative leap beyond previous defense plans: in accordance with the Sato-Nixon Joint Communiqué, it officially advanced Japan's defense perimeter from its own shoreline, as delineated in the third plan, to somewhere on the high seas. The new plan's naval orientation is seen in a building schedule that calls for eighty-six new ships, totaling 103,000 tons, so that by the end of fiscal 1976 the Japanese navy will have 220 ships totaling 247,000 tons, plus a naval air component of 350 planes.[8] (By 1981 the total tonnage may even reach 350,000 tons—125,000 tons less than the 1972 size of the Soviet navy.) This is the equivalent, in just five years, of the total tonnage constructed for the Japanese navy over the past nineteen.[9] This enormously expanded navy will be equipped for the first time with offensive weapons: ship-to-ship missiles.[10] And since the chief conceptual innovation of the fourth plan is air as well as sea control in areas around Japan, the Japanese air force will gain by 1976 six squadrons of F-4E Phantom fighters totaling 158 planes, and its total size will reach approximately 920 planes.

In other respects the fourth plan is a continuation of past policies: it simultaneously increases home production of military hardware and fosters continued Japanese dependency on the United States through heavy reliance on licensed production of American weapons. The most important components of Japan's new Phantom fighters, the engines and gun control systems, will be manufactured in the United States according to American specifications and imported by Japan. All together, Japan may purchase "between $800 million and $1 billion worth of assembled military hardware and parts from the U.S." as part of the fourth plan.[11] And, whereas America spends twenty percent of its annual military budget on research and development (R & D), Japan intends to spend only 3.3 percent of the fourth plan or about 180 billion yen (about $500 million) over the next five years on 120 items. Although this figure represents 3.8 times the R & D allocation under the third plan, it is nevertheless almost inconsequential compared to American levels of spending.[12] For example, on R & D for the ABM program alone, the Pentagon plans to spend, by conservative estimate, about $2.4 billion from 1970 through 1975,[13] or almost five times what Japan has programmed for all military R & D under the fourth plan.

On the other hand, in military R & D the state foots the bill for the development of advanced technology by so-called private industry. The AEW system (airborne early warning), ship-to-ship and air-to-ship missiles, electronic instruments and aircraft components that are scheduled for development under the fourth plan are of inestimable value to private industry. Private firms engaged in such defense production co-opt state-owned resources and funds to strengthen their *overall* monopoly position within a given market. Conversely, the capability that private industries acquire in producing almost any sophisticated technology has wide application to all phases of defense production. Thus in Japan a small "defense" sector is greatly reinforced by a much larger "non-defense" sector. In the 1970s Japan expects to spend the enormous sum of 5000 billion yen ($14 billion) on non-military R & D,[14] with significant impact on military technology anticipated. It is this fact that suggests that Japan's military–industrial complex might in the 1980s become able to disengage from America's. Yet, in considering the billions earmarked for hardware procurement under the fourth plan, one must again stress that it will not only reinforce the oligarchic trend in Japan's own defense industry, but, equally important in the short run, it will bind Japanese defense industry tighter to its American progenitor. The fourth plan's procurement priorities insure that Japan's military–industrial complex will continue to be integrally linked to America's, at least through the seventies.

What, then, can be said about the direction in which Japan's military planners are moving? First, the Japanese government has thus far failed to evolve a clearcut national defense policy, let alone decided whether the Soviet Union or China is its primary hypothetical enemy. Yet postponing these decisions has not dissuaded it in the least from planning a vast military procurement program which envisions:

• Retaining the U.S.–Japan Security Treaty while transforming the Self-Defense Forces into an independent strategic unit within the American alliance system.

• Building an air force and a navy capable of maintaining air and sea supremacy within Japan's defense perimeter—defined variously since April 1971 as including at the least, everything within an area of 1000 nautical miles from Tokyo to, at most, the seas as far south as Indonesia.

• Building a capital-intensive army of thirteen divisions (180,000 first-line troops and 60,000 reserves) with overwhelming fire-power capacity and helicopter mobility, capable of being sent overseas on short notice to fight "limited wars." Since, however, the goal of a thirteen-division army was determined originally by domestic and international conditions obtaining in the early 1950s, demands that it be revised upward are now becoming quite frequent within the GSDF (Ground Self-Defense Forces).[15]

• Lastly, it may be conjectured that in the decade ahead the Defense Agency will, at the least, retain its nuclear options by investigating the possibility of constructing a fleet of nuclear powered Polaris-type submarines and nuclear warheads for its missiles. The United States, however, will oppose a major Japanese effort along these lines because its goal has always been to encourage a dependent military growth in Japan.

In any case, by the time they have completed their fifth five-year plan in the early 1980s, Japan's armed forces will be able to assume an outward, offensive mission of policing Pacific Asia.

The fourth defense plan, in short, explodes the fiction that Japan's primary defense concern is preventing large-scale internal disorders and insuring the security of the home islands. Indeed, the very distinction between defensive and offensive military forces will become meaningless once the fourth plan furnishes Japan with Nike-Hercules missiles which can carry nuclear warheads and F-4E Phantom fighters capable of bombing deep into North Korea, China and the Soviet Far East.

III. The Defense White Paper

The 1970 White Paper (entitled *Japan's Defense*) [16] must be viewed against this background of—in Japan's own eyes—no real defense policy yet enormous military procurement plans, of armed forces imbued with a defensive strategic mission yet rapidly being transformed by technological *faits accomplis* into offensive fighting forces. Its underlying theme was not "defense" but patriotism and the need for a new national consensus supportive of the military. Its credibility, however, was marred by certain contradictions. Twice the White Paper asserted emphatically that "so-called overseas dispatch of forces will not be carried out." [17] Yet during 1971 the Defense Agency hired 300 "civilian" ferry boats for field exercises designed to transport tanks and troops to South Korea, signed an agreement to "exchange military experiences" with Indonesia's armed forces, which will entail dispatching Japanese military instructors to that country, and entered into a separate "arrangement" with the Pentagon on the future deployment of about 6800 Japanese military personnel to Okinawa by the summer of 1973. [18] Or again: Despite repeated assertions that the Self-Defense Forces exist strictly for "defensive defense," the authors of the White Paper could not avoid analyzing international problems in terms of a deterrence concept which, by definition, presupposed deployed forces "to prevent foreign threats and aggression *in advance*." [19] Obviously, this would clearly violate the basic principle of "adhering strictly and exclusively to defense."

And yet, external and internal contradictions notwithstanding, the White Paper is an amazingly candid document which confronts a fundamental weakness of the Self-Defense Forces: their lack of credibility in Japanese and foreign eyes. For that situation to change, for the Defense Forces to become an effective deterrent, the Japanese people as a whole and not just the most oppressed strata of Japanese society—the sons of farmers, small merchants, and small businessmen—must be willing to fight and die for the state. And that they are still not prepared to do. Though lavishly equipped, Japan's armed forces have never been able to meet their full enlistment quotas, except at the time of their initial postwar organization. Even in 1971, when the air force, most prestigious of the services, had achieved 97 percent of its allotted manpower and the navy 96.5 percent, the army still had only 87.4 percent, leaving all of its front-line divisions almost 25 percent undermanned.[20] According to the White Paper, this recruitment problem "is becoming more and more difficult, day by day," making improvement in society's treatment of the military man "the most urgent task."[21] In this respect, the real obstacle to Japanese militarism is certainly not the Security Treaty with the United States, which more than anything else facilitated Japan's rearmament. It is the Japanese people, enough of whom, unlike Americans, refuse to forget the misery and destruction of war because they experienced it directly.[22]

Hence the White Paper's stress on patriotism, public opinion, and education. Hence also its remarkable statement that only a "true patriotism" or "the ardor to give one's life for the defense of the nation . . ." will suffice. "Just loving peace and loving the country" is not enough.[23]

On the occasion of the submission of the fourth draft plan to the cabinet, Prime Minister Sato is alleged to have remarked about the need to harmonize the strengthening of national defense with future educational policy.[24] But when it comes to the nature of the elite consensus on national defense, neither the White Paper nor the fourth defense plan offers any unambiguous conclusions. For that, one must examine the subtle shift in SDF propaganda and recruit indoctrination that first began in the wake of the 1960 struggle against the U.S.–Japan Security Treaty (AMPO) and is continuing today.

IV. The SDF and the New Patriotism

Reestablished covertly and illegally in a repetition of the Weimar military's historic birth[25] and never having enjoyed widespread popular support, Japan's postwar military in addition has suffered the contradiction of a "citizens'" army whose initial primary mission was the counterrevolutionary suppression of other citizens. At the root of its dilemma is a constitution that denies the existence of the military in theory while accepting it in practice.[26] Where the armies of Weimar and imperial Japan of the thirties stressed their ideological distance from society and the superiority of soldier and sailor to ordinary citizen, the army of democratic Japan must, in contrast, insist on its "civilian control," its essential oneness with society and public service nature. It is in the context of this specific legal dilemma that the implications of recent transformations in SDF ideology should be understood. They should also be grasped as one part of an exceedingly broad push toward a new patriotism which emerged in all areas of Japanese life during the 1960s.

From 1950, when the "National Police Reserve" was first established by General MacArthur, to 1960, Japanese military indoctrination consisted almost entirely of straightforward anti-Communism. The 1960 mass struggles to prevent renewal of the U.S.–Japan Security Treaty, led by the Left and participated in by a wide assortment of groups, provided the first real test of the GSDF's anti-Communism. In June, at the height of the crisis, a group of ruling Liberal Democratic Party leaders asked Defense Agency Director-General Akagi Munenori if he would use Ground Self-Defense Forces to protect the Diet and executive buildings from invasion by demonstrators and rioters.[27] Akagi refused—not only because it might have "damaged the image of the 'people's Self-Defense Forces,' "[28] but more likely because he estimated correctly that the troops could not be relied upon to crush the people, who, whatever their political coloration, were still Japanese.

In the 1960s the veteran ex-imperial officers of the SDF, sensitized by this incident to the ideological problem, began gropingly to relate to two new trends in Japanese society. One was the increased activism of the ultranationalist right which had first emerged in the 1950s. Not only did business and government circles lend support to old rightists in the wake of the demonstrations of 1960, but new forms of right-wing activity emerged, such as private "guardsmen companies" which were used, with tacit state support, against striking workers and student activists. The first "guardsman company," the *Nihon Keibi Hoshō Kabushiki Kaisha,* was formed in Tokyo in 1963; the second, *Sōgō Keibi Hoshō,* which is now the largest with 6500 guardsmen, was established in 1965. Between 1965 and 1970 the number of such companies increased from 155 to 310, and the number of guardsmen to nearly 26,000 by October 1970. *Sōgō Keibi's* president, Murai Jun, "was formerly head of the Police Guard Section of the Headquarters of the National Rural Police and the first director of the Cabinet Investigation Office—the Japanese CIA. Its adviser, Yoshio Miwa, was formerly the deputy director-general of the Defense Agency. Most of the chiefs of the company are also of police and secret agent origin."[29] Paralleling the growth of guardsmen companies was an increase in right-wing political organizations which numbered 400 with an estimated 120,000 members in 1970.[30]

In the 1960s, as the new "old right" grew, SDF officers began inviting noted rightists to the training camps. Tōkō Kon, Liberal Democratic Party Dietman and popular novelist, told the men of the Self-Defense Forces at a lecture, "Your mission is to kill; that's not murder. You just kill them; it's all right and it's legal. The state takes responsibility for what you do, so never mind, you can kill with a clear conscience anyone who is not of the Japanese nation."[31] In the spring of 1968 right-wing novelist Mishima Yukio was welcomed by high-ranking officers of the GSDF's Fuji Training School "and given special training for forty-five days as a special soldier. . . . On the basis of what he had learned he organized his own private army, *Tate no kai* ["Shield Society"], made up mainly of students. The SDF provided special training for the group, a concentrated officers' course in 'tactics' at the Fuji Training Camp, by a special arrangement with the GSDF chief."[32]

The SDF was also at the center of the great debate on Japan's recent imperial past which began with the Shōwa History Debate of 1955–1957. Under the government's sponsorship of the Meiji Centennial celebrations during the sixties, the debate affected the national consciousness of Japanese in all walks of life.[33] Part of the new historical awareness was a healthy reaction to the self-hatred that American officials deliberately inculcated during the occupation period, but another part spilled over into recruit indoctrination as a supplement to stepped-up anti-Communist indoctrination.

In March 1963 an SDF Research Association was established to prepare "spiritual education" materials for the troops, including war movies and historical materials. In 1964 the Defense Agency began to encourage establishment of local historical museums to house the records of Pacific War veterans.[34] Soon it was producing its own full-length color films for in-service viewing as well as to propagandize the public. In March 1967, Shōchiku, a leading film company, issued the SDF-made movie "The Japan–U.S. Security Treaty System" under its own title of "The Wonders of Science—Missiles Fly the Heavens" [*Kagaku no kyōi—misairu ozora o tobu*].

That same year the Pentagon returned to the Defense Agency hundreds of war movies that had been confiscated during the Occupation. In 1968 Japan's leading cinema companies released them uncut to the public, touching off a tremendous revival of interest in war movies. Of course, the Defense Agency alone was not responsible for abetting the war movie boom of the late sixties and early seventies. Part of the credit is due its number one defense contractor—the Mitsubishi monopoly group. In the late 1960s Mitsubishi gained control of Japan's leading film making companies. Mitsubishi Realty took over Nikkatsu Cinema; and JASCO, the Mitsubishi supermarket chain, tied up with the famous Tōhō Cinema. Thus it was perhaps not entirely coincidental that the new war movies beautified Japan's past wars of aggression.[35]

But try as the Self-Defense Forces might to raise in-service morale, improve their public image, and win support for militarism, when faced with the fundamental problem of their foreign and domestic credibility as an army in need of constitutional protection they, in Mishima's apt words, "remained as silent as a canary deprived of its song."[36] Nevertheless, by the end of the decade, at least some SDF officers were thinking of solving that problem by resurrecting the still-intact symbol of the emperor, the *Bushidō* spirit, and the notion of a state grounded in mythology. It is still too early to determine what effects Mishima's dramatic suicide at Ichigaya, on November 25, 1970, will have on the SDF. The SDF troops, it is true, gave him a poor reception at the time. But the nostalgia that calls for at least partial restoration of the emperor symbol has been strengthened by his act and cannot be overlooked. The harking back to Japan's mythological origins is exemplified best by General Tsukamoto Masatoshi's talk to the men when he was "special curriculum chief" of the Fuji Training School. As he observed while lecturing on "A General View of Japanese History and National Polity,"

Mythology is mythology; nations rise and fall; but why is it that the emperor system has endured for 2600 years?

Comparison with world history: the United States is only 200 years old; the Soviet Union is only 30. Will they be able to exist as a unified state [like us] for 2600 years?

Imperial Household–State–People are three heads on one body. His Majesty the emperor BANZAI! Japan BANZAI! the Japanese people BANZAI![37]

Nostalgia for Japan's ancient "way of the samurai" is suggested by the emphasis on "fostering morality" which is to be found in the "Self-Defense Force Serviceman's Regulations." It is evidenced most strikingly in certain textbooks for lower-rank officers, in which patriotism is defined as follows:

Loyalty is a feeling peculiar to us Japanese since ancient times. We have been trained in the so-called spirit of *Bushidō* [originally: "the way of the samurai"—the peculiar morality of Japanese military men of the Middle Ages]. Thanks to the Meiji Restoration, the state was unified, and since the emperor became the center of the state, the feeling of loyalty to the way of the warrior became patriotism. We love the state as our highest principle and have come to regard dying for the sake of the state as the highest honor. Precisely this patriotism is the motive force for the development of the state.[38]

Three conclusions can be drawn from the preceding discussion: first, the Self-Defense Forces remain a subordinate military establishment, serving American interests in the Pacific. One hundred twenty-six American bases and 28,000 American servicemen still in Japan, plus another 35,000 on Okinawa, symbolically reinforce their sense of subordination to America. In equipment procurement, in operational planning such as the Three Arrows "map exercise" and in joint deployment exercises with South Korean naval forces, the SDF is a cog in the Pentagon's war machine. Whether they desire rapid or gradual expansion, revival of the emperor symbol or partial revision of the constitution, SDF officers, generally speaking, have a dependent consciousness: nearly all envision continued reliance on American military power. So strong is this reliance on America that it may itself be regarded as a characteristic of Japan's new militarism.

Second, the SDF is an extremely frustrated military, led by former imperial army and navy officers who enjoy the support of conservative business and government leaders who were themselves former imperial officers. It is also a military establishment that finds it increasingly difficult to tolerate a constitution that denies its legitimacy, an imposed and alien principle of civilian control, and, worst of all, a government that perpetuates its strategic aimlessness by refusing to formulate a clearly defined defense policy. The accumulated frustrations of the uniformed SDF officer corps and their friction with Finance Ministry and MITI officials as well as with civilian defense planners may soon become factors to be reckoned with in Japanese politics.

Third, by "gradually weaning the public away from little-Japanism,"[39] by launching successive military consolidation plans that make Japan a "military big power," Japan's conservative leaders deliberately increase the likelihood that these mutually reinforcing developments will precipitate conditions for a revision of the constitution and, ultimately, a "breakthrough to a new state structure."[40] Once that occurs, the internal position and status of both military and emperor in Japanese life are sure to be greatly enhanced: the emperor, or rather the imperial institution, because it has always been used by those in power, as a last resort, to forge consensus on foreign policy and to foster identity between state and society; the military because it can only exist *for itself* when it appears to be defending the values of the Japanese people, values which the living emperor has historically personified.

And yet it must be said that restoration of these two components to more traditional roles will by no means signal a return to the prewar polity. In postwar Japan, the mainstream conception of the national destiny and the individual's proper relation to society and to the military is not being shaped by an ultra-nationalist military elite advantageously positioned within the state structure, hostile to democratic rhetoric, and anti-Western in orientation, but by businessmen and technocrats committed to the ideology of Japanese-style democracy and acting in response to their perception of the needs of the national economy. If conservative politicians, military officers, and an increasing number of university intellectuals desire a quantum leap in military strength, so too do the leaders of big business, and they are the prime movers in the Japanese polity. In order to understand the causes of Japan's new militarism, as well as its recent burst of overseas economic expansion, one must turn to the problems of her business leaders and to the study of her postwar economic history. For it is precisely in Japan that one sees best how advanced monopoly capitalism generates the interrelated evils of budding militarism and economic imperialism.

PART II: THE ECONOMIC DIMENSION

I. The Problem

Since the Korean War in the early 1950s, the strongest sustained impetus for altering the Japanese economy and constitution to serve militaristic ends has come not from military leaders, bureaucrats, or conservative politicians but from the leaders of big business. Herein lies the crucial difference between prewar militarism and the still "nonideological" variety emerging in Japan today.

In prewar Japan militarism antedated both heavy industrialization and completion of the Meiji state structure. To simplify grossly one could say that it sprang primarily from the political–intellectual superstructure: the centuries-long traditions of rule by a military class, later traditions of irrationality, contempt for human rights and hostility toward democracy within the Meiji military establishment, and the persistence of the idea from pre-Tokugawa times of expansion in Asia (particularly Korea, which, ever since Hideyoshi's late-sixteenth-century invasions, was viewed as the bridgehead for Japan's advance on the continent). The new militarism, by contrast, is largely a *substructural phenomenon,* spurred on by the imperatives of economic and technological development.[41] Whereas the old militarism was nurtured by war indemnities (Sino-Japanese War, Liaotung Retrocession, and Boxer Rebellion), by borrowed British and American capital in the decade after 1904, and by state bond issues, the new militarism is fed by Japan's domestically generated surplus yet also grows *parasitically* on American imperialism.[42] Appearing as a major "problem" in Japanese life at the end of a decade of rapid economic growth during which Japanese capitalism underwent a structural transformation, it is clearly a phenomenon of that capitalism's maturity. The Japanese economy by the late 1960s had arrived at a stage where a saturated domestic market was insufficient to sustain high economic growth. In this situation a growing arms budget and access to overseas areas for investment of surplus capital became essential. The new militarism thus has its deepest roots not in the unconstitutional and still psychologically hobbled Self-Defense Forces—though, as we have seen, they can no longer be discounted—but in a defense-industrial sector which is steadily becoming a major growth sector in the Japanese economy.[43]

While the military–industrial complexes of the United States and the U.S.S.R. are nurtured partly for economic–technological reasons and partly to "solve" the political difficulties of administering empires of subject peoples,[44] that of Japan is peculiar in being nurtured, at this stage, primarily to overcome the internal contradictions of advanced monopoly capitalism. (The desire to participate with the United States as an equal rather than a junior partner in policing Pacific Asia is a related but secondary motive.) Ultimately, it is not Japan's new militarism per se that poses a threat to the future of America's imperial hegemony in Asia but its increasing potential for pursuing an independent economic imperialism.

But how did this situation come about? Why does Japanese capitalism impel Japan toward domestic militarism and the imperialism of economic investment abroad? And why have these issues, which first surfaced as long ago as 1948, suddenly acquired such urgency in Japanese domestic politics? Answers to these questions can be had, first, by describing Japan's postwar economic development in relation to international affairs; second, by examining some of the effects of the Japanese economic challenge on the world capitalist system and Japanese–American relations in particular; and, third, by analyzing two constituent elements of the Japanese "success"—technology and agriculture. This last will illuminate both the contradictions of capitalist development and the levers of American manipulation of Japan's economy. It will also set the stage for assessing, in the conclusion, the present level of Japan's ability to break out of the American empire.

II. International Factors

If there was a "reverse course" in U.S. occupation policy for defeated Japan, then its basis was laid months before the Japanese surrender. By retaining intact two of prewar Japan's privileged elites, the imperial institution and the bureaucracy, the Truman administration insured that the formal democratization of Japan would take place within the conservative framework of the old regime. The American plan for postwar Japan was thus highly conservative from its inception; as it progressed it became positively reactionary. Indeed, as soon as the occupation commenced, in late August 1945, the United States took steps "toward preparing Japan for a possible future military role against the Soviet Union."[45] By January 1947, MacArthur had embarked on a program of splitting the Japanese labor movement and crippling the Left. But in the area of our primary concern, the economy, the reverse course made itself felt only by degrees and chiefly in relation to the unfolding of U.S. Cold War policy in Asia.

The first change in U.S. economic policy was a reinterpretation of the meaning of reparations. The original Allied conception of reparations, as stipulated in Article Eleven of the July 26, 1945 Potsdam Proclamation, called for the exaction from Japan of "just reparations in kind." The idea contained two intertwined elements: 1) that reparations were a penalty or retribution that Japan should be made to pay for its aggression against its Asian neighbors, and 2) that reparations were a reminder of Japan's moral responsibility for the harm it had caused in dominating its neighbors. This twofold conception of reparations was soon embodied in the first American reparations report, drawn up by Edwin Pauley in the months immediately following Japan's surrender. The Pauley Report of April 1946 asked the U.S. government to

> ... take no action to assist Japan in maintaining a standard of living higher than that of neighboring Asiatic countries injured by Japanese aggression.... The overall aim should be both to raise and to even up the level of industrialization ["in Eastern Asia as a whole."] This aim can be served by considered allocation, to different countries, of industrial equipment exacted from Japan as reparations. Reconstruction is an urgent need of all the countries against which Japan committed aggression. Reconstruction is also needed in Japan. In the overall comparison of needs Japan should have the last priority.[46]

Linked to this recommendation on reparations was an insight into the relationship between monopoly (in the form of the zaibatsu) and militarism that was profoundly radical in its implications. Pauley called for the dissolution of Japan's great monopolies because

... throughout the modern history of Japan [they] have controlled not only finance, industry and commerce, but also the government. They are the greatest war potential of Japan. It was they who made possible all Japan's conquests and aggressions.... Not only were the Zaibatsu as responsible for Japan's militarism as the militarists themselves, but they profited immensely by it. Even now, in defeat, they have actually strengthened their monopoly position. The industrial facilities owned or controlled by them stand relatively undamaged from the war, compared with thousands and thousands of small businesses which have been wiped out. The "little men" are not only ruined, but heavily indebted to the Zaibatsu. Unless the Zaibatsu are broken up, the Japanese have little prospect of ever being able to govern themselves as free men. As long as the Zaibatsu survive, Japan will be their Japan.[47]

The Occupation made a brief attempt to implement Pauley's reparations and monopoly dissolution proposals but soon abandoned both. In January 1947 the Truman administration sent Clifford Strike at the head of a team of industrial engineering executives to Japan to investigate the reparations question. Three months later, in April, the Strike Commission issued a report "for which the army paid them $750,000, that rejected all but a minor $79 million in reparations payments. It called for the complete rehabilitation of the very industries that the Pauley Commission had recommended be totally dismantled. And, most critically for future policy, the commission criticized all the democratic reforms as adding '... additional difficulties in the process of quickly achieving self-sufficiency.' "[48] In May, following the Strike report, General MacArthur ordered all interim reparations removals stopped and tabled the whole issue until after the conclusion of a peace treaty with Japan. Washington in particular was concerned lest Japanese reparations to the Kuomintang wind up in the hands of the Chinese Communists, as was happening with so much American aid at the time.

Thus by 1947 reparations had ceased to be viewed either as compensation for damage and injury sustained by Japan's neighbors or as a reminder of the past. Instead, Japanese businessmen and American policy-makers alike were starting to see them as a constituent element of Japan's future economic development. When the San Francisco Peace Treaty was signed, on September 8, 1951, Japan agreed to pay war damages "by making available the services of the Japanese people in production, salvaging and other work for the Allied Powers in question." Reparations, like Japanese economic aid a decade later, thus became an instrument for facilitating the advance of Japanese monopoly capital into Southeast Asia.[49]

Washington's decision to drastically scale down Japan's reparations presaged the first real turning point in the postwar revival of Japanese capitalism, which came in 1948 concomitantly with the victories of Mao's armies over United States–backed Kuomintang forces in China and the maturation of a civil war situation in the Korean peninsula in which all nationalist forces were arrayed against the American-installed Rhee government. It took these failures of American Asian policy to finally crystallize the latent implications of the original American decision to retain in power Japan's conservative ruling class minus the military elite. During 1948, as the situation in Asia deteriorated from the perspective of U.S. policy aims, and as economic problems accumulated in the United States, Washington, acting through the Supreme Commander for the Allied Powers (SCAP, or General MacArthur), began to expedite the policy of nurturing Japan as the military workshop of non-Communist Asia. Democratization and demilitarization, formal goals of the Occupation's early months, were downgraded. Economically, from 1948 onward the Occupation reversed the decartelization of Japanese industry and revived Japan's industrial war potential as a subcontracting component of American capitalism.

In December 1948, General MacArthur, having already banned wage increases and strikes in certain key industries, ordered the Yoshida government to take nine measures to stabilize the Japanese economy. These included balancing the budget, strengthening the tax collection system, wage, price, and trade controls, an improved system of allocating raw materials to increase exports, increased production of domestic raw materials and manufactures, and more effective measures for bringing food from the countryside into the cities. Three months later, in March 1949, Joseph M. Dodge, Detroit banker and MacArthur's newly appointed economic adviser, translated the new orientation in occupation policy into an austerity budget based on these "nine principles." The Lower House of the Japanese Diet passed it without revision on April 16, 1949.[50] By eliminating unemployment countermeasures and all funds for school building construction, by tightening up procedures for tax collection in a period of severe price inflation, the Dodge budget met its billing as a harsh austerity measure. Yet its real impact lay not in the rising unemployment and belt-tightening which it occasioned but in a long-term financial–economic orientation to the U.S. economy.[51]

The April 1949 "Dodge budget" contained both a potential military budget and a new mechanism of crucial importance for subordinating Japanese capitalism to American interests. This new mechanism was the U.S. Aid Counterpart Fund for Japanese Stabilization (or the "counterpart fund special account") — though most of the money in it in 1949 came from taxes paid by the Japanese. As the danger of civil war in Korea mounted in the last half of 1949, SCAP used the "counterpart fund special account" to channel Japanese tax money and U.S. loans into direct and indirect Japanese military production.[52]

Finally, on April 23, 1949, SCAP ordered the yen–dollar exchange rate fixed at 360 : 1 and, at the same time, abolished many export subsidies. With the yen firmly subordinated to the dollar, occupied Japan was brought into the United States–dominated international monetary system. The "nine principles," the "Dodge budget," and the uniform currency rate which accompanied it together created an economic framework for recovery which deliberately favored large industrial and commercial concentrations, particularly exporters, at the expense of the small businessman and the working class. The reconstruction of the zaibatsu, the mammoth industrial and trading houses which dominated Japan's prewar economy, proceeded apace.

While these changes were being instituted in the Japanese economy, others, harder to comprehend, were occurring in the psychological orientation of the Japanese people. Here two interrelated but contradictory phenomena can be distinguished within the first two years after the wartime defeat, before the economic "reverse course" got under way in earnest. On the one hand, there was a sense of liberation and acute political awareness as manifested in strikes, demonstrations, and political organizing activities; but, on the other, there was a feeling of "stagnation" and "prostration,"[53] arising in part from the demystification of the nation's central symbols, which left many people temporarily disoriented. These two psychological poles may have reflected the possibilities for genuine revolutionary change that were open to the Japanese people in this critical period. In any case, when deprived of a unifying focus in the person of the emperor, the national loyalties of the Japanese, their nationalism as it were, did not, as many foreigners believed at the time, disintegrate overnight, but shifted instead from the state to the family, village and small local groups—the corporate building blocks of Japanese society.[54]

Not until their own bureaucracy—SCAP's second of the major prewar privileged elites—was endowed with the mission of economic recovery did the Japanese people begin to emerge from this existential syndrome of political awareness and collective depression. As their leaders embarked on their new project, Japanese nationalism gradually assumed an appropriate economic form for a nation relatively isolated from the turmoil of international conflict. Simultaneously, many Japanese employers began to succeed in harnessing the loyalties of their workers toward company goals, thereby transforming decentralized postwar nationalism into a remarkably potent force for economic recovery. Their success, however, was made possible by SCAP's repression of the Left under conditions of massive unemployment induced by Dodge's austerity measures. Shortly before and after the outbreak of the Korean War, SCAP forced a tremendous contraction in the number of unions in Japan. In 1949 there were 34,688 unions with 6,655,483 members representing an estimated 55.8 percent of the work force; by 1951 the number had declined to 27,644 unions with 5,686,774 members representing 42.6 percent of the work force.[55] Thereafter, aided by unions, which were forced to become something like "industrial patriotism clubs,"[56] the companies provided a maximally efficient framework for channeling the energy of Japanese workers into the cause of economic growth.

If the first international event shaping the revival of Japanese capitalism was the triumph of revolution in China and the disintegration of the U.S. position in the Korean peninsula, the Korean War (1950–1953) was the second. The Korean War produced a "special procurements" boom, which, in turn, created sufficient external demand to spark Japan's economic recovery. During and immediately after the Korean War zaibatsu firm names were revived, the antimonopoly act was partially emasculated, and old zaibatsu groups reorganized, this time around banks rather than holding companies, mines, and shipping as in prewar days.[57] In 1951 Japan's mining industry reached its prewar level (1934–1936 average output) and by 1955 exceeded its peak (1944) wartime output.[58] The absolute volume of industrial production and real GNP by that time also exceeded prewar levels,[59] though several more years would be required before Japan recovered its prewar importance in the world economy.

The Korean War also provided the occasion for the start of large-scale capital and technology imports from abroad. Whereas only twenty-seven items of technology were authorized for import in 1949 and 1950, a total of 337 items were brought in between 1951 and 1953. Between 1950 and 1954 royalty payments for imported technology totaled $37,977,000.[60] Since much of this consisted of rights to manufacture standard gauge American weapons or else specific designs and techniques involved in munitions production, this early phase of technological importing can be said to have laid the foundation for the later integration of the Japanese and American defense industries.[61]

By the end of the 1950s six major monopoly groups had emerged: Mitsui, Sumitomo, the Fuji Bank line, the Dai Ichi Bank line, the Sanwa Bank line, and a partially reconstituted Mitsubishi.[62] By 1967 these six accounted for thirty-one percent of the sales and forty percent of the profits of all Japanese companies.[63] And by 1970 a completely reconstituted Mitsubishi group of forty-four companies—nucleus of the Japanese military–industrial complex—had achieved a preeminent position in the economy, outstripping all other monopoly groups.[64]

Throughout the 1950s Japanese capitalism differed qualitatively from its American and European counterparts. Japan's early postwar development had centered almost exclusively on the domestic market, heavy capital investment in plant facilities, and light industrial exports. In the early 1960s, however, this transitory pattern began to change in favor of increased reliance on the world export market and heavy, capital-intensive industrial commodities such as steel, ships, automobiles, and machine tools.[65] Japan's tightly controlled economy was well on its way to becoming fully competitive with the United States at the global level—and even within the United States as was evident when the critical year 1965 brought conditions which enabled Japan to achieve a still higher stage of growth. In this stage Japan became involved economically in nearly all of Pacific Asia and began to interact with American imperialism automatically and through coordination.

The war in Indochina provided the first of the conditions for external expansion of Japanese capitalism. American terror bombing of Laos and Vietnam and, above all, the massive troop buildup in Vietnam during 1965–1968 touched off a new wave of special procurements. The Indochina War also created favorable conditions within the U.S. home market for increased imports of inexpensive Japanese steel and electrical machinery and facilitated expansion of Japan's export trade with South Korea, Taiwan, the Philippines, and Thailand—American client states that fulfilled their own Vietnam War orders by importing raw materials and semifinished products from Japan.[66] The Sato government, which had been worried about a recession and a worsening balance-of-payments deficit during 1964,[67] gave unstinting support to U.S. escalation of the Indochina War, seeing it correctly as the greatest economic stimulant in Asia since the Korean War. The shift of U.S. resources to Southeast Asia forced the United States to push Japan harder than ever to speed up its economic involvement in Southeast Asia and in its former colonies of Taiwan and South Korea. America needed Japan's help for the Indochina War; Japanese big business needed American help in breaking into the markets of Southeast Asia. Furthermore, in the late 1960s one of the factors sparking Japan's rapid growth—contracts and patents for American technology and manufacturing techniques—also worked to channel Japanese exports into these areas by stipulating where the product of the joint venture or subsidiary would be sold.

One key to Japan's new position in Asia after 1965 was South Korea. By September 1965 more than 22,000 South Korean mercenaries had been sent to Vietnam. Dictator Park Chung Hee, having exacted a heavy financial price from U.S. leaders, who were desperate to produce evidence of an allied effort, had linked South Korea firmly to the Vietnam War in a mercenary capacity. Meanwhile, against this background of secret body sales, South Korea's American-trained police and CIA were busy smashing a two-year long student-led campaign to block "normalization" of relations with Japan. On August 14, eve of the twentieth anniversary of Korea's liberation from Japanese colonialism, Park's ruling Democratic-Republican party, in a move later known as the "snatch," unilaterally forced through the National Assembly a treaty and four supplementary agreements normalizing relations with Japan.[68] With equal contempt for democratic procedures, the Sato government completed Diet action on the treaty three months later. At midnight on November 12, 1965, after only six days of full deliberation and in violation of five basic procedural rules of the Lower House, it also secured unilateral Diet ratification of the treaty.[69]

America's "national security managers" had achieved a major victory. By pressuring Japan and South Korea to resolve their long-standing differences, they effectively fused the U.S.–Japan Security Treaty with the October 1953 U.S.–South Korea military alliance, thereby laying the legal foundation for shifting the burden of empire in Northeast Asia to Japan. Building on gains made during the first five years of Park's dictatorship, Japanese business leaders launched a full-scale economic offensive into South Korea. In 1965 direct Japanese investment in South Korea was only $1.2 million; by 1969 it had climbed to $27.1 million. By 1970 Japanese companies controlled about ninety percent of South Korea's fertilizer industry, sixty-four percent of its chemical fiber industry, sixty-two percent of foodstuffs, forty-eight percent of glassmaking and cement, and 43.5 percent of its chemical industry. Furthermore, in joint ventures with South Korean companies, Japanese capital as of March 1970 controlled less than half the stock in nineteen percent of these ventures, half the stock in thirty-three percent over fifty percent but less than 100 percent of the stock in twenty-two percent, and 100 percent of the stock in twenty-six percent.[70] Clearly, after 1965, while concurrently participating in Vietnam "pacification" and opening itself wide to Japanese economic "assistance," South Korea did indeed experience a miraculous transformation, becoming Asia's first mercenary state under dual neocolonial control.

A second turning point in Japan's economic development in 1965 was her relationship with Indonesia. On October 1, 1965, a rightist military coup, probably abetted by the CIA, toppled the Sukarno regime in Indonesia.[71] The post-coup government severed the embryonic Peking–Djakarta "axis" and brought resource-rich Indonesia back into the Western fold in an orgy of mass murder. With this the curtain was also raised for Japan's return to Indonesia as economic patron to a partially Japanese-trained ruling junta led by Suharto. In 1966 the Suharto regime received a $30-million Japanese government loan, in 1967 a $95-million loan, in 1968 $112 million in loans and other forms of assistance, in 1969 $117 million and in 1970 and 1971, jointly with the U.S. government, yen loans of $130 and $155 million respectively. Since 1966 it received a further $37.5 million in free grants, primarily food assistance made available between 1968 and 1970.[72] By 1970 Indonesia had become one of Japan's most important Asian investment markets and bases from which to extract mineral and agricultural wealth. With hundreds of Japanese oil tankers on their way home from the Middle East passing through the Malacca and Sunda Straits, Indonesia also had come to figure in justifications for naval expansion which were advanced by Japanese industrialists tied to the military–industrial complex.[73]

Two other facets of Japan's deepening involvement in Asia after 1965 are worth noting. First, it coincided with China's Cultural Revolution. China's three-year preoccupation with internal affairs may have provided an added incentive to Japanese involvement in Southeast Asia and South Korea. Second is the sudden spurt of Japanese investments in Taiwan, which began with a $150 million government loan in April 1965—two months before Washington cut off its nonmilitary foreign aid. Three years later, in the 1969 Nixon–Sato joint communiqué, Taiwan was referred to as "a most important factor for the security of Japan." By 1971 Japanese firms had invested about $100 million in Taiwan compared with at least $250 million by U.S. firms; but because of myriad technical tieups, "the full extent of Japanese penetration of the Taiwan economy [could] not be measured on the basis of official statistics."[74]

Thus the external conditions for strengthening Japanese capitalism in the late 1960s were provided by a series of events ranging from the Indochina War and the Indonesian coup to the mercenarization of South Korea and China's Cultural Revolution. Added to these factors were the continuing huge imports into Japan of U.S. technology and loan capital. Japan has been the second biggest recipient of United States–controlled World Bank loans. By 1971 it had "received more than $850 million from the World Bank in addition to $150 million in credits from the International Development Association (IDA), the bank's 'soft loan' affiliate."[75] However, according to the breakdown in the chart on page 331, stock acquisitions, chiefly by American investors, have recently become the dominant form of capital import. But only a small percentage of Japanese corporate shares —estimated in 1971 at upwards of 3.3 percent—are foreign owned.

By 1970 Japan ranked third globally in overall industrial production; its GNP was approaching $200 billion (versus $974 billion for the United States) ; its exports, as a percentage of total capitalist world exports, had increased from 3.6 percent in 1961 to 7 percent in 1970 (versus a U.S. total of 15.5 percent and a Western European total of 32.8 percent).[76] In 1971 Japan, its GNP grown to approximately $255 billion, compared to a U.S. GNP of $1073 billion, was the most heavily represented country on *Fortune*'s directory of the 200 largest industrials outside of the United States, with fifty-one companies on the list.[77] For over a decade it had been rationalizing its economic processes (realizing economies of scale) in order to do battle in world export markets. In the unprecedented merger wave that swept the capitalist world in the 1960s, mergers in Japan went from 300 per year in 1958 to about 700 to 800 annually at the end of the sixties.[78] But unlike the conglomerate–merger movement in the United States, the merger movement in Japan was animated chiefly by a desire to meet foreign competition and not to acquire windfall profits for management. This enormous concentration of corporate power gave Japan the world's largest steel company (Nippon Steel) , with eight integrated plants, a capitalization of $637 million, a work force of 80,000 and an output, in 1969, of thirty-five percent of its national steel output.[79] With twenty-seven million tons of merchant shipping—twelve percent of the world's tonnage as of July 1, 1970—it had the world's largest merchant marine.[80] And, although still heavily dependent on the United States for crude oil, it had the world's largest petrochemical industry, an essential foundation for defense prodution.

But Japan's rapid economic growth and its increased industrial and financial concentration has done more than catapult it to the status of a global economic power. These developments have simultaneously produced new forms of dependency on the United States, accelerated the dissolution of Japanese agriculture, impoverished the small and middle business class, and exacerbated the income gap between rich and poor, and between industrial workers and farmers. Moreover, they have generated chronic inflation and wrought ecological havoc on the Japanese islands, devouring land and living space, polluting air and water resources. The maturation of Japanese capitalism has, in brief, introduced new elements of crisis at home while at the same time intensifying contradictions within the world system of capitalism.

FOREIGN CAPITAL INDUCTIONS [IMPORTS] IN JAPAN
1950–1969
Unit: $1000 Dollars

Year	Total	Stock Acquisition	Securities and Private Company Debentures	Loan Investments	Foreign Currency Bond Issues
1950–1954	$ 139,486	$ 35,571	$ 791	$ 103,124	$ —
1955–1959	718,970	64,492	705	623,773	30,000
1960–1964	3,267,096	625,068	6,393	2,027,861	605,775
1960	211,658	74,151	575	127,132	9,800
1961	577,529	116,142	1,357	387,605	72,425
1962	678,823	164,688	736	358,419	155,000
1963	884,302	185,262	1,045	503,945	194,050
1964	912,784	84,845	2,680	650,760	174,500
1965–1969	$6,990,863	$3,183,711	$5,120	$3,200,568	$601,464
1965	528,506	83,331	3,124	379,551	62,500
1966	457,097	126,735	651	329,711	—
1967	847,784	159,836	407	637,544	50,000
1968	1,836,645	670,008	285	947,372	218,980
1969	3,488,240	2,462,897	757	789,602	234,984

(SOURCE: Moriya Fumio, *Sengo Nihon shihonshugi—sono bunseki to hihan* (Postwar Japanese Capitalism—Its Analysis and Criticism) (Tokyo: Aoki Shoten, 1971), p. 306. Statistics compiled from the Bank of Japan's *Economic Statistics Yearbook* and the Finance Ministry's *Economic Survey*.)

III. The Japanese–American Conflict of Interest

At the global level contradictions had been brewing since the Korean War when Japan first showed signs of again developing as a serious competitor of Western industry. In the early 1950s they were reflected in Japan's relation to the United States—sponsored General Agreement on Tariffs and Trade (GATT), the free trade association which began operating in October 1947 on the principle of unconditional most-favored nation treatment. In 1952, after regaining its formal independence, Japan officially requested membership in the GATT but was refused admittance. When it finally gained admittance, in September 1955, fourteen countries, which accounted for about forty percent of Japan's exports, immediately invoked their legal right under GATT to exempt themselves from applying nondiscriminatory treatment where certain categories of Japanese goods were concerned.[81] Having recovered their prewar level of industrial production before Japan, Western Europe, Britain, and the nations of the British Commonwealth were, in effect, exercising their power at the expense of what was then the weakest member of an American-contrived capitalist bloc. That Japan did not feel the effects of this discrimination was due to its position within the GATT as America's economic protégé and to America's sponsorship of Japanese trade expansion in Southeast Asia.

Three years later, in 1958, the economic recovery of both Western Europe and Japan began to impinge on the administration of the Pax Americana. In January the six states of Western Europe formed the European Economic Community (EEC), in June de Gaulle returned to power in France, and in December the states of Western Europe recovered their currency convertibility. The so-called Western alliance now began to split apart as Europe found in de Gaulle a spokesman for its growing sense of self reliance vis-à-vis the United States.[82] The United States meanwhile entered its fourth postwar recession. By the time of the Kennedy regime the contrast between the dynamism of the economies of the EEC and Japan on the one hand and the signs of stagnation in the U.S. economy on the other was even more striking. How did the United States respond to this first structural crisis of empire?

Toward Europe, where the drive toward an independent, nationally oriented capitalism was more advanced, it responded at the private level by stepping up investment in the EEC nations and at the official level by refurbishing its arsenal of weapons for future trade war; the Trade Expansion Act of October 1962 gave the President enormous powers to raise or lower tariffs. Toward Japan, then viewed as the lesser problem, the United States responded by rationalizing its alliance system,[83] pressuring for more "voluntary" restraints on textile exports, for the removal of restrictions on direct U.S. capital investments, and for greater Japanese involvement in the economic development of America's underdeveloped client states.

A decade later, however, as the Indochina crisis came to a climax, the economic problems complicating United States–Japan relations seemed just as serious as the European threat of an eventual market of 250 million pursuing a common external tariff policy. In fact, by 1971, the year of the $3.2 billion American trade deficit with Japan[84] and the Nixon diplomatic and economic shocks, Japanese capitalism had clearly become too powerful to be easily contained within the framework of the American global system. The mercantilisms of the two allies, once complementary,[85] had become antagonistic. Militarily, Japan remained dependent on the United States; economically, it had partially extricated itself from American control and was laying the foundations for a potentially independent economic bloc. But in the summer of 1971 Japan was still at the mercy of Washington, even more dependent on the dollar bloc than Western Europe. Thus when in July, without forewarning Tokyo, Nixon announced his decision to visit Peking, he automatically undercut the essential premise of the very foreign policy that Washington had imposed upon all conservative governments in Japan since the Korean War—that is to say, the policy of insuring that Japan not establish any meaningful economic ties with China, its geographically natural trading partner. When Nixon followed this in August with the unilateral abrogation of the gold–dollar exchange rate and the imposition of direct controls and higher tariffs mainly on Japanese goods— all at a time when Japan was in the midst of a mild economic slump—the effect was both to underline the instability of Japan's new international position and to reinforce trends already under way toward militarism and overseas economic expansion. Finally, in late September, Nixon added insult to injury by threatening to employ the World War I "Trading with the Enemy Act" to stop the flow of Japanese textiles to the United States unless the Sato government quickly signed a three-year agreement unilaterally restricting textile exports. Confronted with threats of unilateral American action if they did not soon acquiesce, the Japanese negotiators gave in and on October 15, 1971, signed a "Memorandum of Understanding" ending the long drawn out textile dispute with the United States.

At this point it is necessary to spell out some of the reasons behind the bitter international competition between Japanese and American multinational corporations. One reason is the pressing need of both for cheap wage labor. The structural transformation of the Japanese economy during the late 1960s had highlighted the problem of rising labor costs. A Keidanren resolution noted the seriousness of·this problem in June 1969. And in 1970 Keidanren's president, Uemura Kogoro, warned that "... the advance of wages can no longer be absorbed by the elevation of labor productivity ... it is ... essential to restrict the advance of wages within the purview of the increase of labor productivity ... [and] to absorb [it] by ... rationalization of management and expansion of labor productivity."[86] In their determination to hold down wages, Japanese capitalists are resorting to two basic approaches. One is to discipline the domestic work force in the ideology of labor–capital cooperation. This involves, among other things, strengthening Dōmei Kaigi, the right-wing national labor federation set up in 1964 with AFL–CIO help to win worker support for the ruling Liberal Democratic party (LDP). The other approach is to undercut the bargaining power of domestic labor by building tax-free factories in South Korea, Taiwan, Southeast Asia, Africa, and Latin America, where labor costs are a fraction of those in Japan.[87]

Besides competing for cheap labor in underdeveloped countries, Japanese and American corporations are also competing for a wide range of limited raw materials. In 1968 Japan consumed ten percent of the raw materials exports of the non-Communist world; by 1980 that figure may rise to thirty percent. The United States, with only six percent of the world's population, is the biggest consumer of raw materials—Japan is second—and its needs are increasing faster than Japan's. Oil, for example, accounts for seventy percent of Japan's energy needs versus forty percent for the United States. But with the United States firmly in control of most of the world's oil and the worth of its own oil imports expected to soar from the current annual $3.5 billion to $20 billion by the early 1980s, the unevenness of the conflict between the two capitalisms is even more striking, in this one critical area, than it was in the 1930s.[88]

A third factor stoking the competition between Japanese and American corporations abroad is pollution. Capitalists in both countries are seeking territorial space in the underdeveloped world for situating their pollution-intensive industries. With every prefecture in Japan affected by industrial pollution and nationwide antipollution rallies eroding support for the LDP, Japanese capitalists are desperately seeking to cure pollution at home by exporting pollution abroad—an approach that is entirely congruent with their goal of holding down industrial costs.[89]

Thus by 1971, with Japanese and American corporations locked in bitter competition abroad, many government and business leaders were enraged at Japan's growing economic independence. The basic economic power relations of the postwar world had been irrevocably undermined; the dollar was no longer the capitalist world's reserve currency; new forms of economic leverage would have to be invoked to contain "selfish allies" who refused to foot the bill for American aggression. All through 1970 and 1971 the Japanese were depicted in U.S. business magazines as "invading, conspiring or plotting to take over" the American economy.[90] Ugly anti-Japanese racial slurs increasingly cropped up in American newspaper headlines. What "the Korean and Vietnamese wars were unable to revive," editorialized the *Wall Street Journal,*

> an economic threat very well may... because of Japan's trade success there have been isolated but increasing examples of anti-Japanese slogans, advertisements, and even a song ("The Import Blues") whose lyrics are crudely anti-Japanese. Like opportunistic prewar politicians who ran on openly "yellow peril" platforms, today some politicans from districts that are losing out to competition from Japan are hammering thinly-disguised anti-Japanese planks and sentiments into their platforms.[91]

Anxious to shift the onus of their own incompetence and greed onto their foreign competitors and to hold down the wages of the American worker, the national elites of government, business and labor have repeatedly invoked the phoney racist image of an American industry fighting for its very survival against a faceless, monolithic entity called "Japan, Inc." No wonder then that against this background of incipient commercial–psychological warfare, the official American response to Japanese competition has been a transmuted version of naval diplomacy, with the modern weapons of tariffs and quotas doing the job that marines and aircraft carriers do against Third World peoples—in short, the tactics of intimidation.[92]

Having subordinated Japanese capitalism to a dependent relationship in the late 1940s, the American ruling class today pursues its "conflict of interest" with Japan through various levers of manipulation. Since these levers are little understood and, indeed, have been totally neglected by academic specialists on Japan, I would like to devote the remainder of this essay to discussing two of them.

IV. Technology

Japan's rapid industrial growth, which averaged 12.9 percent annually for the period 1953–1965,[93] depended upon massive imports of U.S. capital in the form of bank loans and credits, and upon technological borrowing in the form of patent and licensing contracts. Although indispensable for Japan's economic "success," the result of this aid was intensified U.S. economic control. According to one Soviet writer, "By April 1970 Japanese firms had concluded 11,600 technical assistance contracts with foreign companies, over half of them with the U.S."[94] As Halliday and McCormack point out, Japanese industry was then paying out, chiefly to American firms, some $400 million annually or as much as ten times its earnings from technical tieups.[95] Most significant, beginning in the late 1960s, American companies involved in such tieups began to demand 1) a larger voice in management as a condition of exchange, 2) guarantees that goods produced with their borrowed technology would be exported only to Asian countries, and 3) access to new techniques developed with the aid of their capital or scientific knowhow.[96] The new situation, as *Nikkan Kōgyō Shimbun* observed on January 6, 1971, was one in which foreign firms were "becoming hesitant to provide even licensing agreements which in the past they readily agreed to. On the contrary, they demand Japanese techniques through cross-licensing and if the domestic company has no such attractive technical information, then the foreign firm requests managerial participation."

The computer industry provides an instructive example of American capitalism's effort to keep Japan in a client status by maintaining monopoly control over technology "diffusion" and of Japan's struggle to resist and develop its own technology. According to an excellent recent analysis in *Pacific Basin Reports,*

> ... the cost of importing U.S. technology may become prohibitive to a Japanese computer industry intent on becoming internationally competitive. Despite the strides of Japanese

companies in developing an independent computer technology, the industry is still annually paying thirty times more in royalties to foreign interests than it earns in royalty income from abroad.

It is no coincidence that the Japanese [computer] firm which is closest to marketing its products in the U.S.—Fujitsu Ltd.— is the company which has the smallest debt to foreign patent holders. Its products are Japanese-designed, in contrast to the other five which up to now have manufactured computers basically of U.S. design.

But all Japanese computer companies, including Fujitsu, are dependent on the basic computer patents held by IBM, and now it has become clear that IBM's terms for renewing those patents—that is to say, for permitting the Japanese companies to produce computers—is virtually total access to Japan's independently developed computer technology, past and present.

As of October 1970, foreign computers constituted only 45.5 per cent, by value, of all machines in operation in Japan. But foreign producers still dominated sales of large computers. Despite a quota system . . . and despite a basic tariff of 25 per cent applied against all computer imports . . . foreign manufacturers still provided 60.2 per cent of large computers installed.

Now, faced with slippage in market share even of large computers, U.S. makers have mounted an active sales drive to enlarge the share of the total market. The offensive, supported by the U.S. Commerce Department, is concentrating on areas where the Japanese are least strong, such as super-large computers and peripherals. That's the main plot; the sub-plot is the drive by IBM's U.S. rivals to do abroad what they have been unable to do at home: erode IBM's monolithic market share.

The super-large computer competition began last summer when IBM started local production of the IBM 370—Model 155, but was swiftly followed up by Sperry Rand . . . Control Data Corporation, Minneapolis . . . National Cash Register Corporation, Dayton, Ohio [and] Burroughs Corporation, Detroit. . . .

On the Japanese side, Fujitsu has taken the lead in responding to the U.S. super-large computer challenge, although Hitachi and Nippon Electric are also expected to unveil new models shortly. . . . [But] Foreign sales of Japanese computers have been quite minor thus far. According to Honolulu's *Pacific Business News,* a big factor restricting Japan's computer exports has been "an understanding not to compete in overseas markets" with their U.S. technology sources. The "understanding" is said to have been a precondition, in many cases, of the technical tie-ups. Mitsubishi Electric has nonetheless made some sales to Britain, France and West Germany.

Fujitsu Ltd., which has remained free of such ties, has installed machines in Bulgaria, Rumania, the Philippines and Brazil. The company also entered bids last year for two Australian jobs, and although it did not win the contracts, Fujitsu has appointed a permanent representative in Sydney.[97]

The above example of how the United States goes about protecting its global computer monopoly from future Japanese competition suggests that the big corporations are using the U.S. protectionist movement as a club to "threaten Japanese financial and government circles into precipitously opening their most important industries to U.S. penetration."[98] It also illustrates vividly how technological borrowing, in addition to its costliness, represents a critical form of dependency and control. Yet the evidence suggests that Japanese manufacturers, aided by the state, will succeed, eventually, in meeting and overcoming the American quest for control of their domestic computer market, already the world's second largest. In the short run, however, their efforts to resist capture are bound to further embitter Japanese–American economic relations. Clearly, where technological dependency is concerned, contradictions that are not inherently antagonistic at the bilateral (United States–Japan) level become so at the international level. The computer competition ultimately reflects the larger conflict between a newly risen Japanese capitalism struggling to break the fetters of America's global economic hegemony, and a declining American capitalism, desperately seeking to neutralize its foreign competition by waging "preventive commercial warfare" against it.

There is a further aspect of this problem. The technological export process is not limited only to insuring relations of hierarchical subordination among advanced nations; it plays a similar role in binding the underdeveloped countries to their capitalist patrons. Herman Kahn is quite correct in pointing out that there is "now a reverse and increasing flow of 'payments for Japanese technology' in that about 10 percent of the royalties that the Japanese pay to other countries now comes back to them in the form of royalties for their own technology."[99] What Kahn and most liberals altogether ignore, however, is the content of that reverse flow. For example, in South Korea, where Japanese raw materials, chemical products, and machinery accounted for over forty percent of total imports in 1969, and the trade balance in that year was 7 : 1 in Japan's favor, Japanese corporations pass on outmoded technological manuals and ready-to-be-scrapped, surplus production facilities to Korean manufacturers. Liberals call this "technological cooperation" and "private aid," although, even when "diffused" technology is not junk, it only serves to subordinate South Korea's "zaibatsu" monopolies to their Japanese creditors.[100]

Such subordination, moreover, has its own logic which has nothing to do with the content of any reverse flow of technology. The Korean monopolies, it should be remembered, though giants vis-à-vis their domestic competitors, are pygmies vis-à-vis the Japanese and other foreign multinationals. But, precisely because they have been spawned prematurely by foreign capital in an underdeveloped semi-agrarian economy, they need to be integrated into a hierarchy of external subordination if they are 1) to maintain a viable internal domination and 2) avoid the stagnation effects of monopoly growth.[101] It is in this sense that one can speak of the logic of premature monopoly growth creating the need for foreign imperialism. And it is in this sense too that one can see a dual economy of capitalist imperialism emerging in Asia today. In one economy Japan is subordinated to the United States in a hierarchy of technological and capital dependency; in another, thanks to its effective penetration of South Korea, Taiwan, and certain areas of Southeast Asia, Japan itself heads up a hierarchy of technological and capital dependency.

V. Agriculture

Japanese dependency on U.S. capital and technology has given the United States short-term political leverage over Japan. It has also sharpened the global conflict of interest between Japanese and American multinational corporations. This conflict was exacerbated by the dissolution of the Japanese peasantry during the 1960s and early 1970s, which made Japan dependent on U.S. food grains and led the Japanese government to pursue commercial agricultural export and development policies in America's Asian client states. A brief discussion of Japan's postwar agricultural development will illustrate how this situation came about. It will also show how domestic class exploitation is integrally related to foreign trade.

Prior to the structural transformation of the Japanese economy in the late 1960s, agriculture in postwar Japan had gone through two distinct policy phases. The first, following upon the Occupation land reform, witnessed the conversion of some tenants into "owner-farmers" (historically, the most ephemeral of all land-tenure relationships) and the deliberate preservation of a certain amount of tenancy. By 1949 approximately forty-three percent of all farm households in Japan owned less than half a hectare and were unable to sustain themselves on farming alone.[102] From the viewpoint of meeting the export sector's need for cheap labor, the land reform was undoubtedly a success. But it was bought at the cost of 1) creating a stratum of petty owner-farmers who were unable to sustain themselves by farming alone and 2) establishing an exploitative relationship between large industrial concentrations and the countryside. Within twenty years, the mercantilist spirit in Japanese trade encroached upon agriculture, evolving a moden facsimile of the city–countryside relationship of Tokugawa mercantilism.[103]

From completion of the Occupation land reform in 1949 until the ending of the Korean War in 1953, no fundamental change was made in Japanese agricultural policy.[104] The second phase of postwar agricultural policy began only after the signing of the U.S.–Japan Mutual Defense Assistance Agreement (MDA) of March 8, 1954. This agreement, which was based in part on the 1951 United States Mutual Security Act (MSA), pledged the United States to continued support for Japanese rearmament by furnishing weapons and advisers and by helping finance Japan's fledgling defense industries with "counterpart funds." In return, the Japanese government agreed to purchase surplus American grain and to guarantee private American investments in Japan against expropriation or nonconvertibility of currency.[105] One of the first beneficiaries of this arrangement, New Mitsubishi Heavy Industries, received a total of 1.5 billion yen in MSA counterpart funds which it invested in facilities for manufacture of the F-86 fighter which went into production in 1956.[106]

The "counterpart funds" formula thus functioned after the Korean War to convert surplus U.S. grain into Japanese war potential.[107] Under it, Japan bought surplus American grain in yen, the United States returned twenty percent of the total amount paid in yen to Japan for strengthening its defenses and used the remaining eighty percent for its own "off-shore military procurements." Following the March 1954 agricultural agreement, concluded as part of the MDA, three others were concluded under U.S. Public Law 480 (the Agricultural Trade Development and Assistance Act) : one on November 13, 1954, one on May 28, 1955, and another on August 10, 1956.[108] Apart from their crucial military value, these four agreements reflected the growing compatibility of U.S. and Japanese mercantilist trade policies during these years. They also confirmed that postwar Japanese capitalism, no less than the prewar variety, intended to cannibalize the countryside for the development of an urban industrial Japan.

Beginning in 1950 and accelerating steadily throughout the decade, rural Japan provided a steady stream of cheap wage labor. Between 1950 and 1955 an average of 20,000 to 30,000 young people annually left farming for work in the cities, while the number of self-supporting farm families engaged in strictly agricultural pursuits decreased from 50 to 34.8 percent.[109] When this rural surplus labor pool showed signs of drying up in the early 1960s, the Japanese government adopted an agricultural policy based on increased imports of U.S. agricultural produce and maintenance of low prices for home-grown produce. In effect, it abandoned the vast majority of farm households that were unable to be self-supporting.

In the 1960s Japanese agriculture was shaped by two interrelated developments: the uprooting of vast numbers of people from farming and the widening of the U.S. agricultural foothold. The first was implicit in the American-directed land reform. Once agriculture failed to generate a sufficient pool of cheap labor, once it could no longer function to maintain the traditional plasticity of wages, once it had become a financial burden, Japanese capitalism concentrated on keeping farm prices down and squeezing the villages even harder for additional bodies. Between 1960 and 1970 a total of 8,130,000 people left farming for other occupations; in this same period farm households owning 2.5 hectares of land, the amount considered the minimum necessary for a self-supporting farm under the June 1961 Basic Agricultural Law, increased by only 64,000 households. Of that number over sixty percent were forced to engage in temporary occupations outside of agriculture.[110]

However, the Japanese economy as a whole expanded so rapidly during the high growth decade of the sixties that even this vast dislocation of the rural population was insufficient to meet industry's need for cheap wage labor. In 1963 for the first time the demand for labor exceeded its supply among large and medium enterprises. By 1967 fifty to sixty percent of enterprises employing over 1000 people and sixty to seventy percent of those employing less than 1000 people reported difficulties in securing craftsmen and unskilled workers.[111] It was at this point in the late 1960s, when Japanese capitalism itself was entering a higher stage of monopoly concentration, that Japanese agriculture entered a third postwar phase. The new phase has been characterized by big business's efforts to further "liberalize" restrictions on agricultural imports and, ultimately, to substitute ownership of and by large-scale enterprises for land ownership by farm households—the same trend that is today evident in the United States.

The second development shaping Japanese agriculture in the sixties was the accelerating influx of U.S. surplus food grains and feedstuff. The primary incentive for increased U.S. dumping in the Japanese market lay in the decline of U.S. agricultural exports to Western Europe, which began in 1962, the year the Common Market members finally achieved a unified agricultural policy. Throughout the sixties stepped-up pressure on Japan to take more U.S. agricultural products was intimately bound up with the success of the Common Market nations in forging their defensive barriers against U.S. agricultural dumping. (Now that Britain, Ireland, and Denmark, all of whom take large amounts of U.S. grains, are going to join the Common Market agricultural bloc, Washington has become fanatic in urging Japan to lower all tariffs on agricultural imports; but at the same time, recognizing the handwriting on the wall, the United States is exploring ways to gain an agricultural foothold within the Soviet Union and even China.)

In any case, the influx of United States agricultural products contributed directly to the decline in Japanese production of wheat, barley, soybeans, and rapeseed.[112] By 1969 Japanese wheat production had dropped to 750,000 tons compared to 1.78 million in 1961.[113] And by 1971 eighty-five percent of all the wheat and ninety-three percent of all the soybeans consumed in Japan were imported from the United States. Japan had become the largest market ever for U.S. farm products, taking more American soybeans, grains, and cotton than any other single country.[114]

Meanwhile, the Japanese government faced mounting difficulties in meeting big business's demands for lower rice prices. In 1962, the same year that the Common Market nations arrived at a unified agricultural policy, a twenty-eight-billion-pound rice crop made Japan virtually self-sufficient in rice for the first time in its modern history.[115] As its own rice surpluses began accumulating, the Japanese government slowly reduced imports of U.S., Thai, and Taiwanese rice, which dwindled from 967,000 metric tons in 1965 to about 500,000 tons in 1967, and finally to zero in 1971.[116] At the same time, following Yankee precedent, Japan sought to export its rice surpluses despite the disastrous effects such dumping has had in the past on Asia's agrarian economies. Beginning in 1968, while the United States continued dumping its surplus wheat, soybeans, and corn in Japan, subsidized Japanese rice began competing with U.S. rice in Indonesia and South Korea, which in 1970 took 151,000 and 307,000 metric tons of Japanese rice respectively (versus much larger tonnages of U.S. rice). In 1971 the Park dictatorship was forced to more than double its rice imports from Japan.[117] Thus, where rice is concerned, from the start of its third phase of agricultural development, Japan has been able to engage the United States as a competitor in the ruination of backward agricultural economies.

In sum, in order to benefit Japan's more productive exporters and to obtain investment funds for industrial and military development, the Japanese government accepted U.S. surplus agricultural products and received, in return, "direct aid" in the form of yen "counterpart funds" and, eventually, easy access to the American market for its own manufactures. In pursuit of a mercantilist export policy it sacrificed to American agriculture its less productive national grain economy whose reservoir of cheap rural labor had begun to dry up with great rapidity in the late 1960s. Since, however, agricultural dependency is more dangerous than capital and technological dependency, if only because it is more likely to be enduring, this problem forces the Japanese ruling class to undertake structural reforms at home and push economic expansion abroad in competition with the United States. As can be seen today in the Hokuso Plateau,

Mutsu–Ogawara, and Shimokita Peninsula development projects, Japanese monopoly capitalism is extending its rationalizing activities into domestic agriculture.[118] It is also promoting agricultural production-for-export in Southeast Asia and
South Korea, places where rural labor is much cheaper than in
Japan. Underlying these two forms of capitalist expansion—one
internal, against a relatively small domestic peasantry that it now
deems superfluous, the other external, against the peasants in
other Asian lands whom it deems more useful because they are
more abundant—is a common dialectic of expansion.

In the decade ahead Japanese big business envisions two
solutions to its agricultural problems. The internal solution will
lead to further reductions in the number of farm households and
further "liberalization" of import restrictions on foreign agricultural products. Japan has already begun vast, nationwide
development schemes designed to realize sizable economies of
scale in Japanese farming, to free more land for urbanization and
industrial use, to provide an expanded source of cheap labor for
the factories (both along the coast and in the heavy industries
scheduled for the interior), and perhaps even to alleviate the
SDF's recruitment difficulties. Of course, such a restructuring of
domestic agriculture can hardly avoid precipitating more protests
from oppressed groups in the economy, such as farmers, who are
being evicted from their land, as in the Sanrizuka struggles of
1970–1971.[119] In fact, this oppression opens up the possibility of
a new coalition of farmers and urban laborers—though such a
coalition presupposes effective unmasking of big business's hypo-
critical effort to pose as defender of the consumer's need for
cheap food. In any case, "agricultural rationalization" alone is
incapable of meeting big business's need for ever-increasing
amounts of cheap wage labor and land for industrial sites.

Japanese big business, realizing that it must inevitably exhaust
Japan's own supply of land and labor, and realizing also that an
independent agricultural base would by no means be disadvantageous to an overindustrialized Japan, has come to feel compelled to expand abroad. For them the external or foreign trade
approach to the agricultural problem, which is predicated on a
transmuted version of the "greater East Asia co-prosperity
sphere," is just as necessary as domestic "rationalization." In the
Southeast Asian and South Korean countrysides, Japanese multinational corporations, usually of the "integrated trading com-

pany" type (see Appendix), have either started or are planning to develop plantations and factories to process agricultural produce for export to Japan. By the 1980s Japan may well be in the extraordinary position of having built up plantation enclaves within the very agricultural economies that U.S. agricultural policies have consistently undermined. If so, one wonders whether some underdeveloped client states may already be far along the road of substituting Japanese for U.S. economic hegemony.

CONCLUSION

Japan is embarked on a course leading to eventual economic independence from the United States—but at the cost of furthering the growth of domestic militarism, including the beginning of a mixed civilian–military type economy, similar to but smaller than the U.S. military–industrial complex. This new militarism has already become a constituent element of Japan's further economic growth. It is fed by Japan's overseas economic expansion. Eventually, as the U.S. domestic market is eclipsed in importance by Asian and Pacific markets in general and Japan's embryonic *imperio in imperium* in particular, Japan's leaders may be tempted to use military power to protect their commercial, financial, and industrial investments, particularly in Southeast Asia and South Korea. This, in fact, is the direction implicitly envisioned in the Fourth Defense Plan. Despite U.S. setbacks in Indochina and their own disastrous experience there during World War II, Japan's leaders are moving toward closer political and military ties with the client regimes of non-Communist Asia, while simultaneously building their own potential for "counterinsurgency operations."

It is against this background that the present stage in United States–Japan relations should be grasped. The United States–Japan alliance is still viable: Japan continues to be locked into a dependency relationship to U.S. trade, technology, and military cooperation; both countries continue to share common interests in preserving Asia for capitalist investment and trade; and the Asian clients of Japan all have military alliances with the United States. And yet numerous economic contradictions are steadily eroding the United States–Japan military alliance. The competitive quest of the world's first and second capitalist economies for nonrenewable raw materials, cheap labor, high profits, consumer markets, favorable investment conditions and space for situating pollution-intensive industry increasingly borders on economic warfare. With each side beset by mounting domestic contradictions and each seeking to solve its problem of surplus production along national lines—and with the United States' economic frustrations again showing signs of assuming an anti-Japanese racial coloration—United States–Japan relations stand at a crossroads.

In the long run, therefore, the dominant trend is toward deteriorating political–economic relations; but for the next several years the alliance will probably hold. And, while it does, the United States has the upper hand. Indeed, it is reasonable to suppose that United States leverage will be sufficient, at least until the end of this decade, to force Japan to make concessions and to sustain even greater "shocks" than it has to date. But each concession wrought by the Unites States' effort to strengthen its declining control of the Japanese economy will only spur Japan on, in self-defense, to a reorganization of its state structure and economy along increasingly nationalistic and independent lines. Having laid the foundations for an independent imperial dynamic, Japan will move forward, throwing off U.S. control in one area after another, with the possible exception of oil.

All of this means that the system of post–World War II alliances and economic institutions which subordinated Japan and Western Europe to U.S. power is coming undone. That system, originally a continuation of the capitalist wartime economic bloc, incorporated the former Axis partners in the late 1940s and facilitated their economic reconstruction for nearly two decades. During most of this period the unevenness of economic development between the United States and the subordinate bloc members, all of whom had suffered wartime destruction and the loss of their colonial empires, made the mercantilist economic policies which its members practiced against one another essentially nonantagonistic. But, as Western Europe and Japan recovered their prewar strength and then began to draw abreast of the United States, the contradictions of the bloc—actually a reproduction of the 1920s and 1930s—began to erupt in the form of "gold rushes," currency destabilization crises, and dumping conflicts. Although it is impossible to determine where all of this will now lead, it is no accident that the economic policies of the main capitalist units are so intimately bound up with preparations for war.

Ever since the sixteenth century when mercantilist thought was first advanced—against a background of rising commercial capitalism and in concert with the unification of the nation-state—mercantilism *as economic policy,* though not as a body of thought, has continued to exist, assuming different forms in different ages. But always its primary aim, the pursuit of national advantage and relative strength, has tended to promote war. The United States–controlled capitalist bloc which emerged out of the World War II struggle for the redivision of the world's markets has been no exception. Though touted as an arrangement for maintaining "world peace," it has, in fact, fostered a whole succession of unprecedentedly destructive wars in countries of the Third World that were deliberately excluded from it. It has, in addition, fired the greatest arms race in all history. Until recently that race was essentially an interbloc one, limited to the United States and the Soviet Union. The reemergence of economic warfare between the United States, Japan, and Western Europe may now signal the start of a new era of even more intensified and uncontrolled arms races: between the two "superpowers," between the advanced capitalist blocs, and among subordinate mercenary states which are being increasingly relied upon to fight the wars of organized monopoly capitalism.

APPENDIX

A brief word on Japanese multinationals might be helpful. It is useful to make a distinction between the "integrated trading companies" such as Marubeni Iida, Mitsubishi Shoji, Mitsui Bussan, Toyo Menka, C. Itoh, etc., and all the others. The former represent a uniquely Japanese type of multinational corporation marketing anything from noodles to missiles. According to one authority, "The ten leaders in [this] field do an annual business of some $22 billion, or double the amount of the national budget, and carry corresponding weight in national policy." (Source: John G. Roberts in *Burroughs Clearing House,* April 1970, p. 38.)

Because of wage, language, and cultural problems (that is, fear

of provoking white racism), most Japanese multinationals operate primarily in Third World countries rather than in Europe or
the United States. As of March 1971, in fact, one MITI official
estimated that "only 34 Japanese companies were engaged in
manufacturing in the United States and their total investment
stood at only $31.5 million." These insignificant figures con-
trasted (as of June 1970) with "roughly 340 American companies
and a total investment of $616 million in manufacturing facili-
ties in Japan." (Source: Gerd Wilcke, "Investment by Japan in
U.S. Lags," *New York Times,* October 24, 1971.)

In shipbuilding the leading Japanese multinationals are Ishikawajima Harima Industries (IHI), Hitachi, Mitsubishi Heavy
Industries, and Sumitomo Heavy Machinery. IHI presently operates shipyards and machine tool plants in Brazil, Peru, Australia,
and Singapore. In October 1971 Hitachi Shipbuilding and Mitsubishi Heavy Industries separately announced plans to build
shipyards and oceanographic equipment plants in Singapore,
while Sumitomo Heavy Machinery, not to be outdone in Southeast Asia, recently announced plans to build a shipyard under a
joint venture formula with Malaysia's Jehore State. Thus in
shipbuilding at any rate, the charge by European and American
competitors that Japanese companies "will not take advantage of
one another abroad" is a myth. Japanese multinationals do
observe capitalist ethics. (Sources: Ian Stewart, "Japan Stirs
Asian Resentments," *New York Times,* January 10, 1971;
Kikuchi Takao, *"Ugoki dashita Nihonteki 'takokuseki Kigyōka,'"
Gekkan ekonomisuto,* December 1971, pp. 17–18.)

In electronics Japanese industry has only recently begun to go
multinational. The same is true in banking. In 1971 U.S. banks
had 2000 offices in 104 countries and British banks had 5000
overseas branches. Japanese banks, in contrast, were represented
in only "30 countries by about 125 separate offices." This is
changing rapidly. Japanese banks participate in six international
consortia, make formal "alliances" with such U.S. giants as
Chase Manhattan (Mitsubishi) and Bank of America (Sumitomo), and have themselves begun merging to form more powerful units for participation in global competition—a trend evidenced by the recent merger of the Dai Ichi, sixth largest of
Japan's commercial banks, and Nippon Kangyo, eighth largest,
to form the Dai Ichi-Kangyo Bank: largest financial institution

in Japan and twelfth largest in the capitalist world with $1.22 billion in capital and over $9 billion in deposits. (Source: John G. Roberts in *Burroughs Clearing House,* December 1970, p. 43, and May 1971, p. 49.)

NOTES

1. *International Defense Review,* vol. 4, no. 6, December 1971, p. 522.

2. *The Oriental Economist,* April 1970, p. 13. The Defense Production Committee of Keidanren (Federation of Economic Organizations) earlier estimated a smaller budget for the fifth defense program: $22.2 billion or 8000 billion yen. See Goto Moto, "Japan in Asia," *Japan Quarterly,* vol. 16, no. 4, December 1969, p. 391.

3. *Nihon Keizai,* April 28, 1971, p. 24; Kazushige Hirazawa, "Japan's Future World Role and Japanese–American Relations," *Orbis,* vol. 15, no. 1, Spring 1971, p. 339.

4. Sekiya Reiji, *"Seiikika suru bōei yosan"* ["The Sacralization of the Defense Budget"], *Ekonomisuto,* June 1, 1971, p. 28.

5. *Ibid.,* pp. 27–28.

6. The preamble of the Okinawa Restoration Treaty reads as follows: "Japan and the United States of America, Noting that the Prime Minister of Japan and the President of the United States . . . reviewed together on November 19, 20, and 21, 1969, the status of the Ryukyu Islands and the Daito Islands, referred to as 'Okinawa' in the joint communiqué between the Prime Minister and the President issued on November 21, 1969, and agreed that the Government of Japan and the Government of the United States . . . should enter immediately into consultations regarding the specific arrangements for accomplishing the early reversion of these islands to Japan. (Reprinted in *Current History,* vol. 61, no. 364, December 1971, p. 359.)

7. Noguchi Yūichirō, *"Kitaisareru gunji taikokuzō"* ["The Image of a Military Big Power Which Is Being Entertained"], *Ekonomisuto,* June 1, 1971, pp. 16–17; Kawada Kan, *"Teichaku suru sangun fukugō-taisei"* ["The Stabilized Military–Industrial Complex"], *Ekonomisuto,* February 22, 1972, p. 15; *Asahi jānaru,* January 14, 1972, p. 110.

The growing estrangement between uniformed officers of the Self-Defense Forces and civilian officials who work in the central headquarters of the Defense Agency was illuminated several years ago by military critic Horie Yoshitaka. Interviewed in 1965 by an American military historian, Horie observed that the civilian officials were "merely on temporary assignment from other Ministries—Finance, Forestry and

Agriculture, Construction, Transportation, etc. They tend to evince excessive favoritism toward their parent Ministries, and to display negligible enthusiasm for the JSDF duties. . . . As a result, it is difficult for them to work effectively with the uniformed personnel, or to accomplish intensive study of military matters. Since most of these civilians are Tokyo University graduates, they may be able to elicit the support of the Cabinet or of various Ministries. In some instances their ignorance of military affairs arises from arrogance or from hostility toward men in uniform. . . . I have recently heard it said that the Defense College Commander ought to be a soldier, not a civilian—as is the case at West Point and elsewhere." (Source: "Japan's Self-Defense Force Today—Yoshitaka Horie Interviewed by Dr. Alvin D. Coox," in *Marine Corps Gazette* [vol. 49, no. 2, February 1965, p. 53].)

As of March 1972, there were only 499 civilian officials in the 260,000-man Self-Defense Forces. Although a mixed group, ex-police officials monopolized the highest civilian positions, followed by Finance Ministry and MITI bureaucrats *(Ekonomisuto,* March 28, 1972, p. 33) .

8. The full text of the final draft of the Fourth Defense Power Consolidation Plan is printed in the *Mainichi Shimbun,* April 28, 1971. See American Embassy, Tokyo, Political Section, Translation Services Branch—Daily Summary of the Japanese Press, April 29–30, 1971, pp. 21–26.

9. Noguchi Yūichirō, p. 18.

10. On this point see *Armed Forces Journal,* November 1971, where it is pointed out (p. 28) that "A Japanese naval mission is touring the U.S., Norway, Holland, the U.K., France and Italy looking for suitable missiles with which to arm the Japanese Maritime Self-Defense Force. . . . Japan is also developing her own ship-to-ship and air-to-ship missiles, and the Defense Agency has requested $344,000 for basic study and research on ship missiles and $600,000 for the air missile. It would appear likely, therefore, that the touring mission is more interested in picking up techniques than in buying missiles."

11. *International Defense Review,* vol. 4, no. 6, December 1971, p. 522.

12. Sekiya Reiji, *op. cit.,* pp. 28–29; *Aviation Week and Space Technology,* May 24, 1971, p. 47. Also see Kamakura Takao, *"Fukyōka ni Nihonteki sangun fukugotaisei no tenkai"* ["The Development of the Japanese-type Military–Industrial Complex Under the Depression"] *Ekonomisuto,* November 16, 1971, p. 24.

13. I. F. Stone, "The War Machine Under Nixon," in Seymour Melman, ed., *The War Economy of the United States* (New York: St. Martin's Press, 1971) , p. 29. In 1969 Stone cited figures estimating the total cost of the Anti-Ballistic Missile program at over $12 billion, including R & D costs.

14. Nitta Shunzō, *"Shin sangyō seisaku to sangun fukugōtai"* ("The New Industrial Policy and the Military–Industrial Complex"), *Keizai hyōron,* November 1971, p. 42.

15. See General Tsukamoto Masatoshi's diatribe, *"Kyōki shita ka? Umihara kyokuchō"* ("Have You Gone Mad, Director Umihara?"), in *Gunji kenkyū* ("Japan Military Review"), August 1971, pp. 161–65.

16. All quotations are from the official Defense Agency publication *Japan's Defense,* published in October 1970.

17. *Japan's Defense,* pp. 19 and i.

18. *Yomiuri Shimbun,* April 28, 1971; *Hsinhua,* May 10, 1971, as cited in *Foreign Broadcast Information Service* (cited hereafter as FBIS).

In the event of renewed fighting in the Korean peninsula, GSDF troops and their equipment could be deployed to the 38th Parallel in approximately fifteen hours' time (i.e., within a single night). They would be transported by ferry from Shimonoseki to Pusan (seven hours), and thence over high-speed expressway from Pusan to Seoul (seven to eight hours).

19. *Japan's Defense,* p. 14. The emphasis is mine.

20. Sekiya Reiji, *op. cit.,* p. 28.

21. *Japan's Defense,* p. iii.

22. In a revealing phrase, the White Paper calls the public's "revulsion toward the military" one of "the scars of war" (p. 36).

23. *Japan's Defense,* p. 11.

24. *Yomiuri Shimbun,* evening edition, April 27, 1971.

25. For the Weimar analogy see Yoshihara Kōichirō, *70 nen ampo to Nihon no gunjiryoku (The 1970 Ampo and Japan's Military Power)* (Tokyo: Nihon Hyōronsha, 1969), pp. 5–7.

26. Article 9 of the present 1947 constitution states as follows: "Aspiring sincerely to an international peace based on justice and order, the Japanese people forever renounce war as a sovereign right of the nation and the threat or use of force as a means of settling international disputes. In order to accomplish the aim of the preceding paragraph, land, sea and air forces, as well as other war potential, will never be maintained. The right of belligerency of the state will not be recognized."

27. Martin E. Weinstein, *Japan's Postwar Defense Policy, 1947–1968* (New York and London: Columbia University Press, 1971), p. 120.

28. George R. Packard III, *Protest in Tokyo—The Security Treaty Crisis of 1960* (Princeton, N.J.: Princeton University Press, 1966), p. 320.

29. Quoted from New China News Agency (NCNA). International Service, May 13, 1971, in FBIS, China-71-93. Partial, official Japanese

corroboration is provided in the advertisements in *Bōei nenkan 1971* ("Defense Yearbook 1971").

30. Koji Nakamura, "Japan: Nippon on the March," *Far Eastern Economic Review,* May 14, 1970, p. 13.

31. Muto Ichiyo, "Mishima and the Transition from Postwar Democracy to Democratic Fascism," *Ampo—A Report from the Japanese New Left,* nos. 9–10, 1971, p. 42. A useful article for understanding where Japan is headed in the 1970s.

32. *Ibid.,* p. 43.

33. Masao Inaba, "Modern History Documents and the Meiji Centennial Series," *Japan Institute of International Affairs—Annual Review,* vol. 4, 1965–1968, pp. 214–15.

34. Yoshihara Kōichirō, *ibid.,* pp. 246–47.

35. Yamada Kazuo, *"Gunkokushugi fukkatsu to Nihon eiga no dōkō"* ("The Revival of Militarism and Trends in Japanese Cinema"), *Zenei* ("Vanguard"), no. 332, December 1971, pp. 157–58.

36. See *The Japan Interpreter,* Winter 1971, p. 76.

37. Quoted from *Gunji kenkyū* ("Military Review"), January 1971, in Yoshihara Kōichirō, *"Yonjibō ni miru kokubō ishiki—minshushugi guntai no ronri to mujun"* ("Defense Consciousness in the Fourth Plan —The Theory of the Democratic Army and Its Contradiction"), *Ekonomisuto,* June 1, 1971, p. 25.

38. Quoted from Soviet Colonel A. Ebudokimofu (my phonetic transliteration of the Russian name from the Japanese; and my translation), "Japan's New Samurai Spirit," *Red Star,* November 11, 1971, as translated into Japanese in *Gunji kenkyū,* February 1972, p. 116.

39. Writing for an American audience in the October 1969 issue of *Foreign Affairs,* Kiichi Aichi, then foreign minister, had argued (p. 35) that ". . . it is both possible and desirable to devote considerable time and energy to encouraging public interest in outward-looking ideas, gradually weaning the public away from little-Japanism."

40. This provocative phrase is Muto Ichiyo's. See note 31.

41. On this point see Hayashi Naomi, *"Nihon gunkokushugi fukkatsu no keizai kiso"* ("Economic Foundations for the Revival of Japanese Militarism"), *Gendai to shisō,* no. 1, October 1970. Professor Hayashi's excellent work helped me situate Japan's military–industrial complex in the context of postwar economic growth.

42. Late Meiji–Taishō Japan also had a parasitic relationship to Western imperialism. This was due in part to the fact that Japan's prewar economy did not become sufficiently independent to finance its own continental expansion until after it had reaped the economic benefits of three wars. From the Sino-Japanese War of 1894–1895 through the Russo-Japanese War to World War I and the Twenty-One Demands, Japan relied on Western loan capital and war plunder in the form of

indemnities to develop its overseas concessions and spheres of influence. The initiative at all times was taken by the state acting through semi-official enterprises such as the South Manchurian Railway Company, the colonial banks in Taiwan and Korea, the Yokohama Specie Bank, etc., and by large zaibatsu which also relied heavily on diverse forms of state subsidization. Big business itself played an essentially passive role in planning and organizing overseas economic expansion throughout the entire formative phase of Japanese imperialism. Not until the 1920s did this situation begin to change in any significant way. Beginning in the late 1920s and becoming more pronounced in the 1930s, big business, both old and new zaibatsu, played an active role in pushing Japan's continental expansion. This second phase witnessed the emergence of a military–industrial alliance increasingly dependent on Asian sources of critical raw materials.

43. Nitta Shunzō, *"Shin sangyō seisaku to sangun fukugo"* ("The New Industrial Policy and the Military–Industrial Complex"), *Keizai hyōron,* November 1971, pp. 41–42.

44. On the Russian variety of "military–industrial complex" see Richard Armstrong, "Military-Industrial Complex: Russian Style," *Fortune,* vol. 80, August 1, 1969, and *Journal of International Affairs* (Columbia University), vol. 26, no. 2, 1972.

45. John W. Dower, "The Eye of the Beholder: Background Notes on the U.S.-Japan Military Relationship," *Bulletin of Concerned Asian Scholars,* vol. 2, no. 1, October 1969, p. 16.

46. Quoted in Jerome B. Cohen, *Japan's Economy in War and Reconstruction* (Minneapolis: University of Minnesota Press, 1949), p. 420.

47. *Ibid.,* p. 427.

48. Joyce and Gabriel Kolko, *The Limits of Power: The World and United States Foreign Policy, 1945–1954.* (New York: Harper & Row, 1972), p. 512.

49. For an excellent brief discussion of the entire reparations issue see Noguchi Yuichirō, *"Nikkan keizai 'kyōryoku' no kyokō"* ("The Fiction of Japan–ROK Economic 'Cooperation'"), in Saito Takashi and Fujishima Udai, ed., *Nikkan mondai o kangaeru* ("Considerations on Japan–Republic of Korea Problems") (Tokyo: Taihei Shuppansha, 1965), pp. 138–42.

50. Peter Calvocoressi, ed., *Survey of International Affairs 1947–1948* (London: Oxford University Press, 1953), p. 344. Also see Toyama Shigeki, ed., *Shiryō sengo nijū nen shi* ("Historical Materials on Twenty Years of Postwar History"), *Nenpyō* ("Chronology"), vol. 6 (Tokyo: Nihon Hyōronsha, 1967), p. 18.

51. Suzuki Masashi, *Sengo Nihon no shiteki bunseki* ("Historical Analysis of Postwar Japan") (Tokyo: Aoki Shoten, 1969), pp. 71–77.

52. *Ibid.,* p. 78.

53. Maruyama Masao, *Thought and Behavior in Modern Japanese Politics* (London: Oxford University Press, 1963) , p. 148.

54. Maruyama Masao, pp. 150–51.

55. Inoue Kiyoshi, *"Dai niji taisengo no Nihon to sekai"* ("Japan and the World After World War II") , in *Iwanami Kōza-Nihon rekishi,* vol. 21, Gendai *4* (Tokyo: Iwanami Shoten, 1963) , p. 243.

56. On unions as "industrial patriotism clubs," see Nakane Chie, *Japanese Society* (University of California Press, 1970) , p. 18.

57. Kozo Yamamura, *Economic Policy in Postwar Japan—Growth versus Economic Democracy* (Berkeley and Los Angeles: University of California Press, 1967) , pp. 129–31, 148–49.

58. Kurokawa Toshio, *Nihon no teichingin kōzō* ("Japan's Low Wage Structure") (Tokyo: Otsuki Shoten, 1964) , p. 215.

59. G. C. Allen, *A Short Economic History of Modern Japan* (New York: Frederick A. Praeger, 1966) , p. 188.

60. Kurokawa Toshio, p. 216.

61. Masao Kihara, "The Militarization of the Japanese Economy," *The Kyoto University Economic Review,* vol. 38, no. 2, whole no. 85, October 1968, p. 32.

62. Hayashi Naomi, pp. 243–44.

63. A. Kuzminsky, "Behind Japan's 'Economic Miracle,' " *New Times,* March 24, 1971, p. 25.

64. Shirota Noboru, Yamamura Yoshiharu, Shironishi Shinichirō, *Mitsubishi gunjushō—Nihon no sangun fukugotai to shihon shinshutsu* ("The Mitsubishi Arsenal—Japan's Military–Industrial Complex and Capital Expansion") (Tokyo: Gendai Hyoronsha, 1971) , p. 88.

In 1970 the Mitsubishi group accounted for 5.9 percent of the total paid up capital of all Japanese companies (529,700,000,000 yen) , had 9.2 percent (9,403,800,000,000 yen) of the assets of all Japanese companies and gross sales (in 1969) amounting to 4.6 percent (6,828,800,-000,000 yen) of all Japanese company sales (p. 88) .

65. Nitta Shunzō, *"Sangyō saihensei to gōrika"* ("Industrial Reorganization and Rationalization") , *Gendai no me* (Eye of the Present) (November 1969) , pp. 92–99. The shift to a new pattern of exports in the early sixties (1960–1965) is discussed briefly in G. C. Allen, *Japan As a Market and Source of Supply* (London: Pergamon Press, Ltd., 1967) , pp. 117–24. Allen states that "A comparison based on 1961 figures showed that the ratio [of heavy industrial products to total industrial exports] was then 51 per cent for Japan, 82 per cent for the United States, 85 per cent for Germany and 80 per cent for the United Kingdom."

66. "Vietnam Special Procurement and the Economy," in *Japan Quarterly,* vol. 14, no. 1, January–March 1967, p. 14.

67. *Business Week,* March 14, 1964, p. 70.

68. David C. Cole and Princeton N. Lyman, *Korean Development— The Interplay of Politics and Economics* (Harvard University Press, 1971), p. 113. The actual signing of the treaty occurred on June 22, 1965. For Chinese and North Korean press comment on the Normalization Treaty see *BBC-Summary of World Broadcasts, Part 3, The Far East,* November 16, 18, and 19, 1965.

69. Suzuki Masashi, pp. 306–307. Ratification of the treaty in Japan may have been the most unprecedented example of forced voting in Japanese history. The 1960 Security Treaty, which was rammed through the Diet in violation of numerous procedural rules, had been deliberated on from February 5 to May 20, 1960.

70. Quoted from *Chūō Nippō* (April 9, 1970), in Hayashi Naomi, p. 272.

71. Estimates of people summarily executed in Indonesia range from several hundred thousand to a million. One reliable authority points out that "the PKI case is, in fact, that the army, under the leadership of a right-wing 'Council of Generals,' financed and supported by the American CIA . . . had for long been planning to seize power—perhaps on 5 October—to reverse the leftward direction of Indonesia's policies. When news of this leaked, short-notice action by left wing junior army officers and units sympathetic to Sukarno had to be hastily mounted. This afforded the army leaders the perfect justification for the mass murders that followed. The PKI support their version of events by charging that the American Seventh Fleet was in Indonesian waters at the crucial period. It is also alleged that the army moved so swiftly throughout the archipelago to round up communists and supervise their 'elimination' that the operation can only have been one long contemplated and planned." (Source: Malcolm Caldwell, *Indonesia* [Oxford University Press, 1968], pp. 113–14.)

In remembering these mass executions, it is important not to overlook the fact of official U.S. government complicity by virtue of quick recognition and generous aid to the Suharto regime. An obvious comparison can be made here with another resource-rich country—Brazil. Although the military coup in Brazil (April 1964) occurred before the one in Indonesia, the unfolding of tyranny in both countries followed a similar course. In both cases the U.S. government underwrote regimes that could survive only by murdering and torturing their opponents, and in both cases the *quid pro quo* was enormous profits for U.S. and other foreign business enterprises that poured in in the wake of the coups.

72. Kotani Shū, *"Nihon no Tonan Ajia shinshutsu"* ("Japan's Expansion in Southeast Asia"), *Zenei,* no. 324, June 1971, p. 163.

73. In 1969, when Japanese business circles launched their first public campaign for renewal of the U.S.-Japan Security Treaty and in-

creased defense spending for the purpose of creating an "autonomous defense," the boldest argument put forth was that of Keidanren's Kikawada Kazutaka. Kikawada pointed out that since "The Japanese economy . . . is following the policy of securing raw materials from diversified sources abroad for its further expansion and development, . . . efforts must be made to have the people recognize . . . that maintenance of the safety routes of marine transportation is closely connected with the stability of the people's livelihood and the economic prosperity of the country. . . . More concretely, the key problem is to defend the route through the straits of Malacca . . . and the routes from Alaska and Canada across the Western Pacific. *These routes constitute a lifeline for the Japanese economy.* . . . It may well become necessary for Japan, therefore, to strengthen its maritime defense power without concentrating only on the forces to counter civil insurrection or aggression from the air." (Quoted in *Nikkan Kōgyō Shimbun,* April 16, 1969. My italics—H.P.B.)

The last time a "lifeline" metaphor surfaced in Japanese domestic politics was in the late 1920s. Then, rising Chinese nationalism was rapidly undermining Japan's hold on Manchuria, where the bulk of its overseas investments were concentrated. In 1931–1932 the "lifeline" metaphor functioned with telling psychological effect to justify the forcible creation of a client regime in China's Three Eastern Provinces. But when mooted by Kikawada in 1969 the only conceivable threat to Japan's overseas economic interests anywhere in the world was potential rather than actual.

74. *Far Eastern Economic Review,* March 4, 1972, p. 67; *Economic Notes,* published by the Labor Research Association, New York, August 1971, p. 7.

75. *Far Eastern Economic Review,* no. 30, 1970, quoted in Jon Halliday and Gavan McCormack, *'Co-Prosperity in Greater East Asia': Japanese Imperialism Today* (published by the Association for Radical East Asian Studies, 6 Endsleigh Street, London, W1, England, 1971), p. 7. This work is an indispensable reference source for the entire range of postwar Japanese military and economic activities in Asia. This pamphlet, no longer available, has been incorporated into a book by Jon Halliday and Gavan McCormack, *Japanese Imperialism Today* (New York: Monthly Review Press, 1973), pp. 14–15.

76. New China News Agency (Peking), August 28, 1971, as cited in *U.S. Foreign Broadcast Information Service* (China), August 30, 1971, A-3.

77. *Fortune,* August 1971, pp. 150–58.

78. Y. Shishkov, "New Stage in Monopoly Concentration," *New Times,* January 27, 1970, pp. 25–28.

79. R. A. Pense, "The Mineral Industry of Japan," in *Minerals*

Yearbook, vol. 4, Area Reports: International (Washington: U.S. Government Printing Office, 1969), p. 421. In 1969, according to Pense, "Only the U.S. and the U.S.S.R. exceeded Japan in the production of pig iron, ferro alloys, crude steel and special steels, . . . In the smelting and refining of the major nonferrous metals it placed approximately as follows: aluminum (4th) ; copper (5th) ; lead (6th) ; and zinc (3rd) . In mine production of metals, the country ranked somewhat less highly, although holding a position among the top 10 world producers of copper and zinc.

Japan again led the world in producing pyrites and talcsoapstone-pyrophyllite and remained the third largest producer of cement. The country evidently became the third largest petroleum refiner during the year, surpassing Italy, but remained the fourth largest coke producer, after West Germany. The petro-chemical industry, including the important nitrogenous and phosphatic fertilizer producing sectors, claimed to be second only to that of the United States" (p. 422) .

80. Ariyoshi Yoshiya, *"Kaiun gyōkai tōmen no kadai to kongo no tenbō"* ("Urgent Problems Confronting the Shipping Industry and the Future Outlook"), *Keidanren geppō* ("Bulletin of the Federation of Economic Organizations") , September 1971, pp. 7–8.

81. Gardner Patterson, *Discrimination in Internationl Trade, The Policy Issues 1945–1965.* Princeton, New Jersey: Princeton University Press, 1966, pp. 279, 285, 286.

82. Enatsu Michiho, *Kokusai shihonsen to Nihon* ("Japan and the War of International Capital") . Tokyo: Iwanami Shinsho, 1969, pp. 69–76.

83. For example, in January 1960 the United States revised its Security Treaty with Japan in a more equitable form and, shortly thereafter, encouraged the overthrow of its incompetent puppet in South Korea, Syngman Rhee. The connection between these two seemingly unrelated events becomes clear when it is remembered that ever since the making of the 1951 bilateral military pact with Japan, Rhee's anti-Japanese policies had prevented the consolidation of a Northeast Asian defense frontier. By supporting the removal of Rhee and then supporting Park Chung Hee's military coup which destroyed the fruits of the "April Revolution," Washington opened the way for South Korea's incorporation into the Japan sphere of its empire, a move which ultimately widened the area for private American investment in Japanese industry.

84. *New York Times,* May 8, 1972, p. 55

85. The compatibility of the two mercantilisms was reflected in a U.S. trade balance of "plus $4.3 billion yearly from 1955 through 1959." E. Ray Canterbery, *Economics on a New Frontier* (Belmont, California: Wadsworth Publishing Company, Inc., 1968) , p. 198.

86. *Keidanren Review,* no. 15, Summer 1970, pp. 2–3.

87. It is even conceivable, though highly improbable, that the LDP would go so far as to alter Japan's population control policy to bring wages back to their traditional condition of plasticity. For example, Prime Minister Sato in a speech to newspaper editors in the summer of 1969 is alleged to have advocated an increase in Japan's birth rate—this despite a population density in 1968 of 1333 inhabitants per square kilometer. In May 1971, less than two years after Sato's straw-in-the-wind suggestion, the Diet passed a law introducing for the first time "family allowances" into the social security system. While these two pieces of evidence certainly do not support any clearcut official policy in favor of increased population, it is important to remember that, should such a change occur, it would represent, when viewed historically, no real turnabout in the *political perspective* informing official population policy. The rationale behind it, in fact, would be entirely consistent with the Japanese government's original decision to curb population growth: to have done otherwise in the late forties and fifties would have decreased the proportion of capital resources available for economic recovery and industrial investment. Now that their "population problem" has come full circle, producing a rising wage and consumption pattern among Japanese workers, Japanese capitalists seem willing to try anything. (Sources: *Science*, vol. 167, no. 3920, February 13, 1970, p. 960; Toshinobu Kato and Takeshi Takashi, "Family Planning in Industry," in *International Labour Review*, vol. 104, no. 3, September 1971, p. 179; John Walsh, "Population Control and Organized Capital —The Case of Japan," in *Science For the People*, vol. 11, no. 4, December 1970.)

88. *Japan Quarterly*, vol. 18, no. 3, July–September 1971; John M. Lee, *New York Times*, April 9, 1972; Edwin L. Dale, Jr., *New York Times*, June 4, 1972.

89. *The Oriental Economist,* July 1971, p. 12.

90. *Far Eastern Economic Review*, March 1971.

91. The *Wall Street Journal* (September 20, 1972) as cited in the *Congressional Record—Senate*, 92nd Congress, 2nd Session, vol. 118, no. 152, September 27, 1972, S16104.

92. *Forbes,* May 1, 1971, p. 15.

93. Masao Kihara, p. 26.

94. *New Times*, March 24, 1971, p. 24.

95. Jon Halliday and Gavan McCormack, p. 6.

96. Hayashi Naomi, p. 250.

97. *Pacific Basin Reports,* Custom House, Box 26581, San Francisco, California 94126. Report of April 1, 1971, pp. 83–85. I am indebted to Jim Peck for this source.

98. *Pacific Basin Reports,* p. 87.

99. Herman Kahn, *The Emerging Japanese Superstate—Challenge*

and Response (Englewood Cliffs, N.J.: Spectrum Paperback edition, 1971), p. 108.

100. Mainichi Shimbunsha, ed. *Ampo to boei seisan* ("The Security Treaty and Defense Production") (Tokyo: Mainichi Shimbunsha, 1969), p. 167.

101. On this last point see Meir Merhav, *Technological Dependence, Monopoly and Growth* (London: Pergamon Press, Ltd., 1969).

102. Ronald Dore, *Land Reform in Japan* (London: Oxford University Press, 1959), pp. 372–74; American land reform policies in Japan and other Asian countries are ably discussed by Al McCoy in "Land Reform as Counter-Revolution—U.S. Foreign Policy and the Tenant Farmers of Asia," *Bulletin of Concerned Asian Scholars*, vol. 3, no. 1, Winter–Spring 1971, pp. 14–49.

103. For a fascinating reflection on early Japanese mercantilism see E. Herbert Norman, *Japan's Emergence As a Modern State—Political and Economic Problems of the Meiji Period* (New York: Institute of Pacific Relations, 1940), pp. 108–111. Norman observes that "In [Tokugawa] Japan the prevailing type of mercantilism ... exemplifies the metropolis-colony relationship between the city (metropolis) and surrounding countryside (colony) characteristic of primitive European mercantilism" (p. 108).

104. Though no *fundamental* change in policy line was made in this period, the government did try, following the signing of the San Francisco Peace Treaty, to raise agricultural prices above the excessively low ceiling imposed by the Dodge line. This adoption of a seemingly more equitable farm pricing policy through the elimination of some controls on food prices should be grasped in connection with (1) the conservative parties' efforts to protect and to strengthen their electoral base in the countryside and (2) the effort to raise agricultural production to meet the new food needs generated by the Korean War. See, for example, Kato Ichirō and Sakamoto Kusuhiko, *Nihon nōsei no tenkai katei* ("The Development Process of Japan's Agricultural Policy") (Tokyo: Tokyo Daigaku Shuppankai, 1971), p. 144ff.

105. Chitoshi Yanaga, *Big Business in Japanese Politics* (New Haven and London: Yale University Press, 1968), p. 262.

106. Shirota Noboru, Yamamura Yoshiharu, Shironishi Shinichirō, pp. 110–11.

107. Masao Kihara, p. 37, note 26.

108. Arisawa Hiromi and Inaba Shūzō, ed., *Shiryō sengo nijū nen shi* ("Historical Materials on Twenty Years of Postwar History"), vol. 2, *Keizai* (Economics) (Tokyo: Nihon Hyōronsha, 1966), p. 146; Chitoshi Yanaga, pp. 261, 265, 267.

109. Kurokawa Toshio, p. 220.

110. Nishida Yoshiaki, *"Sengo nōsei no kicho to rōnō dōmei ron"*

("The Keynote of Postwar Agricultural Policy and the Farm–Labor Coalition"), *Rekishi hyōron* (Historical Review), no. 255, October 1971, p. 34.

111. Kaichi Maekawa, "Changes of Government Employment Policy in the Face of Economic Growth Since World War II," *The Kyoto University Economic Review*, vol. 40, no. 2, October 1970, p. 48. In the early postwar period an estimated sixteen million persons (as distinguished from farm households) were engaged (full-time or part-time) in agriculture and forestry; "in 1965 the number had been reduced to about 11½ million...." By 1969 the number gainfully employed in agriculture and forestry had fallen to approximately 8,990,000 persons. (Sources: G. C. Allen, *Japan As a Market and Source of Supply*, p. 13; *Economic Picture of Japan 1970–1971*. Published by Keidanren, p. 128.)

112. *The Oriental Economist*, September 1965, p. 517.

113. *Hsinhua* (Peking), February 17, 1971, as cited in FBIS–Chi–71–32, A-30.

114. Between 1965 and 1971 the U.S. accounted for at least seventy percent of Japan's total agricultural imports; other countries furnishing Japan with agricultural imports were Australia (fourteen percent), Canada (five percent), Mexico and Thailand (four percent). (Source: Louise Perkens, "Soybeans Spearhead Record U.S. Farm Sales to Japan," *Foreign Agriculture*, August 30, 1971, p. 506.)

115. Herman M. Southworth and Bruce F. Johnson, ed., *Agricultural Development and Economic Growth* (Ithaca, N.Y.: Cornell University Press, 1967), p. 287.

116. *The Farm Index*. Published by the U.S. Department of Agriculture, March 1971, p. 20.

117. On June 10, 1971 *The Korea Times* reported that "The government is seeking the import of an additional 200,000 tons of rice from Japan this year to meet a possible shortage.... The additional import will bring Korea's total imports from Japan, contracted since last December, to 600,000 tons" (p. 4).

118. *The Oriental Economist*, a Keidanren publication which often publishes discussions of the new farm policy being advocated by the LDP, noted in its July 1970 issue (p. 12) that, "Modernization of agriculture ... cannot be achieved merely by abolition or revision of the Food Control Law ... it will be necessary to revise the Agricultural Land Use Law which severely restricts buying and selling of farm land for promotion of owner-operation with exceptional zeal ... it will be further necessary to permit easier consolidation of fragmented fields, and to promote bigger participation in large-scale farming. It will also be necessary at this juncture to ease the tight restrictions imposed on importation of agricultural produce through lowering of tariff rates and through abolition of the import quota system.... Another basic ob-

jective of the 'comprehensive farm policy' is enlargement of the scale of farm operations through facilitation of change of ownership and tenancy rights. But for successful achievement of this goal, it will be necessary to establish an effective system for absorption of farm workers seeking new jobs. This leads to the third objective of the new approach. Instead of the disorderly migration of farm workers to city and other jobs during the 'off' season, the proposal is that factories be established in the rural areas for properly organized utilization of surplus farm labor."

119. On the Sanrizuka struggles see *AMPO—A Report From the Japanese New Left,* no. 11, 1971.

Notes on the Contributors

HERBERT P. BIX attended Harvard University, earning an M.A. in East Asian studies and a Ph.D. in history and Far Eastern languages. He is Assistant Professor of Japanese History at the University of Massachusetts at Boston. A member of the editorial board of the *Bulletin of Concerned Asian Scholars,* he has been a contributor to the *China Quarterly, The Japan Interpreter,* and a forthcoming volume of essays, *Without Parallel: The American-Korean Relationship Since 1945,* to be published by Pantheon in the spring of 1974.

MALCOLM CALDWELL took First Class Honours in Economics at Nottingham University. He joined the School of Oriental and African Studies, University of London, in 1959 and is the editor of the *Journal of Contemporary Asia.* He contributes to numerous magazines and is the author of *Indonesia, The Chainless Mind* (with J. D. Henderson), *In Whose Pocket* (with Leon Howell and Michael Morrow), and *Cambodia in the Southeast Asian War* (with Lek Tan).

RICHARD DE CAMP was educated at Princeton University (B.A. 1966) and the University of Washington (M.A. in history, 1969). Denied a visa for his Fulbright fellowship in Taiwan, he studied in Japan, and is currently completing his Ph.D. work at the University of Washington with a dissertation on U.S.–China relations during the Kennedy administration. He has contributed articles to various campus newspapers and to the *Bulletin of Concerned Asian Scholars.*

HARRY MAGDOFF spent many years in government where he held positions with the WPA National Research Project on Re-Employment Opportunities and Technical Development, the Civilian Requirements Division of the National Defense Advisory Commission, the War Production Board, and the Current Business Analysis Division of the U.S. Department of Commerce. Finally he was Special Assistant to the U.S. Secretary of Commerce under Henry Wallace and Averell Harriman. He has been a financial consultant, taught economics at the New School for Social Research, and has lectured at universities in the United States, Canada, and Europe. He is the author of *The Age of Imperialism* and *The Dynamics of U.S. Capitalism* (with Paul M. Sweezy) and of many articles and reviews. Since 1969 he has been coeditor of *Monthly Review*.

CHERYL PAYER earned her Ph.D. in political science at Harvard University and was a Fulbright Fellow at the Free University of Berlin. She has taught Asian and world history at Spelman College, Atlanta, and political science and social studies at Harvard University, and traveled as a freelance journalist in Southeast Asia during 1971–1972. She has written for *The Christian Science Monitor* and *Dispatch News Service*, among others, and was a contributor to *The Indochina Story* (Pantheon, 1970). She is currently at work on a book on the IMF and the Third World, to be published by Penguin Books, London.

WILLIAM J. POMEROY attended the University of the Philippines, served in the United States Air Force in the Pacific Theater during World War II, and was a freelance writer in the Philippines after the war. He joined the Huk guerrilla national liberation movement, was captured in 1952, and served ten years of a life sentence as a political prisoner before being pardoned in 1962. Resuming his career as a foreign correspondent, he made his home in England and was recently awarded a Ph.D. in history by the Institute of Oriental Studies, Academy of Sciences of the Union of Soviet Socialist Republics. His many books include *Born of the People, The Forest,* and *American Neo-Colonialism: Its Emergence in the Philippines and Asia, 1898–1920.*

PETER DALE SCOTT took a Ph.D in political science at McGill University and spent four years in the Canadian Foreign Service. He is Associate Professor of English at the University of California, Berkeley. His books include *The War Conspiracy, The Politics of Escalation in Vietnam* (with Franz Schurmann and Reginald Zelnick) , and *Poems.* He contributed to the Beacon Press edition of the Pentagon Papers and has published poetry, literary criticism, translations, and essays on politics and education in numerous Canadian, English, and American journals, among them the *New York Review of Books, The Nation, Canadian Forum,* and the *Times Literary Supplement.*

MARK SELDEN earned his Ph.D. at Yale in modern Chinese history, was a Fulbright scholar in Taiwan and Japan, and is Associate Professor in History at Washington University, St. Louis. He was an editor of the *Bulletin of Concerned Asian Scholars,* and is the author of *The Yenan Way in Revolutionary China, America's Asia: Dissenting Essays on Asian-American Relations* (with Edward Friedman) , and *Open Secret: The Kissinger-Nixon Doctrine in Asia.* He is currently in Japan, doing research and writing.

RALPH THAXTON was a Foreign Area Fellow and a Midwest Universities Consortium for International Activities Fellow in Taiwan, a Fellow in the Stanford Inter-University Program for Chinese Language Studies in Taiwan, and is a Ph.D. candidate at the University of Wisconsin.

THOMAS E. WEISSKOPF took his Ph.D. in economics at MIT. He was Visiting Professor of Economics at the Indian Statistical Institute, New Delhi, consultant to the United Nations Industrial Development Organization, has taught at Harvard, and is now Associate Professor of Economics at the University of Michigan. He edited *Perspectives on the Economic Problem* (with Arthur MacEwan), *Studies in Development Planning* (with Hollis Chenery et al.), and *The Capitalist System: A Radical Analysis of Contemporary Society* (with Richard Edwards and Michael Reich), and has contributed to numerous publications.

Index

Abbott Laboratories, 183
Abramovitz, Moses, 10
Abs, Hermann, 63
Accelerated Rural Devolopment
    (ARD) , 258–64, 268
Acheson, Dean, 110, 136
Adak (naval base) , 281
Adams, John, 8
Afghanistan, 81
Africa, 6, 120
    foreign investment in, 132, 334
Air America, Inc., 128
Alaska, 9, 24
    strategic importance, 280
Aleutian Islands, 9
    strategic importance, 280
Allen, G. C., 354 n.
Alsop, Joseph, 97
Alternative in Southeast Asia
    (Black) , 87 n.
American Bankers Association, 138
American Council for Commerce
    and Industry, 209
American Cyanamid, 183
American Express Company, 292
American Friends of Vietnam, 129
American Indians, 6
American Revolution, 5, 7
American Security Council, 114

*America's Asia: Dissenting Essays
    on Asian-American Relations*
    (Friedman, Selden, eds.) , xv
Amory, Robert, 114
Anderson, B. R. O'G., 49 n.
Anderson, Robert B., 119
Annenberg, Mrs. Walter, 136
Arab oil embargo, 25
Arab states, 25
Arabian Oil Company (Japan) , 26
Arendt, Hannah, 101–2, 103, 104,
    111, 112, 141 n.
Armed Forces Journal, 350 n.
Army Security Agency, 103
Arnold, Matthew, 94
Asia Society, 128
Asia Society Conference, 127
Asian Development Bank (ADB) ,
    x, 71–90, 184
    background, 73–4
    and debt creation, 79
    ideology, 79–80, 84
    infrastructure investments, 80, 83
    and international capitalism, 84–
    6
    Japanese role in, 71–3, 78, 80, 86
    lending policies, 79–86, 88 n.
    and multilateralism, 73–4
    U.S. role in, 78–9, 80, 83, 87 n.

"Asian Development Bank, The" (Watanabe) , 88 n.
Asian elites, xiii, 84, 85, 86, 170–1, 227, 249
    dependence on capitalist powers, 68–70, 85, 191–2
Asian mercenaries, xiv, 138
"Asianization," 194
Atlantic, Gulf and Pacific Company, 183, 184
Attu (naval base) , 281
Australia, 24, 25, 62, 75, 117
    and ADB, 74–5, 78
    Japanese investment in, 75
    and Malaysian insurgency, 34
    U.S. investment in, 75
    and U.S. security, 283
Aviation Week, 131

Baer, Francis S., 144 n.
Bandung Conference, 248
Bangla Desh, 28, 231–2
Bank of America, 184, 292
Barbero, Carmelo, 165
Barnet, Richard, 92–3, 101, 111, 112, 139, 141 n.
Barth, Alfred W., 133
Bell, Peter, 249
Bell Act, 162–3, 173
Bell Mission, 175, 221
Belli, R. David, 87 n.
Benda, H. J., 49 n.
Benguet Consolidated, 184
Benson, Rear Admiral Roy, 47 n.
"Berkeley Mafia," 40
"Berkeley Mafia and the Indonesia Massacre, The" (Ransom) , 48 n.
Beyster Plan, 177
Birla, G. D., 208, 209
Black, Eugene, 71, 74, 78, 79, 86, 87 n., 130, 206, 208
Black Dragon, 42
Blueprint Fallacy, 94–101
Board of National Estimates (of CIA) , 104
Borden Chemicals, 183
Borneo, 37
Boxer Rebellion, 9, 139
Brandi, F. H., 144 n.
Branfman, Fred, 108–9
Brazil, 121, 138
Brazil Squadron, 8

Bretton Woods Conference, 110
British Empire, 3–4, 94
British Special Forces, 34
Brown, Dorris D., 215
Brownell, Herbert, Jr., 164
Brunei, 29, 33
Bulletin of Concerned Asian Scholars, 89 n., 353 n.
Bundy, McGeorge, 124
Bundy, William, 100–1, 103, 111, 115, 124, 136, 138
Burden of Empire: An Appraisal of Western Colonialism in Africa South of the Sahara (Gann, Duignan) , 17 n.
Burma, 29, 32–3, 34
    and oil interests, 32–3
Burmah Oil, 32
Burmah-Shell, 204, 218
Burroughs Clearing House, 347, 349
bushido spirit, 316–17
Business International, 131
Business Week, 120, 122, 131

C. Itoh (corporation) , 347
Caldwell, Malcolm, 44 n., 45 n.
California Standard and Texas Oil Company, 36, 38, 39, 129, 183, 204, 218, 292
Cambodia, 27, 30–1, 32, 78, 102, 118, 116. *See also* Indochina
    and ADB, 81, 83
    Thai troops in, 250–1
    U.S. military operations in, 112
Canada, xii, 6, 8, 23, 24, 157
Canton Island, 281
Cape Horn, 6
capitalism and imperialism, 9–17, 21–49, 74–7, 85, 115, 159–61, 186, 222–30, 310–11, 336–46
capitalism and militarism, 14–16, 22, 30, 82–6, 114–18, 129–30, 135–8, 305–61
Caribbean Sea, 5–7
Central Establishment, 113–16, 126, 144 n.
Central Intelligence Agency (CIA) , 33, 42–3, 47 n., 248
    counterinsurgency, 248, 266, 269, 327
    financial links, 91–154
    intelligence reports, 99–139 *passim*
    and Ivy League, 115

Central Intelligence Agency *(cont.)*
and New York Social Register, 128–9
and oil interests, 33, 114–15
in Thailand, 266, 269
and Vietnam War, 91–154
CIA-DIA-INR Panel Draft, 117
CIA-Financial Establishment, 91–154
Ceylon, 80, 81
Chase Manhattan Bank, 114, 121, 127, 130–1
Checchi and Company, 249
Chiang Kai-shek, 282
Chiengrai (Thailand), 255–8
Chikara, Makino, 76
China, ix, x, 4, 6, 8, 9, 26, 27, 55, 71, 82, 130, 157, 247, 252, 281, 294, 311
early trade, 8, 115
oil resources, 27–8, 29, 35
relations with U.S., x, 181, 342
U.S. counterrevolutionary activity, 264, 282–4, 322–3
and Vietnam War, 106
Chinese Communists, 282, 322–3
Chinese oil industry, 27–9
Chomsky, Noam, 99, 100, 101, 110–11, 140 n.
Chou En-lai, 248
CINCPAC (Commander in Chief, Pacific), 114, 125
classical colonialism, x–xi, 167–72, 190–1, 200–2, 222–3
Clifford, Clark
Club of Rome, 21
Colgate-Palmolive Company, 184
Committee for Coordination of Joint Prospecting for Mineral Resources in Asian Offshore Areas, 30, 31
Committee for Economic Development, 132
"Committee for an Effective and Durable Peace in Asia," 135
Committee of Concerned Asian Scholars, xv
Common Market, 25, 342–3
communism, 37, 43, 96, 98, 99, 117
Communist Party of Indonesia, 43, 59–60
Community Development Program (India), 210

Companies Act (1956), 205
comprador interests, 161, 170–1, 178–9, 190–1
Congress Party (India), 201, 204, 223–5, 228, 230, 231, 232
"Consider Japan," 69 n.
Constantino, Renato, 35
Continental Congress, 135
"Contradictions of Postwar Development in Southeast Asia, The" (Bell, Resnick), 89 n.
Cooper, Chester, 103, 123
"co-prosperity sphere," 137
Corcoran, Foley, Youngman and Rowe (law firm), 114
Council of Foreign Relations, 114, 116–17, 123, 136, 138
counterinsurgency, x, 37–8, 96, 163, 166, 175, 248, 261, 264, 266, 269, 282, 327
"Cowboys," 114
Crescent and the Rising Sun—Indonesian Islam, The (Benda), 49 n.
Cuba, 93, 95, 99, 121, 158
Cultural Revolution (China), 329
currency black-market scandals, 129
currency devaluation, 51–5, 63
beneficiaries of, 54–5
and currency convertibility, 53, 55
and inflation control, 53, 55
Current History, 349 n.

Dai Ichi (Japanese bank), 348
Davies, Derek, 76
Dean, Arthur, 136
debt rescheduling, 61–3
"Decade of Development," 119–20
Defense Agency White Paper (Japan), 312, 315, 316
Defense Production Act, 132
de Gaulle, Charles, 126
Del Monte Corporation, 184, 189
Democratic Republic of Vietnam, 103, 104
Denmark, 342
DePuy, Major William, 108
Desai, Morarji, 231
developing nations, 59, 63–4, 84–5, 120, 175–82, 247–54
as raw materials source, 79–80
Development Assistance Council, 59
development priorities, 63, 64, 84–5

Diem, Ngo Dinh, 95, 96, 118, 122, 124, 128, 264
Dienbienphu, 92, 247
Dillon, C. Douglas, 110, 126, 136
Direction of Trade (IMF, IBRD), 87 n.
Dodge, Joseph M., 323–5
Dodge Company, 183
Dole Pineapple Corporation, 184, 189
Dōmei Kaigi (labor federation), 334
Dominican Republic, 47 n., 121
Dow Chemicals, 183
Du Boff, Richard, 98
Dulles, Allen, 115
Dulles, John Foster, 113, 248, 282
Durbrow, Elbridge, 118
Dutch East Indies, 8

Eames, Alfred, Jr., 188
Earnshaw Docks, 183
East India Squadron, 8
East Kalimantan, 41, 42
Economic Commission for Asia and the Far East (ECAFE), 31, 73, 134
Economic Growth of the United States 1790–1860 (North), 18 n.
economic penetration, x–xv, 26, 33, 40–3, 157–99, 212–20
Economic Stabilization Program, 59
Economic Survey Team, 58
Eisenhower, Dwight D., 98–9, 119
ELINT (electronic intelligence), 102
Ellsberg, Daniel, 96, 97, 139 n.
Emergence of Multination Enterprise: American Business Abroad from the Colonial Era to 1914 (Wilkins), 18 n.
Emmet, Christopher, 129
Empire and Revolution (Horowitz), 139
energy consumption, 23
energy crisis, 21–5, 27
Eniwetok (naval base), 281
Esso Standard, 183, 204, 218
European Economic Community (EEC), 25
Expansion of England, The (Seeley), 3–4
Export and Import Bank (Japan), 41

Exxon, 114
"Eye of the Beholder: Background Notes on the U.S.-Japan Military Relationship" (Dower), 353 n.
Ezaki, Masumi, 309

Fallacy of Neglected Intelligence, 101–7
Fanning Island, 6
Far Eastern Economic Review, 69 n., 76, 81, 352n.
Federal Reserve Bank of New York, 133
Fels, Tony, 89 n.
Fiji, 6
"Filipino First," 176–7, 179
Filoil Corporation, 180, 183
Finletter, Thomas K., 122
Firestone Tire and Rubber Company, 183
First Indochina War, 91–2
First National City Bank Monthly Economic Letter, 109
First National City Bank of New York, 93, 114, 120, 128, 184, 185
Five-Year Plans, 205–13, 230
Flanigan, Horace, 144 n.
For Reasons of State (Chomsky), 140 n.
Ford Foundation, 110, 138, 192, 214–15
Ford Motor Company, 188
Foreign Investment in India (Kidron), 69 n.
Formosa, 29
Fortune, 131
Fourth Republic (France), 91
Fowler, Henry, 78
France, 8, 62, 126, 134, 161
Freidlin, Julius N., 87 n.
French Total Indonesia (oil company), 41
Fuji Bank, 76
Fuji Training School, 316
Fujitsu, Ltd., 337–8

Galbraith, John Kenneth, 122
Gandhi, Indira, 231, 232
Gann, L. H., 17 n.
García, Carlos, 178, 179
Gelb, Leslie, 96, 98–9, 104, 109, 112, 139

General Agreement on Tariffs and Trade (GATT) , 331
General Electric, 183
General Foods, 176, 184
General Petroleum, 128
General Telephone and Electronics Corporation, 184
"General View of Japanese History and National Polity, A" (Tsukamoto) , 316–17
Geneva Conference of Laos, 97, 122
Geology of Indonesia, The (Van Bemmelen) , 36, 47 n.
Germany, 4, 16
Getty Tidewater, 183
Ghana, 121
Gilpatric, Roswell, 118, 121
Globe Wireless, 184
gold reserves, 113, 118–19, 123, 125, 132, 134, 333
Goodyear Tire and Rubber Company, 183
Goulden, Joseph, 141 n.
Great Britain, 8, 9, 22, 25, 33, 34, 60, 62, 116, 332
Great East Asia Co-prosperity Sphere, 26, 41, 45 n., 49 n.
Greece, 121
    U.S. intervention, 130
"Green for Danger" (Nussbaum) , 89 n.
green revolution, 81, 84, 85, 89 n., 215–17
    effects on poor, 81
    in Philippines, 81
    in Thailand, 254–8, 272
Griswold, Deirdre, 48 n.
Guam, 9, 280, 281
"Guided Economy," 39
Gulf Oil, 114, 180, 183, 292

Halliday, Jon, 336
Halperin, Morton, 109
Hankook Caprolactum Corporation, 80
Hannah, John A., 258
Hare-Hawes-Cutting Act, 159–60
Harriman, Averell, 97, 122
Hartke, Vance, 135
Hauge, Gabriel, 136
Hawaii, 9, 280, 281, 291
Hayes, Alfred, 133
Helms, Richard, 113, 115
Henderson, William, 127, 129, 130

Heraclitus, 5
Herter, Christian, 144 n.
Hibben Plan, 177
Hideyoshi, Toyotomi, 319
Higher Circles, The (Domhoff) , 144 n.
Hilsman, Roger, 284
Hitachi Shipbuilding, 348
Hitler, 4
Ho Chi Minh, 111
Hobby, Oveta Culp, 136
Hobson, J. A., 94
Hokuso Plateau (Japan) , 343–4
Holland, 25, 37, 39, 57–8, 62, 161
Hong Kong, xii, 75, 131
Honolulu, 6
Honolulu Conference, 124–5
Honolulu Iron Works, 183
Hoopes, Townsend, 109, 136
Horowitz, David, 139
Huk Rebellion, 163, 167, 173, 175, 177, 182, 190, 193
Hull, Cordell, 22

imperialism, x-xiv, 3–13, 23–7, 40–3, 55, 71–90, 115–22, 157–99, 296–7, 308, 311–12, 317, 327, 339, 345–7
India, x, 27, 28, 118
    agriculture, 202, 210–12, 214–16
    and capitalism, 201–2, 222–30
    classes, 222–8
    Communist Party in, 204–5, 231–2
    and foreign economic domination, 207–46
    and IMF, 56
    independence, 200–7
    nationalist movement, 223–4
    and oil, 29, 217–20
    and Soviet Union, 204–5, 212, 217, 227, 231
    and World Bank, 206, 208, 214, 221
Indian Industrial Mission, 208
Indochina, x, xiv, 4, 30–1, 34, 97, 115, 159
Indochina War, x, 22, 83, 84, 108, 250, 274, 279, 283–5, 288. *See also* Vietnam, Cambodia
    and oil, 30–49
    and U.S. decline, ix, 71, 91, 247
Indonesia, x, 25, 27, 30, 31, 34, 121, 131, 139, 159, 311, 312, 328
    and ADB, 81, 83

Indonesia *(cont.)*
Communist Party in, 37, 43, 57, 59–60
debt burden, 68
and economic crisis, 50–68
Five-Year Plan, 65, 68
and imperialist competition, 35–43, 84, 116–17, 129
and IMF, 50–68, 72
Japanese investment in, 60–3, 70 n., 76–7, 83
and nationalization, 58–60
oil resources, 29, 39, 116–17
repudiated debts, 57, 63, 68
Soviet aid, 45 n.
timber exports, 65, 68
U.S. aid, 58–9
U.S. investment in, 39–40, 42–3, 47 n., 75, 77, 83, 116–18
and Vietnam War, 116–18
"Indonesia in 1964: Towards a 'Peoples' Democracy'?"
(Pauker), 59, 69 n.
Indonesia: Investment—Policies, Procedure, Fields of Investment and Progress Report (Department of Trade), 48 n.
Indonesia: Public Control and Economic Planning (Zahri), 39, 47 n.
Indo-Pakistan War, 220–1
Industrial Finance Corporation of Thailand, 79
Industrial Policy Resolution, 203, 205
Institute of Petroleum (London), 21
Intelligence and Research (State Department), 115
Inter-Governmental Group on Indonesia (IGGI), 40, 48 n., 62–4, 68
International Bank for Reconstruction and Development. *See* World Bank.
International Business Machines (IBM), 126, 134, 237–8
International Development Association (IDA), 209, 329
International Economic Policy Association, 85
International Harvester, 184
International Monetary Fund (IMF), x, xi, 72

and debt creation, 52–3, 68
and foreign investment, 51, 55, 61, 64, 66, 72
and imperialism, 50–70, 72
in India, 56
in Indonesia, 50–70, 72
in Latin America, 55
in Philippines, 53–4, 174–82
and resource transfer, 53–4
and social revolution, 56
stabilization policies, 51–5, 59, 61, 64, 66, 72
and Sukarno, 59–60
and Third World development, 56–7, 68
International Security Affairs, 115, 116
"Investment by Japan in U.S. Lags" (Wilcke), 348
Iran, 22, 30, 121, 138
Iraq, 28
Ireland, 342
Ishikawajima Harima Industries, 348
Italy, 62
Iwo Jima, 281
Iyengar, H. V. R., 208

James, R. Campbell, 128
Janeway, Eliot, 135
Japan, xiii–xiv, 9, 16, 22, 23, 25, 26, 30, 50, 62, 73, 118, 123, 285
and ADB, 74–7
and China, 76, 307
defense spending, 306–13
and imperialism, xiii, 24–7, 40–3, 76–7, 296–7, 308, 311–12, 317, 327, 339, 345–7
and Indonesia, 37, 40–3, 60, 62–3
and Korean War, 319, 325–6
and militarism, xiv, 36, 159, 305–61
and oil, 25–7, 33, 40–2, 76, 346
in Philippines, 65, 159
postwar agricultural development, 339–45
rearmament, 340–1
relations with U.S., 281, 305–6, 308, 331–41
and technology, 336–9
and Thailand, 31, 343
"Japan: Nippon on the March" (Koji), 352 n.

Japan Petroleum Development Corporation, 40
"Japan Stirs Asian Resentments" (Stewart), 348
Japan's Defense (Defense Agency), 351 n.
Japan's Postwar Defense Policy (Weinstein), 351
Japanese-American conflict of interest, xiii, 16, 41, 43, 75, 157, 185, 311, 331–9, 343, 345–7
Japanese Asian investments, 31–3, 40–3, 60–3, 73–4, 76–87, 296, 319, 327–61
Japanese imperialism, xiii–xiv, 24–7, 40–3, 74–7, 296–7, 308, 311–12, 317, 327, 333–6, 339, 345–7
Japanese militarism, xiv, 36, 159, 305–61
Japanese multinationals, 347–9
Japanese naval power, 9, 312, 340
Japanese postwar agriculture, 339–45
Japanese postwar rearmament, 41, 309–13, 340–1
Japex (oil company), 41
Japex-Union Oil Corporation, 42
Jefferson, Thomas, 8
Jehore State (Malaysia), 348
Jennings, B. Brewster, 128
Johns Hopkins University, 74
Johnson, Joseph E., 136
Johnson, Lyndon B., 74, 117, 128, 220–1
and Indochina War, 86, 92, 94–8, 100–10, 118, 123, 127, 130–6, 164, 266
Johnston Island, 281
Joint Economic Committee of Congress, 120
Joint U.S. Military Advisory Group, 164–7
Journal of Contemporary Asia, 46 n., 48 n.

Kadena Air Base, 283–4, 291, 296
Kahn, Herman, 338
Katipunan (revolutionary movement), 168
Kennedy, John F., 92, 93, 95, 96–101, 117, 132–3, 134, 283
American University speech, 122
and balance of payments crisis, 107–33, 147 n.

and defense costs, 118–25, 133
and overseas investments, 118–25
and Vietnam withdrawal, 130
Khmer Serei, 251
Khrushchev, Nikita, 95, 122
Kidron, Michael, 69 n.
Killian, James R., 136
Kirk, Grayson, 128
Kirkpatrick, Lyman, 102, 105
Kissinger, Henry, 92, 136
Kodiak (naval base), 281
Koji, Nakamura, 352 n.
Kolko, Gabriel, 17 n., 18 n., 22, 44 n., 46 n.
Kolko, Joyce, 18 n., 22, 44 n., 46 n.
Korea, 4, 9, 23, 26, 130, 158, 281
Korean War, 15, 108, 109, 132, 166, 204, 282–3, 319, 325, 333, 334, 340
Kra Isthmus (Thailand), 31
Krishnamachari, T. T., 206, 207, 208
Kuomintang, 282, 322–3
Kuwait, 30
Kwajalein, 281

Lamphoutacoul, Siho, 103
Land Reform in Japan (Dore), 359 n.
Lansdale, Edward, 95, 118
Laos, 32, 79, 81, 83, 84, 96, 97, 99, 123, 138, 160, 270
Thai troops in, 250–1
U.S. war effort, 102, 268
Laotian Accords (1962), 122
Latin America, 13, 55, 120, 158
Laurel-Langley Agreement, 178, 189
Lewis, John P., 216
Liaotung Retrocession, 319
Lichauco, Alejandro, 181
Liebman, Marvin, 127
"limited partnership," 95
limited wars, 311
Limits of Growth, The (Meadows et al.), 21, 44 n.
Lindsay, Franklin, 136
Litton Industries, 144 n.
"Logic of Imperialism, The" (Magdoff), 139
Lon Nol, 27, 31, 45 n., 251, 259
Ludwig, Daniel B., 144 n.
"Lying in Politics: Reflections on the Pentagon Papers" (Arendt), 141 n.

Macapagal, Diosdado, 179
MacArthur, General Douglas, 172,
    190, 280, 314, 322–3
Mackay Radio Telegraph Company,
    184
Mackie, J. A. C., 69 n.
Maddox (U.S. destroyer), 102
Madiun affair, 37
Maeda, Rear Admiral Tadashi, 42,
    49 n.
Magdoff, Harry, 92–3, 139
Magsaysay, Ramon, 167, 177, 178
Mahajani, Usha, 69 n.
Mahalanobis, P. C., 205
Majuro (naval base), 281
Malacca Straits, 25, 26, 27, 31
    Japanese strategic interest in,
        293–4, 329, 356 n.
Malaysia, 27, 31, 33, 59, 80, 81, 117,
    131
    and oil, 29, 34
"Malaysia: Changing   Masters"
    (Witton), 46 n.
Manila Chronicle, The, 35–6, 46 n.
Manning, Robert, 124
Mansfield, Mike, 124
Manus (naval base), 281
Mao Tse-tung, 248, 323
Marcopper (copper company), 184
Marcos, Ferdinand, xiii, 53, 181,
    186, 194
Marginal   Establishment,   113–14,
    143 n., 144 n.
Marine Corps Gazette, 350 n.
Marine Counter-Guerrilla Warfare
    School, 284
Marquesas, 6
Marshall Plan, 72, 130
Marubeni-Iida   (corporation),   40,
    347
Marxism, 113, 193
Masuhara, Keikichi, 309
McCarthy, Eugene, 131
McCloy, John J., 136
McCone, John, 105, 113, 115
McCormack, Gavan, 336
McCoy, Thomas F., 138
McGarrah, Richard, 115
McNamara, Robert S., 94, 96, 97,
    98, 105, 106, 108, 109, 111,
    117, 122, 124, 125, 129, 131
McNutt, Paul V., 161, 172
Mead Johnson, 183
Mediterranean Squadron, 8

Meiji, 319
Mekong Delta, 95
Mekong Project, 83–4
"Mekong River Project and Im-
    perialist Interests in South-
    east Asia" (Fels), 89 n.
Melby Mission, 175
Melman, Seymour, 350 n.
Meo tribes (Thailand), 265–73
    and opium, 267–8
mercantilism,   340,   343,   345–7,
    359 n.
Merck, Sharp and Dohme, 183, 217
Mexican War, 6
Mexico, 8, 290
Meyer, John M., Jr., 133
Micronesia, xi, xiv, 280, 283
Middle East, 22, 23, 25, 31, 35, 76
    British influence, 22
    oil, 25, 293–4
    U.S. penetration, 23
Midway, 9, 280, 281
militarism, xv, 36, 159
    and monopoly capitalism, 318–31,
        345–7
Military Assistance Advisory Group
    (Thailand), 248
Military   Assistance   Agreement,
    164–5
Military Bases Agreement, 164–5
military dictatorships, U.S. support
    for, ix, 103, 117, 127, 128
military-industrial complex, 14, 22,
    30, 85, 91–154
    in Japan, 26, 310–11, 345–6
    in Soviet Union, 353 n.
    in U.S., 91–154
Military Review, The (Hilsman),
    284
Mindanao (Southern Philippines),
    43
"Mineral Industry of Japan, The"
    (Pense), 356 n.
Ministry of International Trade
    and Industry (Japan), 294
"miracle rice," 81
Mishima, Yukio, 315, 316
"Mishima and the Transition from
    Postwar Democracy to Demo-
    cratic Fascism" (Moto), 352 n.
Mitsubishi Corporation, 33, 76, 290,
    316, 326
Mitsubishi Heavy Industries, 348
Mitsui (corporation), 40, 290

monopoly capitalism, 318–31, 345
    and agriculture, 344–5
    and militarism, 320–2, 345–7
Monthly Review, 69 n., 87 n.
Moore, General James, 291
Morgan Guaranty Trust, 133
Mossadegh, Premier, 22
multinational corporations, xii–xiii,
    73, 115, 182, 188–90, 216–20,
    333–4, 339, 347–9
Munenori, Akagi, 314
Murai Jun, 315
Murphy, Robert, 136
Mustin, Vice Admiral Lloyd, 100,
    101
Muto, Ichiyo, 352
Mutsu-Ogawara (Japan), 344
Mutual Defense Treaty, 165
Myanma Oil, 32

Nakasone, Yasuhiro, 309
National Association of Manufac-
    turers, 85
National Defense Council (Japan),
    309
National Intelligence Estimate, 95,
    100, 102, 104, 107, 118–19, 123
National Liberation Front (NLF),
    274
national liberation movements, x–
    xi, xiv, 9, 33, 43, 71, 86
    and U.S. intervention, x, 37–8,
    47 n., 96, 163, 166, 175, 193–4,
    247–8, 251, 265–73, 283
National Security Action Mem-
    orandum, 98, 101, 105, 109,
    124–6, 129
National Security Council (NSC),
    99, 100, 102
nationalism, U.S. suppression of,
    179–82, 191–4
*Nationalism and Revolution in
    Indonesia* (Kahin), 49 n.
Nationalist-Citizens Party, 191
Ne Win, 33
Nehru, Jawaharlal, 201–4, 225, 232
neocolonialism in Asia, xiii, 51,
    73–5
    American, xiii, 7–9, 16, 30–7, 71–2,
    157–99
    Japanese, xiii–xiv, 40–1, 279
Nepal, 80, 81
Netherlands. *See* Holland

Netherlands New Guinea Oil
    Company, 36
New England, 6
New Guinea, 36, 131
New Order (Indonesia), 67
New York Review of Books, The,
    102
New York State Bankers Associa-
    tion, 133
New York Times, 98, 109, 122–3,
    193, 195, 220, 221
New York Times Magazine, 103
Newsweek, 283–4
New Zealand, 78
    and Malaysian insurgency, 34
    U.S. investment in, 75
    and U.S. security, 283
Nhu, Ngo Dinh, 123, 124
Nihon Keibi Hoshō Kabushiki
    Kaisha, 314
Nikkan Kōgyō Shimbun, 336
Nippon Kangyo, 348
Nippon Steel, 76, 330
Nishimura, Naomi, 309
Nissen, Bruce, 87 n.
Nixon, Richard M., ix, 30, 73, 86,
    107, 111, 112, 113, 117, 124,
    134, 136, 138, 296, 307, 333
Nixon Doctrine, 71
Nixon-Sato Joint Communiqué,
    308, 329
Nootka Sound, 6
North Atlantic Treaty Organiza-
    tion (NATO), xi, 122, 130
North Korea, xi, 9, 117. *See also*
    Korean War
    economic policies, 59
North Sea, 24
North Vietnam, xi, 95, 112, 122–2.
    See also Indochina War, Viet-
    nam War
    bombing of, 104–5, 117, 132
    U.S. covert operations, 124–5
    and Vietcong, 102–4

Ocean Development Corporation,
    26
Oceania, 131
Office of Strategic Services (OSS),
    104, 133
*OSS: The Secret History of Ameri-
    ca's First Central Intelligence
    Agency* (Smith), 142 n.

Oglesby, Carl, 114
oil, Japanese need for, 24–7, 40–3, 76, 330
Oil—The World's Reserves (Institute of Petroleum) , 21, 44 n.
oil and CIA, 94, 114–15
Oil and Gas Journal, The (King) , 45 n.
oil and imperialism, 21–49, 114–16, 121–2, 127–31, 204, 216–19
"Oil and Imperialism in East Asia" (Caldwell) , 44 n.
oil and Indochina War, 31–2, 49 n.
oil imperialism, 21–49, 114–16
   and Indonesia, 36–43
   and Philippines, 35–6
   and Singapore, 34–5, 43
oil reserves, known, 22, 24, 26, 27, 29–30
   Soviet-U.S.-Japanese cooperation in developing, 26–7
Okinawa, x, xi, xiv, 4, 317
   economic dependence, 288–9
   Japanese era, 279, 289–91, 312
   strategic importance, 279–302, 308
   and U.S.-Japanese tensions, 295–7
   and World War II destruction, 286–7, 291
Okinawa Restoration Treaty, 349 n.
Okinawan Land Adjustment Bureau, 289–90
Omore, 285
Open Door Policy, 9, 74, 77
opium wars, 9
Organic Act (1902) , 159, 169
Organization for Economic Cooperation and Development, 59, 62
OPEC, 25, 27, 28, 40
organized crime, 136
Oriental Economist, The, 287, 349 n.
Osmeña, Sergio, 160

Pacific Basin, xiv, 6–7
Pacific Basin Review, 336
Pacific Commercial Company, 160
Pacific naval bases (U.S.) , 281
Pacific Northwest, 8
Pacific Stars and Stripes, 250
"pacification," 111
Packard, David, 136
Pakistan, 28, 29, 80, 81, 123

Palau, 281
Palmyra, 281
Papers on the War (Ellsberg) , 139 n.
Paris Club, 62, 63
Park, Chung Hee, 259, 308, 327, 328, 343, 357 n.
Parke Davis, 183
Partners in Development (Pearson) , 69 n.
Passman, Otto E., 86
Pathet Lao, 104, 248
Pauker, Guy J., 69 n.
Pauley, Edwin, 321–2
Pax Americana, 280, 332
Pax Americana (Steel) , 4, 17 n.
Payer, Cheryl, 87 n.
Payne-Aldrich Tariff, 171
Peace Corps, 192
Pearson report, 69 n.
peasant resistance, 43, 71, 163, 166, 193–4, 256–65
Pembela Tanah Air, 42
Pense, R. A., 356 n.
Pentagon Papers, 91, 94, 96–118 *passim,* 283
   censorship of, 94, 116–18, 135
Pentagon Studies, 97–8
peonage, 52–3, 68
People's Action Party (Singapore) , 35
People's Oil Company, 32
People's Republic of China. *See* China
Perkins, John A., 136
Permina (oil company) , 39
"Perpetuation of Dependence: The IMF and the Third World, The" (Payer) , 69 n., 87 n.
Perry, Commodore Matthew, 9, 285–6
Persian Gulf, 25
Pertamina (oil company) , 31, 39, 40, 41
Peru, 348
Pfizer Laboratories, 183
"Phased Withdrawal of U.S. Forces, 1962–1964" (Pentagon) , 140 n.
Phelps Dodge Company, 183
Philippines, x, xiii, xiv, 9, 63, 65, 80, 83, 117, 131, 280, 281
   and communism, 166–7, 171, 173, 193

Philippines *(cont.)*
Huk rebellion, 163, 167, 173, 175, 177, 182, 190, 196
and IMF, 53-4
independence, 160-4, 169
industrialization, 174-7
Japanese investment, 77, 161, 327
Katipunan, 168-9
and neocolonialism, 157-99
oil resources, 29
strategic importance, 183
U.S. investment, 65, 75, 77, 161
and U.S. oil interests, 35-6
in World War II, 172-3
Philippine Central Bank, 174, 176
Philippine Commission, 169-70
Philippine Iron Mines, Inc., 184
Pierce, Franklin, 286
Pohang Integrated Steel Works, 82
Political Economy of International Oil and the Underdeveloped Countries (Tanzer), 145 n.
Potsdam, 281, 321
Powell, Lewis F., 136
President's Senior Advisory Group, 107-8, 110, 113, 116, 136, 137
Presidential Task Force on International Development, 73
Proctor and Gamble, 184
Protest in Tokyo—The Security Treaty Crisis of 1960 (Packard), 351 n.
Pueblo, U.S.S., 102
Puerto Rico, xi, 158
Pye, Lucian, 136

"Quarterly Newsletter" (ADB), 88 n.
Quezon y Molina, Manuel, 160
Quirino-Foster Agreement (1950), 175

Raborn, Admiral William F., Jr., 105
RCA Communications, 184
Ransom, David, 48 n.
Rapacki, J., 122
Rapacki Plan, 122
Raskin, Marcus G., 139
Recto, Claro M., 163, 191
Rehabilitation Act, 163
Reischauer, Edwin, 100

"Reluctant Imperialists, The" (Kalb, Abel), 4, 17 n.
Report on India's Food Crisis and Steps to Meet It (Ford Foundation), 215
Research and Development costs, 310, 350 n.
Reston, James, 4
Reuss, Henry, 85
Reynolds Company, 183
Rhee, Syngman, 259, 323, 357 n.
Ribbentrop, Joachim von, 91
Richardson, John, 124
Rising American Empire, The (Van Alstyne), 5-6, 18 n.
Roberts, John G., 347, 349
Rockefeller, David, 131, 136
Rockefeller, John D., III, 128
Rockefeller Brothers Fund Panel II Report, 92, 119
Rolling Thunder program, 106-7
Roosevelt, Kermit, 144 n.
Root-Takahira Agreement, 158
Roots of Involvement: The U.S. in Asia 1784-1971 (Kalb, Abel), 17 n.
Rostow, Walt, 137
Rostow Plan, 95
Roxas, Manuel, 173
Royal Dutch Shell, 36, 38, 39, 130
Rusk, Dean, 96, 110, 136, 137
Russia, 8, 9, 28, 290. *See also* Soviet Union
"Russland, Indonesien und das neue Raj in Asien" (Caldwell), 26, 45 n.
Ryukyu Islands, 278, 280, 281-3, 287, 294

Sabah, 33
Sakkon Nakhon (Thailand), 258-65, 272
Samoa, 9, 280, 281
Sandwich Islands, 6
San Francisco Treaty, 282, 322
Sanwa Bank, 76, 326
Sarawak, 33, 43
Sarit, Thanarat, 248-9, 266
Sato, Eisaku, 296, 308, 313, 328, 333
Saudi Arabia, 30
Scheer, Robert, 95, 99, 111, 139 n.
Schurman, Jacob, 169
Scott, James C., 252

Seeley, J. R., 3
Self-Defense Forces (SDF; Japan),
    311–19
self-sufficiency, economic, 35, 59, 240
Senate Naval Affairs Committee, 281
Senkaku Islands. *See* Tiao-yu Is-
    lands
Seymour, Whitney North, 136
Seymour Company, 183
Sharp, U.S., 138
Shaw, Major Samuel, 6
Shaw and Randall (business firm),
    6
Sheehan, Neal, 104, 109
Shell Oil, 33, 255
Sherman, Vice Admiral Forrest, 281
Sherwin Williams Company, 183
Sherwood, Arthur, 129
"Shield Society," 315
Shimokita Peninsula (Japan), 344
shipbuilding industry, 7–8, 116, 348
Siberia, 24, 25, 26
Sihanouk, Norodom, 31, 45 n., 78,
    83, 251
Sihanoukville, 31
Silent Slaughter, The (Worthy),
    47 n.
Silva, Peer de, 102
Singapore, xii, 27, 31, 35, 43, 80, 82,
    84
    and foreign investors, 75, 77, 82–3
    and oil, 29, 34–5, 131
Sino-Japanese War, 319, 352 n.
Sino-Soviet relations, xiv
Smith, Hedrick, 109
Smith, R. Harris, 104
Social Policy, 139
socialism, 3, 9, 52, 85, 201, 225, 227,
    231
Socony Mobil Corporation, 93, 114,
    127, 128, 183
Sōgō Keibi Hoshō, 314–15
Soriano y Cia, 184
South Atlantic Squadron, 8
South Korea, xii, xiv, 4, 26, 35, 79,
    80, 81, 82, 123, 308, 312, 317
    and ADB, 80–4
    Japanese investment in, 76–7, 294,
        296, 327–8, 334, 338–9, 344
    oil resources, 29
    trade with Japan, 76–7
    U.S. investment in, 75, 77
South Vietnam, xiii, 16, 30–1, 79,
    83, 96, 97, 98, 99, 100

oil resources, 29
U.S. covert operations, 129
U.S. investment in, 77
Southeast Asia, 4, 110, 112
    Japanese investment in, 340–5
    and oil, 21–49
    U.S. policy, 127–8
Southeast Asia Treaty Organization
    (SEATO), xi, 92, 165–6, 248,
    250–1
*Southeast Asia's Economy in the
    1970's* (ADB), 48 n., 79
Southern Manchuria, 158
Soviet Union, x, 27, 62, 71, 93, 282,
    306, 311, 347
    and India, 204–5, 212, 217, 227,
        231
    oil reserves, 28, 30
    U.S. rapprochement, x, 122–3,
        125–6, 342
Spain, 5–6, 91
Spanish-American War, 13
"Special Drawing Rights," 110
Special Forces, 42, 119
Special Message on the Balance of
    Payments (JFK), 118, 125–6
stability, investor need for, 74–9, 84
    and ADB policies, 84–5
Standard Oil, 114, 121, 183, 292
Standard Vacuum, 36, 38, 39, 128–9,
    130
Starr, C. V., 129
*State Department White Paper on
    Vietnam*, 103
State Trading Corporation (India),
    205
Stavins, Ralph, 139, 141 n.
Steel, Ronald, 4
Stewart, Ian, 348
Stone, I. F., 350 n.
strategic resources, U.S. control of,
    xii, 22–3, 30–2, 35–7, 79–80,
    83
Suez Canal, 22
Suharto, General, 27, 39, 60, 42–3,
    45 n., 63–5, 67, 68, 328
"Suharto and the Untung Coup—
    The Missing Link" (Wert-
    heim), 48 n.
Sukarno, 38–9, 47, 57–62, 67, 116,
    166
"Sukarno debts," 63, 68
Sullivan, William, 103, 123

Sullivan and Cromwell (law firm), 114
Sulzberger, C. L., 144 n.
Sumatra, 36, 38
Sumitomo Heavy Machinery, 326, 348
Sunda Straits, 329
Sunday Times (London), 24
Sylvester, Arthur, 124

Taft, William Howard, 169
Taft-Katsura Agreement, 158
Taiwan, xii, xiv, 4, 26, 34, 76, 79, 117, 131, 247, 283, 308
and ADB, 80–4
and cheap labor, 267
Japanese trade, 294, 296, 327, 334, 343
U.S. investment in, 75, 77
Taiwan Straits crisis, 283
Tan Malaka, 37
Tanaka, Prime Minister Kakuei, 307
Tanzer, Michael, 145 n.
Taylor, General Maxwell, 92, 95, 96, 98, 100, 118, 129, 139
technological change, 21, 306, 320, 336–40
and imperialism, 336–9
and munitions, 306
Test Ban Treaty, 122, 125
Texaco, 114
Thai Patriotic Front, 251
Thai Petroleum Committee, 31
Thailand, x, xiv, 23, 24, 30–1, 34, 35, 79, 80, 81, 84, 97, 118, 123, 128, 131
and China, 248–50
expansionism, 250–1
green revolution in, 254–8
and Indochina War, 247–51, 274
Japanese influence, 274–5, 327
Meo tribes, 265–75
modernization, 247–78
oil resources, 29
political structure, 252–4
strategic importance, 46 n., 247–78
USAID in, 258–65
U.S. Military Assistance Program, 251
"Thailand: Bombers and Bases—America's New Frontier" (Morrow), 46 n.

Thanh, San Nogc, 251
Thieu, General Nguyen Van, xiii, 259
Thornton, Charles B., 144 n.
Thuan, Nguyen Dinh, 96
Tiao-yu Islands, 26–7, 45 n., 294
Time, 291
Tōkō, Kon, 315
Tokugawa, 319, 340
Tonkin Gulf, 131
Toyo Menka (corporation), 347
trade agreements, ix, 159–63, 171–4, 181, 342
Trotsky, Leon, 5
Truk (air base), 281
Truman, Harry S., 130, 280–1
Truman Doctrine, 130
Tsukamoto, General Masatoshi, 316
Twentieth Century Petroleum Statistics (DeGolyer, MacNaughton), 29, 44 n.
Tydings-McDuffie Independence Act, 158–9, 160, 171, 172
Tyumen oil field, 26

U Nu, 33
Ulsan Petrochemical Complex, 80, 82
Unilever (corporation), 184, 185
Union Carbide, 183
USSR. *See* Soviet Union
United Fruit, 184, 189
United Kingdom. *See* Great Britain
United Nations, xi, 50, 73, 82
United States, xii, xiii, xiv, 4, 5, 6, 7, 22–3, 62
and ADB, 73, 74
oil reserves, 30
U.S. Agency for International Development (USAID), 58, 192, 214–15, 216, 249
in Thailand, 258–65, 266
US/AID Program in Thailand, The (AID), 258
U.S. Asian hegemony, ix–xiv, 5, 15–16, 30–1, 50–1, 161–2
and anticolonialism, xi
challenges to, x, xiv, 42–3, 71, 73, 137, 338, 346–7
U.S. balance of payments, ix, xiii, 16, 86, 93–4, 107–39
U.S. banks, influence of policy, 92, 107–18, 126–36
U.S. Chamber of Commerce, 118

U.S. dollar crisis, ix, xiii, 16, 92–4, 106–7, 109, 118–19, 125–6, 135–9
U.S. economic crisis, ix–x, 16, 71, 85–7, 93–4, 118–25, 135–7, 293
U.S. global power, decline of, ix–xiii, 42–3, 71, 73, 137, 338, 346
U.S. imperialism, x–xi, 3, 8–9, 157–99
  background, xiii, 5–10
  and capitalism, 9–17, 21–49, 74–7, 85, 115, 159–61, 186, 222–30, 310–11, 336–46
  human costs, xi, xiii, 7, 16–17, 42, 81, 192–7
  institutions of, x, 8–9, 50–70, 71–90, 91–4, 184
  and military bases, 158–60, 164–7
U.S. imperialism in Latin America, 5–7, 13, 23, 55, 120, 158
United States Information Service (USIS), 266, 270–1
U.S. International Chamber of Commerce, 203
U.S.-Japan Security Treaty, 311, 313, 314, 328, 340
U.S. Navy Pacific Squadron, 8
U.S.-Philippine Economic and Technical Cooperation Agreement, 175
U.S. postwar Asian policies, xi–xiii, 5–17, 22–3, 50, 71–3, 91–2, 101, 110–11, 127–8, 157–8, 167–71, 177, 194, 247–8, 279–85
U.S. Public Law 480, 176, 211, 221, 341
U.S. security strategy, 50, 74, 95–9, 105, 164–7, 194, 247–8, 274, 279–302
U.S.-Soviet missile gap, 122, 147
U.S. steel production, 13
U.S. surplus commodities, 210–11
University of the Philippines, 192

Van Alstyne, R. W., 5, 18 n.
Vantage Point, The (Johnson), 117
Venezuela, 23
Vick International, 183
Vietcong, 103, 104, 105
Vietminh, 247, 264, 273
Vietnam, 4, 23, 71, 74, 95, 97, 247, 252, 264, 290. *See also* Vietnam War

Vietnam War, ix, x, 91–154
  and CIA, 91–154
  domestic pressures for, 93–101, 106–7
  economic constraints, 71, 91, 118–25
  and financial establishments, 91–154
Vietnam Working Group (of NSC), 100
Vietnamization, 105, 110–11, 113, 125, 136, 138
Voice of America, 284
Voluntary Program, 132–3

Wake Island, 9, 280, 281
Wall Street, 91, 108, 110, 114, 126
  and CIA, 91–2, 109
Wall Street Journal, 335
war finance crisis, 135–9
"War Machine Under Nixon, The" (Stone), 350 n.
Washington Plans an Aggressive War (Stavins, Barnet, Raskin), 139
Washington Post, 138
Watanabe, Takeshi, 72, 80, 82, 88 n.
Wentworth, Alfred, 131
West Germany, 25, 32, 62, 122, 126
West India Squadron, 8
West Indies, 6
West Irian, 36, 38
West Kalimantan, 43
West Malaysia, 43
West Samoa, 79, 80, 81
Western Europe, 4, 22, 23, 24, 332
Western Java, 40
Westinghouse, Inc., 183
Westmoreland, General William, 110, 138
White Paper on Defense (Japan), 308
Wicker, Tom, 110
Wilcke, Gerd, 348
Wilhelm, Kaiser, 4
Winthrop Stearns Company, 183
Wolf, Walter Reid, 128
"Wonders of Science—Missiles Fly the Heavens, The," 316
World Bank, xi, 50, 60, 62, 66, 70 n., 72, 73, 74, 115, 138, 184–5, 206–7, 209, 214, 218, 220–1, 249, 329

World War I, xi, 76
World War II, x, xi, xii, 5, 13, 14,
    16, 36, 71, 72, 73, 77, 128, 160,
    223
Worthy, William, 47 n.

Yamashita, Taro, 26
"Yankees," 114
Yoshio, Miwa, 315
Young, Kenneth Todd, 127–8, 130,
    136